P...

First ...

Pit 50 Cts Gallery 25 Cts.

Doors Open at a quarter before 7.   Performance commence
at a quarter-past 7 o'clock.

FIRST NIGHT OF A NEW

American Comedy!

IN FIVE ACTS, CALLED

FASHION,

Written for this Theatre, by Mrs. ANNA CORA MOWATT.

Regardless of Expense, the Manager has made every effort to produce this NEW
COMEDY with the STRICTEST FIDELITY, APPROPRIATENESS and SU-
PERIOR EXECUTION of SCENIC ILLUSION, and all that Magnificence of

STAGE APPOINTMENTS!

Which Excited the Admiration and Applause of the Public, on the First Performance of

☞ LONDON ASSURANCE! ☜

Monday Evening, March 24th,

Will be presented, for the 1st time on any stage, a New AMERICAN COMEDY,
(with a Prologue and Epilogue,) called

Fashion!

Written for this Theatre by Mrs. ANNA CORA MOWATT.

New Scenery .... by .... Messrs Hillyard, Smith and P. Grain
The Costumes, Decorations and Appointments .... by .... Mr. Dejonge

Adam Trueman	Mr. Chippendale
Count de Jolimaitre	W. H. Crisp
Colonel Howard	Dyott
Mr. Tiffany	Berry
Mr. T. Tennison Twinkle	De Walden
Mr. Augustus Fog	Bridges
Mr. Snobson	Fisher
Zeke, a colored servant	Skerrett
Master of the Ceremonies	Gallot
Mrs. Tiffany	Mrs. Barry
Gertrude	Miss Clara Ellis
Seraphina Tiffany	Miss Kate Horn
Prudence	Mrs. Knight
Millinette	Dyott

The Prologue will be spoken by .... W. H. CRISP
The Epilogue by .... the Characters.

THE SCENE LIES IN NEW YORK.   TIME 1845!

DRAWING ROOM!

At Mrs. Tiffany's, furnished in the First Style of Modern Elegance, with view of

CONSERVATORY!!

Seen through a French Window—Merchant's Counting House.

INTERIOR of the CONSERVATORY!

VIEW of the BATTERY

BALL ROOM WITH SUPPER ROOM!

IN THE DISTANCE, IN ACT FOURTH

A COTILLION

AND

☞ LA POLKA!

By the Characters, produced under the direction of Mr. PARKER.
In the course of the Evening, the Orchestra will play for the first time, the following
Pieces of Music

OVERTURE—Les Diamans de la Couronne	AUBER
QUADRILLES—Irish Echos	JULLIEN
EDINBURGH WALTZER	LABITZKY
DUET FROM NORMA—Two Cornets ..Messrs. WHOENING	and WILLIS
HAMBURGER ELB GALOPP	LABITZKY

PAS DE DANUBE!

By Miss St. Clair.

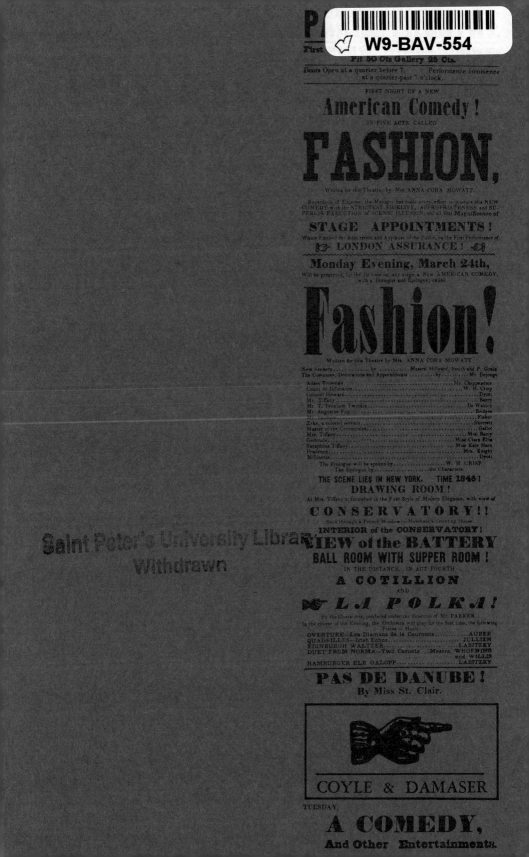

COYLE & DAMASER

TUESDAY,

A COMEDY,

And Other Entertainments.

Six Early American Plays

1798-1890

Performance of *Romeo and Juliet* on the opening night of Booth's Theatre, New York City, February 3, 1869

(J. Clarence Davies Collection, Museum of the City of New York)

SIX EARLY AMERICAN PLAYS

1798-1890

edited by
William Coyle

and
Harvey G. Damaser

WITTENBERG UNIVERSITY

Charles E. Merrill Publishing Company
Columbus, Ohio
A Bell and Howell Company

TABLE OF CONTENTS

v

Introduction

Students of American literature often seem to regard the drama before 1920 as a kind of retarded stepchild, withheld from public view and discussed only in embarrassed whispers with intimate friends. Though often ignored or scornfully dismissed, the plays of the 19th century—crude and inexpert as most of them are—provided entertainment for millions of people and helped create an audience for serious drama in the 20th century. As a matter of fact, British drama in the 19th century was generally imitative and second-rate; most of the plays in this volume are as effective as those enjoyed by Londoners during the same period. We have selected six plays that represent the kinds of dramatic entertainment Americans found enjoyable between 1798 and 1890, when a significant theatre was beginning to emerge. In the introduction preceding each play, we have attempted to relate it to the broad historical pattern sketched below. It is our hope that these plays can be used profitably to supplement survey courses in American literature and to supply the dimension of historical background in courses treating modern American drama.

In some cultures drama has been one of the first literary forms to develop, but in the United States it developed more slowly than either poetry or fiction. Regarded as a waste of time and money and as a possible incitement to vice, the theatre was vigorously condemned as "the devil's workshop" by the Puritans of New England, the Dutch and the Huguenots of New York, and the Quakers, Lutherans, and Scotch-Irish of Pennsylvania. In some cultures drama originated as a supplement or an auxiliary of religious worship, but there was no possibility of this occurring in 17th century America. When the Puritans achieved power in England in 1642, they closed existing theatres; in New England they could not be expected to permit the opening of new ones. Recoiling in horror from such a possibility, Increase Mather wrote in his *Testimony Against Several Profane and Superstitious Customs Now Practiced in New England* (1687): "There is much discourse of beginning Stage-Plays in New England. The last year Promiscuous Dancing was openly practiced."

Because there were neither theatres nor professional actors in America until the mid-18th century, production of plays before that time was extremely sporadic. In 1598 near what is now El Paso, Texas, some Spanish settlers performed a *comedia* written by Marcos Farfán de los Godos. On November 14, 1606, a play by a Frenchman, Marc Lescarbot, *Le Théâtre de Neptune en La Nouvelle-France*, was presented at Port Royal, Acadia. There is also evidence of a play, *The Lost Lady*, written in 1641 by Sir William Berkeley, Governor of Virginia. In 1665 occurred the earliest recorded dramatic performance in English. The play, *Ye Bare and Ye Cubb*, exists only in the court records of Accomac County, Virginia. The three actors were brought to trial and were acquitted of licentiousness after performing the play for the court. There were also some early productions in colleges. At Harvard in 1690, *Gustavus Vasa* by Benjamin Colman, an undergraduate, was acted. In 1702 students at William and Mary performed a "pastoral colloquy" before the governor. Infrequent amateur college productions continued throughout the century, particularly at William and Mary. Between 1699 and 1702 Richard Hunter successfully petitioned the acting Governor of New York for approval of "the acting of Play's in this Citty," but there are no extant records of his productions. It is known, however, that on May 6, 1709, the Governor's Council of New York forbade all "play acting and prize fighting." The first professional actor in America, Anthony Aston, on arriving from Jamaica in 1703, recorded in his journal "We arrived in Charles-Town, full of Lice, Shame, Poverty, Nakedness and Hunger. I turned *Player* and *Poet*, and wrote one Play on the Subject of the Country." All other trace of this play has been lost. The first play to be printed in America, *Androboros* by Robert Hunter, Governor of New York, was published in New York in 1714. A copy of this dramatic satire, in which Hunter attacked his political opponents, is in the Huntington Library, but no record of any production exists.

From this point on, references to dramatic performances become more plentiful, particularly in the Southern colonies, where religious opposition to the stage was not so militant. The first theatre in the colonies was contracted for in Williamsburg, Virginia, in 1716. There is also recorded mention of the New Booth Theatre on Society Hill in Philadelphia in 1724, the New Theatre in New York in 1732, and the New Theatre in Dock Street in Charleston, South Carolina, in 1736.

In August, 1749, the first American professional repertory troupe, the Murray-Kean company, put on their first plays in Philadelphia. They then acted in New York in 1750-51 and moved to Williamsburg to open a new theatre in the fall of 1751. Reorganized as the Virginia Company of Comedians, they played in the South for the next twenty years. Even more important to American dramatic history was the arrival from England in 1752 of Lewis Hallam's company of actors. They played in Virginia in competition with the Virginia Company, appeared in New York for six months in 1753, and then moved to Philadelphia, to Charleston, and finally to Jamaica, where after Hallam's death in 1755 they joined with the company managed by David Douglass. Douglass married

Hallam's widow and brought the troupe back to New York in 1758. To soften the opposition of religious groups and colonial governments, Douglass advertised his plays as "Moral Dialogues" and "Dissertations on Subjects *Moral, Instructive* and *Entertaining*." Anti-British feelings in the colonies induced Douglass to rename his troupe the American Company. They performed in Philadelphia, Maryland, New England, and various parts of the South. In 1766 they built the first permanent theatre in America, the Southwark, just outside the Philadelphia city limits. Here in 1767 they produced the first play by an American to be professionally performed, Thomas Godfrey's posthumous drama, *The Prince of Parthia*. An exotic romantic tragedy set in Parthia at the beginning of the Christian era, the play had no relevance to colonial America or its particular problems. On December 7, 1767, the American Company opened the John Street Theatre in New York. In 1774, however, soon after the Continental Congress forbade all stage entertainments, Douglass took his troupe back to the West·Indies, where both he and his wife died.

During the Revolution the Continental Congress and the colonial legislatures continued their official discouragement of stage plays and other entertainments, but the theatre flourished more than might be expected in wartime. The British produced plays in Boston, Philadelphia, and New York while they occupied those cities; and there is a record of American soldiers' presenting plays at Valley Forge. Dramatic satires and political farces were written by both the British and the Americans for entertainment of the troops and for propaganda purposes. An awakening sense of national identity encouraged the use of native themes, settings, and characters.

After the war the stage was still condemned on religious as well as social and economic grounds. By the mid-1790's, however, New York, Philadelphia, Charleston, and even Boston among other cities had established permanent theatres. In 1784 Lewis Hallam's son and namesake brought the American Company back to Philadelphia, where he evaded the law prohibiting plays by presenting, like Douglass before him, "moral dialogues" and "pantomimical farces." In 1786 Hallam joined with John Henry, the actor-manager of the reopened John Street Theatre in New York, and on April 16, 1787, they produced Royall Tyler's *The Contrast*, the first play on an American subject by an American dramatist to be professionally acted.

Though inspired by *The School for Scandal*, Tyler consciously set out to write an original American play. He made many local geographical and political allusions and attempted to capture American speech patterns. Contrasting sets of British and American characters were deliberately devised to demonstrate the superiority of native American honesty, morality, and manners. Perhaps the first American portrayal of what Henry James later called "the international situation," *The Contrast* reflects Americans' sensitivity to charges of cultural or social inferiority. The play also illustrates satirically the attitude of rural Americans toward the theatre. One character goes into a playhouse without realizing it and thinks that he is looking into the adjacent house through a large hole in the wall. When told that he attended a play, he responds, "Why, I vow, now I come to think on't, the candles seemed to burn blue, and I am sure where I sat it smelt tarnally of brimstone."

This character, Jonathan, is the first of one of the most important character types of the 19th century American theatre—the stage Yankee. Jonathan is a totally American character, unlike anything in European literature. His closest predecessors in American literature were the country bumpkins of the colonial almanacs. Tyler succeeded well in characterizing the inquisitiveness, the shrewdness, and the independence of this naive rural New Englander, but his attempt to suggest Yankee dialect is not as successful. The character of Jonathan was copied by many later dramatists. Among the actors who were popular as stage Yankees were James H. Hackett as Solomon Swop, Joshua Silsbee as Solon Shingle, and George Handel Hill as Jonathan Ploughboy.

The American Company began to dissolve by the early 1790's. Henry sold his interest to Hallam, who took in an English actor, John Hodgkinson, as co-manager. They quarreled constantly, and their difficulties were compounded by Mrs. Hallam's unfortunate habit of appearing on the stage while intoxicated. In 1796 William Dunlap was persuaded to buy a quarter-interest in the company. Hallam withdrew in 1797, Hodgkinson in 1798; a half-century of domination of the American stage by a single company was drawing to a close. The country had developed sufficiently in population, in wealth, and in sophistication to support many theatres and acting groups.

Dunlap supervised the construction of the Park Theatre in New York for the American Company. Although it was the best equipped and most important theatre of the time, he was forced to put it up for auction in 1804, and in 1805 he declared himself bankrupt. The Park, which was opened in 1798, was a three-story stone building, erected at a cost of $130,000. The actors performed on the apron of the stage in front of the proscenium, which was used mainly for the scenic backdrop. Dunlap began the practice of lowering the curtain on a tableau to end each scene; formerly a play was directed to enable all the actors to exit by doors on either side of the proscenium, and the curtain was not lowered to denote a change of scene. The pink and gold interior of the Park contained a small fenced-in area for the orchestra, a pit with uncomfortable backless benches for men, three horseshoe-shaped tiers of boxes, and a steep gallery at the top. Its appearance was more elegant than the manners of the audience. Writing about early 19th century theatres as Jonathan Oldstyle, Washington Irving said, "There is no place of public amusement of which I am so fond as the Theatre. To enjoy this with the greater relish, I go but seldom." He also made the following recommendations:

To the actors—less etiquette, less fustian, less buckram.
To the orchestra—new music, and more of it.
To the pit—patience, clean benches, and umbrellas.
To the boxes—less affectation, less noise, less coxcombs.
To the gallery—less grog and better constable;—and,
To the whole house, inside and out—a total reformation.
And so much for the theatre.

The American stage before the Civil War was dominated by English
actors and by English plays, particularly those of Shakespeare, but there
were some American writers who succeeded in having their plays produced. Notable among those on native subjects were nationalistic plays
like *André* and plays on Indian themes like *Metamora*. Most important
and most numerous, however, were plays on subjects far removed from
the American scene. Under the influence of Shakespeare, Alexandre
Dumas, and Victor Hugo, playwrights turned out tragedies, romantic
melodramas, and some comedies. Plays like *Brutus* (1818) by John Howard
Payne, *Jack Cade* (1835) by Robert T. Conrad, and *The Gladiator* (1831)
by Robert Montgomery Bird combined a romantic interest in the remote
past with democratic sympathy for the man who rebels against established
authority; otherwise, such plays had little relevance to the life of the
time. Most seem dated and highly artificial today. In 1837 Emerson
complained that British playwrights had "Shakespearized" for two hundred years, and American writers were equally imitative. One play, however, *Francesca da Rimini* (1855) by George Henry Boker, transcends
mere imitation and is proof that a masterpiece can occasionally emerge
from an effete tradition. In recreating the story of Paolo and Francesca,
the unhappy lovers described by Dante in Canto V of the *Inferno*, Boker
used a five-act structure, blank verse, soliloquies and asides, alternating
comic and serious scenes, subplots, characters swept toward destruction
by their passions, and other conventions of romantic tragedy. But the
beauty of the verse, the psychological complexity of the major characters,
and the tragic ironies of the conflict raise it far above other plays of a
similar nature and make it appear the best play written in English during
the 19th century. Its inordinate length and its use of an obsolescent stage
tradition have prevented its excellence from being fully recognized.

One of the most important developments in the 19th century American
theatre was the rise of the star system and the decline of the permanent
stock company. Beginning with Thomas Abthorpe Cooper, John Howard
Payne, and George Frederick Cooke, the actor rather than the play
became the attraction for the audience. The star traveled from city to
city, often joining a cast at the last moment in a play that they had not
rehearsed together. He demanded an exorbitant fee, forced the manager
and the other actors to put up with his petty whims, and decided which

plays were to be performed. Dramatists sold him plays outright for small sums, because without a copyright law they had no protection from piracy, and without the star's acceptance there usually was no chance of their plays being produced. The best example of the charismatic star who could draw audiences to see any play in which he chose to appear was Edwin Forrest, once described as "a vast animal bewildered by a grain of genius." Forrest offered prizes of up to $1000 for an American play suited to his robust and declamatory style. He paid out about $20,000 in prizes, a small sum compared with the fortune he made from the prize-winning plays.

Directly or indirectly, Forrest was responsible for the most violent episode in American theatrical history, the Astor Place riots. In 1845 while appearing in London as Macbeth, Forrest was hissed by the audience, probably because many British actors were out of work. Forrest, however, blamed the highly popular star William Charles Macready for his reception, and with characteristic impetuousness went to Edinburgh, where Macready was appearing in *Hamlet,* took a seat in the audience, and hissed his rival's performance. In 1849 when Macready toured the United States, Forrest's admirers packed the galleries of the Astor Place Opera House and created such a disturbance that the production of *Macbeth* could not continue after the third act. Three nights later, on May 10, 1849, Macready attempted the role again and completed the performance, but a mob rioted in protest outside the theatre. Police and militia fired into the crowd; at least twenty-two persons were killed and hundreds were injured. The riot was probably caused by mass hysteria and Know-Nothing prejudice against foreigners rather than by dramatic considerations. Forrest, who denied all connection with the riot, lost favor with actors and managers, but gained in popularity with his audiences.

The American theatre followed quickly the westward expansion of the country. Cincinnati had a theatrical troupe in 1801 and a permanent theatre by 1820. Samuel Drake toured in Kentucky and Ohio after 1815; Noah Ludlow brought his company to Tennessee, New Orleans, and St. Louis soon afterward; and James H. Caldwell followed by establishing theatres along the lower Mississippi. Stars like Forrest and Joseph Jefferson served their dramatic apprenticeship in the rough-and-ready theatres of the frontier. San Francisco and Virginia City had theatres soon after the beginning of the gold rush. The development of showboats also helped spread dramatic entertainment across the nation. The success of William Chapman's *Floating Palace* on the Ohio and Mississippi Rivers in July, 1831, became the inspiration for other showmen. Announced by a whistle or by a steam calliope (after 1887), the boats brought to the riverbanks tragedy, melodrama, comedy, and minstrel shows—almost anything that could be seen in New York. By the end of the century, the increased mobility of touring companies reduced the need for the showboats, and they faded away, the last one, the *Majestic,* being sold in 1959. After operating a Mississippi showboat, P. T. Barnum opened his Museum in New York, where he presented some dramatic entertainments in a "Moral Lecture Room."

Another distinctly American theatrical institution, the minstrel show, originated about the same time. Negro parts had been included in some early plays, and blackface singers like George Washington Dixon had performed in public. In 1828 Thomas Dartmouth Rice, supposedly imitating a crippled Negro, did the first Jim Crow dance. Rice's popularity led to Dan Emmett's Virginia Minstrels of 1843, a full evening of blackface entertainment using the now familiar minstrel show instruments—banjo, fiddle, tambourine, and bones. In 1846 E. P. Christy's Minstrels established a semi-circular line with the Tambo at one end, the Bones at the other, and the white-faced Interlocutor in the center. Although a set routine was developed, the minstrel shows permitted the use of much extemporaneous material. The music of Stephen Foster and Louis Moreau Gottschalk is probably the most lasting contribution of these shows, one of the most popular forms of theatrical entertainment throughout the last half of the 19th century. Beginning in 1848 Frank S. Chanfrau drew Bowery crowds to watch a series of plays in which he starred as Mose the Fireboy. William Niblo and William Mitchell attracted huge crowds to their New York theatres to witness farces, dramatic skits, and variety acts (vaudeville). The theatrical audience in America was further enlarged in 1866 by a musical spectacle, *The Black Crook,* which featured a hundred beautiful French girls wearing short skirts and flesh-colored tights; its run grossed more than a million dollars.

Also popular beginning in 1852 were the Tom Shows, traveling road companies presenting dramatizations of Harriet Beecher Stowe's *Uncle Tom's Cabin.* The adaptation by George L. Aiken was most successful, but at least twelve others were made. Mrs. Stowe received no financial return from the play because she disapproved of the stage and refused to sanction a dramatic version of her novel. Because of its exciting action and colorful characters, the play was more popular after the Civil War than before, and Tom Shows toured the country until the 1930's. Because it was regarded as moral entertainment, *Uncle Tom's Cabin* probably drew into theatres many persons who had been reared to regard the stage as sinful.

By 1865 great progress had been made in the development of an American audience for theatrical entertainment, if not in the creation of a worthwhile native drama. The next generation would see continuing progress toward a mature and significant theatre. Because plays are usually written and produced under the necessity of making an immediate appeal to a varied audience, drama reflects popular taste and attitudes more accurately than any other form of literature. Certainly the American theatre after the Civil War embodies general characteristics of the Gilded Age—large-scale expansion, a trend toward consolidation, uncertainties of taste, and a fondness for elaborate spectacles and emotionalism. In other words, the stage was an integral part of the culture that built the Union

Pacific Railroad, created the Standard Oil Trust, and admired drawing rooms of the wealthy where one might sit on a Louis XIV chair in a Romanesque mansion and examine a Chinese screen at one end of the room or a suit of medieval armor beside a rubber plant at the other.

Most of the characteristics of late 19th century drama had their origins earlier, but after the Civil War they were enormously accelerated. An expanding population with more money to spend for entertainment and a diminishing of the prejudice against the stage resulted in hundreds of new theatres being built. In New York Edwin Booth's million-dollar theatre, which opened in 1869, was the ultimate in Victorian elegance and in ingenious stage machinery. Besides the new theatres which were opened in large cities, every town of any size had an opera house or a town hall where plays could be presented. The more prosperous theatres had resident stock companies, which were sometimes augmented by a traveling star; others depended on road companies that traveled from one town to another, usually spending a week in each. Drama after the Civil War became much more mobile; the expanded railroad network and improved roads made touring easier and gradually reduced the importance of stock companies. The larger number of theatres made it possible for a popular star to specialize in playing the same role year after year. Joseph Jefferson began playing Rip Van Winkle in 1865 and appeared in the part for the next forty years. James O'Neill, father of the playwright, played Edmund Dantes in *The Count of Monte Cristo* more than 6,000 times from 1883 until his death. Part of Eugene O'Neill's bitterness against his father, as revealed in *Long Day's Journey into Night,* resulted from his belief that James O'Neill "sold out" for material gain instead of developing his full potential as an actor.

As the drama became more profitable, combinations inevitably developed to control theatres and bookings. Augustin Daly organized a cooperative association of New York managers in 1873, and managers outside New York sometimes had working agreements on a small scale. In 1896 six men formed the Theatrical Syndicate, which soon monopolized most of the industry. Although the Syndicate was often referred to as Klaw and Erlanger for two of its members, Charles and Daniel Frohman dominated the trust. The Syndicate brought efficiency and system into a chaotic business, but it also discouraged originality and experimentation because it planned its productions to please the widest possible segment of the playgoing public. It controlled most of the major theatres and performers throughout the country, and Broadway became for the stage what Wall Street was for business. David Belasco refused to submit to the Syndicate and won a partial victory. The Shubert brothers later rebelled successfully, but their success meant merely a shift of power to a different monopoly.

Although Charles Frohman and Belasco regarded themselves as star-makers, the star system, which had been somewhat discredited since the Astor Place riots, was weakened, and the importance of the individual actor diminished somewhat. One first thinks of the period in terms of magisterial producers like Lester Wallack, Augustin Daly, Albert M. Palmer, the Frohmans, and Belasco. Each might write or direct plays or even act in them, but his primary function was that of an entrepreneur. Today one is inclined to think of the theatre in terms of playwrights. The shift probably began in 1891 when Bronson Howard formed the Dramatists Club to work for copyright protection. In general, it seems accurate to say that in 1850 a playgoer would plan to see an Edwin Forrest performance, in 1900 to see a David Belasco production, and in 1950 to see a Tennessee Williams play.

As the theatre, like all other aspects of the national life, expanded enormously, a great variety of plays were produced. Shakesperian productions brought the most prestige, if not always the most profit, and Edwin Booth was generally considered America's greatest actor. Adaptations of novels, especially those of Scott and Dickens, were well received. Foreign plays usually had a better chance of success than native ones. Augustin Daly adapted at least sixty-nine plays from French and German dramas. The nostalgic and sentimental regionalism found in local color fiction was also exploited in plays like *Horizon* (1871) by Augustin Daly, *Davy Crockett* (1872) by Frank Murdoch, *The Danites in the Sierras* (1877) by Joaquin Miller, *The Old Homestead* (1886) by Denman Thompson, and *In Mizzoura* (1893) and *Arizona* (1899) by Augustus Thomas.

Whatever the subject matter of a play, audiences preferred tear-jerking scenes and emotional language that today would be ridiculed as blatantly sentimental. One went to the theatre to laugh or to cry or, preferably, to do both alternately. *East Lynne* (1863), one of the most popular plays of the century, evoked sobs from audiences, as did the death of Little Eva in *Uncle Tom's Cabin*. Cruel fathers, unhappy lovers, suffering children, quarrels and reconciliations, deathbeds and funerals—such characters and scenes that most modern audiences would consider maudlin were received with enthusiasm.

The sentimentality of the day was closely related to a fondness for melodrama—plays that subordinate characterization and theme to exciting action and enthrall spectators with thrills and chills, smiles and sobs. Although 19th century melodramas now strike us as extravagantly emotional and crudely unreal, they drew people into theatres and helped create an audience for subsequent playwrights. At their worst, melodramas catered to the same tastes as the dime novels of the period. Audiences admired elaborate spectacles and sensational action. In *The Poor of New York* (1857) by Dion Boucicault, the master of the genre, a tenement fire on stage was a huge success. *Under the Gaslight* (1867) by Augustin Daly was the first play to use the familiar situation of the hero tied to railroad tracks as a full-sized locomotive hurtles toward him. Later plays made the heroine the victim and often substituted a circular saw for the train. Enormous new theatres invited large-scale productions and broad effects. New mechanical devices such as hydraulic lifts and improved gas lighting stimulated the imagination of playwrights and the ingenuity of designers. Perhaps the ultimate in spectacles was the chariot race in the dramatic version of *Ben Hur* (1899). Only a financial depression, however, prevented Steele MacKaye from building a "Spectatorium" to seat 10,000 people at the Chicago World's Fair to witness *The World Finder*, a play about Columbus, which MacKaye had devised for presentation on a stage 500 feet wide and 150 feet deep.

The most important development in American literature after the Civil War was the gradual and grudging acceptance of realism. William Dean Howells, who was a tireless crusader for realism, defined the term again and again, using such phrases as *"democracy in literature," "what is unpretentious and what is true," "the faithful report of our life, its motives and emotions," "the appreciation of the common," "fidelity to experience,"* and *"an honest treatment of our average middle class life, with the rich variety of possibilities in motive and incident native to our society."* The essence of Howells' creed was truth to nature, close observation of everyday life, and rejection of the artifices of false romanticism. He wrote thirty-six plays, most of them satires or farces; although they were not suited to the commercial theatre, many were favorites of amateur dramatic groups. But Howells' major contribution to American drama was his influence as he created a favorable climate for serious realism and encouraged other writers, especially James A. Herne. In his magazine criticism, Howells continually urged writers to deal truthfully with American subjects. Other playwrights he praised included Edward Harrigan, Charles H. Hoyt, Denman Thompson, Clyde Fitch, Augustus Thomas, and Bronson Howard.

Perhaps because the commercial theatre is so directly and so desperately dependent on public acceptance, it usually responds more slowly than other forms of art to drastic changes in taste. It cannot afford the risk of *avant-garde* experiments. At any rate, serious realism developed in drama only after it had been accepted in other forms of literature. That the modern American stage has been for some years in rebellion against the restrictive literalness of realism does not diminish the importance of its influence early in the 20th century.

The term *realism* when applied to drama can refer to stage sets, to acting technique, or to theme and general treatment. The first two, which are somewhat superficial considerations, developed fairly early. Realistic stage sets began with *London Assurance* (1841) by Dion Boucicault, which introduced the box set. Conceiving of the stage as a room with one wall removed encouraged managers to devise realistic interiors. Gradually the action was moved behind the proscenium arch to heighten the illusion of reality. Accuracy in stage settings, however, did not always result in truthful or lifelike productions. Most of the romantic melodramas were staged with close attention to detail. Scenes like the burning steamboat in *The Octoroon* or Sheridan's ride in *Shenandoah* were made as minutely accurate as possible. The ultimate in visual realism came with David

Belasco, who was proud of "the importance and emphasis I place upon every minute detail which makes for truth in my theatre." To equate truth with literal exactness of detail is a self-evident fallacy, but Belasco went to great lengths to be certain that every set was absolutely accurate. If eggs were to be fried onstage, they would be real eggs fried on a real fire, and he would do his best to be certain that they fried with an authentic sputter.

Augustin Daly insisted on realistic sets and also was a pioneer in intro-ducing a quieter and more natural style of acting. Since he controlled the Fifth Avenue Theatre and was a strict disciplinarian who trained his actors carefully, his influence was widely felt. Wallack's Theatre special-ized in British plays and a suave, understated acting style that was widely imitated. Eleanora Duse in 1893 introduced a naturalness of technique similar to modern "method acting." A natural style of acting, however, did not always result in serious drama. William Gillette acted with re-straint and controlled naturalness in such melodramatic plays as *Secret Service* (1895) and *Sherlock Holmes* (1899).

What might be called integral realism, truthfulness of treatment as well as accuracy of representation—truth of the mind and emotions as well as of the eye and ear—made its first tentative appearance in some of the plays of James A. Herne and in plays by Shaw and Ibsen, which were produced despite strong opposition in the 1890's. Valid and truthful treatment of many social issues, however, had to be postponed until the relaxation of social and moral taboos after World War One.

By the last decade of the 19th century, the American theatre had not achieved maturity. No playwrights had emerged who could be compared with Whitman and James or for that matter with Longfellow and Howells. But the next few years would see more serious plays by William Vaughan Moody and Edward Sheldon, productions of Ibsen by Mrs. Fiske, George Pierce Baker's Workshop 47 at Harvard, little theatre groups in many cities, subscription theatre relatively free of commercial domination, and greater freedom to treat serious themes and characters. In 1920 after a long prologue, the curtain would rise on Eugene O'Neill's *Beyond the Horizon* and simultaneously on serious and responsible American drama.

BIBLIOGRAPHY

The texts used for the plays in this volume are identified below. Because of the haphazard conditions under which most 19th century American plays were published, textual purity is a vain illusion. When necessary to facilitate reading, we have silently emended typographical errors and occasionally added a necessary apostrophe or deleted a superfluous comma. We have also simplified the stage directions and have made them as consistent in format as possible.

André. From Dunlap Society Publications, Number 4, 1887.
Metamora. From Richard Moody, *Dramas from the American Theatre 1762-1909.* Cleveland, 1966.
Fashion. From the first London edition, 1850.
The Octoroon. From the privately printed edition, 1864 (?).
Shenandoah. From the edition published by the Society of American Dramatists and Composers, 1897.
Margaret Fleming. From Arthur Hobson Quinn, *Representative Plays of the American Theatre,* New York, 1953.

Texts of many 19th century plays are rather difficult to locate, but most of the plays referred to in the Introductions that follow can be found in the anthologies listed below.

Clark, Barrett H., ed., *America's Lost Plays.* 20 vols. Bloomington, Indiana: Indiana University Press 1963-65.
————, *Favorite American Plays of the Nineteenth Century.* Princeton: Princeton University Press, 1943.
Halline, Allan Gates, ed., *American Plays.* New York: American Book Company, 1935.
Moody, Richard, ed., *Dramas from the American Theatre.* Cleveland: The World Publishing Company, 1966.
Moses, Montrose J., ed., *Representative American Drama, National and Local.* Boston: Little, Brown and Company, 1925.
————, *Representative Plays by American Dramatists.* 3 vols. New York: E. P. Dutton & Co., Inc., 1918-25.
Quinn, Arthur Hobson, ed., *Representative American Plays.* 6th ed. New York: Appleton-Century-Crofts, 1953.

Theatrical history is so ephemeral and so liable to distortions of publicity releases and faulty memories that a standard comprehensive history of the American stage may never be written. The student will find the *Dictionary of American Biography* the most convenient and reliable source of biographical information. Of the historical works listed below, those by Arthur Hobson Quinn are probably the most inclusive and authoritative.

Brown, Thomas Allston, *A History of the New York Stage from 1732 to 1901.* 3 vols. New York: Dodd, Mead & Co., 1903.
Coad, Oral Sumner and Edwin Mims, Jr., *The American Stage.* (*The*

Pageant of America, vol. XIV.) New Haven: Yale University Press, 1929.

Crawford, Mary Caroline, *The Romance of the American Theatre*. Boston: Little, Brown and Company, 1913.

Hewitt, Barnard, *Theatre, U.S.A. 1668 to 1957*. New York: McGraw-Hill Book Company, 1959.

Hornblow, Arthur, *A History of the Theatre in America from Its Beginnings to the Present Time*. 2 vols. Philadelphia: J. B. Lippincott & Co., 1919.

Hughes, Glenn, *A History of the American Theatre 1700-1950*. New York: Samuel French, Inc., 1951.

Mayorga, Margaret, *A Short History of the American Drama*. New York: Dodd, Mead & Co., 1934.

Miller, Jordan Y., *American Dramatic Literature*. New York: McGraw-Hill Book Company, 1961.

Moody, Richard, *America Takes the Stage*. Bloomington, Indiana: Indiana University Press, 1955.

Morris, Lloyd, *Curtain Time: The Story of the American Theatre*. New York: Random House, Inc., 1953.

Moses, Montrose J., *The American Dramatist*. Boston: Little, Brown and Company, 1925.

Odell, George C.D., *Annals of the New York Stage*. 15 vols. New York: Columbia University Press, 1927-49.

Quinn, Arthur Hobson, *A History of the American Drama from the Beginnings to the Civil War*. New York: Harper & Row, Publishers, 1923.

————. *A History of the American Drama from the Civil War to the Present Day*. 2 vols. New York: F. S. Crofts & Co., 1927.

Seilhamer, George O., *A History of the American Theatre*. 3 vols. Philadelphia: Globe Printing House, 1888-91.

Taubman, Howard, *The Making of the American Theatre*. New York: Coward-McCann, Inc., 1965.

Wilson, Garff B., *A History of American Acting*. Bloomington, Indiana: Indiana University Press, 1966.

William Coyle

Harvey G. Damaser

Wittenberg University

January, 1968

ANDRÉ

by
William Dunlap

Introduction

William Dunlap was the first American dramatist to devote himself to the stage as a fulltime profession. His *History of the American Theatre* (1832), though sometimes vague or inaccurate in details, is the best primary source of information on the early American stage. He was also a painter and as a young man studied in London under Benjamin West. He helped found the National Academy of Design and taught there for a number of years. His *History of the Arts of Design* (1834) is a basic source of information on artists of the period. The only full-scale account of his busy life is *William Dunlap: A Study of His Life and Works* (New York, 1917) by Oral S. Coad.

Dunlap was born February 19, 1766, in Perth Amboy, New Jersey. His father, an Irish merchant who had served in the British army, was a Loyalist and in 1777 moved his family to New York City, where young William undoubtedly saw plays produced by British soldiers. A pleasant but unjustified supposition is that he may have seen Major John André, who was fond of theatricals and is said to have appeared as an actor and also to have designed a backdrop for the Theatre Royal, as the British renamed the John Street Theatre. In 1783 at the home of a family friend, Dunlap painted Washington's portrait from life, an experience that may have helped engender the veneration later expressed in *André*. Dunlap's three years in London (1784-87) were enjoyable ones and may have been partially responsible for the friendly attitude toward England that is evident in *André*. His stay abroad also afforded him additional opportunities to attend plays. Soon after his return, the success of *The Contrast* by Royall Tyler inspired him to try his hand at playwriting. His first attempt, *The Modest Soldier*, was accepted but was not produced. His second, *The Father*, was produced on September 7, 1789. From that time until 1828 he was responsible for at least fifty-seven plays, some of them original works and some adaptations of German or French plays. His greatest success was achieved with the plays of Kotzebue, which were in vogue briefly around 1800. In 1796 Dunlap bought a quarter-share of the Old American Company and for eight hectic years struggled to keep the enterprise solvent. Both its personnel and its past history made success unlikely from the start. His two partners appeared in *André*—Lewis Hallam as Washington and John Hodgkinson as André. Quarrels within the company, frequent outbreaks of yellow fever in New York, and too many complimentary tickets for shareholders forced Dunlap into bankruptcy in 1805. He afterward supported his family by painting miniatures, portraits, and religious and historical scenes; but until his death on September 28, 1839, he occasionally returned to the theatre as a playwright or as a manager.

André is a strongly nationalistic, even chauvinistic play. The reverence for George Washington is closely related to the patriotic theme. Moreover, although the Prologue begs for the playwright that "no party spirit blast his views," Dunlap obviously was expressing Federalist ideas. The necessity of a strong Federal government ("How all-resistless is a union'd people"), the distrust of Europe ("No foreign force, no European influence"), and the conciliatory attitude toward England ("Never let memory of the sire's offence/Descend upon the son") represent the Federalist position. Since Dunlap was reared in a Loyalist home and had lived in England, the essential conservatism of the play probably reflects his sincere convictions at the time, but he may also have believed that he was expressing the predominant views of his audience. If a playwright wants to stress a particular theme, he is likely to use a character as a spokesman. It is always a bit risky to identify a character as the "voice of the dramatist," but in *André* M'Donald seems to state the message that Dunlap wished to convey to his fellow countrymen.

Its unified action and dignified though somewhat stilted blank verse make *André* the best American play of its time, but it is not wholly successful from a literary point of view. One reason may have been a divided intention of which Dunlap himself was unaware. On the one hand, he was writing a fervently patriotic play; on the other, he was glorifying an enemy spy. As he confessed in the preface to the published version, he "adorned the poetical character of André with every virtue."

One of the most mysterious of the many legends associated with the American Revolution is the way in which Major John André (1750-80) came to be regarded as a martyr-hero by many Americans. The son of a Swiss merchant, André joined the British army in 1771 after his engagement to Honora Sneyd, a ward of the Seward family of Lichfield, was broken off. Honora had married a widower by 1780, and Dunlap's introducing her into his play was a bit of dramatic license. André was serving as adjutant to Sir Henry Clinton in New York when the British received intimations that General Benedict Arnold was willing to defect from the American army and to surrender West Point. On September 20, 1780, André, wearing his military uniform, went up the Hudson to negotiate with Arnold. His sloop, the *Vulture*, was forced downstream, and André was abandoned behind enemy lines. After hiding for some time, he put on civilian clothes and attempted to return to New York. Being out of uniform, he was in danger of being executed as a spy if captured. When he was within sight of the British lines, he was stopped by three foraging militiamen. Apparently because one of them was wearing a captured Hessian's coat, André revealed his identity. Word of the capture was sent to Arnold, who was able to escape. Some indication of the importance Americans attached to this incident is suggested by the fact that the three privates who apprehended André more or less by accident were the only men below the rank of major to be decorated during the Revolution. André was tried by a military board and sentenced to hang.

Some Americans, the British, and André himself urged that he should face a firing squad instead of being hanged like a common criminal. Several of Washington's closest advisors sympathized with André. Alexander Hamilton pleaded for him; Nathaniel Greene and Anthony Wayne were overcome with emotion when he was hanged. Washington refused to alter the sentence because doing so would have implied some reservations concerning André's guilt, and André was hanged on October 2.

Three factors, all of them evident in Dunlap's play, help to account for the somewhat unusual circumstance of an enemy spy becoming a legendary hero: André's gallantry and courage in facing death (His last words, according to Alexander Hamilton, were "It will be but a momentary pang"), rumors of his unhappy love affair, and the ironic fact that Benedict Arnold, the master-plotter, escaped.

Despite the widespread interest in André, Dunlap's play was not successful. It was first presented on March 30, 1798, by the Old American Company at the Park Theatre, New York, which had opened just two months before. On opening night the receipts were $817, but on the second night they dwindled to $271. In the opening performance, Thomas Abthorpe Cooper (Bland), an English tragedian recently arrived in America and a notoriously slow study, did not know his lines and had to be prompted. Dunlap believed that the failure of the play was due to the scene in which Bland tears the cockade from his hat and denounces Washington. The audience hissed the action at the first performance, and Dunlap added a short scene in which M'Donald tells Bland that Washington has forgiven his impetuous act. Despite this concession to nationalistic sensibilities, the play grossed only $329 on the third night, and it was not performed again.

Although *André* was a financial failure, Dunlap, an energetic if often unsuccessful opportunist, did not abandon his materials. On July 4, 1803, *The Glory of Columbia—Her Yeomanry* was produced at the Park Theatre. Though a weaker play than *André* in almost every respect, it remained a stage favorite and a surefire moneymaker for the next fifty years. A comparison of the two plays reveals much about popular taste of the time. *The Glory of Columbia* opens with a prose soliloquy by Benedict Arnold, a satanic but tormented villain. André's three captors (Paulding, VanWert, and Williams) are incorruptible rustic patriots, and the virtues of the citizen soldier are stressed much more than in *André*. Williams' sister dresses herself as a soldier in order to join the army, adding a touch of farce. The capture of André takes place on stage, and at frequent intervals the actors break into song. André is executed at the close of Act IV. The final act is a spectacle of Yorktown; at the close a transparency is lowered on which an eagle is pictured holding a laurel wreath above the head of Washington.

For a variety of reasons, historical plays, like historical novels, are often somewhat unsatisfactory from a literary point of view. One difficulty is that if the plot is based on an actual event, the audience already knows the outcome; a foregone conclusion generates little suspense. Dunlap probably included the Bland subplot in *André* to furnish a dramatic conflict. Furthermore, if the major characters are well-known figures like Washington or Lincoln, there can be little depth of characterization since they already exist as stereotypes in the minds of the audience. Another difficulty results from the patriotic themes of most historical dramas. Although patriotism is a noble sentiment, thousands of political speeches and Fourth of July orations have unfortunately reduced most expressions of it to clichés. Fresh, credible dialogue is rare in historical plays.

Plays about the American Revolution with which *André* might be compared include *The Group* (1775) by Mrs. Mercy Warren, *The Battle of Bunker's Hill* (1776) by Hugh Henry Brackenridge, *The Fall of British Tyranny* (1776) probably written by John Leacock, *Bunker Hill* (1797) by John Daly Burk, *A Tale of Lexington* (1823) by S. B. H. Judah, *Marion* (1821) by Mordecai M. Noah, *Anthony Wayne* (1845) by James Rees, *Love in '76* (1857) by Oliver B. Bunce, and *Nathan Hale* (1898) and *Major André* (1903) by Clyde Fitch. Two successful modern plays on Revolutionary subjects are *Valley Forge* (1934) by Maxwell Anderson and *The Patriots* (1943) by Sidney Kingsley.

"The Unfortunate Death of Major Andre." An engraving by John Goldar, 1783.

From Henry Steele Commager and Richard B. Morris, eds., *The Spirit of 'Seventy-Six*. New York: Harper & Row, Publishers, 1967. By permission of the editors.

ANDRÉ;

A *TRAGEDY*, IN FIVE ACTS:

AS PERFORMED BY THE OLD AMERICAN COMPANY,

NEW-YORK, MARCH 30, 1798.

TO WHICH ARE ADDED

AUTHENTIC DOCUMENTS

RESPECTING

MAJOR ANDRÉ;

CONSISTING OF

LETTERS TO MISS SEWARD,

THE

COW CHACE,

PROCEEDINGS OF THE COURT MARTIAL, &c.

COPY RIGHT SECURED.

NEW-YORK:

Printed by T. & J. SWORDS, No. 99 Pearl-ftreet.

— 1798.—

Facsimile Title Page

From the Dunlap Society Reprint, 1887.

Cast of Characters

GENERAL, dress, American staff uniform, blue, faced with buff, large gold epaulets, cocked hat, with the black and white cockade, indicating the union with France, buff waistcoat and breeches, boots

M'DONALD, a man of forty years of age, uniform nearly the same as the first

SEWARD, a man of thirty years of age, staff uniform

ANDRÉ, a man of twenty-nine years of age, full British uniform after the first scene

BLAND, a youthful but military figure, in the uniform of a Captain of horse—dress, a short blue coat, faced with red, and trimmed with gold lace, two small epaulets, a white waistcoat, leather breeches, boots and spurs; over the coat, crossing the chest from the right shoulder, a broad buff belt, to which is suspended a manageable hussar sword; a horseman's helmet on the head, decorated as usual, and the union cockade affixed

MELVILLE, a man of middle age, and grave deportment; his dress a Captain's uniform when on duty; a blue coat with red facings, gold epaulet, white waistcoat and breeches, boots and cocked hat, with the union cockade

BRITISH OFFICER

AMERICAN OFFICER

CHILDREN

AMERICAN SERGEANT

AMERICAN OFFICERS AND SOLDIERS, &C.

MRS. BLAND

HONORA

Scene, the Village of Tappan, Encampment, and adjoining country. Time, ten hours.

Prologue

Spoken by Mr. Martin (Seward)

A native bard, a native scene displays,
And claims your candor for his daring lays,
Daring so soon, in mimic scenes to show,
What each remembers as a real woe.
Who has forgot when gallant ANDRÉ died?
A name by Fate to Sorrow's self allied.
Who has forgot, when o'er the untimely bier,
Contending armies paus'd to drop a tear.

　　Our Poet builds upon a fact to-night;
Yet claims in building, every Poet's right;
To choose, embellish, lop, or add, or blend,
Fiction with truth, as best may suit his end;
Which, he avows, is pleasure to impart,
And move the passions but to mend the heart.

　　O, may no party spirit blast his views,
Or turn to ill the meanings of the Muse;
She sings of wrongs long past, men as they were,
To instruct, without reproach, the men that are;
Then judge the story by the genius shown,
And praise, or damn it, for its worth alone.

ACT I
Scene 1

*A wood seen by star-light; an encampment at a distance
appearing between the trees.*

(Enter Melville)

MELVILLE.　　The solemn hour, "when night and morning meet,"
Mysterious ties, to Superstition dear,
And Superstition's guides, now passes by;
Deathlike in solitude. The sentinels,

10

In drowsy tones, from post to post send on
The signal of the passing hour. "All's well,"
Sounds through the camp. Alas, all is not well;
Else, why stand I, a man, the friend of man,
At midnight's depth, deck'd in this murderous guise,
The habiliment of death, the badge of dire
Necessitous coercion. 'T is not well.
—In vain the enlighten'd friends of suffering man
Point out, of war, the folly, guilt, and madness.
Still, age succeeds to age, and war to war;
And man, the murderer, marshals out in hosts
In all the gaiety of festive pomp,
To spread around him death and desolation.
How long! how long!——
—Methinks I hear the tread of feet this way.
My meditating mood may work me woe. (*Draws*)
Stand, whoso'er thou art. Answer. Who's there?

(*Enter Bland*)

BLAND.   A friend.
MELVILLE.   Advance and give the countersign.
BLAND.   Hudson.
MELVILLE.   What, Bland!
BLAND.   Melville, my friend, you here?
MELVILLE.   And *well*, my brave young friend. But why do you,
At this dead hour of night, approach the camp
On foot, and thus alone?
BLAND.   I have but now
Dismounted, and from yon sequester'd cot,
Whose lonely taper through the crannied wall
Sheds its faint beams and twinkles midst the trees,
Have I, adventurous, grop'd my darksome way.
My servant and my horses, spent with toil,
There wait till morn.
MELVILLE.   Why waited not yourself?
BLAND.   Anxious to know the truth of those reports
Which, from the many mouths of busy fame,
Still, as I pass'd, struck varying on my ear,
Each making th' other void. Nor does delay
The color of my hasteful business suit.
I bring dispatches for our great commander;
And hasted hither with design to wait
His rising, or awake him with the sun.
MELVILLE.   You will not need the last, for the blest sun
Ne'er rises on his slumbers; by the dawn

We see him mounted gaily in the field,
Or find him wrapt in meditation deep,
Planning the welfare of our war-worn land.
BLAND.   Prosper, kind Heaven, and recompense his cares.
MELVILLE.   You're from the South, if I presume aright?
BLAND.   I am; and, Melville, I am fraught with news.
The South teems with events—convulsing ones.
The Briton, there, plays at no mimic war;
With gallant face he moves, and gallantly is met.
Brave spirits, rous'd by glory, throng our camp;
The hardy hunter, skill'd to fell the deer,
Or start the sluggish bear from covert rude;
And not a clown that comes, but from his youth
Is trained to pour from far the leaden death,
To climb the steep, to struggle with the stream,
To labor firmly under scorching skies,
And bear, unshrinking, winter's roughest blast.
This, and that heaven-inspir'd enthusiasm
Which ever animates the patriot's breast,
Shall far outweigh the lack of discipline.
MELVILLE.   Justice is ours; what shall prevail against her?
BLAND.   But as I pass'd along, many strange tales
And monstrous rumors have my ears assail'd:
That Arnold had prov'd false; but he was ta'en
And hung, or to be hung—I know not what.
Another told that all our army, with their
Much-lov'd chief, sold and betray'd, were captur'd.
But as I nearer drew, at yonder cot
'T was said that Arnold, traitor like, had fled;
And that a Briton, tried and prov'd a spy,
Was, on this day, as such, to suffer death.
MELVILLE.   As you drew near, plain truth advanced to meet you.
'T is even as you heard, my brave young friend.
Never had people on a single throw
More interest at stake; when he who held
For us the die prov'd false and play'd us foul.
But for a circumstance of that nice kind,
Of cause so microscopic that the tongues
Of inattentive men call it the effect
Of chance, we must have lost the glorious game.
BLAND.   Blest, blest be heaven! whatever was the cause!
MELVILLE.   The blow ere this had fallen that would have bruis'd
The tender plant which we have striven to rear,
Crush'd to the dust, no more to bless this soil.
BLAND.   What warded off the blow?
MELVILLE.   The brave young man, who this day dies, was seiz'd

Within our bounds, in rustic garb disguis'd.
He offer'd bribes to tempt the band that seiz'd him;
But the rough farmer, for his country arm'd,
That soil defending which his ploughshare turn'd,
Those laws his father chose and he approv'd,
Cannot, as mercenary soldiers may,
Be brib'd to sell the public weal for gold.
BLAND. 'T is well. Just Heaven! O grant that thus may fall
All those who seek to bring this land to woe,
All those, who, or by open force, or dark
And secret machinations, seek to shake
The Tree of Liberty, or stop its growth,
In any soil where thou hast pleased to plant it.
MELVILLE. Yet not a heart but pities and would save him;
For all confirm that he is brave and virtuous,
Known, but till now, the darling child of Honor.
BLAND (*Contemptuously*). And how is call'd this honorable spy?
MELVILLE. André's his name.
BLAND (*Much agitated*). André!
MELVILLE. Aye! Major André.
BLAND. André! O no, my friend, you're sure deceiv'd—
I'll pawn my life, my ever sacred fame,
My general's favor, or a soldier's honor,
That gallant André never yet put on
The guise of falsehood. O, it cannot be!
MELVILLE. How might I be deceiv'd? I've heard him, seen him,
And what I tell, I tell from well-prov'd knowledge;
No second tale-bearer who heard the news.
BLAND. Pardon me, Melville. O, that well-known name,
So link'd with circumstances infamous!
My friend must pardon me. Thou wilt not blame
When I shall tell what cause I have to love him;
What cause to think him nothing more the pupil
Of Honor stern, than sweet Humanity.
Rememberest thou, when cover'd o'er with wounds
And left upon the field, I fell the prey
Of Britain? To a loathsome prison-ship
Confin'd, soon had I sunk, victim of death,
A death of aggravated miseries;
But, by benevolence urg'd, this best of men,
This gallant youth, then favor'd, high in power,
Sought out the pit obscene of foul disease,
Where I and many a suffering soldier lay,
And, like an angel, seeking good for man,
Restor'd us light and partial liberty.
Me he mark'd out his own. He nurst and cur'd,

He lov'd and made his friend. I liv'd by him,
And in my heart he liv'd, till, when exchang'd,
Duty and honor call'd me from my friend.
Judge how my heart is tortur'd.—Gracious Heaven,
Thus, thus to meet him on the brink of death—
A death so infamous. Heav'n grant my prayer.

(Kneels)

That I may save him, O, inspire my heart
With thoughts, my tongue with words that move to pity. *(Rises)*
Quick, Melville, show me where my André lies.
MELVILLE.   Good wishes go with you.
BLAND.   I'll save my friend.   *(Exeunt)*

Scene, *the encampment by star-light.*

(Enter the General, M'Donald, and Seward)

GENERAL.   'T is well. Each sentinel upon his post
Stands firm, and meets me at the bayonet's point;
While in his tent the weary soldier lies,
The sweet reward of wholesome toil enjoying;
Resting secure as erst within his cot
He careless slept, his rural labor o'er;
Ere Britons dar'd to violate those laws,
Those boasted laws by which themselves are govern'd,
And strove to make their fellow-subjects slaves.
SEWARD.   They know to whom they owe their present safety.
GENERAL.   I hope they know that to themselves they owe it;
To that good discipline which they observe,
The discipline of men to order train'd
Who know its value, and in whom 't is virtue;
To that prompt hardihood with which they meet
Or toil or danger, poverty or death.
Mankind who know not whence that spirit springs,
Which holds at bay all Britain's boasted power,
Gaze on their deeds astonish'd. See the youth
Start from his plough and straightway play the hero;
Unmurmuring bear such toils as veterans shun;
Rest all content upon the dampsome earth;
Follow undaunted to the deathful charge;
Or, when occasion asks, lead to the breach,
Fearless of all the unusual din of war,
His former peaceful mates. O patriotism!
Thou wondrous principle of godlike action.
Wherever liberty is found, there reigns

The love of country. Now the self-same spirit
Which fill'd the breast of great Leonidas
Swells in the hearts of thousands on these plains,
Thousands who never heard the hero's tale.
'T is this alone which save thee, O my country!
And, till that spirit flies these western shores,
No power on earth shall crush thee.
SEWARD. 'T is wondrous!
The men of other climes from this shall see
How easy 't is to shake oppression off;
How all-resistless is a union'd people;
And hence, from our success (which, by my soul,
I feel as much secur'd as though our foes
Were now within their floating prisons hous'd,
And their proud prows all pointing to the east),
Shall other nations break their galling fetters,
And re-assume the dignity of man.
M'DONALD.   Are other nations in that happy state,
That, having broke Coercion's iron yoke,
They can submit to Order's gentle voice,
And walk on earth self-ruled? I much do fear it.
As to ourselves, in truth, I nothing see,
In all the wond'rous deeds which we perform,
But plain effects from causes full as plain.
Rises not man forever 'gainst oppression?
It is the law of life; he can't avoid it.
But when the love of property unites
With sense of injuries past and dread of future,
Is it then wonderful that he should brave
A lesser evil to avoid a greater?
GENERAL (*Sportively*).   'T is hard, quite hard, we may not please
    ourselves,
By our great deeds ascribing to our virtue.
SEWARD.   M'Donald never spares to lash our pride.
M'DONALD.   In truth I know of naught to make you proud.
I think there 's none within the camp that draws
With better will his sword than does M'Donald.
I have a home to guard. My son is—butcher'd—
SEWARD.   Hast thou no nobler motives for thy arms
Than love of property and thirst of vengeance?
M'DONALD.   Yes, my good Seward, and yet nothing wond'rous.
I love this country for the sake of man.
My parents, and I thank them, cross'd the seas,
And made me native of fair Nature's world,
With room to grow and thrive in. I have thriven;
And feel my mind unshackled, free, expanding,

Grasping with ken unbounded mighty thoughts,
At which, if chance my mother had, good dame,
In Scotia, our revered parent soil,
Given me to see the day, I should have shrunk
Affrighted. Now, I see in this new world
A resting spot for man, if he can stand
Firm in his place, while Europe howls around him,
And all unsettled as the thoughts of vice,
Each nation in its turn threats him with feeble malice.
One trial, now, we prove; and I have met it.
GENERAL.   And met it like a man, my brave M'Donald.
M'DONALD.   I hope so; and I hope my every act
Has been the offspring of deliberate judgment;
Yet feeling seconds reason's cool resolves.
O! I could hate, if I did not more pity
These bands of mercenary Europeans,
So wanting in the common sense of nature,
As, without shame, to sell themselves for pelf
To aid the cause of darkness; murder man—
Without inquiry murder, and yet call
Their trade the trade of honor—high-soul'd honor—
Yet honor shall accord in act with falsehood.
O! that proud man should e'er descend to play
The tempter's part, and lure men to their ruin.
Deceit and honor badly pair together.
SEWARD.   You have much shew of reason; yet, methinks
What you suggest of one, whom fickle Fortune,
In her changeling mood, hath hurl'd, unpitying,
From her topmost height to lowest misery,
Tastes not of charity. André, I mean.
M'DONALD.   I mean him, too; sunk by misdeed, not fortune.
Fortune and chance; O, most convenient words!
Man runs the wild career of blind ambition,
Plunges in vice, takes falsehood for his buoy,
And when he feels the waves of ruin o'er him,
Curses, "in good set terms," poor Lady Fortune.
GENERAL (*Sportively to Seward*).   His mood is all untoward; let us leave
   him.
Tho' he may think that he is bound to rail,
We are not bound to hear him.   (*To M'Donald*) Grant you that?
M'DONALD.   O, freely, freely! You I never rail on.
GENERAL.   No thanks for that; you've courtesy for office.
M'DONALD.   You slander me.
GENERAL.   Slander that would not wound.
Worthy M'Donald, though it suits full well
The virtuous man to frown on all misdeeds,

Yet ever keep in mind that man is frail;
His tide of passion struggling still with Reason's
Fair and favorable gale, and adverse
Driving his unstable bark upon the
Rocks of error. Should he sink thus shipwreck'd,
Sure, it is not Virtue's voice that triumphs
In his ruin. I must seek rest. Adieu!

(Exeunt General and Seward)

M'DONALD.   Both good and great thou art; first among men;
By nature, or by early habit, grac'd
With that blest quality which gives due force
To every faculty, and keeps the mind
In healthful equipoise, ready for action;
Invaluable temperance—by all
To be acquired, yet scarcely known to any.   *(Exit)*

END OF THE FIRST ACT.

ACT II.

Scene, *a prison.*

André discovered, in a pensive posture, sitting at a table; a book by him and candles; his dress neglected, his hair dishevelled; he rises and comes forward.

ANDRÉ.   Kind Heaven be thank'd for that I stand alone
In this sad hour of life's brief pilgrimage!
Single in misery; no one else involving,
In grief, in shame, and ruin. 'T is my comfort.
Thou, my thrice honor'd sire, in peace went'st down
Unto the tomb, nor knew to blush, nor knew
A pang for me. And thou, revered matron,
Could'st bless thy child, and yield thy breath in peace.
No wife shall weep, no child lament my loss.
Thus may I consolation find in what
Was once my woe. I little thought to joy
In not possessing, as I erst possest,
Thy love, Honora! André's death, perhaps,
May cause a cloud pass o'er thy lovely face;
The pearly tear may steal from either eye;
For thou mayest feel a transient pang, nor wrong
A husband's rights: more than a transient pang

O mayest thou never feel! The morn draws nigh
To light me to my shame. Frail nature shrinks—
And *is* Death then so fearful? I have brav'd
Him, fearless, in the field, and steel'd my breast
Against his thousand horrors; but his cool,
His sure approach, requires a fortitude
Which naught but conscious rectitude can give.

(Retires, and sits leaning)

(Enter Bland, unperceived by André)

BLAND.   And is that André? O, how changed! Alas!
Where is that martial fire, that generous warmth,
Which glow'd his manly countenance throughout,
And gave to every look, to every act,
The tone of high chivalrous animation?
André, my friend, look up!
ANDRÉ.   Who calls *me* friend?
BLAND.   Young Arthur Bland.
ANDRÉ (*Rising*).   That name sounds like a friend's. (*With emotion*)
I have inquired for thee—wish'd much to see thee—
I prythee take no note of these fool's tears—
My heart was full—and seeing thee—
BLAND (*Embracing him*).   O André!
I have but now arrived from the South—
Nor heard—till now—of this—I cannot speak;
Is this a place?—O, thus to find my friend!
ANDRÉ.   Still dost thou call me friend? I, who dared act
Against my reason, my declared opinion;
Against my conscience and a soldier's fame?
Oft in the generous heat of glowing youth,
Oft have I said how fully I despis'd
All bribery base, all treacherous tricks in war:
Rather my blood should bathe these hostile shores,
And have it said, "He died a gallant soldier,"
Than with my country's gold encourage treason,
And thereby purchase gratitude and fame.
BLAND.   Still mayest thou say it, for thy heart's the same.
ANDRÉ.   Still is my heart the same, still may I say it;
But now my deeds will rise against my words;
And should I dare to talk of honest truth,
Frank undissembling probity and faith,
Memory would crimson o'er my burning cheek,
And actions retrospected choke the tale.
Still is my heart the same. But there has past
A day, an hour, which ne'er can be recall'd.

Unhappy man! Tho' all thy life pass pure;
Mark'd by benevolence thy every deed;
The out-spread map, which shows the way thou 'st trod,
Without one devious track or doubtful line;
It all avails thee naught, if in one hour,
One hapless hour, thy feet are led astray;—
Thy happy deeds all blotted from remembrance;
Cancel'd the record of thy former good.
Is it not hard, my friend? Is 't not unjust?
BLAND. Not every record cancel'd. O, there are hearts
Where Virtue's image, when 't is once engraved,
Can never know erasure.
ANDRÉ. Generous Bland! (*Takes his hand*) The hour draws nigh which
ends my life's sad story.
I should be firm—
BLAND. By heaven, thou shalt not die!
Thou dost not sure deserve it. Betray'd, perhaps—
Condemn'd without due circumstance made known?
Thou didst not mean to tempt our officers?
Betray our yeoman soldiers to destruction?
Silent! Nay, then 't was from a duteous wish
To serve the cause thou wast in honor bound.
ANDRÉ. Kind is my Bland, who to his generous heart
Still finds excuses for his erring friend;
Attentive hear and judge me:
Pleas'd with the honors daily shower'd upon me,
I glow'd with martial heat my name to raise
Above the vulgar herd, who live to die,
And die to be forgotten. Thus I stood,
When avarice or ambition Arnold tempted,
His country, fame, and honor to betray,
Linking his name to infamy eternal.
In confidence it was to me propos'd
To plan with him the means which should ensure
Thy country's downfall. Nothing then I saw
But confidential favor in the service,
My country's glory, and my mounting fame;
Forgot my former purity of thought,
And high-ton'd honor's scruples disregarded.
BLAND. It was thy duty so to serve thy country.
ANDRÉ. Nay, nay; be cautious ever to admit
That duty can beget dissimulation.
On ground, unoccupied by either part,
Neutral esteem'd, I landed, and was met.
But ere my conference was with Arnold clos'd,
The day began to dawn; I then was told

That till the night I must my safety seek
In close concealment. Within your posts convey'd,
I found myself involved in unthought dangers.
Night came. I sought the vessel which had borne
Me to the fatal spot; but she was gone.
Retreat that way cut off, again I sought
Concealment with the traitors of your army.
Arnold now granted passes, and I doff'd
My martial garb, and put on curs'd disguise.
Thus in a peasant's form I pass'd your posts;
And when, as I conceiv'd, my danger o'er,
Was stopt and seiz'd by some returning scouts.
So did ambition lead me, step by step,
To treat with traitors, and encourage treason;
And then, bewilder'd in the guilty scene,
To quit my martial designating badges,
Deny my name, and sink into the spy.
BLAND.   Thou didst no more than was a soldier's duty,
To serve the part on which he drew his sword.
Thou shalt not die for this. Straight will I fly—
I surely shall prevail—
ANDRÉ.   It is in vain.
All has been tried. Each friendly argument—
BLAND.   All has not yet been tried. The powerful voice
Of friendship in thy cause has not been heard.
My General favors me, and loves my father—
My gallant father, would that he were here!
But he, perhaps, now wants an André's care,
To cheer his hours—perhaps now languishes
Amidst those horrors whence thou sav'dst his son.
The present moment claims my thought. André,
I fly to save thee!
ANDRÉ.   Bland, it is in vain.
But, hold—there is a service thou may'st do me.
BLAND.   Speak it.
ANDRÉ.   O, think, and as a soldier think,
How I must die—the *manner* of my death—
Like the base ruffian, or the midnight thief,
Ta'en in the act of stealing from the poor,
To be turn'd off the felon's—murderer's cart,
A mid-air spectacle to gaping clowns;—
To run a short, an envied course of glory,
And end it on a gibbet.—
BLAND.   Damnation!
ANDRÉ.   Such is my doom. O, have the manner changed,
And of mere death I'll think not. Dost thou think—?

Perhaps thou canst gain that?
BLAND (*Almost in a frenzy*).   Thou shalt not die.
ANDRÉ.   Let me, O, let me die a soldier's death,
While friendly clouds of smoke shroud from all eyes
My last convulsive pangs, and I'm content.
BLAND (*With increasing emotion*).   Thou shalt not die! Curse on the laws
   of war!
If worth like thine must thus be sacrificed
To policy so cruel and unjust,
I will forswear my country and her service;
I'll hie me to the Briton, and with fire,
And sword, and every instrument of death
Or devastation, join in the work of war.
What! shall worth weigh for naught? I will avenge thee!
ANDRÉ.   Hold, hold, my friend! thy country's woes are full.
What! wouldst thou make me cause another traitor?
No more of this; and, if I die, believe me,
Thy country for my death incurs no blame.
Restrain thy ardor—but ceaselessly entreat
That André may at least die as he lived,
A soldier.
BLAND.   By heaven! thou shalt not die!

(*Bland rushes off; André looks after him with an expression of love
and gratitude, then retires up the stage. Scene closes.*)

Scene, *the General's quarters.*

(*Enter M'Donald and Seward, in conversation*)

M'DONALD (*Coming forward*).   Three thousand miles the Atlantic wave
   rolls on,
Which bathed Columbia's shores, ere, on the strand
Of Europe, or of Africa, their continents,
Or sea-girt isles, it chafes.
SEWARD.   O, would to heaven
That in midway between these sever'd worlds
Rose barriers, all impassable to man,
Cutting off intercourse, till either side
Had lost all memory of the other!
M'DONALD.   What spur now goads thy warm imagination?
SEWARD.   Then might, perhaps, one land on earth be found,
Free from th' extremes of poverty and riches;
Where ne'er a scepter'd tyrant should be known,
Or tyrant lordling, curses of creation;—

Where the faint shrieks of woe-exhausted age,
Raving, in feeble madness, o'er the corse
Of a polluted daughter, stained by lust
Of viand-pampered luxury, might ne'er be heard;
Where the blasted form of much abused
Beauty, by villainy seduced, by knowledge
All unguarded, might ne'er be viewed, flitting
Obscene, 'tween lamp and lamp, i' th' midnight street
Of all-defiling city; where the child—
M'DONALD.   Hold! Shroud thy raven imagination.
Torture not me with images so curst.
SEWARD.   Soon shall our foes inglorious fly these shores.
Peace shall again return. Then Europe's ports
Shall pour a herd upon us, far more fell
Than those, her mercenary sons, who now
Threaten our sore chastisement.
M'DONALD.   Prophet of ill,
From Europe shall enriching commerce flow,
And many an ill attendant; but from thence
Shall likewise flow blest science. Europe's knowledge,
By sharp experience bought, we should appropriate;
Striving thus to leap from that simplicity,
With ignorance curst, to that simplicity,
By knowledge blest; unknown the gulf between.
SEWARD.   Mere theoretic dreaming.
M'DONALD.   Blest wisdom
Seems, from out the chaos of the social world,
Where good and ill in strange commixture float,
To rise, by strong necessity impell'd;
Starting, like Love divine, from womb of Night,
Illuming all, to order all reducing;
And showing by its bright and noontide blaze
That happiness alone proceeds from justice.
SEWARD.   Dreams, dreams! Man can know naught but ill on earth.
M'DONALD.   I'll to my bed, for I have watch'd all night;
And may my sleep give pleasing repetition
Of these my waking dreams! Virtue's incentives.

(*Exit*)

SEWARD.   Folly's chimeras rather: guides to error.

(*Enter Bland, preceded by a sergeant*)

SERGEANT.   Pacquets for the General.   (*Exit*)
BLAND.   Seward, my friend!
SEWARD.   Captain, I'm glad to see the hue of health

Sit on a visage from the sallow South.
BLAND.   The lustihood of youth hath yet defied
The parching sun, and chilling dew of even.
The General—Seward—?
SEWARD.   I will lead you to him.
BLAND.   Seward, I must make bold. Leave us together,
When occasion offers. 'T will be friendly.
SEWARD.   I will not cross your purpose.   (*Exeunt*)

Scene, *a chamber. Enter Mrs. Bland.*

MRS. BLAND.   Yes, ever be this day a festival
In my domestic calendar. This morn
Will see my husband free. Even now, perhaps,
Ere yet Aurora flies the eastern hills,
Shunning the sultry sun, my Bland embarks.
Already, on the Hudson's dancing wave,
He chides the sluggish rowers, or supplicates
For gales propitious; that his eager arms
May clasp his wife, may bless his little ones.
O, how the tide of joy makes my heart bound,
Glowing with high and ardent expectation!

(Enter two children)

FIRST CHILD.   Here we are, Mamma, up, and dress'd already.
MRS. BLAND.   And why were ye so early?
FIRST CHILD.   Why, did not you tell us that Papa was to be home to-day?
MRS. BLAND.   I said, perhaps.
SECOND CHILD (*Disappointed*).   Perhaps!
FIRST CHILD.   I don't like perhaps's.
SECOND CHILD.   No, nor I neither; nor "may-be-so's."
MRS. BLAND.   We make not certainties, my pretty loves;
I do not like "perhaps's" more than you do.
SECOND CHILD.   O, don't say so, Mamma! for I'm sure I hardly ever ask
you anything but you answer me with "may be so," "perhaps," or "very
likely." "Mamma, shall I go to the camp to-morrow, and see the General?"
"May be so, my dear." Hang "may be so," say I!
MRS. BLAND.   Well said, Sir Pertness!
FIRST CHILD.   But I am sure, Mamma, you said that to-day Papa would
have his liberty.
MRS. BLAND.   So your dear father, by his letters, told me.
SECOND CHILD.   Why, then, I am sure he will be here to-day. When he can
come to us, I'm sure he will not stay among those strange Englishmen and

Hessians. I often wish'd that I had wings to fly, for then I would soon be
with him.

MRS. BLAND.   Dear boy!

(Enter servant, and gives a letter to Mrs. Bland)

SERVANT.   An express, Madam, from New York to head-quarters, in passing, delivered this.

SECOND CHILD.   Papa's coming home to-day, John.

(Exeunt servant and children)

MRS. BLAND.   What fears assail me! O, I did not want
A letter now! *(She reads in great agitation, exclaiming, while her eyes are
fixed on the paper)* My husband doomed to die! Retaliation! *(She looks
forward with wildness, consternation, and horror)*
To die, if André dies! *He* dies to-day!
My husband to be murdered! And to-day!
To-day, if André dies! Retaliation!
O curst contrivance! Madness relieve me!
Burst, burst, my brain! Yet—André is not dead;
My husband lives. *(Looks at the letter)* "One man has power."
I fly to save the father of my children!

(Rushes out)

END OF THE SECOND ACT.

ACT III.

Scene, *the General's quarters.*

(The General and Bland come forward.)

GENERAL *(Papers in his hand)*   Captain, you are noted here with honorable
Praises. Depend upon that countenance
From me, which you have prov'd yourself so richly
Meriting. Both for your father's virtues
And your own, your country owes you honor—
The sole return the poor can make for service.

BLAND.   If from my country aught I've merited,
Or gain'd the approbation of her champion,
At any other time I should not dare,
Presumptuously, to show my sense of it;

But now my tongue, all shameless, dares to name
The boon, the precious recompense, I wish,
Which, granted, pays all service, past or future,
O'erpays the utmost I can e'er achieve.
GENERAL. Brief, my young friend, briefly, your purpose.
BLAND. If I have done my duty as a soldier;
If I have brav'd all dangers for my country;
If my brave father has deserved aught;
Call all to mind—and cancel all—but grant
My one request—mine, and humanity's.
GENERAL. Be less profuse of words, and name your wish;
If fit, its fitness is the best assurance
That not in vain you sue; but, if unjust,
Thy merits, nor the merits of thy race,
Cannot its nature alter, nor my mind,
From its determined opposition change.
BLAND. You hold the fate of my most lov'd of friends;
As gallant soldier as e'er faced a foe,
Bless'd with each polish'd gift of social life,
And every virtue of humanity.
To me, a savior from the pit of death,
To me, and many more, my countrymen.
Oh, could my words portray him what he is!
Bring to your mind the blessings of his deeds,
While thro' the fever-heated, loathsome holds
Of floating hulks, dungeons obscene, where ne'er
The dewy breeze of morn, or evening's coolness,
Breath'd on our parching skins, he pass'd along,
Diffusing blessings; still his power exerting,
To alleviate the woes which ruthless war,
Perhaps thro' dire necessity, heap'd on us;
Surely the scene would move you to forget
His late intent—tho' only serving then
As duty prompted—and turn the rigor
Of War's iron law from him, the best of men,
Meant only for the worst.
GENERAL. Captain, no more.
BLAND. If André lives, the prisoner finds a friend;
Else helpless and forlorn—
All men will bless the act, and bless thee for it.
GENERAL. Think'st thou thy country would not curse the man
Who, by a clemency ill-tim'd, ill-judg'd,
Encourag'd treason? That pride encourag'd,
Which, by denying us the rights of nations,
Hath caus'd those ills which thou hast now portray'd?
Our prisoners, brave and generous peasantry,

As rebels have been treated, not as men.
'T is mine, brave yeomen, to assert your rights;
'T is mine to teach the foe, that, though array'd
In rude simplicity, ye yet are men,
And rank among the foremost. Oft their scouts,
The very refuse of the English arms,
Unquestion'd, have our countrymen consign'd
To death, when captur'd, mocking their agonies.
BLAND.   Curse them! (*Checking himself*) Yet, let not censure fall on André.
O, there are Englishmen as brave, as good,
As ever land on earth might call its own;
And gallant André is among the best!
GENERAL.   Since they have hurl'd war on us, we must show
That by the laws of war we will abide;
And have the power to bring their acts for trial
To that tribunal, eminent 'mongst men,
Erected by the policy of nations,
To stem the flood of ills, which else fell war
Would pour, uncheck'd, upon the sickening world,
Sweeping away all trace of civil life.
BLAND.   To pardon him would not encourage ill.
His case is singular; his station high;
His qualities admired; his virtues lov'd.
GENERAL.   No more, my good young friend: it is in vain.
The men entrusted with thy country's rights
Have weigh'd, attentive, every circumstance.
An individual's virtue is by them
As highly prized as it can be by thee.
I know the virtues of this man and love them.
But the destiny of millions, millions
Yet unborn, depends upon the rigor
Of this moment. The haughty Briton laughs
To scorn our armies and our councils. Mercy,
Humanity, call loudly, that we make
Our now depised power be felt, vindictive.
Millions demand the death of this young man.
My injur'd country, he his forfeit life
Must yield, to shield thy lacerated breast
From torture. (*To Bland*) Thy merits are not overlook'd.
Promotion shall immediately attend thee.
BLAND (*With contemptuous irony*).   Pardon me, sir, I never shall deserve
    it.
(*With increasing heat*) The country that forgets to reverence virtue;
That makes no difference 'twixt the sordid wretch
Who, for reward, risks treason's penalty,
And him unfortunate, whose duteous service

Is, by mere accident, so chang'd in form
As to assume guilt's semblance, I serve not:
Scorn to serve. I have a soldier's honor,
But 't is in union with a freeman's judgment,
And when I act, both prompt. Thus from my helm
I tear what once I proudly thought the badge
Of virtuous fellowship. (*Tears the cockade from his helmet*) My sword I
  keep. (*Puts on his helmet*)
Would, André, thou hadst never put thine off.
Then hadst thou through opposers' hearts made way
To liberty, or bravely pierc'd thine own! (*Exit*)
GENERAL. Rash, headstrong, maddening boy!
Had not this action past without a witness,
Duty would ask that thou shouldst rue thy folly—
But, for the motive, be the deed forgotten. (*Exit*)

Scene, *a village.*

*At a distance some tents. In front muskets, drums, and other indica-
tions of soldiers' quarters.*

(*Enter Mrs. Bland and children, attended by Melville*)

MELVILLE. The General's doors to you are ever open.
But why, my worthy friend, this agitation?
Our colonel, your husband—
MRS. BLAND (*In tears, gives him the letter*). Read, Melville.
FIRST CHILD. Do not cry, Mamma, for I 'm sure if Papa said he would
come home to-day, he will come yet; for he always does what he says he
will.
MRS. BLAND. He cannot come, dear love; they will not let him.
SECOND CHILD. Why, then, they told him lies. O, fye upon them!
MELVLLE (*Returning the letter*). Fear nothing, Madam, 't is an empty
  threat:
A trick of policy. They dare not do it.
MRS. BLAND. Alas, alas! what dares not power to do?
What art of reasoning, or what magic words,
Can still the storm of fears these lines have raised?
The wife's, the mother's fears? Ye innocents,
Unconscious on the brink of what a perilous
Precipice ye stand, unknowing that to-day
Ye are cast down the gulph, poor babes, ye weep
From sympathy. Children of sorrow, nurst,

Nurtur'd, 'midst camps and arms; unknowing man,
But as man's fell destroyer; must ye now,
To crown your piteous fate, be fatherless?
O, lead me, lead me to him! Let me kneel,
Let these, my children, kneel, till André, pardon'd,
Ensures to me a husband, them a father.
MELVILLE. Madam, duty forbids further attendance.
I am on guard to-day. But see your son;
To him I leave your guidance. Good wishes
Prosper you.   (*Exit Melville*)

(*Enter Bland*)

MRS. BLAND. My Arthur, O my Arthur!
BLAND. My mother! (*Embracing her*)
MRS. BLAND. My son, I have been wishing
For you—(*Bursts into tears, unable to proceed*)
BLAND. But whence this grief, these tears, my mother?
Why are these little cheeks bedew'd with sorrow?
(*He kisses the children, who exclaim*, Brother, brother!)
Have I done aught to cause a mother's sadness?
MRS. BLAND. No, my brave boy! I oft have fear'd, but never
Sorrow'd for thee.
BLAND. High praise! Then bless me, Madam;
For I have pass'd through many a bustling scene
Since I have seen a father or a mother.
MRS. BLAND. Bless thee, my boy! O, bless him, bless him, Heaven!
Render him worthy to support these babes,
So soon, perhaps, all fatherless—dependent.
BLAND. What mean'st thou, Madam? Why these tears?
MRS. BLAND. Thy father—
BLAND. A prisoner of war,—I long have known it,—
But made so without blemish to his honor,
And soon exchang'd, returns unto his friends,
To guard these little ones, and point and lead
To virtue and to glory.
MRS. BLAND. Never, never! His life, a sacrifice to André's manes,
Must soon be offer'd. Even now, endungeon'd,
Like a vile felon, on the earth he lies,
His death expecting. André's execution
Gives signal for the murder of thy father.
André now dies!
BLAND (*Despairingly*). My father and my friend!
MRS. BLAND. There is but one on earth can save my husband—
But one can pardon André.

BLAND.   Haste, my mother!
Thou wilt prevail. Take with thee in each hand
An unoffending child of him thou weep'st.
Save—save them both! This way—haste—lean on me.   (*Exeunt*)

Scene, *the General's quarters.*

(*Enter the General and M'Donald*)

GENERAL.   Here have I intimation from the foe,
That still they deem the spy we have condemn'd,
Merely a captive; by the laws of arms
From death protected; and retaliation,
As they term it, threaten, if we our purpose hold.
Bland is the victim they have singled out,
Hoping his threaten'd death will André save.
M'DONALD.   If I were Bland I boldly might advise
My General how to act. Free, and in safety,
I will now suppose my counsel needless

(*Enter an American officer*)

OFFICER.   Another flag hath from the foe arrived,
And craves admittance.
GENERAL.   Conduct it hither.   (*Exit officer*)
Let us, unwearied hear, unbias'd judge,
Whate'er against our martial court's decision,
Our enemies can bring.

(*Enter British officer, conducted by the American officer*)

GENERAL.   You are welcome, sir.
What further says Sir Henry?
BRITISH OFFICER.   This from him.
He calls on you to think what weighty woes
You now are busy bringing on your country.
He bids me say, that if your sentence reach
The prisoner's life—prisoner of arms he deems him,
And no spy—on him alone it falls not.
He bids me loud proclaim it, and declare,
If this brave officer, by cruel mockery
Of war's stern law, and justice' feign'd pretence,
Be murder'd, the sequel of our strife, bloody,
Unsparing and remorseless, you will make.

Think of the many captives in our power.
Already one is mark'd; for André mark'd;—
And when his death, unparallel'd in war,
The signal gives, then Colonel Bland must die.
GENERAL.   'T is well, sir; bear this message in return.
Sir Henry Clinton knows the laws of arms:
He is a soldier, and, I think, a brave one.
The prisoners he retains he must account for.
Perhaps the reckoning 's near. I, likewise, am
A soldier; entrusted by my country.
What I shall judge most for that country's good,
That shall I do. When doubtful, I consult
My country's friends; never her enemies.
In André's case there are no doubts; 't is clear:
Sir Henry Clinton knows it.
BRITISH OFFICER.   Weigh consequences.
GENERAL.   In strict regard to consequence I act;
And much should doubt to call that action right,
Howe'er specious, whose apparent end
Was misery to man. That brave officer
Whose death you threaten, for himself drew not
His sword—his country's wrongs arous'd his mind;
Her good alone his aim; and if his fall
Can further fire that country to resistance,
He will, with smiles, yield up his glorious life,
And count his death a gain; and tho' Columbians
Will lament his fall, they will lament in blood.
                                   (*General walks up the stage.*)
M'DONALD.   Hear this, hear this, mankind!
BRITISH OFFICER.   Thus am I answered?

(*Enter a sergeant with a letter*)

SERGEANT.   Express from Colonel Bland.   (*Delivers it and exit*)
GENERAL.   With your permission.   (*Opens it*)
BRITISH OFFICER.   Your pleasure, sir. It may my mission further.
M'DONALD.   O Bland, my countryman, surely I know thee!
GENERAL.   'T is short; I will put form aside, and read it.
(*Reads*) "Excuse me, my Commander, for having a moment doubted your
virtue; but you love me. If you waver, let this confirm you. My wife and
children, to you and my country. Do *your* duty."
Report this to your General.
BRITISH OFFICER.   I shall, sir.

(*Bows and exit with American officer*)

GENERAL.   O Bland, my countryman!   (*Exit, with emotion*)
M'DONALD.   Triumph of virtue!
Like him and thee, still be Americans.
Then, tho' all-powerful Europe league against us,
And pour in arms her legions on our shores;
Who is so dull would doubt their shameful flight?
Who doubt our safety, and our glorious triumph?

Scene, *the prison.*

(*Enter Bland*)

BLAND.   Lingering, I come to crush the bud of hope
My breath has, flattering, to existence warmed.
Hard is the task to friendship—hard to say
To the lov'd object, there remains no hope,
No consolation for thee; thou *must* die
The worst of deaths, no circumstance abated.

(*Enter André in his uniform*)

ANDRÉ.   Is there that state on earth which friendship cannot cheer?
BLAND.   Little *I* bring to cheer thee, André.
ANDRÉ.   I understand. 'T is well. 'T will soon be past.
Yet, 't was not much I asked. A soldier's death,
A trifling change of form.
BLAND.   Of that I spoke not.
By vehemence of passion hurried on,
I pleaded for thy precious life alone;
The which denied, my indignation barr'd
All further parley. But strong solicitation
Now is urg'd to gain the wish'd-for favor.
ANDRÉ.   What is 't o'clock?
BLAND.   'T is past the stroke of nine.
ANDRÉ.   Why, then, 't is almost o'er. But to be hung—
Is there no way to escape that infamy?
What then *is* infamy?—no matter—no matter.
BLAND.   Our General hath received another flag.
ANDRÉ.   Soliciting for me?
BLAND.   On thy behalf.
ANDRÉ.   I have been ever favor'd.
BLAND.   Threat'nings, now;
No more solicitations. Harsh, indeed,
The import of the message; harsh, indeed.

ANDRÉ.   I am sorry for it. Would that I were dead,
And all was well with those I leave behind.
BLAND.   Such a threat! Is it not enough, just Heaven,
That I must lose this man? Yet there was left
One for my soul to rest on. But, to know
That the same blow deprives them both of life—
ANDRÉ.   What mean'st thou, Bland? Surely my General
Threats not retaliation. In vengeance
Dooms not some better man to die for me?
BLAND.   The best of men.
ANDRÉ.   Thou hast a father, captive—
I dare not ask—
BLAND.   That father dies for thee.
ANDRÉ.   Gracious Heaven, how woes are heap'd upon me!
What! cannot one, so trifling in life's scene,
Fall, without drawing such a ponderous ruin?
Leave me, my friend, awhile—I yet have life—
A little space of life—let me exert it
To prevent injustice; from death to save
Thy father, thee to save from utter desolation.
BLAND.   What mean'st thou, André?
ANDRÉ.   Seek thou the messenger
Who brought this threat. I will my last entreaty
Send by him. My General, sure, will grant it.
BLAND.   To the last thyself!   (*Exit*)
ANDRÉ.   If, at this moment,
When the pangs of death already touch me,
Firmly my mind against injustice strives,
And the last impulse to my vital powers
Is given by anxious wishes to redeem
My fellow-men from pain; surely my end,
Howe'er accomplish'd, is not infamous.   (*Exit*)

END OF THE THIRD ACT.

ACT IV.

Scene, *the encampment.*

(*Enter M'Donald and Bland*)

BLAND.   It doth in truth appear, that as a—spy—
Detested word!—brave André must be view'd.
His sentence he confesses strictly just.
Yet sure, a deed of mercy, from thy hand,

Could never lead to ill. By such an act,
The stern and blood-stain'd brow of War
Would be disarmed of half its gorgon horrors;
More humanized customs be induced;
And all the race of civilized man
Be blest in the example. Be it thy suit;
'T will well become thy character and station.
M'DONALD. Trust me, young friend, I am alone the judge
Of what becomes my character and station;
And having judg'd that this young Briton's death,
Even 'though attended by thy father's murder,
Is necessary, in these times accurs'd,
When every thought of man is ting'd with blood,
I will not stir my finger to redeem them.
Nay, much I wonder, Bland, having so oft
The reasons for this necessary rigor
Enforced upon thee, thou wilt still persist
In vain solicitations. Imitate
Thy father!
BLAND. My father knew not André.
I know his value; owe to him my life;
And gratitude, that first, that best of virtues,—
Without the which man sinks beneath the brute,—
Binds me in ties indissoluble to him.
M'DONALD. That man-created virtue blinds thy reason.
Man owes to man all love; when exercised,
He does no more than duty. Gratitude,
That selfish rule of action, which commands
That we our preference make of men,
Not for their worth, but that they did *us* service,
Misleading reason, casting in the way
Of justice stumbling-blocks, cannot be virtue.
BLAND. Detested sophistry! 'T was André sav'd me.
M'DONALD. He sav'd thy life, and thou art grateful for it.
How self intrudes, delusive, on man's thoughts.
He sav'd thy life, yet strove to damn thy country;
Doom'd millions to the haughty Briton's yoke;
The best and foremost in the cause of virtue
To death, by sword, by prison, or the halter;
His sacrifice now stands the only bar
Between the wanton cruelties of war
And our much-suffering soldiers; yet when weigh'd
With gratitude, for that he sav'd *thy* life,
These things prove gossamer, and balance air;—
Perversion monstrous of man's moral sense!
BLAND. Rather perversion monstrous of all good

Is thy accurs'd, detestable opinion.
Cold-blooded reasoners, such as thee, would blast
All warm affection; asunder sever
Every social tie of humanized man.
Curst be thy sophisms, cunningly contriv'd
The callous coldness of thy heart to cover,
And screen thee from the brave man's detestation!
M'DONALD.   Boy, boy!
BLAND.   Thou knowest that André's not a spy.
M'DONALD.   I know him one. Thou hast acknowledg'd it.
BLAND.   Thou liest!
M'DONALD.   Shame on thy ruffian tongue! How passion
Mars thee! I pity thee. Thou canst not harm,
By words intemperate, a virtuous man.
I pity thee; for passion sometimes sways
My older frame, through former uncheck'd habit;
But when I see the havoc which it makes
In others, I can shun the snare accurst,
And nothing feel but pity.
BLAND (*Indignantly*).   Pity me! (*Approaches him, and speaks in an under
    voice*)
Thou canst be cool, yet, trust me, passion sways thee.
Fear does not warm the blood, yet 't is a passion.
Hast thou no feeling? I have call'd thee liar!
M'DONALD.   If thou could'st make me one, I then might grieve.
BLAND.   Thy coolness goes to freezing; thou 'rt a coward!
M'DONALD.   Thou knowest thou tell'st a falsehood.
BLAND.   Thou shalt know
None with impunity speaks thus of me.
That to rouse thy courage! (*Touches him gently with his open hand, in
    crossing him. M'Donald looks at him unmoved.*) Dost thou not yet feel?
M'DONALD.   For *thee* I feel. And, tho' another's acts
Cast no dishonor on the worthy man,
I still feel for thy father. Yet, remember,
I may not, haply, ever be thus guarded;
I may not always the distinction make,
However just, between the blow intended
To provoke, and one that's meant to injure.
BLAND.   Hast thou no sense of honor?
M'DONALD.   Truly, yes:
For I am honor's votary. Honor, with me,
Is worth; 't is truth; 't is virtue; 't is a thing
So high preëminent, that a boy's breath,
Or brute's, or madman's blow can never reach it.
My honor is so much, so truly mine,
That none hath power to wound it, save myself.

BLAND. I will proclaim thee through the camp a coward.
M'DONALD. Think better of it. Proclaim not thine own shame.
BLAND. I'll brand thee,—damnation! *(Exit)*
M'DONALD. O passion, passion!
A man who values fame far more than life;
A brave young man; in many things a good;
Utters vile falsehood; adds injury to insult;
Striving with blood to seal such foul injustice;
And all from impulse of unbridled feeling. *(Pause)*
Here comes the mother of this headstrong boy,
Severely rack'd. What shall allay her torture?
For common consolation, *here*, is insult.

(Enter Mrs. Bland and children)

MRS. BLAND. O my good friend!
M'DONALD *(Taking her hand)*. I know thy cause of sorrow.
Art thou now from our Commander?
MRS. BLAND *(Drying her tears and assuming dignity)*. I am.
But vain is my entreaty. All unmov'd
He hears my words, he sees my desperate sorrow.
Fain would I blame his conduct, but I cannot.
Strictly examin'd, with intent to mark
The error which so fatal proves to *me*,
My scrutiny but ends in admiration.
Thus when the prophet from the hills of Moab
Look'd down upon the chosen race of Heaven,
With fell intent to curse, ere yet he spake,
Truth all resistless, emanation bright
From great Adonai, fill'd his froward mind,
And chang'd the curses of his heart to blessings.
M'DONALD. Thou payest high praise to virtue. Whither now?
MRS. BLAND. I still must hover round this spot until
My doom is known.
M'DONALD. Then to my quarters, lady;
There shall my mate give comfort and refreshment:
One of your sex can best your sorrows soothe. *(Exeunt)*

Scene, *the prison.*

(Enter Bland)

BLAND. Where'er I look, cold desolation meets me.
My father—André—and self-condemnation.
Why seek I André now? Am *I* a man
To soothe the sorrows of a suffering friend?

The weather-cock of passion! fool inebriate!
Who could with ruffian hand strive to provoke
Hoar wisdom to intemperance! Who could lie!
Aye, swagger, lie, and brag!—Liar! Damnation!
O, let me steal away and hide my head,
Nor view a man, condemned to harshest death,
Whose words and actions, when by mine compar'd,
Show white as innocence and bright as truth.
I now would shun him, but that his shorten'd
Thread of life gives me no line to play with.
He comes with smiles, and all the air of triumph,
While *I* am sinking with remorse and shame;
Yet *he* is doom'd to death, and *I* am free.

(*Enter André*)

ANDRÉ.   Welcome, my Bland! Cheerly, a welcome hither!
I feel assurance that my last request
Will not be slighted. Safely thy father
Shall return to thee. (*Holding out a paper*) See what employment
For a dying man. Take thou these verses;
And, after my decease, send them to her
Whose name is woven in them; whose image
Hath controul'd my destiny. Such tokens
Are rather out of date. Fashions
There are in love as in all else; they change
As variously. A gallant knight, erewhile,
Of Cœur de Lion's day, would, dying, send
His heart home to its mistress; degenerate
Soldier, I send but some blotted paper.
BLAND.   If 't would not damp thy present cheerfulness,
I would require the meaning of thy words.
I ne'er till now did hear of André's mistress.
ANDRÉ.   Mine is a story of that common kind,
So often told, with scanty variation,
That the pall'd ear loaths the repeated tale.
Each young romancer chuses for his theme
The woes of youthful hearts, by the cold hand
Of frosty age, arm'd with parental power,
Asunder torn. But I long since have ceas'd
To mourn; well satisfied that she I love,
Happy in holy union with another,
Shares not my wayward fortunes, nor would I
Now these tokens send, remembrance to awaken,
But that I know her happy; and the happy
Can think on misery and share it not.

BLAND (*Agitated*).   Some one approaches.
ANDRÉ.   Why, 't is near the time!
But tell me, Bland, say, is the manner chang'd?
BLAND.   I hope it, but I yet have no assurance.
ANDRÉ.   Well, well!
HONORA (*Without*).   I must see him.
ANDRÉ.   Whose voice was that?
My senses! Do I dream? (*Leans on Bland*)

(*Enter Honora*)

HONORA.   Where is he?
ANDRÉ.   'T is she! (*Starts from Bland and advances towards Honora; she rushes into his arms.*)
HONORA.   It is enough! He lives, and *I* shall save him.
                    (*She faints in the arms of André.*)
ANDRÉ.   She sinks—assist me, Bland! O, save her, save her! (*Places her in a chair and looks tenderly on her*)
Yet, why should she awake from that sweet sleep?
Why should she ope her eyes—(*Wildly*)—to see me hung!
What does she here? Stand off—(*Tenderly*)—and let her die.
How pale she looks! How worn that tender frame!
She has known sorrow! Who could injure her?
BLAND.   She revives—André—soft, bend her forward.
                    (*André kneels and supports her.*)
HONORA.   André!—
ANDRÉ.   Lov'd excellence!
HONORA.   Yes, it is André! (*Rises and looks at him*)
No more deceived by visionary forms,
By him supported—(*Leans on him*)
ANDRÉ.   Why is this?
Thou dost look pale, Honora—sick and wan—
Languid thy fainting limbs—
HONORA.   All will be well.
But was it kind to leave me as thou did'st?
So rashly to desert thy vow-link'd wife?
ANDRÉ.   When made another's both by vows and laws—
HONORA (*Quitting his support*).   What meanest thou?
ANDRÉ.   Did'st thou not marry him?
HONORA.   Marry!
ANDRÉ.   Did'st thou not give thy hand away
From me?
HONORA.   O, never, never.
ANDRÉ.   Not married?
HONORA.   To none but thee, and but in will to thee.
ANDRÉ.   O blind, blind wretch! Thy father told me—

HONORA. Thou wast deceived. They hurried me away,
Spreading false rumors to remove thy love—
(*Tenderly*) Thou did'st too soon believe them.
ANDRÉ. Thy father—How could I but believe Honora's father?
And he did tell me so. I reverenc'd age,
Yet knew age was not virtue. I believed
His snowy locks, and yet they did deceive me.
I have destroy'd myself and thee!—Alas,
Ill-fated maid, why did'st thou not forget me?
Hast thou rude seas and hostile shores explor'd
For this? To see my death? Witness my shame?
HONORA. I come to bless thee, André, and shall do it.
I bear such offers from thy kind Commander
As must prevail to save thee. Thus the daughter
May repair the ills her cruel sire inflicted.
My father, dying, gave me cause to think
That arts were us'd to drive thee from thy home;
But what those arts I knew not. An heiress left,
Of years mature, with power and liberty,
I straight resolv'd to seek thee o'er the seas.
A long-known friend, who came to join her lord,
Yielded protection and lov'd fellowship.—
Indeed, when I did hear of thy estate,
It almost kill'd me;—I was weak before—
ANDRÉ. 'T is I have murder'd thee!
HONORA. All shall be well.
Thy General heard of me, and instant form'd
The plan of this my visit. I am strong,
Compar'd with what I was. Hope strengthens me;
Nay, even solicitude supports me now;
And when thou shalt be safe,*thou* wilt support me.
ANDRÉ. Support thee!—O Heaven! What!—and *must* I die?
Die!—and leave her *thus*—suffering—unprotected!

(*Enter Melville and guard*)

MELVILLE. I am sorry that my duty should require
Service, at which my heart revolts; but, sir,
Our soldiers wait in arms. All is prepar'd—
HONORA. To death! Impossible! Has my delay,
Then, murder'd him? A momentary respite—
MELVILLE. Lady, I have no power.
BLAND. Melville, my friend,
This lady bears dispatches of high import,
Touching this business; should they arrive too late—
HONORA. For pity's sake, and heaven's, conduct me to him;

And wait the issue of our conference.
O, 't would be murder of the blackest dye,
Sin execrable, not to break thy orders—
Inhuman, thou art not.
MELVILLE.   Lady, thou say'st true;
For rather would I lose my rank in arms,
And stand cashier'd for lack of discipline,
Than gain 'mongst military men all praise,
Wanting the touch of sweet humanity.
HONORA.   Thou grantest my request?
MELVILLE.   Lady, I do. Retire!   (*Soldiers go out.*)
BLAND.   I know not what excuse, to martial men,
Thou canst advance for this; but to thy heart
Thou wilt need none, good Melville.
ANDRÉ.   O Honora!
HONORA.   Cheer up, I feel assur'd. Hope wings my flight,
To bring thee tidings of much joy to come.
                    (*Exit Honora, with Bland and Melville*)
ANDRÉ.   Eternal blessings on thee, matchless woman!
If Death now comes, he finds the veriest coward
That e'er he dealt withal. I cannot think
Of dying. Void of fortitude, each thought
Clings to the world—the world that holds Honora!
                                        (*Exit*)

END OF THE FOURTH ACT.

ACT V.

Scene, *the encampment.*

(*Enter Bland*)

BLAND.   Suspense—uncertainty—man's bane and solace,
How racking now to me! My mother comes.
Forgive me, O my father, if in this war,
This wasting conflict of my 'wildering passions,
Memory of thee holds here a second place.
M'Donald comes with her. I would not meet him;
Yet I will do it. Summon up some courage—
Confess my fault, and gain, if not his love,
At least the approbation of my judgment.

(*Enter Mrs. Bland and children, with M'Donald*)

BLAND. Say, Madam, is there no change of counsel,
Or new determination?
MRS. BLAND. Naught new, my son.
The tale of misery is told unheard.
The widow's and the orphans' sighs
Fly up, unnoted by the eye of man,
And mingle, undistinguish'd, with the winds.
My friend (*To M'Donald*), attend thy duties. I must away.
SECOND CHILD. You need not cry, Mamma, the General will do it, I am
sure, for I saw him cry. He turn'd away his head from *you*, but I saw it.
MRS. BLAND. Poor thing! Come, let us home and weep. Alas! I can no
more, for war hath made men rocks.

(*Exeunt Mrs. Bland and children*)

BLAND. Colonel, I used thee ill this morning.
M'DONALD. No!
Thyself thou used'st most vilely, I remember.
BLAND. Myself sustained the injury, most true;
But the intent of what I said and did
Was ill to thee alone; I 'm sorry for it.
See'st thou these blushes? They proceed from warmth
As honest as the heart of man e'er felt;
But not with shame unmingled, while I force
This tongue, debased, to own it slander'd thee,
And utter'd—I could curse it—utter'd falsehood.
Howe'er misled by passion, still my mind
Retains that sense of honest rectitude
Which makes the memory of an evil deed
A troublesome companion. I was wrong.
M'DONALD. Why, now, this glads me; for thou now art right.
O, may thy tongue, henceforward, utter naught
But Truth's sweet precepts, in fair Virtue's cause!
Give me thy hand. (*Takes his hand*) Ne'er may it grasp a sword
But in defence of justice.
BLAND. Yet, erewhile,
A few short hours scarce past, when this vile hand
Attempted on *thee* insult; and was raised
Against thy honor; ready to be raised
Against thy life. If this my deep remorse—
M'DONALD. No more, no more! 'T is past. Remember it
But as thou would'st the action of another,
By thy enlighten'd judgment much condemn'd;
And serving as a beacon in the storms
Thy passions yet may raise. Remorse is vice;

Guard thee against its influence debasing.
Say to thyself: "I *am* not what I *was;*
I am not *now* the instrument of vice;
I'm changed; I am a man; Virtue's firm friend;
Sever'd forever from my former self;
No link, but in remembrance salutary."
BLAND.   How all men tower above me!*
M'DONALD.   Nay, not so.
Above what once thou wast, some few do rise;
None above what thou art.
BLAND.   It shall be so.
M'DONALD.   It is so.
BLAND.   Then to prove it.
For I must yet a trial undergo,
That will require a consciousness of virtue.   (*Exit*)
M'DONALD.   O, what a temper doth in man reside!
How capable of yet unthought perfection!   (*Exit*)

---

*After the first performance, this speech and the next five were deleted, and the fol-
lowing exchange, praising Washington, was substituted:*
BLAND.   Noble M'Donald, truth and honor's champion!
Yet think not strange that my intemperance wrong'd thee.
Good as thou art! for, would'st thou, can'st thou, think it?
My tongue, unbridled, hath the same offence,
With action violent, and boisterous tone,
Hurl'd on that glorious man, whose pious labors
Shield from every ill his grateful country.
That man, whom friends to adoration love,
And enemies revere. Yes, M'Donald,
Even in the presence of the first of men
Did I abjure the service of my country,
And reft my helmet of that glorious badge
Which graces even the brow of Washington.
How shall I see him more?
M'DONALD.   Alive himself to every generous impulse,
He hath excused the impetuous warmth of youth,
In expectation that thy fiery soul,
Chasten'd by time and reason, will receive
The stamp indelible of godlike virtue.
To me, in trust, he gave this badge disclaim'd,
With power, when thou should'st see thy wrongful error,
From him, to reinstate it in thy helm,
And thee in his high favor. (*Gives the cockade*)
BLAND (*Takes the cockade and replaces it*).   Shall I speak my thoughts of thee and
   him?
No! let my actions henceforth show what thou
And he have made me. Ne'er shall my helmet
Lack again its proudest, noblest ornament,
Until my country knows the rest of peace,
Or Bland the peace of death.   (*Exit*)

Scene, *the General's quarters.*

(*Enter General and Seward*)

GENERAL.   Ask her, my friend, to send by thee her pacquets.

(*Exit Seward*)

O, what keen struggles must I undergo!
Unbless'd estate; to have the power to pardon;
The court's stern sentence to remit;—give life;—
Feel the strong wish to use such blessed power;
Yet know that circumstances strong as fate
Forbid to obey the impulse. O, I feel
That man should never shed the blood of man!

(*Enter Seward*)

SEWARD.   Naught can the lovely suitor satisfy,
But conference with thee, and much I fear
Refusal would cause madness.
GENERAL.   Yet to admit,
To hear, be tortur'd, and refuse at last—
SEWARD.   Sure never man such spectacle of sorrow
Saw before. Motionless the rough-hewn soldiers
Silent view her, or walk aside and weep.
GENERAL (*After a pause*).   Admit her. (*Seward goes out.*) O, for the art, the precious art,
To reconcile the sufferer to his sorrows!

(*Honora rushes in and throws herself wildly on her knees before him; he endeavors to raise her.*)

HONORA.   Nay, nay, here is my place, or here, or lower,
Unless thou grant'st his life. All forms away!
Thus will I clasp thy knees, thus cling to thee—
I am his wife—'t is I have ruin'd him—
O, save him! Give him to me! Let us cross
The mighty seas, far, far—ne'er to offend again—

(*The General turns away and hides his eyes with his hand.*)

(*Enter Seward and an officer*)

GENERAL.   Seward, support her; my heart is torn in twain. (*Honora, as if exhausted, suffers herself to be raised, and leans on Seward.*)

OFFICER. This moment, sir, a messenger arrived
With well confirm'd and mournful information,
That gallant Hastings, by the lawless scouts
Of Britain taken, after cruel mockery
With show of trial and of condemnation,
On the next tree was hung.
HONORA (*Wildly*). O, it is false,
GENERAL. Why, why, my country, did I hesitate? (*Exit*)

(*Honora sinks, faints, and is borne off by Seward and officer.*)

Scene, *the prison.*

(*André meeting Bland*)

ANDRÉ. How speeds Honora? (*Pause*) Art thou silent, Bland?
Why, then, I know my task. The mind of man,
If not by vice debas'd, debilitated,
Or by disease of body quite unton'd,
Hath o'er its thoughts a power—energy divine.
Of fortitude the source and every virtue—
A godlike power, which e'en o'er circumstance
Its sov'reignty exerts. Now from my thoughts,
Honora! Yet she is left alone—expos'd—
BLAND. O, André, spurn me, strike me to the earth;
For what a wretch am I in André's mind,
That he can think he leaves his love alone,
And I retaining life!
ANDRÉ. Forgive me, Bland,
My thoughts glanc'd not on thee. Imagination
Pictur'd only, then, her orphan state, helpless;
Her weak and grief-exhausted frame. Alas!
This blow will kill her.
BLAND (*Kneeling*). Here do I myself
Devote, my fortune consecrate, to thee,
To thy remembrance, and Honora's service.
ANDRÉ. Enough! Let me not see her more—nor think of her—
Farewell, farewell, sweet image! Now for death.
BLAND. Yet that thou should'st the felon's fate fulfil—
Damnation! My blood boils. Indignation
Makes the current of my life course wildly
Through its round and maddens each emotion.
ANDRÉ. Come, come, it matters not.
BLAND. I do remember,
When a boy at school, in our allotted tasks,

We, by our puny acts, strove to pourtray
The giant thoughts of Otway. I was Pierre.
O, thou art Pierre's reality—a soldier,
On whose manly brow sits fortitude enamor'd;
A Mars, abhorring vice, yet doom'd to die
A death of infamy; thy corse expos'd
To vulgar gaze—halter'd—distorted—oh—(*Pauses, and then adds in a low hollow voice:*)
Pierre had a friend to save him from such shame—
And so hast thou.
ANDRÉ.   No more, as thou dost love me.
BLAND.   I have a sword, and arm, that never fail'd me.
ANDRÉ.   Bland, such an act would justly thee involve,
And leave that helpless one thou sworest to guard
Expos'd to every ill. O, think not of it!
BLAND.   If thou wilt not my aid—take it thyself. (*Draws and offers his sword*)
ANDRÉ.   No, men will say that cowardice did urge me.
In my mind's weakness, I did wish to shun
That mode of death which error represented
Infamous: now let me rise superior;
And with a fortitude too true to start
From mere appearances, show your country
That she, in me, destroys a man who might
Have liv'd to virtue.
BLAND (*Sheathing his sword*).   I will not think more of it;
I was again the sport of erring passion.
ANDRÉ.   Go thou and guide Honora from this spot.
HONORA (*Entering*).   Who shall oppose his wife? I will have way!
They, cruel, would have kept me from thee, André.
Say, am I not thy wife? Wilt thou deny me?
Indeed I am not dress'd in bridal trim.
But I have travelled far:—rough was the road—
Rugged and rough—that must excuse my dress.
(*Seeing André's distress*) Thou art not glad to see me.
ANDRÉ.   Break my heart!
HONORA.   Indeed, I feel not much in spirits. I wept but now.

(*Enter Melville and guard*)

BLAND (*To Melville*).   Say nothing.
ANDRÉ.   I am ready.
HONORA (*Seeing the guard*). Are *they* here?
Here again—the same—but they shall not harm me.
I am with *thee*, my André—I am safe—
And *thou* art safe with me. Is it not so? (*Clinging to him*)

(*Enter Mrs. Bland*)

MRS. BLAND.   Where is this lovely victim?
BLAND.   Thanks, my mother.
MRS. BLAND.   M'Donald sent me hither. My woes are past.
Thy father, by the foe released, already
Is in safety. This be forgotten now;
And every thought be turn'd to this sad scene.
Come, lady, home with me.
HONORA.   Go home with thee?
Art thou my André's mother? We will home
And rest, for thou art weary—very weary. (*Leans on Mrs. Bland*)

(*André retires to the guard, and goes off with them, looking on her to the last, and with an action of extreme tenderness takes leave of her. Melville and Bland accompany him.*)

HONORA.   Now we will go. Come, love! Where is he?
All gone!—I do remember—I awake—
They have him. Murder! Help! O, save him! save him!

(*Honora attempts to follow, but falls. Mrs. Bland kneels to assist her. Scene closes.*)

Scene, *the encampment.*

Procession to the execution of André. First enter Pioneers—detachment of Infantry—military Band of Music—Infantry. The music having passed off, enter André between Melville and American officer; they sorrowful, he cheerfully conversing as he passes over the stage.

ANDRÉ.   It may in me be merely prejudice,
The effect of young opinion deep engraved
Upon the tender mind by care parental;
But I must think your country has mistook
Her interests. Believe me, but for this I should
Not willingly have drawn a sword against her.
                 (*They bow their heads in silence*)
Opinon must, nay, ought to sway our actions;
Therefore—

(*Having crossed the stage, he goes out as still conversing with them. Another detachment of Infantry, with muffled and craped drums, closes the procession; as soon as they are off—*

Scene

draws and discovers the distant view of the encampment.)

(Procession enters in same order as before, proceeds up the stage, and goes off on the opposite side.)

(Enter M'Donald, leading Bland, who looks wildly back)

BLAND.   I dare not *thee* resist. Yet why, O why
Thus hurry me away?—
M'DONALD.   Would'st thou behold—
BLAND.   O, name it not!
M'DONALD.   Or would'st thou, by thy looks
And gestures wild, o'erthrow that manly calmness
Which, or assumed or felt, so well becomes thy friend?
BLAND.   What means that cannon's sound?
M'DONALD (*After a pause*).   Signal of death
Appointed. André, thy friend, is now no more.
BLAND.   Farewell, farewell, brave spirit! O! let my countrymen,
Henceforward when the cruelties of war
Arise in their remembrance; when their ready
Speech would pour forth torrents in their foe's dispraise,
Think on this act accurst, and lock complaint in silence. (*Bland throws
himself on the earth.*)
M'DONALD.   Such are the dictates of the heart, not head.
O, may the children of Columbia still
Be taught by every teacher of mankind,
Each circumstance of calculative gain,
Or wounded pride, which prompted our oppressors;
May every child be taught to lisp the tale;
And may, in times to come, no foreign force,
No European influence, tempt to misstate,
Or awe the tongue of eloquence to silence.
Still may our children's children deep abhor
The motives, doubly deep detest the actors;
Ever remembering that the race who plann'd,
Who acquiesced, or did the deeds abhor'd,
Has pass'd from off the earth; and, in its stead,
Stand men who challenge love or detestation
But from their proper, individual deeds.
Never let memory of the sire's offence
Descend upon the son.

CURTAIN DROPS.

METAMORA

or

The Last of the Wampanoags*

by

John Augustus Stone

*Metamora, or *The Last of the Wampanoags* by John Augustus Stone, reprinted by permission of the publisher and editor from *Dramas from the American Theatre,* 1762-1909, edited by Richard Moody, published by The World Publishing Company, Cleveland, Ohio, © 1966 by Richard Moody.

Introduction

John Augustus Stone, author of *Metamora*, is a somewhat mysterious figure. Born in Concord, Massachusetts, on December 15, 1800, he made his debut as an actor at the age of twenty, and the following year he married an actress, Mrs. Amelia Legge. Never a star, he specialized in character parts and comic roles. He appeared in New York and Philadelphia and also toured the South. Although he wrote seven or eight other plays, none achieved the popularity of *Metamora*, which opened at the Park Theatre on December 15, 1829, and became one of the most popular plays of the time. With Edwin Forrest playing the leading role, it drew packed houses wherever it was shown. Stone wrote the play in response to Forrest's announcement in *The Critic* for November 28, 1828, offering $500 plus a half-benefit for "the best tragedy in five acts, of which the hero, or principal character, shall be an aboriginal of this country." A committee with William Cullen Bryant as chairman served as judges; and, as Forrest probably had anticipated, the contest stirred considerable advance interest in the play. The Prologue and Epilogue, which were written by members of the committee, reflect some apprehension that audiences would not accept a play by an American playwright on an American theme, but the play was received enthusiastically. On May 29, 1834, despondent and ill, Stone committed suicide by leaping into the Schuylkill River in Philadelphia. Forrest placed a monument over his grave inscribed "To the Memory of John Augustus Stone, Author of Metamora, by His Friend Edwin Forrest."

Nothing illustrates the actors' domination of the early American stage more vividly than Forrest's relationship with Stone and other dramatists. The playwright received a pittance; the star made a fortune. The best illustration of this inequity is Robert Montgomery Bird of Philadelphia, who wrote prize-winning plays in four of Forrest's subsequent contests but never received a financial return comparable with Forrest's. Between 1829 and 1833, Bird wrote four plays, including *The Gladiator*, one of Forrest's most popular roles. For a time the two men were close friends, but soon they began quarreling over money. Forrest insisted that Bird should return $2000 paid him for a revision of *Metamora* that had not been acted; Bird claimed that Forrest owed him $6000 on an oral promise. The result was that Bird, who was developing into an accomplished dramatist, turned to writing fiction and verse and seldom even attended a theatre for the rest of his life. In 1869 Forrest refused to permit Bird's son to publish his father's plays, claiming (falsely) that he owned the copyrights.

Edwin Forrest dominated the American stage during the second quarter of the 19th century. Born in Philadelphia, he made his stage debut at eleven and was a star at twenty. Muscular and vigorous, he excelled in roles that displayed his physique and afforded scope for his booming voice. Late in 1823 he went to New Orleans, where he enjoyed considerable success and became a close friend of the famous Colonel Bowie. Lawrence Barrett, one of his biographers, believed that his acquaintance in New Orleans with the Choctaw chief Pushmataha (*c.* 1765-December 24, 1824) influenced his conception of the role of Metamora. At any rate, the part of the Indian chief ("the grandest model of a mighty man") pitted against the forces of civilization suited Forrest's style perfectly. A scandalous divorce suit in 1851 brought Forrest considerable notoriety but did not diminish his popularity with audiences at the Bowery Theatre. Some measure of his taste is suggested by the fact that after the court battles with his wife began he played the role of Othello with particular zest and sometimes delivered addresses to his audiences attacking his wife and vindicating his own conduct. A man of enormous energy and impetuous vigor, Forrest established a flamboyant and declamatory acting style for his generation. When he died in Philadelphia, he bequeathed enough money to found the Edwin Forrest Home for Aged and Infirm Actors.

Stone's play has a tenuous basis in American colonial history. He probably borrowed from *Superstition* (1824), a play by James Nelson Barker, the legend that one of the regicides (the men responsible for the execution of Charles I) found refuge in America. He based his main plot on King Philip's War (1675-76). Massasoit, chief of the Wampanoags, made a treaty with the first Pilgrim settlers. His son, Metacom, called King Philip by the colonists, professed a desire to continue his father's peaceful policies, but secretly plotted to destroy the settlements. In the series of raids and skirmishes that resulted from this plot, Philip's tribe was virtually annihilated.

Beginning in the 1820s Americans became fascinated with the Indian as subject matter for literature and painting. This fascination was a corollary of the primitivism evident in various phases of the Romantic Movement. The mysterious red man stirred the imaginations of Easterners, for whom he was no longer a menace but a vague memory. Colorful costumes, religious ceremonies, burial customs, and other picturesque details appealed to the romantic imagination. Beautiful Indian princesses, defiant warriors, and wise old chieftains abounded in the literature of the time. They spoke with natural eloquence, using a figurative style which authors derived from interpreters' versions of treaty parleys, from *Ossian*, and from their own imaginations. The Indian was always presented as a member of a doomed race. One can speculate as to the psychological and social origins of this interest, as Americans apparently took a morbid satisfaction from the pathos of a primitive people fated to be destroyed by the inevitable extension of civilization. This "vanishing redman" concept, which was encouraged by the Indian removals in the 1830s and 1840s, is reflected in titles and subtitles of many literary works that begin *The Last of the*. . . .

The Indian invited epic treatment, and beginning in the 1820's a number of lengthy, now forgotten narrative poems appeared; for example, *Logan* (1821) by Samuel Webber, *Traits of the Aboriginees* (1822) by Lydia Sigourney, *Sannilac* (1831) by Henry Whiting, *Powhatan* (1841) by Seba Smith, *Tecumseh* (1842) by George H. Colton, and *Alhalla* (1843) by Henry Rowe Schoolcraft. The culmination of the poetic treatments of Indian themes was Longfellow's *Hiawatha* (1855).

In fiction James Fenimore Cooper's novels were both cause and effect of the Indian vogue. His *Last of the Mohicans* (1826) contains most of the themes, character types, and situations exploited by other writers. Two opposite views of the Indian's true nature prevailed—that he was a treacherous child of Satan and that he was a guileless child of nature. The first, which might be termed the "pesky redskin" theory, prevailed on the frontier. The second or "noble savage" theory, derived largely from Rousseau, predominated in literature. Cooper presented both sides with no apparent awareness that he was straddling the issue. Some of his Indians (chiefly Iroquois and Sioux) are bloodthirsty savages whom he frequently compares to animals. Others (Mohicans, Delawares, and Pawnees) are generous, brave and chivalrous; Cooper compares them to Apollo or to medieval knights. Other authors often embodied the antithesis of nobility and savagery in the same character; Metamora is both an implacable enemy of civilization and its pathetic victim.

Until recently, only two texts of *Metamora*, both incomplete, were known—a manuscript at the Edwin Forrest Home in Philadelphia which gives only Metamora's speeches and cues and one at the University of Utah which lacks the fourth act. Richard Moody of Indiana University discovered a third copy (lacking Act V) among the Lord Chamberlain's plays in the British Museum. A transcription of the composite play with textual notes is included in his *Dramas from the American Theatre 1762-1909* (Cleveland, World Publishing Company, 1966).

That *Metamora* is generally regarded as the best of the Indian plays indicates the literary quality of this genre. Other plays with which it might be compared include *Ponteach* (1766) written by Major Robert Rogers but never produced, *The Indian Princess* (1808) by James Nelson Barker, *The Indian Prophecy* (1827) and *Pocahontas* (1830) by George William Custis, and *The Forest Princess* (1848) by Mrs. Charlotte Barnes Conner. In general, for a variety of reasons good and bad, the Indian has been presented as a melodramatic stereotype in all media from Stone's day to the present.

Edwin Forrest as Metamora

(Hoblitzelle Theatre Arts Library, University of Texas)

(Harvard Theatre Collection)

Cast of Characters

INDIANS

METAMORA, chief of the Wampanoags
KANESHINE, an Indian prophet
ANNAWANDAH, the traitor
OTAH, an Indian boy
INDIAN BOY, child of Metamora
NAHMEOKEE, wife of Metamora
INDIANS, WARRIORS, ETC.

ENGLISH

LORD FITZARNOLD
SIR ARTHUR VAUGHAN
MORDAUNT
ERRINGTON, chief of the council
WALTER, an orphan
CAPTAIN CHURCH
WOLFE
GOODENOUGH
TRAMP
OCEANA, Mordaunt's daughter
SOLDIERS, SAILORS, PEASANTS, ETC.

Prologue

Written by Mr. Prosper M. Wetmore.
Spoken by Mrs. Barrett, New Park Theater,
New York, December 15, 1829.

Not from the records of Imperial Rome,
Or classic Greece—the muses' chosen home—
From no rich legends of the olden day
Our bard hath drawn the story of his play;
Led by the guiding hand of genius on,
He here hath painted Nature on her throne;
His eye hath pierced the forest's shadowy gloom,
And read strange lessons from a nation's tomb:
Brief are the annals of that blighted race—
These halls usurp a monarch's resting-place—
Tradition's mist-enshrouded page alone
Tells that an empire was—we know 'tis gone!
From foreign climes full oft the muse has brought
Her glorious treasures of gigantic thought;
And here, beneath the witchery of her power,
The eye hath poured its tributary shower:
When modern pens have sought th' historic page,
To picture forth the deeds of former age—
O'er soft Virginia's sorrows ye have sighed,
And dropt a tear when spotless beauty died;
When Brutus "cast his cloud aside"; to stand
The guardian of the tyrant-trampled land—
When patriot Tell his clime from thraldom freed,
And bade th' avenging arrow do its deed,
Your bosoms answered with responsive swell,
For freedom triumphed when th' oppressors fell!
These were the melodies of humbler lyres,
The lights of Genius, yet without his fires;
But when the master-spirit struck the chords,
And inspiration breathed her burning words—
When passion's self stalked living o'er the stage,
To plead with love, or rouse the soul to rage—
When Shakespeare led his bright creations forth,
And conjured up the mighty dead from earth—
Breathless—entranced—ye've listened to the line,

And felt the minstrel's power, all but divine!
While thus your plaudits cheer the stranger lay,
Shall native pens in vain the field essay?
To-night we test the strength of native powers,
Subject, and bard, and actor, all are ours—
'Tis yours to judge, if worthy of a name,
And bid them live within the halls of fame!

ACT I

Scene 1

Sunset. A wild, picturesque scene; high, craggy rocks in distance; dark pine trees, etc. Rocks cross stage, with platform cross behind. Steps, etc., at back. A rude tomb, flowers growing around it. Half dark. Mordaunt discovered leaning on tomb. Slow music.

MORDAUNT. The sun has sunk behind yon craggy rocks; and day's last beams are fading from the clouds that fleet in hurrying masses through the sky, like tattered banners of a flying host! England, my home! When will thy parent arms again enfold me? Oh! When for me will dawn a day of hope? Will not sincere repentance from my scathed brow efface the brand of regicide?

TRAMP. (*Outside*) What ho! Good Master Mordaunt! (*Cannon*)

MORDAUNT. Ha! What mean those sounds? Now, your news? (*Enter Tramp*)

TRAMP. A gallant bark, urged by the favoring breeze, makes for the crowded shore.

MORDAUNT. From England! Ha!

TRAMP. St. George's banner floats from her high mast, and her long signal pennon gleams with green and gold.

MORDAUNT. 'Tis he—he comes and with him hope arrives. Go, hasten, fellow; seek my daughter; say the Lord Fitzarnold comes to greet her. (*Tramp crosses to the right behind.*) Marshal my followers in their best array—away to the beach and let loud music welcome him ashore. (*Exit Tramp*) What mingled feelings crowd about my heart, blended so strange and wild? Sunned by his sovereign's smile, Fitzarnold comes to woo and wed my daughter. Born on the heaving deep, the child of storms, and reared in savage wilds, her worth and beauty well may grace the courtly halls of England. And yet, to force her gentle will, whose every thought has been to soothe my sorrows and relieve my cares! Yet must she wed

Fitzarnold. His alliance can with oblivion shroud the past, clear from my scutcheon every rebel stain, and give my franchised spirit liberty.

(*Exit. Slow music, four bars. Enter Oceana, looking around as if in search.*)

OCEANA.   Sure, 'twas my father's voice, and loud in converse. Father! Dear father! Not here? And yet I thought—(*Flute heard, distant*) Ha! whence that strain? So soft yet strange. Methinks some pious minstrel seeks the moonlight hour to breathe devotion forth in melody. (*Music changes.*) Hark! It changes place and measure, too. Now deeper in the woods it warbles, now it seems aloft floating in plaintive tones through the air. This place—the hour—the day—heavens! 'tis my mother's birthday, and her grave undecked with flowers! O my mother, my dear mother! Perhaps her angel spirit hovers here o'er her lone daughter's steps, a guardian still. (*Kneels to tomb*) Ah, what flower is this? "Forgetmenot!" (*Music ceases.*) My mother, look from thy seraph home upon thy child, and when for those thou lovest on earth thou breathest a prayer, oh, then forget me not. (*Places flower in bosom. Enter Walter*)
WALTER.   Oceana!
OCEANA.   Walter, was thine the strain but now I heard?
WALTER.   'Twas but an humble tribute to thy beauty, but could not match the sweetness of thy voice, whose every tone, attuned to dulcet sounds, can melt the soul to nature's harmony.
OCEANA.   Walter, this from thee.
WALTER.   Nay, blame me not; although dependent on Sir Arthur Vaughan, nameless and poor, yet do I not despair, for in my heart a sacred treasure lies I would not barter for my patron's gold.
OCEANA.   What means't thou, Walter?
WALTER.   Thine own sweet image, which naught on earth can banish or efface—a whispered hope I dare not speak aloud—a light thine own bright eyes have kindled up.
OCEANA.   Nay, Walter, you ask not of the danger I escaped!
WALTER.   Danger! What danger? When?
OCEANA.   'Twas yestere'en, when I was lingering on the eastern beach, all heedless of the coming night, a panther growling from the thicket rushed and marked me for his prey. Powerless I stood—my blood stood still—I shrieked as I strove to fly, when at the instant, from a ready hand, swift as the lightning's flash, an arrow came and felled the monster as he crouched to spring.
WALTER.   Didst mark who sent it?
OCEANA.   Full well I did. High on a craggy rock an Indian stood, with sinewy arm and eye that pierced the glen. His bowstring drawn to wing a second death, a robe of fur was o'er his shoulder thrown, and o'er his long,

dark hair an eagle's plume waved in the breeze, a feathery diadem. Firmly he stood upon the jutting height, as if a sculptor's hand had carved him there. With awe I gazed as on the cliff he turned—the grandest model of a mighty man.

WALTER.   'Twas Haups' great chieftain, Metamora called; our people love him not, nor is it strange; he stands between them and extended sway, ready alike with words of power to urge, or gleaming weapon force his princely dues.

METAMORA.   (*Outside*) Hah! Ha!

OCEANA.   (*Going up*) Behold his dread encounter with a wolf. His vanquished foe with mighty arm he hurls down the steep height where mortal never trod.

METAMORA.   Hah! Hah! (*Enters on rock, passes across and off*)

WALTER.   (*At Metamora's exit*) 'Tis Metamora, the noble sachem of a valiant race—the white man's dread, the Wampanoag's hope. (*Enter Metamora*)

METAMORA.   Ha, ha, ha! Turned on me—brave beast; he died like a red man.

OCEANA.   Chief, you are hurt; this scarf will staunch the wound. (*Offers it*)

METAMORA.   No! (*Rejects it*)

WALTER.   'Tis Oceana—she whose life you saved.

METAMORA.   Metamora will take the white maiden's gift. (*Oceana ties his arm with scarf.*)

OCEANA.   But yestere'en thou savedst my life, great chief; how can I pay thee for the generous deed?

METAMORA.   Hearken, daughter of the pale face; Metamora forgives not a wrong and forgets not a kindness. In the days of his age, Massasoit, my father, was in the white man's dwelling; while there, the spirit of the grave touched him and he laid down to die. A soft hand was stretched out to save him; it was the hand of thy mother. She that healed him sleeps in yonder tomb; but why should Metamora let his arrows sleep in the quiver when her daughter's life was in danger and her limbs shook with fear? Metamora loves the mild-eyed and the kind, for such is Nahmeokee.

WALTER.   Such words, and more than all, such deeds, should win you, chief, the love of all our people. Would you were more among us. Why never seek our homes? Sir Arthur Vaughan's doors will open to the Indian chief.

OCEANA.   My sire will thank thee for his daughter's life.

METAMORA.   The red man's heart is on the hills where his father's shafts have flown in the chase. Ha! I have been upon the high mountain top where the grey mists were beneath my feet, and the Great Spirit passed by me in his wrath. He spake in anger and the old rocks crumbled beneath the flash of his spear. Then I was proud and smiled, for I had slain the great bird whose wing never tires, and whose eye never shrinks; and his feathers would adorn the long black hair of Nahmeokee, daughter of Miantonemo, the great hunter. The war and the chase are the red man's brother and sister. The storm cloud in its fury frights him not. Wrapt in the spoils he has won, he lays him down and no one comes near to steal. The Great Spirit hears his evening prayer, and he sleeps amidst the roar of a mighty cataract.

WALTER. Were all thy nation mild and good like thee, how soon the fire of discord might be quenched.

METAMORA. Metamora has been the friend of the white man; yet if the flint be smitten too hard it will show that in its heart is fire. The Wampanoag will not wrong his white brother who comes from the land that is first touched by the rising sun; but he owns no master, save that One who holds the sun in his right hand, who rides on a dark storm, and who cannot die. (*Crosses to the left*)

WALTER. That lofty bearing—that majestic mien—the regal impress sits upon his brow, and earth seems conscious of her proudest son. (*Conch shell heard sounding from the right*)

METAMORA. Ha! My young men return from their evening toil, and their hands are filled with the sweet fish of the lake. Come to my wigwam; ye shall eat of fish that the Great Spirit of the waters sends, and your hearts shall be made glad. (*Going to the right, but returns and takes from his head an eagle plume*) Maiden, take this; it means speed and safety; when the startling whoop is heard and the war hatchet gleams in the red blaze, let it be found in thy braided hair. Despise not the red man's gift; it will bring more good to you than the yellow earth the white man worships as his god. Take it—no Wampanoag's hand will e'er be raised against the head or hand that bears the eagle plume. (*Crosses to Walter*) Young man, be thou like the oak in its spreading power and let thy tough branches shelter the tender flower that springs up under them. Look to the maiden of the eagle plume, and—come to my wigwam. (*Exit*)

OCEANA. Teach him, Walter; make him like to us.

WALTER. 'Twould cost him half his native virtues. Is justice goodly? Metamora's just. Is bravery virtue? Metamora's brave. If love of country, child and wife and home, be to deserve them all—he merits them.

OCEANA. Yet he is a heathen.

WALTER. True, Oceana, but his worship though untaught and rude flows from his heart, and Heaven alone must judge of it. (*Enter Tramp*)

TRAMP. Your father, lady, requires your presence.

OCEANA. Say I come. (*A distant drum*)

WALTER. What is that?

TRAMP. The drum that summons Lord Fitzarnold's escort. He comes a suitor for my lady's hand. (*Exit Tramp*)

WALTER. Deny it, Oceana—say 'tis false!

OCEANA. It is—

WALTER. Untrue?

OCEANA. Oh, most unwelcome.

WALTER. Heavens! You tremble—and your cheek is pale—my Lord Fitzarnold, that most courtly gentleman, and must my hopes—

OCEANA. Walter, dost thou mean—

WALTER. Obey thy sire. I cannot say farewell. But, oh, when highborn revelers carouse, and proud Fitzarnold lords it at the board, give one brief thought to me! That blessed thought shall soothe the fond complainings of my heart and hush them to repose. (*Exit Walter and Oceana*)

Scene 2

Lights up. A room in Sir Arthur's house. Enter Sir Arthur and Walter.

WALTER. Yet hear me, sir.

SIR ARTHUR. Forebear; thou art too hot.

WALTER. 'Tis not the meanness of our state that galls us, but men's opinions. Poverty and toil and consciousness of lowly destiny sit lightly where no scorn is heaped upon them. But yesterday I was indeed content, for none despised, none had learned to scoff the son of charity, the wretched ship boy who could trace existence no further than the wreck from which you plucked him; but now 'tis changed, all suddenly begin to find me base.

SIR ARTHUR. Marry, go to! You wrong yourself and me. Have I not fostered you—like a father tutored you? In early life bereft of wife and child, wearied of discord and fierce civil strife, I left the haunts of wild and factious men, to woo contentment in this wilderness. My heart was vacant and received thee in. Do not by any rash, unworthy act forsake that heart. Who is it finds thee base?

WALTER. All, since Fitzarnold is expected here.

SIR ARTHUR. Fitzarnold! What a plague! There is naught talked of or thought of but Lord Fitzarnold! And yet this noble viscount, but for his coat and title were a man to look with scorn upon—a profligate and spendthrift as fame already has too truly shown him.

WALTER. And 'tis for such a man that Master Mordaunt sets me aside—for such a man his daughter must cast me off.

SIR ARTHUR. Tut! Master Mordaunt is too wise a man to give his daughter to this Lord Fitzarnold. Patience awhile, and watch the progress of this meteor. Patience, and trust to fortune. (*Exit*)

WALTER. This lordly suitor comes to wake me from my cherished dreams, and crush the hopes which lately looked so fair. And shall I yield the glorious prize I deemed was wholly mine? Yield, and without a struggle? No, by heaven! Look to thyself, Fitzarnold. Let Oceana be but true, I heed not all thy power, thy wealth, thy titles, backed though they be by Mordaunt's selfish views. (*Exit*)

Scene 3

The harbor. Ships anchored in the distance. Military music. Mor-daunt, Errington, Goodenough, Church, Soldiers, Citizens (male and female) discovered. A boat comes on from the left with Fitzarnold, Wolfe, and Sailors, who land. Shout.

MORDAUNT.   Long live the king! Welcome Fitzarnold! Rest to the sea-worn! Joy to each and all!
FITZARNOLD.   I thank thee, Mordaunt! But I did not think to see such faces in the wilderness! Thy woody shores are bright with sparkling eyes, like Argonaut's adventurous sailors. But where's the golden boon we look for, sir? Fair Oceana—Mordaunt, where is she? (*Walter enters from the left and stands against the wing.*)
MORDAUNT.   So please you, my lord, at home, eager to pay your lordship's kindness back, and prove she can discern thy courtesy.
WALTER.   (*Aside*) Indeed! Dost say so, worldling?
MORDAUNT.   Pray thee, regard these gentlemen, my lord—our council's father, Errington—and this our army's leader; elders of the State.

(*Introducing them severally; Fitzarnold salutes them, and at last ap-proaching Walter, extends his hand; Walter bows coldly but does not take it. Music eight bars.*)

FITZARNOLD.   How now, young sir? Mordaunt, who is this?
MORDAUNT.   My noble lord, I pray thee, heed him not! A wayward youth, somewhat o'er worn with study. (*Crosses to Walter*) Rash boy! Be wise and tempt me not; I can destroy—
WALTER.   Thy daughter's peace and wed her there. (*Mordaunt gives Walter a look of hate and turns from him.*)
MORDAUNT.   Forth to the hall—a strain of music there. (*Crosses to the right*)
FITZARNOLD.   Young sir, I shall desire some further converse with you.
WALTER.   At injury's prompting, deeds, not words, were best. My lord, you shall find me. (*Touches his sword*)
FITZARNOLD.   Now for thy fair daughter, Mordaunt, come.

(*Music. Exeunt all but Walter and Wolfe. Peasants and Soldiers exeunt.*)

WOLFE.   Thou goest not with them?
WALTER.   No, nor before, nor follow after. But why dost thou ask?
WOLFE.   Because I know thee.
WALTER.   Then thou knowest one who will not take a lordling by the hand, because his fingers shine with hoops of gold—nor shun the beggar's grasp if it be honest. Thou knowest me?

WOLFE. Yes!

WALTER. To know oneself was thought task enough in olden time. What dost thou know?

WOLFE. That thou wert wrecked and saved.

WALTER. Aye, more's the pity! (*Aside*) Had I been drowned I had not lived to love and have no hope.

WOLFE. Thou art a good man's son.

WALTER. A pity then, again. Were I a rascal's offspring, I might thrive. What more?

WOLFE. Thou shalt possess thy mistress.

WALTER. Didst mark that lord?

WOLFE. He is my master.

WALTER. Then I am dumb. Be faithful to him, and now farewell. (*Crosses to the left*)

WOLFE. Yet in good time I will say that you will bestow a blessing for.

WALTER. Indeed! What mean you?

(*Enter Tramp with packet*)

TRAMP. News from the Indians. (*Shows packet*) 'Tis for the council by a horseman left, who bade me see it with all haste delivered. The Indian tribes conspire from east to west and faithful Sasamond has found his grave! This packet must be borne to Mordaunt.

WALTER. Trust it with me.

TRAMP. That I will readily, so thou wilt bear it safely.

WALTER. Aye, and quickly, too. (*Takes packet, crosses to the right*) Let me remember Metamora's words—"Look to the maiden of the eagle plume."

(*Exit hastily, followed by Wolfe, and Tramp. Quick curtain.*)

ACT II

Scene 1

Music. Interior of a wigwam; a skin rolled. Stage covered with skins, etc. Child on skin near entrance. Nahmeokee near it. Metamora at the left, preparing for the chase.

NAHMEOKEE. Thou wilt soon be back from the chase.

METAMORA. Yes, before the otter has tasted his midday food on the bank of the stream, his skin shall make a garment for Nahmeokee when the snow whitens the hunting grounds and the cold wind whistles through the trees. Nahmeokee, take our little one from his rest; he sleeps too much.

NAHMEOKEE. Oh, no! But thou, Metamora, sleepst too little. In the still hour of midnight when Wekolis has sung his song, and the great light has gone down behind the hills, when Nahmeokee's arms like the growing vine were round thee—as if some danger lay waiting in the thick wood— thou didst bid me bring thy tomahawk and the spear that Massasoit had borne when the war cry of the Wampanoags was loudest in the place of blood! Why is thy rest like the green lake when the sudden blast passes across its bosom?

METAMORA. Nahmeokee, the power of dreams has been on me, and the shadows of things that are to be have passed before me. My heart is big with a great thought. When I sleep I think the knife is red in my hand, and the scalp of the white man is streaming.

NAHMEOKEE. Metamora, is not the white man our brother? And does not the Great Spirit look on him as he does on us? Do not go towards his home today because thy wrath is kindled and it spreads like the flames which the white man makes in the dark bosom of the forest. Let Nahmeokee clasp her arms around thee; rest thy head upon her bosom, for it is hot and thy eye is red with the thoughts that burn! Our old men counsel peace, and the aim of the white man will spare.

METAMORA. Yes, when our fires are no longer red, on the high places of our fathers; when the bones of our kindred make fruitful the fields of the stranger, which he has planted amidst the ashes of our wigwams; when we are hunted back like the wounded elk far toward the going down of the sun, our hatchets broken, our bows unstrung and war whoop hushed; then will the stranger spare, for we will be too small for his eye to see.

(Trumpet. Enter Otah.)

OTAH. O son of Massasoit, the power of the white man approaches, and he looks not like one who seeks the Wampanoag's friendship! Look where the bright weapons flash through the clouds of his track.

METAMORA. Ha! Let the paleface come with the calumet or with the knife, Metamora does not fear their power. Where is Annawandah, skilled in talk? Let him approach me.

(Exit Otah)

NAHMEOKEE. Our child would not rest in the mid-hour of night for the hidden snake had bitten him as he lay stretched in the rays of the sun. I rose from my seat to get the dried leaves the Good Spirit has filled with power to heal; the moon was bright and a shadow passed me. It was Annawandah passed our wigwam; his step was like the course of the serpent and he paused and listened. My eye followed him to the seaside, and his light canoe shot like an arrow across the slumbering waters.

METAMORA. Humph! Was he alone?

NAHMEOKEE. Alone.

METAMORA. And he went with fear?
NAHMEOKEE. Like one who goes to steal.

(Trumpet. Enter Otah.)

OTAH. Look! The white warrior comes.

(Enter Church, Sir Arthur Vaughan, and Goodenough, with musqueteers.)

CHURCH. Although we come unbidden, chieftain, yet is our purpose friendly.
METAMORA. Why do you bring your fire weapons if you come to hold a talk of peace?
CHURCH. It is our custom.
METAMORA. Well, speak; my ears are open to hear.
SIR ARTHUR. Philip, our mission is—
METAMORA. Philip! I am the Wampanoag chief, Metamora.
SIR ARTHUR. We are directed by our council's head, for the times are filled with doubt, and to make *sure* our bond of peace and love to urge your presence at the council.
NAHMEOKEE. *(Aside)* Do not go.
METAMORA. Daughter of Miantinemo, peace! *(To them)* I will go.
CHURCH. Our troops shall form thy escort there.
METAMORA. I know the path.
SIR ARTHUR. We must not go without thee, chief.
METAMORA. I have breasted the cold winds of forty winters and to those that spoke kindly to me in the words of love I have been pliant—aye, very yielding like the willow that droops over the stream, but till with a single arm you can move the mighty rock that mocks the lightning and the storm seek not to stir Metamora when his heart says no. I will come! *(Crosses to the right)*
CHURCH. We shall expect thee, chief.
METAMORA. Metamora cannot lie.
CHURCH. Stand to your arms.

(Trumpet. Exit Church, Goodenough, Otah and Soldiers.)

SIR ARTHUR. Be thou not rash, but with thy tongue of manly truth dispel all charge that wrongs thy noble nature. Throw not the brand that kindles bloody war lest thou thyself should be the victim. *(Sir Arthur going to the left)*
METAMORA. My father's deeds shall be my counsellors, and the Great Spirit will hear the words of my mouth. *(Exit Sir Arthur)* Now, Nahmeokee, I will talk to thee. Dost thou not love this little one, Nahmeokee?
NAHMEOKEE. Oh, yes!

METAMORA. When first his little eyes unclosed, thou saidst they were like mine; and my people rejoiced with a mighty joy, that the grandson of Massasoit, the white man's friend, should rule in the high places of his kindred; and hoped that his days would be long and full of glory. Nahmeokee, by the blood of his warlike race, he shall not be the white man's slave.

NAHMEOKEE. Thy talk is strange, and fear creeps over me. Thy heart is beating at thy side, as if thy bosom could not hold it.

METAMORA. Because 'tis full of thee—and thee, my little one. Humph! Bring me the knife thy brother wore in battle—my hatchet—the spear that was thy father's when Uncas slew him for the white man's favor. Humph! These things thou gavest me with thyself; thinkest thou this arm can wield them in the fight?

NAHMEOKEE. Ah! Thy bravery will lose thee to me.

METAMORA. Let not thy heart be troubled. If I require assistance from my people, I will lift up a flame on the lofty hill that shall gleam afar through the thick darkness.

NAHMEOKEE. I shall remember thy words.

METAMORA. Take in thy babe; I am going. (*Crosses to the left*)

NAHMEOKEE. Metamora, dost thou go alone?

METAMORA. No; Manito is with me.

(*Exit. Nahmeokee exit.*)

Scene 2

A room in the house of Mordaunt. Enter Oceana.

OCEANA. Free from Fitzarnold's gaze, I feel myself again. Why came he here? His looks appalled me yet my father smiled—ah! he comes.

(*Enter Mordaunt*)

MORDAUNT. How now, my daughter; how is this? Why have you left his lordship thus?

OCEANA. I thought 'twas time.

MORDAUNT. It is not time to play the prude, when noble men confess thy charms and come fair suitors to thee. Fitzarnold loves thee and his alliance is so dear to me, I'll have no scruples of a timid girl to weigh against it. For long years I've nursed this fondness and I now command obedience.

OCEANA. That union must remain unblessed wherein the helpless hand is giving no heart to bear it company. O my father, how at the altar can I take that vow my heart now whispers never can be kept.

MORDAUNT. Hear me, rash girl, now that none o'erhear our converse. Learn thy father's destiny—the name I bear is not my own!

OCEANA. My father!

MORDAUNT. Thou didst not know my former life and deeds. Hardy ad
venture and the shock of arms, civil contention and a monarch's death
make up the past, and poison all who come! 'Tis thou alone can clothe
my future days with peace and shed one cheering ray o'er a dark scene
of terror.

OCEANA. Art thou distraught?

MORDAUNT. Do not deny me, girl, and make me so! I am an outcast and
a man forbid. Fitzarnold knows me and he asks my child—has power, and
gaining thee preserves thy sire. Speak, Oceana! Thy resolve: what is it?

OCEANA. Thou canst not mean it, father! No, it cannot be!

MORDAUNT. Girl, it is as certain as our earthly doom. Decide, then, now
between my honor and my instant death! For by thy mother's memory
and by my soul, if my despair do find thee pitiless, my own right hand
shall end a wretched life and leave thee nothing for a bridal dower but
my curses and a blighted name. (*Crosses to the right*)

OCEANA. My throat is parched! I pray a moment's peace, a moment's
pause.

(*Business. Mordaunt paces the stage in great agitation, at last falls
on his knee to Oceana. Walter enters, starts at seeing them and
remains at back.*)

MORDAUNT. Look at thy father, lowly begging life of thee. I will not
swear, I will not rave, my child, but I'll implore thee! If thou hast ever
loved me and dost so still, show that affection now! Let not thy father's
name forever stand a mark for men to heap their curses on—relent, my
child.

OCEANA. I can endure no more—rise, my father.

MORDAUNT. Dost thou promise?

OCEANA. All, all!

MORDAUNT. Swear, by truth! by honor! By the dead—

OCEANA. To wed Fitzarnold—

WALTER. (*Comes up*) Hold! Hold, rash girl, forebear! Thou art ensnared
and wouldst pronounce thy doom.

MORDAUNT. Lightning consume thee, meddling fool! What bringst thou
here?

WALTER. No pleasant duty, sir; a message which the council sends thee
here. (*Gives packet to Mordaunt*) I am no spy, nor do I care to know
secrets too dread for thine own heart to hold.

MORDAUNT. Beggar, begone!

(*Strikes him with packet and crosses to the left. Walter draws sword.
Oceana interposes.*)

OCEANA. It is my father, Walter, mine.

WALTER. A blow.

OCEANA.   Oh, thou wilt forgive him!

WALTER.   Never! I will forth, and ere he shall enforce thee where thou hast no joy, will rend the mask he cheats us with. (*Crosses to the left*)

OCEANA.   And if thou dost, by heaven I'll ne'er be thine.

WALTER.   (*Sheathes sword*) Old man, an angel's bosom shelters thine. Instruct Fitzarnold in our quarrel's cause. No daughter bars my way to him.

(*Exit. Enter Fitzarnold.*)

FITZARNOLD.   How now, you tremble; what has chanced?

MORDAUNT.   A moody beggar who abused my love and I chastised him for it—that's all.

OCEANA.   My father—

MORDAUNT.   Go to thy chamber.

OCEANA.   Would it were my grave. (*Exit*)

MORDAUNT.   My noble lord, that moody stripling whom you saw last night—whether set on by Vaughan, his patron, or by the vainness of his own conceits, resolves to break my daughter's marriage.

FITZARNOLD.   And wilt thou suffer this? What is the villain's state?

MORDAUNT.   Dependence on Sir Arthur Vaughan; his wealth, a goodly person, and the law of schools. (*Bell tolls.*) Hark! I am summoned to the council. Wilt thou along?

(*Fitzarnold crosses to the left.*)

FITZARNOLD.   I trust he finds no favor with your daughter.

MORDAUNT.   She shall be thine, my lord; thine with free will and full contentment. Now for the council.

(*Exeunt*)

Scene 3

Flourish. The council chamber. Errington, Sir Arthur and Church on raised platform. Mordaunt and Fitzarnold seated at table at the left; Elders, etc. Goodenough and Soldiers at the right. Villagers, etc. Walter and Tramp.

ERRINGTON.   'Tis news that asks from us most speedy action. Heaven has in sounds most audible and strange, in sights, too, that amazed the lookers-on, forewarned our people of their peril. 'Tis time to lift the arm so long supine, and with one blow cut off this heathen race, who spite of reason and the word revealed, continue hardened in their devious ways, and make the chosen tremble. Colleagues, your voices—speak—are you for peace or war?

SIR ARTHUR. What is your proof your Indian neighbors mean not as fairly towards our settlements as did King Philip's father, Massasoit?

ERRINGTON. Sir, we have full proof that Philip is our foe. Sasamond, the faithful servant of our cause, has been dispatched by Philip's men, set on to murder him. One of his tribe confessed the horrid truth—and will, when time shall call, give horrid proof on't. I say this chieftain is a man of blood, and Heaven will bless the valiant arm that slays him.

(*Metamora enters suddenly and remains at the center. When Metamora enters, all start and grasp their swords. The soldiers prepare to fire. All are silent and confused.*)

METAMORA. You sent for me and I am come. Humph! If you have nothing to say I will go back—if you fear to question, Metamora does not fear to answer.

ERRINGTON. Philip, 'tis thought you love us not, and all unmindful of our league of peace, plot with the Narragansetts, and contrive fatal disorder to our colony.

METAMORA. Do your fears counsel you? What is it makes your old men grave? And your young men grasp their fire weapons as if they awaited the onset of the foe? Brothers, what has Metamora done that doubt is in all your faces and your spirits seem troubled? The good man's heart is a stranger to fear, and his tongue is ready to speak the words of truth.

ERRINGTON. We are informed that thou gavest shelter to a banished man, whose deeds unchristian met our just reproof—one by our holy synod doomed—whom it is said you housed, and thereby hast incurred our church's censure—and given just cause to doubt thy honesty.

METAMORA. Why was that man sent away from the home of his joy? Because the Great Spirit did not speak to him as he had spoken to you? Did you not come across the great waters and leave the smoke of your father's hearth because the iron hand was held out against you, and your hearts were sorrowful in the high places of prayer. Why do you that have just plucked the red knife from your own wounded sides, strive to stab your brother?

ERRINGTON. Indian, this is no reply for us. Didst thou not know the sentence of the court on him whom thou didst shelter?

METAMORA. If my rarest enemy had crept unarmed into my wigwam and his heart was sore, I would not have driven him from my fire nor forbidden him to lie down upon my mat. Why then should the Wampanoag shut out the man of peace when he came with tears in his eyes and his limbs torn by the sharp thorns of the thicket? Your great book, you say, tells you to give good gifts to the stranger and deal kindly with him whose heart is sad; the Wampanoag needs no such counselor, for the Great Spirit has with his own fingers written it upon his heart.

MORDAUNT. Why dost thou put arms into thy people's hands, thereby engendering mischief towards us?

METAMORA.   If my people do wrong, I am quick to punish. Do you not set a snare for them that they may fall, and make them mad with the fire water the Great Spirit gave you in his wrath? The red man sickens in the house of the palefaces, and the leaping stream of the mountains is made impure by the foul brooks that mingle with it.

SIR ARTHUR.   Chieftain, since these things are so, sell us thy lands and seek another biding place.

METAMORA.   And if I did, would you not stretch out your hand to seize that also? No! White man, no! Never will Metamora forsake the home of his fathers, and let the plough of the strangers disturb the bones of his kindred.

CHURCH.   These are bold words, chief.

METAMORA.   They are true ones.

ERRINGTON.   They give no token of thy love of peace. We would deal fairly with thee—nay, be generous.

METAMORA.   Then would you pay back that which fifty snows ago you received from the hands of my father, Massasoit. Ye had been tossed about like small things upon the face of the great waters, and there was no earth for your feet to rest on; your backs were turned upon the land of your fathers. The red man took you as a little child and opened the door of his wigwam. The keen blast of the north howled in the leafless wood, but the Indian covered you with his broad right hand and put it back. Your little ones smiled when they heard the loud voice of the storm, for our fires were warm and the Indian was the white man's friend.

ERRINGTON.   Such words are needless now.

METAMORA.   I will speak no more; I am going.

MORDAUNT.   Hold! A moment, Philip; we have yet to tell of the death of Sasamond, who fell in secret and by treachery.

METAMORA.   So should the treacherous man fall, by the keen knife in the darkness and not ascend from the strife of battle to the bright haven where the dead warrior dwells in glory.

ERRINGTON.   Didst thou contrive his murder?

METAMORA.   I will not answer.

ERRINGTON.   We have those can prove thou didst.

METAMORA.   I have spoken.

ERRINGTON.   Bring in the witness. (*Exit Goodenough*)We, too, long have stayed the arm of power from execution. Come, we parley with a serpent and his wiles are deep.

METAMORA.   Injurious white man! Do not tread too hard upon the serpent's folds. His fangs are not taken out, nor has its venom lost the power to kill.

ERRINGTON.   Approach!

(*Goodenough returns with Annawandah.*)

METAMORA.   Annawandah!

ERRINGTON.   Behold, deceitful man, thy deeds are known.

METAMORA. Let me see his eye. Art thou he whom I snatched from the war club of the Mohigan, when thou hadst sung thy death song, and the lips of the foe were thirsty for thy blood? Has Metamora cherished thee in his wigwam and hast thou put a knife into the white man's hand to slay him! The foul spirit hath entered thee, and the pure blood of the Wampanoag has left thy veins. Thy heart is a lie, and thine eye cannot rest upon the face of truth, when like the great light it shines on thee in unclouded glory. Elders, can he speak to you the words of truth, when he is false to his brother, his country and his god?

ERRINGTON. He was thy trusty agent, Philip, and conscience-smote revealed thy wickedness.

METAMORA. You believe his words?

ERRINGTON. We do, and will reward his honesty.

METAMORA. Wampanoag! No, I will not call thee so. Red man, say unto these people they have bought thy tongue, and thou hast uttered a lie!

ERRINGTON. He does not answer.

METAMORA. I am Metamora, thy father and thy king.

ERRINGTON. Philip o'erawes him—send the witness home.

METAMORA. I will do that! Slave of the white man, go follow Sasamond.

(*Stabs Annawandah, who staggers off. All stand up, general movement.*)

ERRINGTON. Seize and bind him.

(*Soldiers make a forward movement.*)

METAMORA. Come! My knife has drunk the blood of the false one, yet it is not satisfied! White man, beware! The mighty spirits of the Wampanoag race are hovering o'er your heads; they stretch out their shadowy arms to me and ask for vengeance; they shall have it. The wrath of the wronged Indian shall fall upon you like a cataract that dashes the uprooted oak down the mighty chasms. The war whoop shall start you from your dreams at night, and the red hatchet gleam in the blaze of your burning dwellings! From the east to the west, in the north and in the south shall cry of vengeance burst, till the lands you have stolen groan under your feet no more!

ERRINGTON. Secure him!

METAMORA. Thus do I smite your nation and defy your power.

ERRINGTON. Fire on him.

(*Business. Metamora hurls hatchet into stage, and rushes out. Soldiers fire after him. Mordaunt, who has moved forward, receives a shot and falls in chair. Tableau. Drums, trumpets, and general confusion. Quick curtain.*)

ACT III

Scene 1

A chamber in Mordaunt's house. Enter Fitzarnold.

FITZARNOLD.   Mordaunt wounded, and perhaps to death, struck by a shot that was leveled at the chief; and the fierce storm of war at distance heard, which soon may burst tremendous o'er our heads! This is no place for me. She must be mine tonight! Aye, this night, for fear his death may snatch his gold and daughter from me. Within there, Wolfe! (*Enter Wolfe*) Go get a surgeon for this Mordaunt's wounds, a scribe and priest for me—wilt be silent?

WOLFE.   I will observe! Does my lord wed tomorrow?

FITZARNOLD.   No, this night; and with tomorrow's sun I spread my sail for England.

WOLFE.   Ha!

FITZARNOLD.   How now! What meanest thou? Wouldst thou to rival me?

WOLFE.   My lord!

FITZARNOLD.   Well, well; go see thy duty done. (*Exit*)

WOLFE.   My lord, be sure on't. Now for young Walter. I will fulfill my duty but not to thee, my Lord Fitzarnold! Thou wilt not thank me for the priest I'll bring. (*Exit*)

Scene 2

An Indian village, deep wood, wigwam. Lights half down. Conch shell heard. Nahmeokee enters from wigwam.

NAHMEOKEE.   Sure 'twas the shell of Metamora, and spoke the strain it was wont when the old men were called to council, or when the scout returns from his long travel.

METAMORA.   (*Outside*) Nahmeokee!

NAHMEOKEE.   It is—it is Metamora.

(*Enter Metamora*)

METAMORA.   Is our little one well, Nahmeokee?

NAHMEOKEE.   He is. How didst thou leave the white man with whom thou hast been to hold a talk?

METAMORA.   Like the great stream of the mountain when the spirit of the storm passes furiously over its bosom. Where are my people?

NAHMEOKEE.   Here in the deep woods where Kaneshine, the aged priest, tells them the mighty deeds of their people, and interprets to them the will of the Great Spirit.

METAMORA.   Otah! (*Otah enters*) Summon my warriors; bid them with speed to council. (*Exit Otah*) I have escaped the swift flight of the white man's bullets but like the bounding elk when the hunters who follow close upon his heels. (*Reenter Otah with Kaneshine and all the Indians. Indian march, eight bars. Indians form at the left.*) Warriors, I took a prisoner from the uplifted weapon of the Mohigan, when the victor's limbs were bloody and the scalps at his belt had no number. He lived in my wigwam; I made him my brother. When the spirit of sleep was upon me, he crept like a guilty thing away, and put into the white man's hand a brand of fire to consume me, and drive my people far away where there are no hunting grounds and where the Wampanoag has no protecting Spirit.

KANESHINE.   Annawandah?

METAMORA.   Annawandah!

KANESHINE.   Where is he, chief of thy people, and where is the dog whose head the Great Spirit will smite with fire?

METAMORA.   Where the ravenous bird of night may eat the flesh of his body. Here is the blood of the traitor's heart! (*Shows knife*) My people, shall I tell you the thoughts that fill me?

KANESHINE.   Speak, Metamora, speak!

METAMORA.   When the strangers came from afar off, they were like a little tree; but now they are grown up and their spreading branches threaten to keep the light from you. They ate of your corn and drank of your cup, and now they lift up their arms against you. Oh my people, the race of the red man has fallen away like the trees of the forest before the axes of the palefaces. The fair places of his father's triumphs hear no more the sound of his footsteps. He moves in the region his proud fathers bequeathed him, not like a lord of the soil, but like a wretch who comes for plunder and for prey.

(*Distant thunder and lightning*)

KANESHINE.   The chief has spoken truly and the stranger is worthy to die! But the fire of our warriors is burnt out and their hatchets have no edge. O son of Massasoit, thy words are to me like the warm blood of the foe, and I will drink till I am full! Speak again!

METAMORA.   "Chief of the people," said a voice from the deep as I lay by the seaside in the eyes of the moon—"Chief of the people, wake from thy dream of peace, and make sharp the point of thy spear, for the destroyer's arm is made bare to smite. O son of my old age, arise like the tiger in great wrath and snatch thy people from the devourer's jaws!" My father spoke no more; a mist passed before me, and from the mist the Spirit bent his eyes imploringly on me. I started to my feet and shouted the shrill battle cry of the Wampanoags. The high hills sent back the echo, and rock, hill and ocean, earth and air opened their giant throats and cried with me, "Red man, arouse! Freedom! Revenge or death!" (*Thunder and lightning. All quail but Metamora.*) Hark, warriors! The Great Spirit hears me and pours forth his mighty voice with mine. Let your voice in battle be like his, and the flash from your fire weapons as quick to kill. Nahmeokee, take this knife, carry it to the Narragansett, to thy brother; tell him the hatchet is dug from the grave where the grass is grown old above it; thy tongue will move him more than the voice of all our tribe in the loud talk of war.

NAHMEOKEE.   Nahmeokee will not fail in her path; and her eyes will be quick to see where the stranger has set his snare.

METAMORA.   Warriors! Your old and infirm must you send into the country of the Narragansett, that your hearts may not be made soft in the hour of battle.

NAHMEOKEE.   Go you tonight, Metamora?

METAMORA.   Tonight! I will not lay down in my wigwam till the foe has drawn himself together and comes in his height to destroy. Nahmeokee, I still will be the red man's father and his king, or the sacred rock whereon my father spoke so long the words of wisdom shall be made red with the blood of his race.

(*Hurried music. Metamora and Indians exeunt. Nahmeokee goes in wigwam.*)

Scene 3

A chamber in Mordaunt's house. Clock strikes twelve as scene opens. Thunder distant. Enter Oceana in plain attire.

OCEANA.   I know not how it is but every thunder peal seems to bear words portentous. The moaning blast has meaning in its sound and tells of distant horror—it is the hour when I bade Walter come! Can he have braved the tempest? Hark, I hear a step! (*Knock*) How my heart beats. (*Enter Fitzarnold*) It is—it is Fitzarnold!

FITZARNOLD.   Fitzarnold, lady! Why this wonder? Is it fear? Can she whom thunder frights not shrink from me?

OCEANA.   My lord, the hour is late; I feign would know who sent thee hither.

FITZARNOLD.   Thy honored father.

OCEANA.   Thy purpose?

FITZARNOLD.   Read it there. (*Gives letter*)

OCEANA.   Ha! Tonight! Be thine tonight?

FITZARNOLD. Aye, tonight. I have thy father's secret.

OCEANA. I know thou hast, and in that mean advantage wouldst mar his daughter's happiness forever—away! I blush that thus I parley words with thee—get thee gone. (*Crosses to the left*)

FITZARNOLD. Yes, when thou goest with me; not till then, lady. I will not waste the time that grows more precious every moment to me. (*Thunder*) What though the lightning flash and thunder roll—what though the tempest pours its fury down, Fitzarnold's soul does swell above the din! Nay more, dares brave the storm within thy breast, and shrinks not from the lightning of thine eye.

OCEANA. Would it could kill thee!

FITZARNOLD. It can do more—can conquer like the fiery serpent. It pierces, and as it pierces charms—Oceana!

OCEANA. Stand back! I will alarm my sire.

FITZARNOLD. And if thou dost, he will not aid thee. My treasures are embarked, aye, all but thee; thy father gives consent, the priest waits and ere morning, father, daughter, son, shall all be riding on the wave for England.

OCEANA. No, never!

FITZARNOLD. Convince thyself—(*Stamps his foot. Walter enters disguised as a priest.*) Now, scornful lady, thy bridal hour has come; thy tauntings do but fan the flame that rages here.

OCEANA. Is there no refuge?

FITZARNOLD. None, but in these arms.

OCEANA. No hope—no rescue!

FITZARNOLD. None! None!

OCEANA. Walter, on thee I call—Walter, where art thou?

WALTER. (*Throws off disguise*) Walter is here.

FITZARNOLD. Villain! Thy life or mine!

(*Fitzarnold draws, Oceana throws herself between them.*)

OCEANA. Forebear! No blood! (*To Walter*) Thou must come stainless to these arms.

WALTER. Sayest thou? Wilt thou take me to them?

OCEANA. I will—I do.

(*They embrace.*)

FITZARNOLD. Thy father's blood be on thee; he is Fitzarnold's victim.

(*Exit. Bell rings. Enter Tramp.*)

TRAMP. The savages approach! The Wampanoag chieftain and his crew, at distance, peal their startling yell of war! Haste, sir, to meet them.

WALTER. Retire thee for a while, my Oceana—thou, sir, on the instant follow me—your sword! your sword!

(*Exit with Oceana; Tramp follows.*)

Scene 4

A view of Mordaunt's house on the beach. Sea in distance, ship on fire. Garden and staircase leading down to the water. Lights down at opening of scene. Distant yells heard. Enter Fitzarnold hastily.

FITZARNOLD. Almighty powers! Hemmed in on every side! No hope. (*War whoop*) Hark to their savage yells! No means are left for flight, for on the waves my precious vessel burns—by the fell savage mastered! No retreat!

(*War whoops. Exit Fitzarnold hastily. Metamora and all the Indians enter up staircase entrances. Music hurried, forte till all are on.*)

METAMORA. (*Pointing to Fitzarnold*) Follow him! (*To others*) Go into the white man's dwelling and drag him to me that my eye can look upon his torture and his scalp may tell Metamora's triumph to his tribe—go.

(*Otah and Kaneshine are about to enter the house when Oceana appears.*)

OCEANA. Forebear, ye shall not enter.
METAMORA. Warriors, have I not spoken.
    (*Throws her around to the left; Indians go in.*)
OCEANA. Great Chieftain! Dost thou not know me?
METAMORA. I am a Wampanoag in the home of mine enemy; I ride on my wrongs, and vengeance cries out for blood.
OCEANA. Wilt thou not hear me?
METAMORA. Talk to the rattling storm or melt the high rocks with tears; thou canst not move me. My foe! my foe! my foe!
OCEANA. Have mercy, Heaven!

(*The Indians return dragging in Mordaunt.*)

METAMORA. Hah!
MORDAUNT. Mercy! Mercy!
OCEANA. My father! Spare my father! (*Rushes to Mordaunt*)
METAMORA. He must die! Drag him away to the fire of the sacrifice that my ear may drink the music of his dying groans.
OCEANA. Fiends and murderers!
METAMORA. The white man has made us such. Prepare.

(*Business*)

OCEANA. Then smite his heart through mine; our mangled breasts shall meet in death—one grave shall hold us. Metamora, dost thou remember this? (*Shows eagle plume*)

METAMORA. Yes.

OCEANA. It was thy father's. Chieftain, thou gavest it to me.

METAMORA. Say on.

OCEANA. Thou saidst it would prove a guardian to me when the conflict raged. Were thy words true when with thy father's tongue thou saidst, whatever being wore the gift, no Indian of thy tribe should do that being harm.

METAMORA. The Wampanoag cannot lie.

OCEANA. Then do I place it here. (*Places it on Mordaunt's bosom*)

METAMORA. Hah!

OCEANA. The Wampanoag cannot lie, and I can die for him who gave existence to me.

MORDAUNT. My child! my child!

(*Red fire in house*)

METAMORA. Take them apart! (*Indians separate them.*) Old man, I cannot let the tomahawk descend upon thy head, or bear thee to the place of sacrifice; but here is that shall appease the red man's wrath. (*Seizes Oceana; flames seen in house*) The fire is kindled in thy dwelling, and I will plunge her in the hot fury of the flames.

MORDAUNT. No, no, thou wilt not harm her.

OCEANA. Father, farewell! Thy nation, savage, will repent this act of thine.

METAMORA. If thou art just, it will not. Old man, take thy child. (*Throws her to him*) Metamora cannot forth with the maiden of the eagle plume; and he disdains a victim who has no color in his face nor fire in his eye.

(*Bugle sounds.*)

MORDAUNT. Gracious heavens!

METAMORA. Hark! The power of the white man comes! Launch your canoes! We have drunk blood enough. Spirit of my father, be at rest! Thou art obeyed, thy people are avenged.

(*Exit hastily followed by the Indians. Drums and trumpet till curtain. Enter Walter, Goodenough, Church, Soldiers, Peasants, male and female, all from behind house. Soldiers are about to fire, when Walter throws himself before them and exclaims.*)

WALTER. Forebear! Forebear!

(*Walter and Oceana embrace. Tableau. Curtain.*)

ACT IV

Scene 1

Enter Errington—Lord Fitzarnold—Walter and Church. A room in Sir Arthur's house.

SIR ARTHUR. Welcome my brother.

ERRINGTON. The strife is over: but the wail of those who mourn some captive friend still wounds the ear and fills our hearts with sadness.

FITZARNOLD. The follower of mine, surprised or else too venturous in the fight, was dragged away in bondage.

SIR ARTHUR. Old Wolfe.

FITZARNOLD. The same—a moody but a faithful man doomed no doubt to torture or to death.

WALTER. Faithful indeed. But not to him thou think'st. (*Aside*)

ERRINGTON. He will avenge the captives' fall.

WALTER. But must they fall—is there no way to save them?

ERRINGTON. None, young sir, unless thy wisdom find it.

WALTER. They might be ransomed.

SIR ARTHUR. True they might. And from my wealth I'll pay whatever price the Indians' power will yield them for.

ERRINGTON. But who so rash to bear such offer unto Philip in his present mood?

FITZARNOLD. (*Aside*) Could I but tempt this stripling to his death.

ERRINGTON. Say is there one so reckless and so brave will dare the peril to preserve his fellows?

FITZARNOLD. Grave sirs, I know of none more truly fit than young Walter to achieve the deed. How proud the name required by such an act. How vast the joy his daring heart must feel. Whose arm against such terror shall prevail. And rescue numbers from a lingering death.

WALTER. If my Lord so dearly holds the prize,
Why not himself adventure to attain it?
But I will go—for I have reasons for it
Would move me, felt I not my Lord's great pity for the captives' woe.

SIR ARTHUR. Bravely said, thou deserve'st our thanks,
And if thou canst persuade the hostile chief
To draw his arm'd bands away and save the blood, that else must flow so terribly.

ERRINGTON. Take swiftest horse young man and Heaven protect thee.

WALTER. No tongue so blest as that which heralds peace—
No heart so mailed as that which beats, warm for his fellow man.
Fare you well. (*Exit Walter*)

ERRINGTON. Now to our labours—those new levies made—
We may exterminate, with one full blow

This savage race, hated of man—unblessed of Heaven—
Surely a land so fair was ne'er designed to feed the heartless infidel.

(*Cry: "Indians! Indians!"*)

ERRINGTON. Hah! More massacre! Mercy, Heaven!

(*Enter Oceana*)

OCEANA. Oh, Sirs, shew pity to a captive wretch whom heartless men abuse with taunts and blows. If ye are men oh let the helpless find in you kind pity—mercy and protection.
ERRINGTON. Maiden,
Whom dost thou speak of?
OCEANA. An Indian woman
And her infant child, by these made prisoners. Look there, they have ta'en her child from her.

(*Enter Nahmeokee with Officer, two Guards, as prisoner. Good-enough with the child.*)

ERRINGTON. How now, who hast thou there?
GOODENOUGH. An Indian woman, we captured in the glen.
A spy, 'tis thought sent by the cursed foe.
ERRINGTON. Came she alone?
GOODENOUGH. No, a young and nimble man
Was with her, but he 'scap'd pursuit.
I am sure he is wounded, for I saw him fall.
ERRINGTON. Woman what art thou?
NAHMEOKEE. Give poor woman her child?
ERRINGTON. Dost thou hear my question?
NAHMEOKEE. Give poor Indian woman her child?
OCEANA. Do so.
GOODENOUGH. Why 'twas I that caught the creature—and—
OCEANA. Man, didst thou hear me? (*Takes child from him*)
GOODENOUGH. Hard times indeed to lose so good a prize. The brat is saleable. 'Tis mine.
OCEANA. Measureless brute.
GOODENOUGH. For what? 'Tis only an Indian boy.

(*Oceana gives Nahmeokee her child, who touch'd with her kindness, takes her scarf to wipe Oceana's eyes. The latter recognises it to be the one bound round Metamora's arm in first scene.*)

OCEANA. Nahmeokee!
NAHMEOKEE. Hush!

ERRINGTON.   Who art thou, woman?

NAHMEOKEE.   I am the servant of the Great Spirit.

ERRINGTON.   Who is thy husband?

NAHMEOKEE.   One thou dost not love.

ERRINGTON.   His name?

NAHMEOKEE.   I will not tell thee.

ERRINGTON.   We can enforce an answer.

NAHMEOKEE.   Poor Indian woman cannot keep her limbs from pain; but she can keep silence.

ERRINGTON.   Woman, what is thy nation & thy race?

NAHMEOKEE.   White man, the Sun is my father and the Earth my mother —I will speak no more.

ERRINGTON.   Captain, take charge of this same stubborn wretch
Who neither will her name nor purpose tell.
If she do prove as alleg'd a spy,
Nothing shall save her from a public death;
We must o'erawe our treacherous foe.
And this obdurate & blasphemous witch
May in her death, keep death from many more.
Summon our Elders—my Lord Fitzarnold,
Your counsel now may aid us.

FITZARNOLD.   'Tis thine,—& my poor service.

ERRINGTON.   Take her away. (*Cross to right*) Justice is sometimes slow,
Yet is she sure.

NAHMEOKEE.   Thy nation, white man, yet may find it so.

(*Exeunt Errington, Goodenough, Church, Nahmeokee and Soldiers*)

OCEANA.   Fitzarnold of the Council—could I move
His sympathy? (*Approaching him tremblingly*) My lord.

FITZARNOLD.   Well lady?

OCEANA.   I have offended thee.

FITZARNOLD.   I have forgotten it.

OCEANA.   I have a boon to ask.

FITZARNOLD.   Sayst thou—of me?

OCEANA.   It will not cost thee much.

FITZARNOLD.   No price too great to purchase thy sweet smiles of thee.

OCEANA.   Then be this female's advocate, my lord.
Thou canst be eloquent and the heart of good,
But much misguided men may by thy speech
Be moved to pity and to pardon her.

FITZARNOLD.   How so—a wandering wretch unknown?

OCEANA.   Metamora has helpless prisoners.

FITZARNOLD.   'Tis true—and thou dost deeply feel for them.
Young Walter now seeks their enfranchisement.

OCEANA.   I know it sir. (*Aside*) Be still my throbbing heart.
My lord, what vengeance will her husband take.

Think you will aught appease dread Philip's wrath—
When he is told—chieftain, thy wife's a slave?
FITZARNOLD.   His wife—the Queen! Indeed! Dost say so?
OCEANA.   Give not the secret unto mortal ear—
It might destroy all hopes of unity.
Preserve this captive from impending doom
And countless prayers shall pay thee for it.
FITZARNOLD.   Thy kind approval is reward enough.
OCEANA.   Shall she be saved?
FITZARNOLD.   She shall be free—a word of mine can do it.
OCEANA.   Thanks! Thanks! My Lord deceive me not.
FITZARNOLD.   Fear not, fair Lady. I have pledged my word.

(*Exit Oceana*)

FITZARNOLD.   Thou thinks't me kind—ha! ha! I will be so. Philip has
Captives—& young Walter's there.
The Council dare not take this woman's life for that would doom their
captive countrymen. Imprisoned she is free from danger for the law
protects her. But turn her loose to the wild fury of the senseless crowd
she dies ere justice or the Elders' arms can reach her. Ah! This way con-
ducts me straight to the goal. I am resolved to reach and seal at once
my hated rival's doom. Oh! I will plead as Angels do in Heaven
For mortals when they err and mourn for it.
Her freedom is her death—the zealot crowd
Will rush upon her like the loosen'd winds
And prove as merciless—while the lion husband,
Madden'd with his loss, sheds blood to surfeiting.
Oh yes, dear pleader for the captive one,
Thy boon is granted. She shall be free! (*Exit*)

Scene 2

One-half dark. An Indian Retreat. Wolfe bound to the Stake at the
right. Metamora at a distance leaning on his rifle. Kaneshine & War-
riors. Lights one-half down.

KANESHINE.   Warriors, our enemies have been met, and the blood of the
Stranger has sunk deep into the sand—yet the spirit of those who have
fallen by the power of the foe are not yet appeas'd—prepare the captives
for their hour of death. Come round the tree of sacrifice and lift up the
flame, till it devour in its fiery rage, the abhor'd usurpers (*Gun*) of the
red man's soil! Come, my lips are dry for the captives' blood.

(*As they are about to fire the pile, a shot is heard. Enter Walter.*)

METAMORA.   Hold! Let the young man say why he comes into our country unbidden. Why does he tempt the ire of our warriors, when their weapons are red with the blood of the battle?

WALTER.   That I come friendly let this emblem speak.
To check the dire advance of bloody war,
To urge the Wampanoag to disarm his band
And once again renew with us the bond
That made the white and red man brothers.

METAMORA.   No, young man, the blood my warriors have tasted, has made their hearts glad and their hands are thrust out for more. Let the white man fear. The arrow he has shot into the mountain has turned back and pierced his own side. What are the Elders' words?

WALTER.   Let Philip take our wampum and our coin
Restore his captives and remove his dead
And rest from causeless and destructive war,
Until such terms of lasting peace are made
As shall forever quell our angry feuds
And sink the hatchet to be raised no more.

METAMORA.   *Humph!* And meanwhile he sharpens his long weapons in secret, and each day grows more numerous. When the great stream of the mountains first springs from the earth it is very weak, and I can stand up against its waters, but when the great rain descends, it is swift and swollen, death dwells in its white bosom and it will not spare.

WALTER.   By Him who moves the stars and lights the Sun,
If thou dost shed the trembling captives' blood,
A thousand warlike men will rush to arms
And terribly avenge their countrymen.

METAMORA.   Well, let them come! Our arms are as strong as the white man's. And the use of the fire-weapon he has taught us. My ears are shut against thee.

WALTER.   (*To Wolfe*) Oh, my friend! I will achieve thy rescue if gold or prayers can move them.

WOLFE.   I was prepared to die, and only mourned
For I am childless and a lonely man.
I had not told the secret of thy birth.
And shewn thy father to thee.

WALTER.   My Father! Sayst thou?

WOLFE.   Walter, listen to me.

OTAH.   (*Speaks without*) Metamora!

METAMORA.   Ha! (*Enter Otah*)

OTAH.   Nahmeokee!

METAMORA.   Dead!

OTAH.   Our feet grew weary in the path, and we sate down to rest in the dark wood—the fire-weapons blazed in the thicket, and my arm was wounded, with the other I grasped the keen knife you gave Nahmeokee, but I sank down powerless and the white men bore off the queen a captive.

METAMORA. *Humph*—Nahmeokee is the white man's prisoner. Where is thy horse?

WALTER. Beneath yonder tree.

METAMORA. Unbind the captive! Young man! You must abide with the Wampanoag till Nahmeokee returns to her home. Woe unto you if the hard hand has been laid upon her. Take the white man to my wigwam.

WALTER. I thank thee, Chieftain, this is kindness to me. Come, good Wolfe, tell me my father's name.

METAMORA. If one drop fall from Nahmeokee's eye, one hair from her head, the axe shall hew your quivering limbs asunder and the ashes of your bones be carried away on the rushing winds. Come, old man.

(*Exeunt*)

Scene 3

(*Enter Fitzarnold*)

FITZARNOLD. Nahmeokee now is free, and the fanatic herd all cry aloud, "Oh mad rulers! Mercy to her"—she comes—and witch, hag and Indian din her ears. They come this way—I must avoid their clamor. (*Enter Nahmeokee*)

NAHMEOKEE. Let them not kill the poor Indian woman.

FITZARNOLD. Woman away.

NAHMEOKEE. They will murder my child.

FITZARNOLD. Hold off—I cannot help thee. (*Exit Fitzarnold*)

NAHMEOKEE. They come upon me from every side of the path. My limbs can bear me no farther. Mercy! Hah! They have missed my track and seek in the wood, and in the caves for my blood. Who is he that rides a swift horse there, through the narrow path way of the glen! The shade of the coming night is over him and he dimly appears a red man riding the swift cloud. (*Shouts*) Ha, they have traced me by the white garment, the brambles tore from me in my flight. They come. Cling to me my child. Cling to thy mother's bosom. (*Enter Goodenough and 4 Peasants*)

GOODENOUGH. Foul Indian witch, thy race is run. Drag her to the lake. Take her child from her. (*Enter Metamora*)

METAMORA. Stand back! or the swift death shall take wing. Which of you has lived too long? Let him lift up his arm against her.

OFFICER. How is this? King Philip ventures here? What comest thou for?

METAMORA. Boy! Thou art a child, there is no mark of the war upon thee. Send me thy Elder, or thy Chief. I'll make my talk to him.

GOODENOUGH. Here comes Master Errington. (*Enter Errington & Soldiers*)

ERRINGTON. Philip a Prisoner!

METAMORA. No! He has arms in his hand and courage in his heart, he comes near you of his own will, and when he has done his work, he'll go back to his wigwam.

ERRINGTON. Indian, you answer boldly.

METAMORA. What is there I should fear?

ERRINGTON. Savage! The wrath of him who hates the Heathen and the man of blood.

METAMORA. Does he love mercy; and is he the white man's friend?

ERRINGTON. Yes.

METAMORA. How did Nahmeokee and her infant wrong you, that you hunted her through the thorny pathway of the glen, and scented her blood like the fierce red wolf in his hunger?

CHURCH. Why hold parley with him! Call our musqueteers and bear them both to trial and to doom. Heaven smiles on us—Philip in our power. His cursed followers would sue for peace.

METAMORA. Not till the blood of twenty English captives be poured out as a sacrifice. Elders beware, the knife is sharpened—the stake is fixed—and the captives' limbs tremble under the burning gaze of the prophet of wrath. Woe come to them when my people shall hear their chief has been slain by the pale faces or is bound in the dark place of doom.

NAHMEOKEE. Do not tempt them, Metamora, they are many like the leaves of the forest and we are but as two lone trees standing in their midst.

METAMORA. Which can easier escape the hunter's spear? The tiger that turns on it in his wrath, or the lamb that sinks down and trembles? Thou has seen me look unmoved at a torturing death—shall mine eye be turned downward when the white man frowns?

ERRINGTON. Philip, the peace our young man offered thee. Didst thou regard his words?

METAMORA. Yes.

ERRINGTON. And wilt thou yield compliance?

METAMORA. I will. Nahmeokee shall bear the tidings to my people that the prisoners may return to their homes, and the war-whoop shall not go forth on the evening gale.

ERRINGTON. Let her set forth. Friends, let me advise you,
Keep the Chieftain prisoner, let's muster men.
And in unlook'd for hour with one blow we will overwhelm
This accursed race. And furthermore—(*Converses apart*)

NAHMEOKEE. (*To Metamora*) I will remember thy words.

METAMORA. Grieve not that I linger in the dark place of the condemned, for the eye of the Great Spirit will be on me there.

ERRINGTON. We greet thee, Philip, and accept thy love. Nahmeokee may return.

METAMORA. 'Tis very good. The horse stands 'neath the brow of the hill —speak not—I read thy thought in thy eye. Go—go, Nahmeokee. I am ready to follow you.

ERRINGTON. Conduct him forth to prison. (*Soldiers attempt to take his gun.*)

METAMORA. No! This shall be to me as my child and I will talk to it, until I go back to my people.

GOODENOUGH. Right well conceived, could it but talk.

METAMORA. It can—when the land of my great fore-fathers is trampled on by the foot of the foe—or when treachery lurks round the Wampanoag, while he bides in the white man's home.

END OF ACT FOURTH

ACT V

Scene 1

Same as Act I, Scene 1. Lights down. Oceana discovered leaning against tomb. Slow music, four bars.

OCEANA. Tomb of the silent dead, thou seemest my only refuge! O Walter, where art thou? Alas! the kindly promptings of thy noble heart have led thee to captivity, perhaps to death! Welcome the hour when these dark portals shall unfold again, and reunite parent and child in the long sleep of death. (*Enter Fitzarnold*) Ah! Fitzarnold here!

FITZARNOLD. I come with words of comfort to thee and fain would soothe thy sorrow.

OCEANA. I do not ask your sympathy, my lord.

FITZARNOLD. A sea of danger is around thee, lady, and I would be the skillful pilot to guide thy struggling bark to safety.

OCEANA. Nay, but let me rather perish in the waves than reach a haven to be shared with thee.

FITZARNOLD. Thou hast no choice; thy father willed thee mine, and with his latest breath bequeathed thee to me. Walter, my stripling rival in thy love, has left thee here defenseless and alone. I deem as nothing thy unnatural hate, and only see thy fair and lovely form; and though thy flashing eyes were armed with lightning, thus would my arms enfold thee.

OCEANA. (*Clings to tomb*) Now, if thou darest, approach me—now whilst with my mother's spirit hovering o'er me—whilst thus with tearful eyes and breaking heart I call on Heaven to blast the bold audacious wretch, who seeks a daughter's ruin o'er her parent's grave.

FITZARNOLD. Aye, despite of all.

METAMORA. (*In tomb*) Hold! Touch her not!

OCEANA. Hark to that voice! Kind Heaven has heard my prayers.

(The door of the tomb opens, and Metamora appears. Oceana faints and falls.)

FITZARNOLD.   Philip here!

METAMORA.   He is. The Great Spirit has sent me; the ghosts are waiting for thee in the dark place of doom! Now thou must go. Tremble, for the loud cry is terrible and the blaze of their eyes, like the red fire of war, gleams awfully in the night.

FITZARNOLD.   I have not wronged thee.

METAMORA.   Not? Didst thou not contrive the death of Nahmeokee, when the treacherous white man thirsted for her blood? Did she not with bended knees, her eyes streaming with woes of the heart, catch hold of thy shining broad garment thinking it covered man? Was not thy hand upraised against her, and thy heart, like thy hand, flint that wounds the weary one who rests upon it?

FITZARNOLD.   No! no!

METAMORA.   I saw thee when my quick step was on the hills, and the joy of Metamora's eyes felt thy blows. I feel them now! "Revenge!" cried the shadow of my father as he looked on with me. I, too, cried revenge and now I have it! The blood of my heart grows hotter as I look on him who smote the red cheek of Nahmeokee.

FITZARNOLD.   As reparation I will give thee gold.

METAMORA.   No! Give me back the happy days, the fair hunting ground, and the dominion my great forefathers bequeathed me.

FITZARNOLD.   I have not robbed thee of them.

METAMORA.   Thou art a white man, and thy veins hold the blood of a robber! Hark! The spirits of the air howl for thee! Prepare—*(Throws him around to the right)*

FITZARNOLD.   Thou shalt not conquer ere thou killest me. This sword a royal hand bestowed! This arm can wield it still.

(Draws; Metamora disarms and kills him.)

METAMORA.   Metamora's arm has saved thee from a common death; who dies by me dies nobly! *(Turns to Oceana)* For thee, Metamora's home shall screen thee from the spreading fury of his nation's wrath.

(Hurry till change. Exit bearing Oceana.)

Scene 2

A chamber. Enter Sir Arthur, meeting Errington and Church.

SIR ARTHUR.   I have news will startle you.

ERRINGTON.   Is't of the chief?

SIR ARTHUR.   It is; he has escaped our power!

ERRINGTON.   Escaped! Confusion! How?

SIR ARTHUR.   But now we sought his prison and found it tenantless.

ERRINGTON.   But how escaped he? There was no egress thence, unless some treacherous hand unlocked the door.

SIR ARTHUR.   And so we thought, at first; but on minute search we found some stones displaced, which showed a narrow opening into a subterranean passage, dark and deep, through which we crept until, to our surprise, we reached the tomb of Mordaunt.

ERRINGTON.   The tomb of Mordaunt?

SIR ARTHUR.   The ruined pile which now serves as our prison was, years since, when first he sought these shores, the residence of Mordaunt, and this secret passage, doubtless, was formed by him for concealment or escape in time of danger.

ERRINGTON.   Indeed!

SIR ARTHUR.   Yes, and he had cause to be so guarded, for once, unseen by him, I heard that wretched man commune with Heaven, and sue for pardon for the heinous sin of Hammond of Harrington!

ERRINGTON.   Hammond! The outlawed regicide?

SIR ARTHUR.   Even so; it was himself he prayed for, the guilty man who gave to death the king, his lord, the royal martyr Charles. As Mordaunt, he here sought refuge from the wrath of the rightful heir now seated on the throne.

ERRINGTON.   Think you the chieftain knew this secret way?

SIR ARTHUR.   'Tis likely that he did, or else by chance discovered it and thus has won his freedom and his life.

CHURCH.   We must summon our men. Double the guard and have their range extended.

(Exeunt Church and Errington)

WOLFE.   *(Without)* Where is Sir Arthur Vaughan?

SIR ARTHUR.   Who calls? *(Enter Wolfe)* Now, who art thou?

WOLFE.   A suppliant for pardon.

SIR ARTHUR.   Pardon—for what?

WOLFE.   A grievous sin, I now would fain confess.

SIR ARTHUR.   Indeed! Go on! Declare it then; I will forgive thee!

WOLFE.   Long years have passed since then, but you must still remember when at Naples with your wife and child.

SIR ARTHUR.   Ha! Dost thou mean—

WOLFE.   The flames consumed thy dwelling and thou together with thy wife and boy, escaped almost by miracle.

SIR ARTHUR.   Ha!

WOLFE.   I there looked on midst the assembled throng, a stranger mariner. Urged by the fiend, and aided by the wild confusion of the scene, I snatched your boy and through the noisy throng I bore him to my anchored bark, thinking his waiting parents soon would claim with gold their darling. Next day came on a tempest and the furious winds far from the city drove us and thy child.

SIR ARTHUR.   Heavens! Can this be true?

WOLFE.   He grew up the sharer of my sea-born perils. One awful night our vessel struck upon the rocks near these shores and the greedy ocean swelled over her shattered frame—thy son—

SIR ARTHUR.   Go on—go on—

WOLFE.   Was by mysterious power preserved and guided to his unconscious father. Walter is thy son.

SIR ARTHUR.   Man! Why didst thou not tell me?

WOLFE.   I feared thy just anger and the force of law. I became Fitzarnold's follower but to this hour has memory tortured me.

SIR ARTHUR.   And Walter is a hostage to the savage foe; perchance they have murdered him!

WOLFE.   No! Oceana's kindness to the Indian queen has purchased his freedom and my own.

SIR ARTHUR.   Where is he?

WOLFE.   Looking for her he loves, fair Oceana! Whom 'tis said, a party of the foe carried off.

SIR ARTHUR.   Quick, let us arm and follow him. For thee, this act of justice pardons thee.

(Exeunt)

Scene 3

Indian village. Groups of Indians. Kaneshine and Otah discovered. Kaneshine has been addressing them. His looks are gloomy and bewildered.

METAMORA.   *(Outside, at change of scene)* Where are my people?

KANESHINE.   Ha! 'Tis our chief—I know the sound of his voice, and some quick danger follows him.

(Metamora enters, bearing Oceana. Nahmeokee enters from wigwam.)

METAMORA.   Nahmeokee, take the white maiden in; I would speak to my people; go in and follow not the track of the warrior's band.

NAHMEOKEE.   Come in, my mat is soft, and the juice of the sweet berry shall give joy to thy lips. Come in, thou art pale and yielding, like the lily, when it is borne down by the running waters.

(She leads Oceana into wigwam.)

METAMORA.   Warriors, I have escaped from the hands of the white man, when the fire was kindled to devour me. Prepare for the approaching hour if ye love the high places your fathers trod in majesty and strength. Snatch your keen weapons and follow me! If ye love the silent spots where the bones of your kindred repose, sing the dread song of war and follow me! If you love the bright lakes which the Great Spirit gave you when the sun first blazed with the fires of his torch, shout the war song of the Wampanoag race, and on to the battle follow me! Look at the bright glory that is wrapped like a mantle around the slain in battle! Call on the happy spirits of the warriors dead, and cry, "Our lands! Our nation's freedom! Or the grave!"

KANESHINE. O chieftain, take my counsel and hold out to the palefaces the pipe of peace. Ayantic and the great Mohigan join with our foes against us, and the power of our brother, the Narragansett, is no more! List, o chieftain, to the words that I tell of the time to come.

METAMORA. Ha! Dost thou prophesy?

KANESHINE. In the deep wood, when the moon shone bright, my spirit was sad and I sought the ear of Manito in the sacred places; I heard the sound as of one in pain, and I beheld gasping under a hemlock, the lightning had sometime torn, a panther wounded and dying in his thick red gore. I thought of the tales of our forefathers who told us that such was an omen of coming evil. I spoke loudly the name of Metamora, and the monster's eyes closed instantly and he writhed no more. I turned and mourned, for I said, Manito loves no more the Wampanoag and our foes will prevail.

METAMORA. Didst thou tell my people this?

KANESHINE. Chieftain, yes; my spirit was troubled.

METAMORA. Shame of the tribe, thou art no Wampanoag, thy blood is tainted—thou art half Mohigan, thy breath has sapped the courage of my warriors' hearts. Begone, old man, thy life is in danger.

KANESHINE. I have spoken the words of truth, and the Great Manito has heard them.

METAMORA. Liar and coward! Let him preserve thee now!

(About to stab him when Nahmeokee enters from wigwam and interposes)

NAHMEOKEE. He is a poor old man—he healed the deep wound of our little one. (*Gets to the left of Metamora*)

METAMORA. Any breast but Nahmeokee's had felt the keen edge of my knife! Go, corrupted one, thy presence makes the air unwholesome round hope's high places. Begone!

KANESHINE. Metamora drives me from the wigwam before the lightning descends to set it on fire. Chieftain, beware the omen. (*Exit*)

NAHMEOKEE. (*Aside*) Will he not become the white man's friend and show him the secret path of our warriors? Manito guard the Wampanoag!

METAMORA. Men of Po-hon-e-ket, the palefaces come towards your dwellings and no warrior's hatchet is raised for vengeance. The war whoop is hushed in the camp and we hear no more the triumph of battle. Manito hates you, for you have fallen from the high path of your fathers and Metamora must alone avenge the Wampanoag's wrongs.

OMNES. Battle! Battle!

METAMORA.   Ha! The flame springs up afresh in your bosoms; a woman's breath has brought back the lost treasure of your souls. (*Distant march, drums and trumpet heard*) Ha! they come! Go, warriors, and meet them, and remember the eye of a thousand ages looks upon you. (*Warriors exeunt silently*) Nahmeokee, should the palefaces o'ercome our strength, go thou with our infant to the sacred place of safety. My followers slain, there will the last of the Wampanoags pour out his heart's blood on the giant rock, his father's throne.

NAHMEOKEE.   O Metamora!

METAMORA.   Come not near me or thou wilt make my heart soft, when I would have it hard like the iron and gifted with many lives. Go in, Nahmeokee. (*Distant trumpets. Nahmeokee goes in wigwam. Metamora kneels.*) The knee that never bent to man I bend to thee, Manito. As the arm was broken that was put out again Nahmeokee, so break thou the strength of the oppressor's nation, and hurl them down from the high hill of their pride and power, with the loud thunder of thy voice. Confound them—smite them with the lightning of thine eye—while thus I bare my red war arm—while thus I wait the onset of the foe—(*Loud alarm*) They come! Death! Death, or my nation's freedom!

(*Rushes off. Loud shouts. Drums and trumpets till change.*)

Scene 4

Rocky pass. Trumpet sounds retreat. Enter Errington and Church.

ERRINGTON.   They fly! They fly—the field is ours! This blow destroys them. Victory cheaply bought at twice our loss; the red man's power is broken now forever. (*Enter Walter*) Is Oceana slain?

WALTER.   No; the chieftain Metamora rescued her from the base passions of the Lord Fitzarnold whom Metamora slew to avenge the wrongs he offered to his wife, and Oceana by the chief was borne in safety to his lodge.

ERRINGTON.   In safety?

WALTER.   Yes; from the hands of Nahmeokee I received her, just as some Indians, maddened by defeat, prepared to offer her a sacrifice.

ERRINGTON.   Away then, Walter. (*Walter crosses to the right.*) Sir Arthur now seeks thee out to claim thee as his own son.

WALTER.   My father! I fly to seek him. (*Exit*)

ERRINGTON.   The victory is ours; yet while Philip lives we are in peril! Come, let us find this Indian prophet whom Metamora banished from his tribe. He may be bribed to show us the chieftain's place of safety.

(*Exeunt. Change.*)

Scene 5

Metamora's stronghold. Rocks, bridge and waterfall. Nahmeokee discovered listening. The child lies under a tree at the right, covered with furs. Slow music, four bars.

NAHMEOKEE. He comes not, yet the sound of the battle has died away like the last breath of a storm! Can he be slain? O cruel white man, this day will stain your name forever.

(Slow music, sixteen bars. Metamora enters on bridge.)

METAMORA. Nahmeokee, I am weary of the strife of blood. Where is our little one? Let me take him to my burning heart and he may quell its mighty torrent.

NAHMEOKEE. *(With broken utterance)* He is here!

(Lifts the furs and shows the child dead)

METAMORA. Ha! Dead! Dead! Cold!

NAHMEOKEE. Nahmeokee could not cover him with her body, for the white men were around her and over her. I plunged into the stream and the unseen shafts of the fire weapons flew with a great noise over my head. One smote my babe and he sunk into the deep water; the foe shouted with a mighty shout, for he thought Nahmeokee and her babe had sunk to rise no more.

METAMORA. His little arms will never clasp thee more; his little lips will never press the pure bosom which nourished him so long! Well, is he not happy? Better to die by the stranger's hand than live his slave.

NAHMEOKEE. O Metamora! *(Falls on his neck)*

METAMORA. Nay, do not bow down thy head; let me kiss off the hot drops that are running down thy red cheeks. Thou wilt see him again in the peaceful land of spirits, and he will look smilingly as—as—as I do now, Nahmeokee.

NAHMEOKEE. Metamora, is our nation dead? Are we alone in the land of our fathers?

METAMORA. The palefaces are all around us, and they tread in blood. The blaze of our burning wigwams flashes awfully in the darkness of their path. We are destroyed—not vanquished; we are no more, yet we are forever—Nahmeokee.

NAHMEOKEE. What wouldst thou?

METAMORA. Dost thou not fear the power of the white man?

NAHMEOKEE. No.

METAMORA. He may come hither in his might and slay thee.

NAHMEOKEE. Thou art with me.

METAMORA. He may seize thee, and bear thee off to the far country, bind these arms that have so often clasped me in the dear embrace of love, scourge thy soft flesh in the hour of his wrath, and force thee to carry burdens like the beasts of the fields.

NAHMEOKEE. Thou wilt not let them.

METAMORA. We cannot fly, for the foe is all about us; we cannot fight, for this is the only weapon I have saved from the strife of blood.

NAHMEOKEE. It was my brother's—Coanchett's.

METAMORA. It has tasted the white man's blood, and reached the cold heart of the traitor; it has been our truest friend; it is our only treasure.

NAHMEOKEE. Thine eye tells me the thought of thy heart, and I rejoice at it. (*Sinks on his bosom*)

METAMORA. Nahmeokee, I look up through the long path of thin air, and I think I see our infant borne onward to the land of the happy, where the fair hunting grounds know no storms or snows, and where the immortal brave feast in the eyes of the giver of good. Look upwards, Nahmeokee, the spirit of thy murdered father beckons thee.

NAHMEOKEE. I will go to him.

METAMORA. Embrace me, Nahmeokee—'twas like the first you gave me in the days of our strength and joy—they are gone. (*Places his ear to the ground*) Hark! In the distant wood I faintly hear the cautious tread of men! They are upon us, Nahmeokee—the home of the happy is made ready for thee. (*Stabs her, she dies.*) She felt no white man's bondage— free as the air she lived—pure as the snow she died! In smiles she died! Let me taste it, ere her lips are cold as the ice.

(*Loud shouts. Roll of drums. Kaneshine leads Church and Soldiers on bridge.*)

CHURCH. He is found! Philip is our prisoner.

METAMORA. No! He lives—last of his race—but still your enemy—lives to defy you still. Though numbers overpower me and treachery surround me, though friends desert me, I defy you still! Come to me—come singly to me! And this true knife that has tasted the foul blood of your nation and now is red with the purest of mine, will feel a grasp as strong as when it flashed in the blaze of your burning dwellings, or was lifted terribly over the fallen in battle.

CHURCH. Fire upon him!

METAMORA. Do so, I am weary of the world for ye are dwellers in it; I would not turn upon my heel to save my life.

CHURCH. Your duty, soldiers.

(*They fire. Metamora falls. Enter Walter, Oceana, Wolfe, Sir Arthur, Errington, Goodenough, Tramp, and Peasants. Roll of drums and trumpet till all on.*)

METAMORA. My curses on you, white men! May the Great Spirit curse you when he speaks in his war voice from the clouds! Murderers! The last of the Wampanoags' curse be on you! May your graves and the graves of your children be in the path the red man shall trace! And may the wolf and the panther howl o'er your fleshless bones, fit banquet for the destroyers! Spirits of the grave, I come! But the curse of Metamora stays with the white man! I die! My wife! My Queen! My Nahmeokee!

(Falls and dies; a tableau is formed. Drums and trumpet sound a retreat till curtain. Slow curtain)

Epilogue

Written by Mr. James Lawson.
Spoken by Mrs. Hilson, New Park Theater,
New York, December 15, 1829.

Before this bar of beauty, taste, and wit,
This host of critics, too, who throng the pit,
A trembling bard has been this night arraigned;
And I am counsel in the cause retained.
Here come I, then, to plead with nature's art,
And speak, less to the law, than to the heart.
    A native bard—a native actor too,
Have drawn a native picture to your view;
In fancy, this bade Indian wrongs arise,
While that embodied all before your eyes;
Inspired by genius, and by judgment led,
Again the Wampanoag fought and bled;
Rich plants are both of our own fruitful land,
Your smiles the sun that made their leaves expand;
Yet, not that they are native do I plead,
'Tis for their worth alone I ask your meed.
How shall I ask ye? Singly? Then I will—
But should I fail? Fail! I must try my skill.
    Sir, I know you—I've often seen your face;
And always seated in that selfsame place;
Now, in my ear—what think you of our play?
That it has merit truly, he did say;
And that the hero, prop'd on genius' wing,
The Indian forest scoured, like Indian king!
    See that fair maid, the tear still in her eye,
And hark! hear not you now that gentle sigh?
Ah! these speak more than language could relate,
The woe-fraught heart o'er Nahmeokee's fate;
She scans us not by rigid rules of art,
Her test is feeling, and her judge the heart.
    What dost thou say, thou bushy-whiskered beau?
He nods approval—whiskers are the go.
    Who is he sits the fourth bench from the stage?
There; in the pit!—why he looks wondrous sage!
He seems displeased, his lip denotes a sneer—
O! he's a critic that looks so severe!

Why, in his face I see the attic salt—
A critic's merit is to find a fault.
What fault find you, sir? eh! or you, sir?
  None!
Then, if the critic's mute, my cause is won.
Yea, by that burst of loud heartfelt applause,
I feel that I have gained my client's cause.
  Thanks, that our strong demerits you forgive,
And bid our bard and Metamora live.

FASHION

or

Life in New York

by
Anna Cora Mowatt

Introduction

The career of Anna Cora Ogden Mowatt Ritchie not only reveals her as a courageous and talented woman but also suggests a great deal about the mores of her day. A member of an established, well-to-do family, she was the first American woman from her social class to be associated with the theatre. She appeared on the stage at a time when many ladies would not appear in an audience. She was born March 5, 1819, in Bordeaux, France, where her father, a New York merchant, had business interests. Samuel Ogden enjoyed the theatre and encouraged his nine children to present home theatricals. Anna was something of a prodigy and, according to her autobiography, had read all of Shakespeare by the age of ten. In 1825 the family returned to live in New York, where she attended a fashionable academy for young ladies and on Sundays listened to sermons at Grace Church condemning the stage. When she was fourteen, she saw Fanny Kemble in *The Hunchback*, her first visit to the theatre. At about this time, James Mowatt, a lawyer twice her age, fell in love with her. They were secretly married in 1834, and she was for a short time estranged from her family. The sixteen-year-old bride wrote a long epic, *Pelayo, or the Cavern of Cavadonga*. Her husband arranged for its publication by Harper's, and when critics attacked it she promptly counterattacked with a long rhymed satire, *Reviewers Reviewed*.

In 1837, after doctors diagnosed a chronic bronchial ailment as tuberculosis and recommended a sea voyage, she went to Europe, accompanied by an aunt. She attended plays in London and Paris, noted the respect accorded actresses like Madame Vestris and Rachel, and also observed American tourists aping European fashions and manners. The central theme of *Fashion* was expressed in a letter she wrote her sister: "The customs and fashions which we imitate as Parisian are not infrequently mere caricatures of those that exist in Paris." While abroad she wrote travel articles and a six-act play, *Gulzara, or the Persian Slave*, which her family performed after she returned home.

By 1841 James Mowatt had lost his entire fortune in real estate and stock speculations and was unable to work because of failing sight. Despite the protests of her family, Mrs. Mowatt presented a series of public recitations in Boston and New York. She also wrote articles and sentimental fiction for *Godey's*, *Graham's*, and other magazines. The success of her dramatic readings may have given her courage to extend her career to the professional stage. Travel abroad and residence in rapidly expanding New York City furnished material for a lively comedy satirizing the newly rich and their competition for social status. In her autobiography she modestly observed that her natural inclination toward sarcasm made

Fashion an easy play for her to write. Probably the enormous success of her play in March of 1845 emboldened her to take the much more daring step of appearing on the stage herself. Actresses were not received in polite society. Exceptions to this prejudice were Fanny Kemble, who toured America in 1832 and two years later married Pierce Butler of Philadelphia Main Line society, and Charlotte Cushman, a native of Boston, who made her stage debut in 1835. In general, however, actresses were regarded—frequently with good reason—as being outside the pale of respectability. Mrs. Mowatt's appearance as Pauline in Bulwer-Lytton's *The Lady of Lyons* on June 6, 1845, was an unprecedented event. The audience rose to cheer her and showered the stage with flowers when she appeared for a curtain call. Her debut in Philadelphia was also a success despite the intoxication of her dramatic coach and leading man, W. H. Crisp, which she innocently interpreted as nervousness. In her first year as a star, she mastered more than twenty roles, and in 1847 she wrote *Armand, the Child of the People*, which included a part for herself. She toured the United States and also was well received in England. She occasionally played Gertrude in *Fashion*, but it was not one of her favorite roles. That a gentlewoman should appear as a professional actress did much to make acting a respectable career for women and smooth the way for such actresses of the next generation as Laura Keene, Maude Adams, Mrs. Leslie Carter, Mrs. Fiske, Clara Morris, and Georgiana Drew.

James Mowatt died in 1851, and on June 6, 1854, after making a triumphant final tour, she married William F. Ritchie, editor of the Richmond, Virginia, *Enquirer*. For reasons never fully explained but apparently involving differences of opinion over the slavery question, their marriage was not happy, and she lived abroad after 1861. She died at Twickenham, England, on July 29, 1870. Her professional pride is suggested by the title she chose for her life-story: *The Autobiography of an Actress* (1854), a valuable account of the American stage in the late 1840's and early 1850's. After her retirement she also wrote three stories about theatrical life which were published as *Mimic Life; or, Before and Behind the Curtain* (1856). The standard biography is *The Lady of Fashion* (New York, 1954) by Eric W. Barnes.

Fashion opened on March 24, 1845, at the Park Theatre in New York. At a time when a play seldom ran more than three or four nights, it held the stage for three weeks, and after closing because of the actors' other commitments it was presented in Philadelphia with a different cast. It remained a favorite of American audiences and in 1850 was well received in London. It has been revived several times in the present century. During the first run of the play, a prologue by Epes Sargent, spoken by W. H. Crisp, who played the role of Count Jolimaitre, was designed to forestall criticism. The closing sixteen lines touch on the general prejudice against the stage and on the tendency to underrate both native American subjects and women authors:

And now, come forth, thou man of sanctity!
How shall I venture a reply to thee?
The *Stage*—what is it, though beneath *thy* ban,
But a *Daguerreotype* of life and man?
Arraign poor human nature, if you will,
But let the *Drama* have her mission still!
Let her, with honest purpose, still reflect
The faults which keen-eyed Satire may detect.
For there *be* men, who fear not an hereafter,
Yet tremble at the Hell of public laughter!

Friends, from these scoffers we appeal to you!
Condemn the *false*, but O! applaud the *true*.
Grant that *some* wit may grow on native soil,
And Art's fair fabric rise from woman's toil—
While we exhibit but to reprehend
The social vices, 'tis for you to mend!

Discussions of *Fashion* always make much of the two reviews of the play written by Poe. The first, which appeared in the *Broadway Journal* for March 29, was rather harsh. Although he described it as "superior to any American play," Poe found *Fashion* too conventional and artificial. He objected to the clumsy asides and to Trueman's long speeches at the close. The following week he published a longer article in which he said that he had attended every performance. He did not wholly recant from his original judgment, but he predicted that *Fashion* might be the "clearest indication of a revival of the American drama." He closed by calling on American writers to stop imitating dramatists of the past and to write of and for their own day. Poe later commented favorably on Mrs. Mowatt's acting and condemned the popular prejudice against the stage. Himself the son of an actress, Poe appreciated Mrs. Mowatt's courage as well as her ability.

Although *Fashion* is often described as a comedy of manners, this designation, strictly speaking, does not altogether fit the play. A true comedy of manners does not moralize but accepts the code of a sophisticated, often decadent society even while satirizing the affectation and intrigues of its members. Mrs. Mowatt's satire is more didactic and less cynical than one would expect to find in a comedy of manners. Her major target is the fatuous pretentiousness of social climbers, but at least a dozen foibles of fashionable society can be identified as minor targets. This diffusion may weaken the force of her satire somewhat. Some aspects of the play clearly are not satirical. The subplot involving Gertrude is a sentimental Cinderella story; that involving Snobson, the villainous clerk, is crude melodrama; Mrs. Tiffany's misuse of French words and her other blunders belong to farce; and Zeke, the comic butler, is on the level of minstrel show buffoonery. Despite the multiple effects, which remove some of the sting from the satire, the play acts well, largely because of the lively dialogue. Poe praised the "colloquy" as "spirited, generally terse, and well seasoned at points with sarcasm of much power," and his judgment seems sound today. Although the Negro dialect and the French phrases seem rather clumsy attempts at humor, much of the dialogue is fast-moving and often epigrammatic. Certainly the speeches are more natural than most, whether blank verse or prose, in other plays of the time.

The characters in *Fashion* are familiar comic types: the wealthy businessman who is a slave to his office and his wife's extravagance, the middle-aged social climber, the pert French maid, and the bogus European nobleman. Adam Trueman is a type found in many 19th century American plays—the blunt, sensible man who speaks the truth as he sees it, whatever the consequences. Trueman undoubtedly serves as the voice of the dramatist when he denounces hypocrisy and extravagance. Modern revivals have usually portrayed him as a caricature, but there is little indication in the play that Mrs. Mowatt did not intend him to be taken seriously. In her autobiography she wrote "the only character in the play which was sketched from life was that of the blunt, warm hearted old farmer. I was told that the original was seen in the pit vociferously applauding Adam Trueman's strictures of fashionable society."

The true comedy of manners has been comparatively rare on the American stage, perhaps because such plays are best suited to a stable, rigidly stratified society. Plays with which *Fashion* might be compared include *The Contrast* (1787) by Royall Tyler, *Fashionable Follies* (1815) by Joseph Hutton, *Self* (1856) by Mrs. Sidney F. Bateman, *Saratoga* (1870) and *Diamonds* (1872) by Bronson Howard, *The Mighty Dollar* (1875) by Benjamin E. Woolf, *The Climbers* (1901) by Clyde Fitch, and *The New York Idea* (1906) by Langdon Mitchell. On the modern stage the comedies of S. N. Behrman and Philip Barry most nearly fulfill the definition of comedy of manners.

Anna Cora Mowatt as painted by John James Audubon
(Museum of the City of New York)

PARK THEATRE

First Tier 75 Cts.   Boxes, 2d & 3d Tiers 50 Cts.
Pit 50 Cts   Gallery 25 Cts.

Doors Open at a quarter before 7.   Performance commence
at a quarter-past 7 o'clock.

FIRST NIGHT OF A NEW

American Comedy !

IN FIVE ACTS, CALLED

FASHION,

Written for this Theatre, by Mrs. ANNA CORA MOWATT.

Regardless of Expense, the Manager has made every effort to produce this NEW
COMEDY with the STRICTEST FIDELITY, APPROPRIATENESS and SU-
PERIOR EXECUTION of SCENIC ILLUSION, and all that Magnificence of

STAGE   APPOINTMENTS !

Which Excited the Admiration and Applause of the Public, on the First Performance of

☞ LONDON ASSURANCE ! ☜

Monday Evening, March 24th,

Will be presented, for the 1st time on any stage, a New AMERICAN COMEDY,
(with a Prologue and Epilogue) called

Fashion!

Written for this Theatre by Mrs. ANNA CORA MOWATT.

New Scenery . . . . by . . . . Messrs. Hillyard, Smith and P. Grain
The Costumes, Decorations and Appointments . . . . . . by . . . . Mr. Dejonge

Adam Trueman	Mr. Chippendale
Count de Jolimaitre	W. H. Crisp
Colonel Howard	Dyott
Mr. Tiffany	Barry
Mr. T. Tennison Twinkle	De Walden
Mr. Augustus Fog	Bridges
Mr. Snobson	Fisher
Zeke, a colored servant	Sherrett
Master of the Ceremonies	Gallot
Mrs. Tiffany	Mrs. Barry
Gertrude	Miss Clara Ellis
Seraphina Tiffany	Miss Kate Horn
Prudence	Mrs. Knight
Millinette	Dyott

The Prologue will be spoken by . . . . W. H. CRISP
The Epilogue by . . . . the Characters.

THE SCENE LIES IN NEW YORK.   TIME 1845 !

DRAWING ROOM !

At Mrs. Tiffany's, furnished in the First Style of Modern Elegance, with view of

CONSERVATORY!!

Seen through a French Window.—Merchant's Counting House.

INTERIOR of the CONSERVATORY!

VIEW of the BATTERY

BALL ROOM WITH SUPPER ROOM !

IN THE DISTANCE.   IN ACT FOURTH

A COTILLION

AND

☞ LA POLKA !

By the Characters, produced under the direction of Mr. PARKER.
In the course of the Evening, the Orchestra will play for the first time, the following
Pieces of Music.

OVERTURE—Les Diamans de la Couronne	AUBER
QUADRILLES—Irish Echos	JULLIEN
EDINBURGH WALTZER	LABITZKY
DUET FROM NORMA—Two Cornets . . Messrs. WHOENING and WILLIS
HAMBURGER ELB GALOPP	LABITZKY

PAS DE DANUBE !

By Miss St. Clair.

To conclude with the Comedy of

USED UP !

As written for Mr. Charles Matthews, and played by him upwards of 300 nights
with Unprecedented Success.

Sir Charles Coldstream	. . . . . .	. . . . . .	W. H. Crisp
Sir Adonis Leech	De Walden	Lattiat	Freeland
Hon. Tom Saville	Crocker	Officers	Heath & Gourlay
John Ironbrace	Barry	Boy	Mast. King
Brisk	Povey	Lady Chatterbuck . .	Mrs. Dyott
Farmer	Anderson	Mary	Sherrett

TUESDAY,

A COMEDY,

And Other Entertainments.

Various Novelties are in Preparation.

(Harvard Theatre Collection)

Cast of Characters

ADAM TRUEMAN, a Farmer from Catteraugus
COUNT JOLIMAITRE, a fashionable European Importation
COLONEL HOWARD, an Officer in the U. S. Army
MR. TIFFANY, a New York Merchant
T. TENNYSON TWINKLE, a Modern Poet
AUGUSTUS FOGG, a Drawing-Room Appendage
SNOBSON, a rare species of Confidential Clerk
ZEKE, a colored Servant
MRS. TIFFANY, a Lady who imagines herself fashionable
PRUDENCE, a Maiden Lady of a certain age
MILLINETTE, a French Lady's Maid
GERTRUDE, a Governess
SERAPHINA TIFFANY, a Belle
LADIES AND GENTLEMEN OF THE BALL-ROOM

ACT I

A splendid Drawing-Room in the House of Mrs. Tiffany. Open folding doors discovering a Conservatory. On either side glass windows down to the ground. Doors on right and left. Mirror, couches, ottomans, a table with albums, etc., beside it an arm-chair. Millinette dusting furniture, Zeke in a dashing livery, scarlet coat, etc.

ZEKE. Dere's a coat to take de eyes ob all Broadway! Ah! Missy, it am de fixins dat make de natural *born* gemman. A libery for ever! Dere's a pair ob insuppressibles to 'stonish de coloured population.

MILLINETTE. Oh, *oui*, Monsieur Zeke. (*Very politely*) I not *comprend* one word he say! (*Aside*)

ZEKE. I tell 'ee what, Missy, I'm 'stordinary glad to find dis a bery 'spectabul like situation! Now as you've made de acquaintance ob dis here family, and dere you've had a supernumerary advantage ob me—seeing dat I only receibed my appointment dis morning. What I wants to know is your publicated opinion, privately expressed, ob de domestic circle.

MILLINETTE. You mean vat *espèce*, vat kind of personnes are Monsieur and Madame Tiffany? Ah! Monsieur is not de same ting as Madame,—not at all.

ZEKE. Well, I s'pose he ain't altogether.

MILLINETTE. Monsieur is man of business,—Madame is lady of fashion. Monsieur make the money,—Madame spend it. Monsieur nobody at all,—Madame everybody altogether. Ah! Monsieur Zeke, de money is all dat is *necessaire* in dis country to make one lady of fashion. Oh! it is quite anoder ting in *la belle France!*

ZEKE. A bery lucifer explanation. Well, now we've disposed ob de heads of de family, who come next?

MILLINETTE. First, dere is Mademoiselle Seraphina Tiffany. Mademoiselle is not at all one proper *personne*. Mademoiselle Seraphina is one coquette. Dat is not de mode in *la belle France;* de ladies, dere, never learn *la coquetrie* until dey do get one husband.

ZEKE. I tell 'ee what, Missy, I disreprobate dat proceeding altogeder!

MILLINETTE. Vait! I have not tell you all *la famille* yet. Dere is Ma'mselle Prudence—Madame's sister, one very *bizarre* personne. Den dere is Ma'mselle Gertrude, but she is not anybody at all; she only teach Mademoiselle Seraphina *la musique.*

ZEKE. Well, now, Missy, what's your own special defunctions?

MILLINETTE. I not understand, Monsieur Zeke.

ZEKE. Den I'll amplify. What's de nature ob your exclusive services?

MILLINETTE. *Ah, oui! je comprend.* I am Madame's *femme de chambre* —her lady's maid, Monsieur Zeke. I teach Madame *les modes de Paris,* and Madame set de fashion for all New York. You see, Monsieur Zeke, dat it is me, *moi-même*, dat do lead de fashion for all de American *beau monde!*

ZEKE. Yah! yah! yah! I hab de idea by de heel. Well now, p'raps you can 'lustrify my officials?

MILLINETTE. Vat you will have to do? Oh! much tings, much tings. You vait on de table,—you tend de door,—you clean de boots,—you run de errands,—you drive de carriage,—you rub de horses,—you take care of de flowers,—you carry de water,—you help cook de dinner,—you wash de dishes,—and den you always remember to do everyting I tell you to!

ZEKE. Wheugh, am dat *all?*

MILLINETTE. All I can tink of now. To-day is Madame's day of reception, and all her grand friends do make her one *petite* visit. You mind run fast ven de bell do ring.

ZEKE. Run? If it wasn't for dese superfluminous trimmings, I tell 'ee what, Missy, I'd run—

MRS. TIFFANY. (*Outside*) Millinette!

MILLINETTE. Here comes Madame! You better go, Monsieur Zeke.

ZEKE. Look ahea, Massa Zeke, doesn't dis open rich! (*Aside*)

(*Exit Zeke*)

(*Enter Mrs. Tiffany right, dressed in the most extravagant height of fashion*)

MRS. TIFFANY. Is everything in order, Millinette? Ah! very elegant, very elegant indeed! There is a *jenny-says-quoi* look about this furniture,—an air of fashion and gentility perfectly bewitching. Is there not, Millinette?

MILLINETTE. Oh, *oui*, Madame!

MRS. TIFFANY. But where is Miss Seraphina? It is twelve o'clock; our visitors will be pouring in, and she has not made her appearance. But I hear that nothing is more fashionable than to keep people waiting.—None but vulgar persons pay any attention to punctuality. Is it not so, Millinette?

MILLINETTE. Quite *comme il faut*.—Great personnes always do make little personnes wait, Madame.

MRS. TIFFANY. This mode of receiving visitors only upon one specified day of the week is a most convenient custom! It saves the trouble of keeping the house continually in order and of being always dressed. I flatter myself that *I* was the first to introduce it amongst the New York *ee-light*. You are quite sure that it is strictly a Parisian mode, Millinette?

MILLINETTE. Oh, *oui*, Madame; entirely *mode de Paris*.

MRS. TIFFANY. This girl is worth her weight in gold. (*Aside*) Millinette, how do you say *arm-chair* in French?

MILLINETTE. *Fauteuil*, Madame.

MRS. TIFFANY. *Fo-tool!* That has a foreign—an out-of-the-wayish sound that is perfectly charming—and so genteel! There is something about our

American words decidedly vulgar. *Fowtool!* how refined. *Fowtool! Arm-chair!* what a difference!

MILLINETTE.   Madame have one charmante pronunciation. *Fowtool!* (*Mimicking aside*) Charmante, Madame!

MRS. TIFFANY.   Do you think so, Millinette? Well, I believe I have. But a woman of refinement and of fashion can always accommodate herself to everything foreign! And a week's study of that invaluable work— "*French without a Master,*" has made me quite at home in the court language of Europe! But where is the new valet? I'm rather sorry that he is black, but to obtain a white American for a domestic is almost impossible; and they call this a free country! What did you say was the name of this new servant, Millinette?

MILLINETTE.   He do say his name is Monsieur Zeke.

MRS. TIFFANY.   Ezekiel, I suppose. Zeke! Dear me, such a vulgar name will compromise the dignity of the whole family. Can you not suggest something more aristocratic, Millinette? Something *French!*

MILLINETTE.   *Oh, oui,* Madame; *Adolph* is one very fine name.

MRS. TIFFANY.   A-dolph! Charming! Ring the bell, Millinette! (*Millinette rings the bell*) I will change his name immediately, besides giving him a few directions. (*Enter Zeke, left. Mrs. Tiffany addresses him with great dignity.*) Your name, I hear, is *Ezekiel.*—I consider it too plebeian an appellation to be uttered in my presence. In future you are called A-dolph. Don't reply,—never interrupt me when I am speaking. A-dolph, as my guests arrive, I desire that you will inquire the name of every person, and then announce it in a loud, clear tone. *That* is the fashion in Paris.

(*Millinette retires up the stage.*)

ZEKE.   Consider de office discharged, Missus. (*Speaking very loudly*)

MRS. TIFFANY.   Silence! Your business is to obey and not to talk.

ZEKE.   I'm dumb, Missus!

MRS. TIFFANY.   (*Pointing up stage*) A-dolph, place that *fowtool* behind me.

ZEKE.   (*Looking about him*) I habn't got dat far in de dictionary yet. No matter, a genus gets his learning by nature.

(*Takes up the table and places it behind Mrs. Tiffany, then expresses in dumb show great satisfaction. Mrs. Tiffany, as she goes to sit, discovers the mistake.*)

MRS. TIFFANY.   You dolt! Where have you lived not to know that *fowtool* is the French for *arm-chair?* What ignorance! Leave the room this instant.

(*Mrs. Tiffany draws forward an arm-chair and sits. Millinette comes forward suppressing her merriment at Zeke's mistake and removes the table.*)

ZEKE. Dem's de defects ob not having a libery education.

(*Exit Zeke*)

(*Prudence peeps in.*)

PRUDENCE. I wonder if any of the fine folks have come yet. Not a soul,—
I knew they hadn't. There's Betsy all alone. (*Walks in*) Sister Betsy!

MRS. TIFFANY. Prudence! how many times have I desired you to call
me *Elizabeth? Betsy* is the height of vulgarity.

PRUDENCE. Oh! I forgot. Dear me, how spruce we do look here, to be
sure,—everything in first rate style now, Betsy. (*Mrs. Tiffany looks at her
angrily.*) *Elizabeth*, I mean. Who would have thought, when you and I
were sitting behind that little mahogany-coloured counter, in Canal
Street, making up flashy hats and caps—

MRS. TIFFANY. Prudence, what *do* you mean? Millinette, leave the room.

MILLINETTE. *Oui*, Madame.

(*Millinette pretends to arrange the books upon a side table, but
lingers to listen.*)

PRUDENCE. But I always predicted it,—I always told you so, Betsy—I
always said you were destined to rise above your station!

MRS. TIFFANY. Prudence! Prudence! have I not told you that—

PRUDENCE. No, Betsy, it was *I* that told *you*, when we used to buy our
silks and ribbons of Mr. Antony Tiffany—"*talking Tony*" you know we
used to call him, and when you always put on the finest bonnet in our
shop to go to his,—and when you staid so long smiling and chattering
with him, I always told you that *something* would grow out of it—and
didn't it?

MRS. TIFFANY. Millinette, send Seraphina here instantly. Leave the room.

MILLINETTE. *Oui*, Madame. So dis Americaine ladi of fashion vas one
milliner? Oh, vat a fine country for *les marchandes des modes!* I shall
send for all my relation by de next packet! (*Aside*)

(*Exit Millinette*)

MRS. TIFFANY. Prudence! never let me hear you mention this subject
again. Forget what we *have* been, it is enough to remember that we *are*
of the *upper ten thousand!*

(*Prudence goes left and sits. Enter Seraphina, very extravagantly
dressed.*)

MRS. TIFFANY. How bewitchingly you look, my dear! Does Millinette
say that that head-dress is strictly Parisian?

SERAPHINA. Oh yes, Mamma, all the rage! They call it a *lady's tarpaulin*, and it is the exact pattern of one worn by the Princess Clementina at the last court ball.

MRS. TIFFANY. Now, Seraphina, my dear, don't be too particular in your attentions to gentlemen not eligible. There is Count Jolimaitre, decidedly the most fashionable foreigner in town,—and so refined,—so much accustomed to associate with the first nobility in his own country that he can hardly tolerate the vulgarity of Americans in general. You may devote yourself to him. Mrs. Proudacre is dying to become acquainted with him. By the by, if she or her daughters should happen to drop in, be sure you don't introduce them to the Count. It is not the fashion in Paris to introduce—Millinette told me so.

(Enter Zeke)

ZEKE. (*In a very loud voice*) Mister T. Tennyson Twinkle!
MRS. TIFFANY. Show him up. (*Exit Zeke*)
PRUDENCE. I must be running away. (*Going*)
MRS. TIFFANY. Mr. T. Tennyson Twinkle—a very literary young man and a sweet poet! It is all the rage to patronize poets! Quick, Seraphina, hand me that magazine.—Mr. Twinkle writes for it.

(Seraphina hands the magazine; Mrs. Tiffany seats herself in an arm-chair and opens the book.)

PRUDENCE. (*Returning*) There's Betsy trying to make out that reading without her spectacles. (*Takes a pair of spectacles out of her pocket and hands them to Mrs. Tiffany*) There, Betsy, I knew you were going to ask for them. Ah! they're a blessing when one is growing old!
MRS. TIFFANY. What do you mean, Prudence? A woman of fashion *never* grows old! Age is always out of fashion.
PRUDENCE. Oh, dear! what a delightful thing it is to be fashionable. (*Exit Prudence. Mrs. Tiffany resumes her seat.*)

(Enter Twinkle. He salutes Seraphina.)

TWINKLE. Fair Seraphina! The sun itself grows dim,
    Unless you aid his light and shine on him!
SERAPHINA. Ah! Mr. Twinkle, there is no such thing as answering you.
TWINKLE. (*Looks around and perceives Mrs. Tiffany*) The "New Monthly Vernal Galaxy." Reading my verses, by all that's charming! Sensible woman! I won't interrupt her. (*Aside*)
MRS. TIFFANY. (*Rising and coming forward*) Ah! Mr. Twinkle, is that you? I was perfectly *abimé* at the perusal of your very *distingué* verses.
TWINKLE. I am overwhelmed, Madam. Permit me. (*Taking the magazine*) Yes, they do read tolerably. And you must take into consideration,

ladies, the rapidity with which they were written. Four minutes and a half by the stop watch! The true test of a poet is the *velocity* with which he composes. Really, they do look very prettily, and they read tolerably—*quite* tolerably—*very* tolerably,—especially the first verse. (*Reads*) "To Seraphina T_____."

SERAPHINA.   Oh! Mr. Twinkle!

TWINKLE.   (*Reads*) "Around my heart"—

MRS. TIFFANY.   How touching! Really, Mr. Twinkle, quite tender!

TWINKLE.   (Recommencing) "Around my heart"—

MRS. TIFFANY.   Oh, I must tell you, Mr. Twinkle! I heard the other day that poets were the aristocrats of literature. That's one reason I like them, for I do dote on all aristocracy!

TWINKLE.   Oh, Madam, how flattering! Now pray lend me your ears! (*Reads*)
    "Around my heart thou weavest"—

SERAPHINA.   That is such a *sweet* commencement, Mr. Twinkle!

TWINKLE.   (*Aside*) I wish she wouldn't interrupt me! (*Reads*)
"Around my heart thou weavest a spell"—

MRS. TIFFANY.   Beautiful! But excuse me one moment, while I say a word to Seraphina! Don't be too affable, my dear! Poets are very ornamental appendages to the drawing-room, but they are always as poor as their own verses. They don't make eligible husbands! (*Aside to Seraphina*)

TWINKLE.   (*Aside*) Confound their interruptions! My dear Madam, unless you pay the utmost atteniton you cannot catch the ideas. Are you ready? Well, now you shall hear it to the end! (*Reads*)
"Around my heart thou weavest a spell
"Whose"—

(*Enter Zeke*)

ZEKE.   Mister Augustus Fogg! A bery misty lookin' young gemman? (*Aside*)

MRS. TIFFANY.   Show him up, A-dolph! (*Exit Zeke*)

TWINKLE.   This is too much!

SERAPHINA.   Exquisite verses, Mr. Twinkle,—exquisite!

TWINKLE.   Ah, lovely Seraphina! your smile of approval transports me to the summit of Olympus.

SERAPHINA.   Then I must frown, for I would not send you so far away.

TWINKLE.   Enchantress! It's all over with her. (*Aside*)

(*Retire up right and converse*)

MRS. TIFFANY.   Mr. Fogg belongs to one of our oldest families,—to be sure he is the most difficult person in the world to entertain, for he never takes the trouble to talk, and never notices anything or anybody,—but then I hear that nothing is considered so vulgar as to betray any emotion, or to attempt to render oneself agreeable!

(*Enter Mr. Fogg, fashionably attired but in very dark clothes*)

FOGG. (*Bowing stiffly*) Mrs. Tiffany, your most obedient. Miss Seraphina, yours. How d'ye do, Twinkle?

MRS. TIFFANY. Mr. Fogg, how do you do? Fine weather,—delightful, isn't it?

FOGG. I am indifferent to weather, Madam.

MRS. TIFFANY. Been to the opera, Mr. Fogg? I hear that the *bow monde* make their *debutt* there every evening.

FOGG. I consider operas a bore, Madam.

SERAPHINA. (*Advancing*) You must hear Mr. Twinkle's verses, Mr. Fogg!

FOGG. I am indifferent to verses, Miss Seraphina.

SERAPHINA. But Mr. Twinkle's verses are addressed to me!

TWINKLE. Now pay attention, Fogg! (*Reads*)—
"Around my heart thou weavest a spell
"Whose magic I"—

(*Enter Zeke*)

ZEKE. Mister—No, he say he ain't no Mister—

TWINKLE. "Around my heart thou weavest a spell
      "Whose magic I can never tell!"

MRS. TIFFANY. Speak in a loud, clear tone, A-dolph!

TWINKLE. This is terrible!

ZEKE. Mister Count Jolly-made-her!

MRS. TIFFANY. Count Jolimaitre! Good gracious! Zeke, Zeke,—A-dolph, I mean.—Dear me, what a mistake! (*Aside*) Set that chair out of the way,—put that table back. Seraphina, my dear, are you all in order? Dear me! dear me! Your dress is so tumbled! (*Arranges her dress*) What are you grinning at? (*To Zeke*) Beg the Count to *honour* us by walking up! (*Exit Zeke*) Seraphina, my dear (*Aside to her*) remember now what I told you about the Count. He is a man of the highest,—good gracious! I am so flurried; and nothing is so ungenteel as agitation! what will the Count think! Mr. Twinkle, pray stand out of the way! Seraphina, my dear, place yourself on my right! Mr. Fogg, the conservatory—beautiful flowers,—pray amuse yourself in the conservatory.

FOGG. I am indifferent to flowers, Madam.

MRS. TIFFANY. Dear me! the man stands right in the way,—just where the Count must make his *entray!* (*Aside*) Mr. Fogg,—pray—

(*Enter Count Jolimaitre, very dashingly dressed; he wears a
moustache.*)

MRS. TIFFANY. Oh, Count, this unexpected honour—

SERAPHINA. Count, this inexpressible pleasure—

COUNT. Beg you won't mention it, Madam! Miss Seraphina, your most devoted!

MRS. TIFFANY. What condescension! (*Aside*) Count, may I take the liberty to introduce—Good gracious! I forgot. (*Aside*) Count, I was about to remark that we never introduce in America. All our fashions are foreign, Count.

(*Twinkle, who has stepped forward to be introduced, shows great indignation.*)

COUNT. Excuse me, Madam, our fashions have grown antediluvian before you Americans discover their existence. You are lamentably behind the age—lamentably! 'Pon my honour, a foreigner of refinement finds great difficulty in existing in this provincial atmosphere.

MRS. TIFFANY. How dreadful, Count! I am very much concerned. If there is anything which I can do, Count—

SERAPHINA. Or I, Count, to render your situation less deplorable—

COUNT. Ah! I find but one redeeming charm in America—the superlative loveliness of the feminine portion of creation,—and the wealth of their obliging papas. (*Aside*)

MRS. TIFFANY. How flattering! Ah! Count, I am afraid you will turn the head of my simple girl here. She is a perfect child of nature, Count.

COUNT. Very possibly, for though you American women are quite charming, yet, demme, there's a deal of native rust to rub off!

MRS. TIFFANY. *Rust?* Good gracious, Count! where do you find any rust? (*Looking about the room*)

COUNT. How very unsophisticated!

MRS. TIFFANY. Count, I am so much ashamed,—pray excuse me! Although a lady of large fortune, and one, Count, who can boast of the highest connections, I blush to confess that I have never travelled,—while you, Count, I presume are at home in all the courts of Europe.

COUNT. *Courts?* Eh? Oh, yes, Madam, *very* true. I believe I am pretty well known in some of the courts of Europe—(*Aside*) police courts. In a word, Madam, I had seen enough of civilized life—wanted to refresh myself by a sight of barbarous countries and customs—had my choice between the Sandwich Islands and New York—chose New York!

MRS. TIFFANY. How complimentary to our country! And, Count, I have no doubt you speak every conceivable language? You talk English like a native.

COUNT. Eh, what? Like a native? Oh, ah, demme, yes, I am something of an Englishman. Passed one year and eight months with the Duke of Wellington, six months with Lord Brougham, two and a half with Count d'Orsay—knew them all more intimately than their best friends—no heroes to me—hadn't a secret from me, I assure you,—*especially of the toilet.* (*Aside*)

MRS. TIFFANY. Think of that, my dear! Lord Wellington and Duke Broom! (*Aside to Seraphina*)

SERAPHINA. And only think of Count d'Orsay, Mamma! (*Aside to Mrs. Tiffany*) I am so wild to see Count d'Orsay!

COUNT. Oh! a mere man milliner. Very little refinement out of Paris! Why, at the very last dinner given at Lord—Lord Knowswho, would you believe it, Madam, there was an individual present who wore a *black* cravat and took *soup twice!*

MRS. TIFFANY. How shocking! the sight of him would have spoilt my appetite! Think what a great man he must be, my dear, to despise lords and counts in that way. (*Aside to Seraphina*) I must leave them together. (*Aside*) Mr. Twinkle, your arm. I have some really very *foreign exotics* to show you.

TWINKLE. I fly at your command. I wish all her exotics were blooming in their native soil! (*Aside, and glancing at the Count*)

MRS. TIFFANY. Mr. Fogg, will you accompany us? My conservatory is well worthy a visit. It cost an immense sum of money.

FOGG. I am indifferent to conservatories, Madam; flowers are such a bore!

MRS. TIFFANY. I shall take no refusal. Conservatories are all the rage,— I could not exist without mine! Let me show you,—let me show you.

(*Places her arm through Mr. Fogg's, without his consent. Exeunt Mrs. Tiffany, Fogg, and Twinkle into the conservatory, where they are seen walking about.*)

SERAPHINA. America, then, has no charms for you, Count?

COUNT. Excuse me,—some exceptions. I find you, for instance, particularly charming! Can't say I admire your country. Ah! if you had ever breathed the exhilarating air of Paris, ate creams at Tortoni's, dined at the Café Royale, or if you had lived in London—felt at home at St. James's, and every afternoon driven a couple of Lords and a Duchess through Hyde Park, you would find America—where you have no kings, queens, lords, nor ladies—insupportable!

SERAPHINA. Not while there was a Count in it!

(*Enter Zeke, very indignant*)

ZEKE. Where's de Missus?

(*Enter Mrs. Tiffany, Fogg, and Twinkle, from the conservatory*)

MRS. TIFFANY. Whom do you come to announce, A-dolph?

ZEKE. He said he wouldn't trust me—no, not eben wid so much as his name; so I wouldn't trust him up stairs; den he ups wid *his stick* and I *cuts mine.*

MRS. TIFFANY. Some of Mr. Tiffany's vulgar acquaintances. I shall die with shame. (*Aside*) A-dolph, inform him that I am *not at home.* (*Exit Zeke*) My nerves are so shattered, I am ready to sink. Mr. Twinkle, that *fowtool,* if you please!

TWINKLE. What? What do you wish, Madam?

MRS. TIFFANY. The ignorance of these Americans! (*Aside*) Count, may I trouble you? That *fowtool,* if you please!

COUNT. She's not talking English, nor French, but I suppose it's American. (*Aside*)

TRUEMAN. (*Outside*) Not at home!

ZEKE. No, Sar—Missus say she's not at home.

TRUEMAN. Out of the way, you grinning nigger!

(*Enter Adam Trueman, dressed as a farmer, a stout cane in his hand, his boots covered with dust. Zeke jumps out of his way as he enters. Exit Zeke.*)

TRUEMAN. Where's this woman that's not *at home* in her own house? May I be shot! if I wonder at it! I shouldn't think she'd ever feel *at home* in such a show-box as this! (*Looking round*)

MRS. TIFFANY. What a plebeian looking old farmer! I wonder who he is? (*Aside*) Sir—(*Advancing very agitatedly*) What do you mean, sir, by this *ow*dacious conduct? How dare you intrude yourself into my parlor? Do you know who I am, sir? (*With great dignity*) You are in the presence of Mrs. Tiffany, sir!

TRUEMAN. Antony's wife, eh? Well now, I might have guessed that— ha! ha! ha! for I see you make it a point to carry half your husband's shop upon your back! No matter; that's being a good helpmate—for he carried the whole of it once in a pack on his own shoulders—now you bear a share!

MRS. TIFFANY. How dare you, you impertinent, *ow*dacious, ignorant old man! It's all an invention. You're talking of somebody else. What will the Count think! (*Aside*)

TRUEMAN. Why, I thought folks had better manners in the city! This is a civil welcome for your husband's old friend, and after my coming all the way from Catteraugus to see you and yours! First a grinning nigger tricked out in scarlet regimentals—

MRS. TIFFANY. Let me tell you, sir, that liveries are all the fashion!

TRUEMAN. The fashion, are they? To make men wear the *badge of servitude* in a free land,—that's the fashion, is it? Hurrah for republican simplicity! I will venture to say now, that you have your coat-of-arms too!

MRS. TIFFANY. Certainly, sir; you can see it on the panels of my *voyture.*

TRUEMAN. Oh! no need of that. I know what your escutcheon must be! A bandbox *rampant,* with a bonnet *couchant,* and a pedlar's pack *passant!* Ha! ha! ha! that shows both houses united!

MRS. TIFFANY. Sir! You are most profoundly ignorant,—what do you mean by this insolence, sir? How shall I get rid of him? (*Aside*)

TRUEMAN. (*Looking at Seraphina*) I hope that is not Gertrude! (*Aside*)

MRS. TIFFANY. Sir, I'd have you know that—Seraphina, my child, walk with the gentlemen into the conservatory. (*Exeunt Seraphina, Twinkle, Fogg into conservatory*) Count Jolimaitre, pray make due allowances for the errors of this rustic! I do assure you, Count—(*Whispers to him*)

TRUEMAN. Count! She calls that critter with a shoebrush over his mouth, Count! To look at him, I should have thought he was a tailor's walking advertisement! (*Aside*)

COUNT. (*Addressing Trueman, whom he has been inspecting through his eye-glass*) Where did you say you belonged, my friend? Dug out of the ruins of Pompeii, eh?

TRUEMAN. I belong to a land in which I rejoice to find that you are a foreigner.

COUNT. What a barbarian! He doesn't see the honour I'm doing his country! Pray, Madam, is it one of the aboriginal inhabitants of the soil? To what tribe of Indians does he belong—the Pawnee or Choctaw? Does he carry a tomahawk?

TRUEMAN. Something quite as useful,—do you see that? (*Shaking his stick. Count runs to right, behind Mrs. Tiffany.*)

MRS. TIFFANY. Oh, dear! I shall faint! Millinette! (*Approaching right*) Millinette!

(*Enter Millinette, without advancing into the room*)

MILLINETTE. *Oui*, Madame.

MRS. TIFFANY. A glass of water! (*Exit Millinette*) Sir, (*Crossing to Trueman*) I am shocked at your plebeian conduct! This is a gentleman of the highest standing, sir! He is a *Count*, sir!

(*Enter Millinette, bearing a salver with a glass of water. In advancing towards Mrs. Tiffany, she passes in front of the Count, starts and screams. The Count, after a start of surprise, regains his composure, plays with his eye-glass, and looks perfectly unconcerned.*)

MRS. TIFFANY. What is the matter? What *is* the matter?

MILLINETTE. Noting, noting,—only—(*Looks at Count and turns away her eyes again*) only—noting at all!

TRUEMAN. Don't be afraid, girl! Why, did you never see a live Count before? He's tame—I dare say your mistress there leads him about by the ears.

MRS. TIFFANY. This is too much! Millinette, send for Mr. Tiffany instantly! (*Crosses to Millinette, who is going*)

MILLINETTE. He just come in, Madame!

TRUEMAN. My old friend! Where is he? Take me to him—I long to have one more hearty shake of the hand!

MRS. TIFFANY. Shake of the fist, you mean. (*Crosses to him*) If I don't make him shake his in your face, you low, *ow*dacious—no matter, we'll see. Count, honour me by joining my daughter in the conservatory, I will return immediately.

(*Count bows and walks towards conservatory, Mrs. Tiffany following part of the way and then returning to Trueman.*)

TRUEMAN. What a Jezebel! These women always play the very devil with a man, and yet I don't believe such a damaged bale of goods as *that* (*Looking at Mrs. Tiffany*) has smothered the heart of little Antony!
MRS. TIFFANY. This way, sir, sal vous plait. (*Exit, with great dignity*)
TRUEMAN. *Sal vous plait.* Ha, ha, ha! We'll see what Fashion has done for him. (*Exit*)

ACT II

Scene 1

Inner apartment of Mr. Tiffany's Counting-House. Mr. Tiffany seated at a desk looking over papers. Mr. Snobson on a high stool at another desk, with a pen behind his ear.

SNOBSON. (*Rising, advances to the front of the stage, regards Tiffany and shrugs his shoulders*) How the old boy frets and fumes over those papers, to be sure! He's working himself into a perfect fever—ex-actly,—therefore *bleeding's* the prescription! So here goes! (*Aside*) Mr. Tiffany, a word with you, if you please, sir?
TIFFANY. (*Sitting still*) Speak on, Mr. Snobson. I attend.
SNOBSON. What I have to say, sir, is a matter of the first importance to the credit of the concern—the *credit* of the concern, Mr. Tiffany!
TIFFANY. Proceed, Mr. Snobson.
SNOBSON. Sir, you've a handsome house—fine carriage—nigger in livery—feed on the fat of the land—everything first rate—
TIFFANY. Well, sir?
SNOBSON. My salary, Mr. Tiffany!
TIFFANY. It has been raised three times within the last year.
SNOBSON. Still it is insufficient for the necessities of an honest man,—mark me, an *honest* man, Mr. Tiffany.
TIFFANY. (*Crossing*) What a weapon he has made of that word! (*Aside*) Enough—another hundred shall be added. Does that content you?
SNOBSON. There is one other subject, which I have before mentioned, Mr. Tiffany,—your daughter,—what's the reason you can't let the folks at home know at once that I'm to be *the man?*

TIFFANY.   Villain! And must the only seal upon this scoundrel's lips be placed there by the hand of my daughter? (*Aside*) Well, sir, it shall be as you desire.

SNOBSON.   And Mrs. Tiffany shall be informed of your resolution?

TIFFANY.   Yes.

SNOBSON.   Enough said! That's the ticket! The CREDIT *of the concern's safe,* sir. (*Returns to his seat*)

TIFFANY.   How low have I bowed to this insolent rascal! To rise himself, he mounts upon my shoulders, and unless I can shake him off he must crush me! (*Aside*)

(*Enter Trueman*)

TRUEMAN.   Here I am, Antony, man! I told you I'd pay you a visit in your money-making quarters. (*Looks around*) But it looks as dismal here as a cell in the State's prison!

TIFFANY.   (*Forcing a laugh*) Ha, ha, ha! State's prison! You are so facetious! Ha, ha, ha!

TRUEMAN.   Well, for the life of me I can't see anything so amusing in that! I should think the State's prison plaguy uncomfortable lodgings. And you laugh, man, as though you fancied yourself there already.

TIFFANY.   Ha, ha, ha!

TRUEMAN.   (*Imitating him*) Ha, ha, ha! What on earth do you mean by that ill-sounding laugh, that has nothing of a laugh about it! This *fashion*-worship has made heathens and hypocrites of you all! *Deception* is your household God! A man laughs as if he were crying, and cries as if he were laughing in his sleeve. Everything is something else from what it seems to be. I have lived in your house only three days, and I've heard more lies than were ever invented during a Presidential election! First your fine lady of a wife sends me word that she's not at home—I walk upstairs, and she takes good care that *I* shall not be *at home*—wants to turn me out of doors. Then *you* come in—take your old friend by the hand—whisper, the deuce knows what, in your wife's ear, and the tables are turned in a tangent! Madam curtsies—says she's enchanted to see me—and orders her grinning nigger to show me a room.

TIFFANY.   We were exceedingly happy to welcome you as our guest.

TRUEMAN.   Happy? *You* happy? Ah! Antony! Antony! that hatchet face of yours, and those criss-cross furrows tell quite another story! It's many a long day since you were *happy* at anything! You look as if you'd melted down your flesh into dollars, and mortgaged your soul in the bargain! Your warm heart has grown cold over your ledger—your light spirits heavy with calculation! You have traded away your youth—your hopes—your tastes for wealth! and now you *have* the wealth you coveted, what does it profit you? Pleasure it cannot buy; for you have lost your *capacity* for enjoyment. Ease it will not bring; for the love of gain is never satisfied! It has made your counting-house a penitentiary, and your home a fashionable *museum* where there is no niche for you! You have spent so much time *ciphering* in the one, that you find yourself at last a very *cipher* in the other! See me, man! Seventy-two last August!—strong as a hickory and every whit as sound!

TIFFANY. I take the greatest pleasure in remarking your superiority, sir.

TRUEMAN. Bah! no man takes pleasure in remarking the superiority of another! Why the deuce can't you speak the truth, man? But it's not the *fashion*, I suppose! I have not seen one frank, open face since—no, no, I can't say that either, though lying *is* catching! There's that girl, Gertrude, who is trying to teach your daughter music—but Gertrude was bred in the country!

TIFFANY. A good girl; my wife and daughter find her very useful.

TRUEMAN. Useful? Well, I must say you have queer notions of *use!*— But come, cheer up, man! I'd rather see one of your old smiles, than know you'd realized another thousand! I hear you are making money on the true, American high-pressure system—better go slow and sure—the more steam, the greater danger of the boiler's bursting! All sound, I hope? Nothing rotten at the core?

TIFFANY. Oh, sound—quite sound!

TRUEMAN. Well, that's pleasant—though I must say you don't look very pleasant about it!

TIFFANY. My good friend, although I am solvent, I may say, perfectly solvent—yet you—the fact is, you can be of some assistance to me!

TRUEMAN. That's the *fact*, is it? I'm glad we've hit upon one *fact* at last! Well—

(*Snobson, who during this conversation has been employed in writing, but stops occasionally to listen, now gives vent to a dry, chuckling laugh.*)

TRUEMAN. Hey? What's that? Another of those deuced ill-sounding, city laughs! (*Sees Snobson*) Who's that perched up on the stool of repentance —eh, Antony?

SNOBSON. The old boy has missed his text there—*that's* the stool of repentance! (*Aside, and looking at Tiffany's seat*)

TIFFANY. One of my clerks—my confidential clerk!

TRUEMAN. Confidential? Why, he looks for all the world like a spy—the most inquisitorial, hang-dog face—ugh! the sight of it makes my blood run cold! Come, (*Crosses*) let us talk over matters where this critter can't give us the benefit of his opinion! Antony, the next time you choose a confidential clerk, take one that carries his credentials in his face—those in his pocket are not worth much without!

(*Exeunt Trueman and Tiffany*)

SNOBSON. (*Jumping from his stool and advancing*) The old prig has got the tin, or Tiff would never be so civil! All right—Tiff will work every shiner into the concern—all the better for me! Now I'll go and make love to Seraphina. The old woman needn't try to knock me down with any of her French lingo! Six months from to-day, if I ain't driving my two foot-men tandem, down Broadway—and as fashionable as Mrs. Tiffany her-self, then I ain't the trump I thought I was! that's all. (*Looks at his watch*) Bless me! eleven o'clock, and I haven't had my julep yet? Snobson, I'm ashamed of you! (*Exit*)

Scene 2

The interior of a beautiful conservatory; a walk through the centre; stands of flower-pots in bloom; a couple of rustic seats. Gertrude, attired in white, with a white rose in her hair, watering the flowers. Colonel Howard, regarding her.

HOWARD.   I am afraid you lead a sad life here, Miss Gertrude?
GERTRUDE.   (*Turning round gaily*) What! amongst the flowers? (*Continues her occupation*)
HOWARD.   No, amongst the thistles, with which Mrs. Tiffany surrounds you; the tempests, which her temper raises!
GERTRUDE.   They never harm me. Flowers and herbs are excellent tutors. I learn prudence from the reed, and bend until the storm has swept over me!
HOWARD.   Admirable philosophy! But still this frigid atmosphere of fashion must be uncongenial to you? Accustomed to the pleasant com-panionship of your kind friends in Geneva, surely you must regret this cold exchange?
GERTRUDE.   Do you think so? Can you suppose that I could possibly pre-fer a ramble in the woods to a promenade in Broadway? A wreath of scented wild flowers to a bouquet of these sickly exotics? The odour of new-mown hay to the heated air of this crowded conservatory? Or can you imagine that I could enjoy the quiet conversation of my Geneva friends, more than the edifying chit-chat of a fashionable drawing-room? But I see you think me totally destitute of taste?
HOWARD.   You have a merry spirit to jest thus at your grievances!
GERTRUDE.   I have my *mania*,—as some wise person declares that all men have,—and mine is a love of independence! In Geneva, my wants were supplied by two kind old maiden ladies, upon whom I know not that I have any claim. I had abilities, and desired to use them. I came here at my own request; for here I am no longer *dependent! Voilà tout*, as Mrs. Tiffany would say.
HOWARD.   Believe me, I appreciate the confidence you repose in me!
GERTRUDE.   Confidence! Truly, Colonel Howard, the *confidence* is en-tirely on your part, in supposing that I confide that which I have no

reason to conceal! I think I informed you that Mrs. Tiffany only received visitors on her reception day—she is therefore not prepared to see you. Zeke—Oh! I beg his pardon—Adolph made some mistake in admitting you.

HOWARD.   Nay, Gertrude, it was not Mrs. Tiffany, nor Miss Tiffany, whom I came to see; it—it was—

GERTRUDE.   The conservatory perhaps? I will leave you to examine the flowers at leisure! (*Crosses left*)

HOWARD.   Gertrude—listen to me. If I only dared to give utterance to what is hovering upon my lips! (*Aside*) Gertrude!

GERTRUDE.   Colonel Howard!

HOWARD.   Gertrude, I must—must—

GERTRUDE.   Yes, indeed you *must*, must leave me! I think I hear somebody coming—Mrs. Tiffany would not be well pleased to find you here—pray, pray leave me—that door will lead you into the street. (*Hurries him out through door, takes up her watering-pot, and commences watering flowers, tying up branches, etc.*) What a strange being is man! Why should he hesitate to say—nay, why should I prevent his saying, what I would most delight to hear? Truly, man *is* strange—but woman is quite as incomprehensible! (*Walks about gathering flowers*)

(*Enter Count Jolimaitre*)

COUNT.   There she is—the bewitching little creature! Mrs. Tiffany and her daughter are out of ear-shot. I caught a glimpse of their feathers floating down Broadway, not ten minutes ago. Just the opportunity I have been looking for! Now for an engagement with this captivating little piece of prudery! 'Pon my honour, I am almost afraid she will not resist a *Count* long enough to give value to the conquest. (*Approaches her*) *Ma belle petite*, were you gathering roses for me?

GERTRUDE.   (*Starts on first perceiving him, but instantly regains her self-possession*) The roses here, sir, are carefully guarded with thorns—if you have the right to gather, pluck for yourself!

COUNT.   Sharp as ever, little Gertrude! But now that we are alone, throw off this frigidity, and be at your ease.

GERTRUDE.   Permit me to *be alone*, sir, that I *may be* at my ease.

COUNT.   Very good, *ma belle*, well said! (*Applauding her with his hands*) Never yield too soon, even to a *title!* But, as the old girl may find her way back before long, we may as well come to particulars at once. I love you; but that you know already. (*Rubbing his eye-glass unconcernedly with his handkerchief*) Before long I shall make Mademoiselle Seraphina my wife, and, of course, you shall remain in the family!

GERTRUDE.   (*Indignantly*) Sir—

COUNT.   'Pon my honour you shall! In France we arrange these little matters without difficulty!

GERTRUDE. But I am an *American!* Your conduct proves that you are not one! (*Going*)

COUNT. (*Preventing her*) Don't run away, my immaculate *petite Americaine!* Demme, you've quite over-looked my condescension—the difference of our stations—you a species of upper servant—an orphan—no friends.

(*Enter Trueman unperceived*)

GERTRUDE. And therefore more entitled to the respect and protection of every *true gentleman!* Had you been one, you would not have insulted me!

COUNT. My charming little orator, patriotism and declamation become you particularly! (*Approaches her*) I feel quite tempted to taste—

TRUEMAN. (*Thrusting him aside*) An American hickory switch! (*Strikes him*) Well, how do you like it?

COUNT. Old matter-of-fact! (*Aside*) Sir, how dare you?

TRUEMAN. My stick has answered that question!

GERTRUDE. Oh! now I am quite safe!

TRUEMAN. Safe! not a bit safer than before! All women would be safe, if they knew how virtue became them! As for you, Mr. Count, what have you to say for yourself? Come, speak out!

COUNT. Sir,—aw—aw—you don't understand these matters!

TRUEMAN. That's a fact! Not having had *your* experience, I don't believe I *do* understand them!

COUNT. A piece of pleasantry—a mere joke—

TRUEMAN. A joke, was it? I'll show you a joke worth two of that! I'll teach you the way we natives joke with a puppy who don't respect an honest woman! (*Seizing him*)

COUNT. Oh! oh! demme—you old ruffian! let me go. What do you mean?

TRUEMAN. Oh! a piece of pleasantry—a mere joke—very pleasant, isn't it?

(*Attempts to strike him again; Count struggles with him. Enter Mrs. Tiffany hastily, in her bonnet and shawl.*)

MRS. TIFFANY. What is the matter? I am perfectly *abimé* with terror. Mr. Trueman, what has happened?

TRUEMAN. Oh! we have been *joking!*

MRS. TIFFANY. (*To Count, who is re-arranging his dress*) My *dear* Count, I did not expect to find you here—how kind of you!

TRUEMAN. Your *dear* Count has been showing his *kindness* in a very *foreign* manner. Too *foreign*, I think, he found it to be relished by an *unfashionable native!* What do you think of a puppy, who insults an innocent girl all in the way of *kindness?* This Count of yours—this importation of—

COUNT. My dear Madam, demme, permit me to explain. It would be unbecoming—demme—particularly unbecoming of you—aw—aw—to pay any attention to this ignorant person. (*Crosses to Trueman*) Anything that he says concerning a man of my standing—aw—the truth is, Madam—

TRUEMAN. Let us have the truth, by all means,—if it is only for the novelty's sake!

COUNT. (*Turning his back to Trueman*) You see, Madam, hoping to obtain a few moments' private conversation with Miss Seraphina—with *Miss Seraphina*, I say—and—aw—and knowing her passion for flowers, I found my way to your very tasteful and *recherché* conservatory. (*Looks about him approvingly*) *Very* beautifully arranged—does you great credit, Madam! Here I encountered this young person. She was inclined to be talkative; and I indulged her with—with a—aw—demme—a few *commonplaces!* What passed between us was mere *harmless badinage*—on *my* part. You, Madam, you—so conversant with our European manners—you are aware that when a man of fashion—that is, when a woman—a man is bound—amongst noblemen, you know—

MRS. TIFFANY. I comprehend you perfectly—*parfittement*, my dear Count.

COUNT. 'Pon my honour, that's very obliging of her. (*Aside*)

MRS. TIFFANY. I am shocked at the plebeian forwardness of this conceited girl!

TRUEMAN. (*Walking up to Count*) Did you ever keep a reckoning of the lies you tell in an hour?

MRS. TIFFANY. Mr. Trueman, I blush for you! (*Crosses to Trueman*)

TRUEMAN. Don't do that—you have no blushes to spare!

MRS. TIFFANY. It is a man of rank whom you are addressing, sir!

TRUEMAN. A rank villain, Mrs. Antony Tiffany! A *rich one* he would be, had he as much *gold* as *brass!*

MRS. TIFFANY. Pray pardon him, Count; he knows nothing of *how ton!*

COUNT. Demme, he's beneath my notice. I tell you what, old fellow—(*Trueman raises his stick as Count approaches; the latter starts back*) the sight of him discomposes me—aw—I feel quite uncomfortable—aw—let us join your charming daughter? I can't do you the honour to shoot you, sir,—(*To Trueman*) you are beneath me—a nobleman can't fight a commoner! Good-bye, old Truepenny! I—aw—I'm insensible to your insolence!

(*Exeunt Count and Mrs. Tiffany*)

TRUEMAN. You won't be insensible to a cow-hide in spite of your nobility! The next time he practises any of his foreign fashions on you, Gertrude, you'll see how I'll wake up his sensibilities!

GERTRUDE. I do not know what I should have done without you, sir.

TRUEMAN. Yes, you do—you know that you would have done well enough! Never tell a lie, girl! not even for the sake of pleasing an old man! When you open your lips, let your heart speak! Never tell a lie! Let your face be the looking-glass of your soul—your heart its clock—while your tongue rings the hours! But the glass must be clear, the clock true, and then there's no fear but the tongue will do its duty in a woman's head!

GERTRUDE.   You are very good, sir!

TRUEMAN.   That's as it may be!—How my heart warms towards her! (*Aside*) Gertrude, I hear that you have no mother?

GERTRUDE.   Ah! no, sir; I wish I had.

TRUEMAN.   So do I! Heaven knows, so do I! (*Aside, and with emotion*) And you have no father, Gertrude?

GERTRUDE.   No, sir—I often wish I had!

TRUEMAN.   (*Hurriedly*) Don't do that, girl! don't do that! Wish you had a mother—but never wish that you had a father again! Perhaps the one you had did not deserve such a child!

(*Enter Prudence*)

PRUDENCE.   Seraphina is looking for you, Gertrude.

GERTRUDE.   I will go to her. (*Crosses*) Mr. Trueman, you will not permit me to thank you, but you cannot prevent my gratitude! (*Exit*)

TRUEMAN.   (*Looking after her*) If falsehood harbours there, I'll give up searching after truth!

(*Retires up the stage musingly, and commences examining the flowers*)

PRUDENCE.   What a nice old man he is, to be sure! I wish he would say something! (*Aside. Walks after him, turning when he turns—after a pause*) Don't mind me, Mr. Trueman!

TRUEMAN.   Mind you? Oh! no, don't be afraid (*Crosses*)—I wasn't minding you. Nobody seems to mind you much!

(*Continues walking and examining the flowers.—Prudence follows.*)

PRUDENCE.   Very pretty flowers, ain't they? Gertrude takes care of them.

TRUEMAN.   Gertrude? So I hear—(*Advancing*) I suppose you can tell me now who this Gertrude—

PRUDENCE.   Who she's in love with? I *knew* you were going to say that! I'll tell you all about it! Gertrude, she's in love with—Mr. Twinkle! and he's in love with her. And Seraphina, she's in love with Count Jolly—what-d'ye-call-it: but Count Jolly don't take to her at all—but Colonel Howard—he's the man—he's desperate about her!

TRUEMAN.   Why, you feminine newspaper! Howard in love with that quintessence of affectation! Howard—the only frank, straightforward fellow that I've met since—I'll tell him my mind on the subject! And Gertrude hunting for happiness in a rhyming dictionary! The girl's a greater fool than I took her for! (*Crosses right*)

PRUDENCE.   So she is—you see I know all about them!

TRUEMAN.   I see you do! You've a wonderful knowledge—wonderful—of *other people's concerns!* It may do here, but take my word for it, in the county of Catteraugus you'd get the name of a great *busy-body*. But perhaps you know that, too?

PRUDENCE.   Oh! I always know what's coming. I feel it beforehand all over me. I knew something was going to happen the day you came here—and what's more I can always tell a married man from a single—I felt right off that you were a bachelor!

TRUEMAN.   Felt right off I was a bachelor, did you? you were sure of it—sure?—quite sure? (*Prudence assents delightedly.*) Then you felt wrong!—a bachelor and a widower are not the same thing!

PRUDENCE.   Oh! but it all comes to the same thing—a widower's as good as a bachelor any day! And besides, I knew that you were a farmer *right off.*

TRUEMAN.   On the spot, eh? I suppose you saw cabbages and green peas growing out of my hat?

PRUDENCE.   No, I didn't—but I knew all about you. And I knew—(*Looking down and fidgeting with her apron*)—I knew you were for getting married soon! For last night I dreamt I saw your funeral going along the streets, and the mourners all dressed in white. And a funeral is a sure sign of a wedding, you know! (*Nudging him with her elbow*)

TRUEMAN.   (*Imitating her voice*) Well, I can't say that I *know* any such thing! you know! (*Nudging her back*)

PRUDENCE.   Oh! it does, and there's no getting over it! For my part, I like farmers—and I know all about setting hens and turkeys, and feeding chickens, and laying eggs, and all that sort of thing!

TRUEMAN.   May I be shot! if mistress newspaper is not putting in an advertisement for herself! This is your city mode of courting, I suppose, ha, ha, ha! (*Aside*)

PRUDENCE.   I've been west, a little; but I never was in the county of Catteraugus, myself.

TRUEMAN.   Oh, you were not? And you have taken a particular fancy to go there, eh?

PRUDENCE.   Perhaps I shouldn't object—

TRUEMAN.   Oh!—ah!—so I suppose. Now pay attention to what I am going to say, for it is a matter of great importance to yourself.

PRUDENCE.   Now it's coming—I know what he's going to say! (*Aside*)

TRUEMAN.   The next time you want to tie a man for life to your apron-strings, pick out one that don't come from the county of Catteraugus—for green-horns are scarce in those parts, and modest women plenty! (*Exit*)

PRUDENCE.   Now, who'd have thought he was going to say that! But I won't give him up yet—I won't give him up. (*Exit*)

ACT III
Scene 1

Mrs. Tiffany's Parlor. Enter Mrs. Tiffany, followed by Mr. Tiffany.

TIFFANY. Your extravagance will ruin me, Mrs. Tiffany!

MRS. TIFFANY. And your stinginess will ruin me, Mr. Tiffany! It is totally and *toot a fate* impossible to convince you of the necessity of *keeping up appearances.* There is a certain display which every woman of fashion is forced to make!

TIFFANY. And pray who made *you* a woman of fashion?

MRS. TIFFANY. What a vulgar question! All women of fashion, Mr. Tiffany—

TIFFANY. In this land are *self-constituted*, like you, Madam—and *fashion* is the cloak for more sins than charity ever covered! It was for *fashion's* sake that you insisted upon my purchasing this expensive house—it was for *fashion's* sake that you ran me in debt at every exorbitant upholsterer's and extravagant furniture warehouse in the city—it was for *fashion's* sake that you built that ruinous conservatory—hired more servants than they have persons to wait upon—and dressed your footman like a harlequin!

MRS. TIFFANY. Mr. Tiffany, you are thoroughly plebeian, and insufferably *American*, in your grovelling ideas! And, pray, what was the occasion of these very *mal-ap-pro-pos* remarks? Merely because I requested a paltry fifty dollars to purchase a new style of head-dress—a *bijou* of an article just introduced in France.

TIFFANY. Time was, Mrs. Tiffany, when you manufactured your own French head-dresses—took off their first gloss at the public balls, and then sold them to your shortest-sighted customers. And all you knew about France, or French either, was what you spelt out at the bottom of your fashion-plates—but now you have grown so fashionable, forsooth, that you have forgotten how to speak your mother tongue!

MRS. TIFFANY. Mr. Tiffany, Mr. Tiffany! Nothing is more positively vulgarian—more *unaristocratic* than any allusion to the past!

TIFFANY. Why, I thought, my dear, that *aristocrats* lived principally upon the past—and traded in the market of fashion with the bones of their ancestors for capital!

MRS. TIFFANY. Mr. Tiffany, such vulgar remarks are only suitable to the counting-house; in my drawing-room you should—

TIFFANY. Vary my sentiments with my locality, as you change your *manners* with your *dress!*

MRS. TIFFANY. Mr. Tiffany, I desire that you will purchase Count d'Orsay's "Science of Etiquette," and learn how to conduct yourself—

especially before you appear at the grand ball, which I shall give on Friday!

TIFFANY. Confound your balls, Madam; they make *footballs* of my money, while you dance away all that I am worth! A pretty time to give a ball when you know that I am on the very brink of bankruptcy!

MRS. TIFFANY. So much the greater reason that nobody should suspect your circumstances, or you would lose your credit at once. Just at this crisis a ball is absolutely *necessary* to save your reputation! There is Mrs. Adolphus Dashaway—she gave the most splendid fête of the season —and I hear on very good authority that her husband has not paid his baker's bill in three months. Then there was Mrs. Honeywood—

TIFFANY. Gave a ball the night before her husband shot himself—perhaps you wish to drive me to follow his example? (*Crosses right*)

MRS. TIFFANY. Good gracious! Mr. Tiffany, how you talk! I beg you won't mention anything of the kind. I consider black the most unbecoming color. I'm sure I've done all that I could to gratify you. There is that vulgar old torment, Trueman, who gives one the lie fifty times a day— haven't I been very civil to him?

TIFFANY. Civil to his *wealth*, Mrs. Tiffany! I told you that he was a rich old farmer—the early friend of my father—my own benefactor—and that I had reason to think he might assist me in my present embarrassments. Your civility was *bought*—and like most of your *own* purchases has yet to be *paid* for.

MRS. TIFFANY. And will be, no doubt! The condescension of a woman of fashion should command any price. Mr. Trueman is insupportably inde- corous—he has insulted Count Jolimaitre in the most outrageous manner. If the Count was not so deeply interested—so *abimé* with Seraphina, I am sure he would never honour us by his visits again!

TIFFANY. So much the better—he shall never marry my daughter!—I am resolved on that. Why, Madam, I am told there is in Paris a regular matri- monial stock company, who fit out indigent dandies for this market. How do I know but this fellow is one of its creatures, and that he has come here to increase its dividends by marrying a fortune?

MRS. TIFFANY. Nonsense, Mr. Tiffany. The Count, the most fashionable young man in all New York—the intimate friend of all the dukes and lords in Europe—not marry my daughter? Not permit Seraphina to be- come a Countess? Mr. Tiffany, you are out of your senses!

TIFFANY. That would not be very wonderful, considering how many years I have been united to you, my dear. Modern physicians pronounce lunacy infectious!

MRS. TIFFANY. Mr. Tiffany, he is a man of fashion—

TIFFANY. Fashion makes fools, but cannot *feed* them. By the bye, I have a request,—since you are bent upon ruining me by this ball, and there is no help for it,—I desire that you will send an invitation to my confidential clerk, Mr. Snobson.

MRS. TIFFANY. Mr. Snobson! Was there ever such an *you-nick* demand!

Mr. Snobson would cut a pretty figure amongst my fashionable friends! I shall do no such thing, Mr. Tiffany.

TIFFANY.   Then, Madam, the ball shall not take place. Have I not told you that I am in the power of this man? That there are circumstances which it is happy for you that you do not know—which you cannot comprehend,—but which render it essential that you should be civil to Mr. Snobson? Not you merely, but Seraphina also? He is a more appropriate match for her than your foreign favorite.

MRS. TIFFANY.   A match for Seraphina, indeed! (*Crosses*) Mr. Tiffany, you are determined to make a *fow pas*.

TIFFANY.   Mr. Snobson intends calling this morning. (*Crosses to left*)

MRS. TIFFANY.   But, Mr. Tiffany, this is not reception day—my drawing-rooms are in the most terrible disorder—

TIFFANY.   Mr. Snobson is not particular—he must be admitted.

(*Enter Zeke*)

ZEKE.   Mr. Snobson.

(*Enter Snobson; exit Zeke*)

SNOBSON.   How d'ye do, Marm? (*Crosses to center*) How are you? Mr. Tiffany, your most!—

MRS. TIFFANY.   (*Formally*) *Bung jure. Comment vow porte vow, Monsur Snobson?*

SNOBSON.   Oh, to be sure—very good of you—fine day.

MRS. TIFFANY.   (*Pointing to a chair with great dignity*) *Sassoyez vow, Monsur Snobson.*

SNOBSON.   I wonder what she's driving at? I ain't up to the fashionable lingo yet! (*Aside*) Eh? what? Speak a little louder, Marm?

MRS. TIFFANY.   What ignorance! (*Aside*)

TIFFANY.   I presume Mrs. Tiffany means that you are to take a seat.

SNOBSON.   Ex-actly—very obliging of her—so I will. (*Sits*) No ceremony amongst friends, you know—and likely to be nearer—you understand? O. K., all correct. How *is* Seraphina?

MRS. TIFFANY.   Miss Tiffany is not visible this morning. (*Retires up*)

SNOBSON.   Not visible? (*Jumping up, crosses*) I suppose that's the English for can't see her? Mr. Tiffany, sir—(*Walking up to him*) what am I to understand by this *de-fal-ca-tion*, sir? I expected your word to be as good as your bond—beg pardon, sir—I mean *better*—considerably *better*—no humbug about it, sir.

TIFFANY.   Have patience, Mr. Snobson. (*Rings bell*)

(*Enter Zeke*)

Zeke, desire my daughter to come here.

MRS. TIFFANY. (*Coming down centre*) A-dolph—I say, A-dolph—

(*Zeke straightens himself and assumes foppish airs, as he turns to Mrs. Tiffany.*)

TIFFANY. Zeke.

ZEKE. Don't know any such nigga, Boss.

TIFFANY. Do as I bid you instantly, or off with your livery and quit the house!

ZEKE. Wheugh! I'se all dismission. (*Exit*)

MRS. TIFFANY. A-dolph, A-dolph! (*Calling after him*)

SNOBSON. I brought the old boy to his bearings, didn't I though! Pull that string, and he is sure to work right. (*Aside*) Don't make any stranger of me, Marm—I'm quite at home. If you've got any odd jobs about the house to do, I sha'n't miss you. I'll amuse myself with Seraphina when she comes—we'll get along very cosily by ourselves.

MRS. TIFFANY. Permit me to inform you, Mr. Snobson, that a French mother never leaves her daughter alone with a young man—she knows your sex too well for that!

SNOBSON. Very *dis*-obliging of her—but as we're none French—

MRS. TIFFANY. You have yet to learn, Mr. Snobson, that the American *ee-light*—the aristocracy—the *how-ton*—as a matter of conscience, scrupulously follow the foreign fashions.

SNOBSON. Not when they are foreign to their interests, Marm—for instance—(*Enter Seraphina*) There you are at last, eh, Miss? How d'ye do? Ma said you weren't visible. Managed to get a peep at her, eh, Mr. Tiffany?

SERAPHINA. I heard you were here, Mr. Snobson, and came without even arranging my toilette; you will excuse my negligence?

SNOBSON. Of everything but *me*, Miss.

SERAPHINA. I shall never have to ask your pardon for *that*, Mr. Snobson.

MRS. TIFFANY. Seraphina—child—really—

(*As she is approaching Seraphina, Mr. Tiffany plants himself in front of his wife.*)

TIFFANY. Walk this way, Madam, if you please. To see that she fancies the surly fellow takes a weight from my heart. (*Aside*)

MRS. TIFFANY. Mr. Tiffany, it is highly improper and not at all *distingué* to leave a young girl—

(*Enter Zeke*)

ZEKE. Mr. Count Jolly-made-her!

MRS. TIFFANY. Good gracious! The Count—Oh, dear!—Seraphina, run and change your dress,—no, there's not time! A-dolph, admit him. (*Exit*

Zeke) Mr. Snobson, get out of the way, will you? Mr. Tiffany, what are you doing at home at this hour?

(*Enter Count Jolimaitre, ushered by Zeke*)

ZEKE. Dat's de genuine article ob a gemman. (*Aside. Exit.*)

MRS. TIFFANY. My dear Count, I am overjoyed at the very sight of you.

COUNT. Flattered myself you'd be glad to see me, Madam—knew it was not your *jour de reception*.

MRS. TIFFANY. But for you, Count, all days—

COUNT. I thought so. Ah, Miss Tiffany, on my honour, you're looking beautiful. (*Crosses to the right*)

SERAPHINA. Count, flattery from you—

SNOBSON. What? Eh? What's that you say?

SERAPHINA. Nothing but what etiquette requires. (*Aside to him*)

COUNT. (*Regarding Mr. Tiffany through his eye-glass*) Your worthy Papa, I believe? Sir, your most obedient.

(*Mr. Tiffany bows coldly; Count regards Snobson through his glass, shrugs his shoulders and turns away.*)

SNOBSON. (*To Mrs. Tiffany*) Introduce me, will you? I never knew a Count in all my life—what a strange-looking animal!

MRS. TIFFANY. Mr. Snobson, it is not the fashion to introduce in France!

SNOBSON. But, Marm, we're in America. (*Mrs. Tiffany crosses to Count.*) The woman thinks she's somewhere else than where she is—she wants to make an *alibi*? (*Aside*)

MRS. TIFFANY. I hope that we shall have the pleasure of seeing you on Friday evening, Count?

COUNT. Really, Madam, my invitations—my engagements—so numerous —I can hardly answer for myself: and you Americans take offence so easily—

MRS. TIFFANY. But, Count, everybody expects you at our ball—you are the principal attraction—

SERAPHINA. Count, you *must* come!

COUNT. Since you insist—aw—aw—there's no resisting you, Miss Tiffany.

MRS. TIFFANY. I am so thankful. How can I repay your condescension. (*Count and Seraphina converse.*) Mr. Snobson, will you walk this way?— I have *such* a cactus in full bloom—remarkable flower! Mr. Tiffany, pray come here—I have something particular to say.

TIFFANY. Then speak out, my dear—I thought it was highly improper just now to leave a girl with a young man? (*Aside to her*)

MRS. TIFFANY. Oh, but the Count,—that is different!

TIFFANY. I suppose you mean to say there's nothing of *the man* about him?

(*Enter Millinette with a scarf in her hand*)

MILLINETTE. A-dolph tell me he vas here. (*Aside*) Pardon, Madame, I bring dis scarf for Mademoiselle.

MRS. TIFFANY. Very well, Millinette; you know best what is proper for her to wear.

(*Mr. and Mrs. Tiffany and Snobson retire up stage; she engages the attention of both gentlemen.*)

(*Millinette crosses towards Seraphina, gives the Count a threatening look, and commences arranging the scarf over Seraphina's shoulders.*)

MILLINETTE. Mademoiselle, *permettez-moi. Perfide!* (*Aside to Count*) If Mademoiselle vil stand *tranquille* one *petit moment.* (*Turns Seraphina's back to the Count, and pretends to arrange the scarf*) I must speak vid you to-day, or I tell all—you find me at de foot of de stair ven you go. *Prends garde!* (*Aside to Count*)

SERAPHINA. What is that you say, Millinette?

MILLINETTE. Dis scarf make you so very beautiful, Mademoiselle—*Je vous salue, mes dames. (Curtsies. Exit)*

COUNT. Not a moment to lose! (*Aside*) Miss Tiffany, I have an unpleasant—a particularly unpleasant piece of intelligence—you see, I have just received a letter from my friend the—aw—the Earl of Airshire; the truth is, the Earl's daughter—beg you won't mention it—has distinguished me by a tender *penchant.*

SERAPHINA. I understand—and they wish you to return and marry the young lady; but surely you will not leave us, Count?

COUNT. If *you* bid me stay—I shouldn't have the conscience—I couldn't *afford* to tear myself away. I'm sure that's honest. (*Aside*)

SERAPHINA. Oh, Count!

COUNT. Say but one word—say that you shouldn't mind being made a Countess—and I'll break with the Earl to-morrow.

SERAPHINA. Count, this surprise—but don't think of leaving the country, Count—we could not pass the time without you! I—yes, yes, Count— I do consent!

COUNT. I thought she would! (*Aside, while he embraces her*) Enchanted, rapture, bliss, ecstasy, and all that sort of thing—words can't express it, but you understand. But it must be kept a secret—positively it *must!* If the rumour of our engagement were whispered abroad—the Earl's daughter— the delicacy of my situation, aw—you comprehend? It is even possible that our nuptials, my charming Miss Tiffany, *our nuptials* must take place in private!

SERAPHINA. Oh, that is quite impossible!

COUNT. It's the latest fashion abroad—the very latest! Ah, I knew that would determine you. Can I depend on your secrecy?

SERAPHINA. Oh, yes! Believe me.

SNOBSON. (*Coming forward in spite of Mrs. Tiffany's efforts to detain him*) Why, Seraphina, haven't you a word to throw to a dog?

TIFFANY.   I shouldn't think she had after wasting so many upon a puppy. (*Aside*)

(*Enter Zeke, wearing a three-cornered hat*)

ZEKE.   Missus, de bran new carriage am below.

MRS. TIFFANY.   Show it up,—I mean,—very well, A-dolph. (*Exit Zeke*) Count, my daughter and I are about to take an airing in our new *voyture,* —will you honour us with your company?

COUNT.   Madam, I—I have a most *pressing* engagement. A letter to write to the *Earl of Airshire*—who is at present residing in the *Isle of Skye.* I must bid you good-morning.

MRS. TIFFANY.   Good-morning, Count. (*Exit Count*)

SNOBSON.   I'm quite at leisure, (*Crosses to Mrs. Tiffany*) Marm. Books balanced—ledger closed—nothing to do all the afternoon—I'm for you.

MRS. TIFFANY.   (*Without noticing him*) Come, Seraphina, come!

(*As they are going, Snobson follows them.*)

SNOBSON.   But, Marm—I was saying, Marm, I am quite at leisure—not a thing to do; have I, Mr. Tiffany?

MRS. TIFFANY.   Seraphina, child—your red shawl—remember—Mr. Snob-son, *bon swear!* (*Exit, leading Seraphina*)

SNOBSON.   Swear! Mr. Tiffany, sir, am I to be fobbed off with a *bon swear?* D——n it, I will swear!

TIFFANY.   Have patience, Mr. Snobson, if you will accompany me to the counting-house—

SNOBSON.   Don't count too much on me, sir. I'll make up no more accounts until these are settled! I'll run down and jump into the carriage in spite of her *bon swear.* (*Exit*)

TIFFANY.   You'll jump into a hornet's nest, if you do! Mr. Snobson, Mr. Snobson! (*Exit after him*)

Scene 2

Housekeeper's Room. Enter Millinette.

MILLINETTE.   I have set dat *bête,* Adolph, to vatch for him. He say he would come back so soon as Madame's *voiture* drive from de door. If he not come—but he vill—he vill—he *bien étourdi,* but he have *bon coeur.*

(*Enter Count*)

COUNT.   Ah! Millinette, my dear, you see what a good-natured dog I am to fly at your bidding—

MILLINETTE.   Fly? Ah! *trompeur!* Vat for you fly from Paris? Vat for you leave me—and I love you so much? Ven you sick—you almost die—did I not stay by you—take care of you—and you have no else friend? Vat for you leave Paris?

COUNT.   Never allude to disagreeable subjects, *mon enfant!* I was forced by uncontrollable circumstances to fly to the land of liberty—

MILLINETTE.   Vat you do vid all de money I give you? The last sou I had—did I not give you?

COUNT.   I dare say you did, *ma petite*—wish you'd been better supplied! (*Aside*) Don't ask any questions here—can't explain now—the next time we meet—

MILLINETTE.   But, ah! ven shall ve meet—ven? You not deceive me, not any more.

COUNT.   Deceive you! I'd rather deceive myself—I wish I could! I'd persuade myself you were once more washing linen in the Seine! (*Aside*)

MILLINETTE.   I vil tell you ven we shall meet—On Friday night Madame give one grand ball—you come *sans doute*—den ven de supper is served—de Americans tink of noting else ven de supper come—den you steal out of de room, and you find me here—and you give me one grand *explanation!*

(*Enter Gertrude, unperceived*)

COUNT.   Friday night—while supper is serving —*parole d'honneur* I will be here—I will explain every thing—my sudden departure from Paris—my—demme, my countship—every thing! Now let me go—if any of the family should discover us—

GERTRUDE.   (*Who during the last speech has gradually advanced*) They might discover more than you think it advisable for them to know!

COUNT.   The devil!

MILLINETTE.   *Mon Dieu!* Mademoiselle Gertrude!

COUNT.   (*Recovering himself*) My dear Miss Gertrude, let me explain—aw—aw—nothing is more natural than the situation in which you find me—

GERTRUDE.   I am inclined to believe that, sir.

COUNT.   Now—'pon my honour, that's not fair. Here is Millinette will bear witness to what I am about to say—

GERTRUDE.   Oh, I have not the slightest doubt of that, sir.

COUNT.   You see, Millinette happened to be lady's-maid in the family of —of—the Duchess Chateau D'Espagne—and I chanced to be a particular friend of the Duchess—*very particular* I assure you! Of course I saw Millinette, and she, demme, she saw me! Didn't you, Millinette?

MILLINETTE.   Oh! *oui*—Mademoiselle, I knew him ver well.

COUNT.   Well, it is a remarkable fact that—being in correspondence with this very Duchess—at this very time—

GERTRUDE.   That is sufficient, sir—I am already so well acquainted with your extraordinary talents for improvisation, that I will not further tax your invention—

MILLINETTE. Ah! Mademoiselle Gertrude, do not betray us—have pity!

COUNT. (*Assuming an air of dignity*) Silence, Millinette! My word has been doubted—the word of a nobleman! I will inform my friend, Mrs. Tiffany, of this young person's audacity. (*Going*)

GERTRUDE. His own weapons alone can foil this villain! (*Aside*) Sir—sir— Count! (*At the last word the Count turns.*) Perhaps, sir, the least said about this matter the better!

COUNT. (*Delightedly*) The least said? We won't say anything at all. She's coming round—couldn't resist me! (*Aside*) Charming Gertrude—

MILLINETTE. *Quoi?* Vat that you say?

COUNT. My sweet, adorable Millinette, hold your tongue, will you? (*Aside to her*)

MILLINETTE. (*Aloud*) No, I vill not! If you do look so from out your eyes at her again, I vill tell all!

COUNT. Oh, I never could manage two women at once,—jealousy makes the dear creatures so spiteful. The only valour is in flight. (*Aside*) Miss Gertrude, I wish you good-morning. Millinette, *mon enfant, adieu.* (*Exit*)

MILLINETTE. But I have one word more to say. Stop! Stop! (*Exit after him*)

GERTRUDE. (*Musingly*) Friday night, while supper is serving, he is to meet Millinette here and explain—what? This man is an impostor! His insulting me—his familiarity with Millinette—his whole conduct—prove it. If I tell Mrs. Tiffany this, she will disbelieve me, and one word may place this so-called Count on his guard. To convince Seraphina would be equally difficult, and her rashness and infatuation may render her miserable for life. No—she shall be saved! I must devise some plan for opening their eyes. Truly, if I *cannot* invent one, I shall be the first woman who was ever at a loss for a stratagem—especially to punish a villain or to shield a friend. (*Exit*)

ACT IV

Scene 1

Ball-room splendidly illuminated. A curtain hung at the further end. Mr. and Mrs. Tiffany, Seraphina, Gertrude, Fogg, Twinkle, Count, Snobson, Colonel Howard, a number of guests—some seated, some standing. As the curtain rises, a cotillion is danced; Gertrude dancing with Howard, Seraphina with Count.

COUNT. (*Advancing with Seraphina to the front of the stage*) To-morrow then—to-morrow—I may salute you as my bride—demme, my Countess!

(Enter Zeke with refreshments)

SERAPHINA.   Yes, to-morrow.

(As the Count is about to reply, Snobson thrusts himself in front of Seraphina.)

SNOBSON.   You said you'd dance with me, Miss—now take my fin, and we'll walk about and see what's going on.

(Count raises his eye-glass, regards Snobson, and leads Seraphina away; Snobson follows, endeavouring to attract her attention, but encounters Zeke, bearing a waiter of refreshments; stops, helps himself, and puts some in his pockets.)

Here's the treat! get my to-morrow's luncheon out of Tiff.

(Enter Trueman, yawning and rubbing his eyes)

TRUEMAN.   What a nap I've had, to be sure! *(Looks at his watch)* Eleven o'clock, as I'm alive! Just the time when country folks are comfortably turned in, and here your grand *turnout* has hardly begun yet! *(To Tiffany, who approaches)*
GERTRUDE.   *(Advancing)* I was just coming to look for you, Mr. Trueman. I began to fancy that you were paying a visit to dream-land.
TRUEMAN.   So I was child—so I was—and I saw a face—like yours—but brighter!—even brighter! *(To Tiffany)* There's a smile for you, man! It makes one feel that the world has something worth living for in it yet! Do you remember a smile like that, Antony? Ah! I see you don't—but I do—I do! *(Much moved)*
HOWARD.   *(Advancing)* Good evening, Mr. Trueman. *(Offers his hand)*
TRUEMAN.   That's right, man; give me your whole hand! When a man offers me the tips of his fingers, I know at once there's nothing in him worth seeking beyond his fingers' ends.

(Trueman and Howard, Gertrude and Tiffany converse.)

MRS. TIFFANY.   *(Advancing)* I'm in such a fidget lest that vulgar old fellow should disgrace us by some of his plebeian remarks! What it is to give a ball, when one is forced to invite vulgar people!

(Mrs. Tiffany advances towards Trueman; Seraphina stands conversing flippantly with the gentlemen who surround her; amongst them is Twinkle, who, having taken a magazine from his pocket, is reading to her, much to the undisguised annoyance of Snobson.)

Dear me, Mr. Trueman, you are very late—quite in the fashion, I declare!
TRUEMAN.   Fashion! And pray what is *fashion*, Madam? An agreement
between certain persons to live without using their souls! to substitute
etiquette for virtue—decorum for purity—manners for morals! to affect a
shame for the works of their Creator! and expend all their rapture upon
the works of their tailors and dressmakers!
MRS. TIFFANY.   You have the most *ow-tray* ideas, Mr. Trueman—quite
rustic, and deplorably *American!* But pray walk this way. (*Mrs. Tiffany
and Trueman go up stage.*)
COUNT.   (*Advancing to Gertrude, who stands centre, Howard a short
distance behind her*) Miss Gertrude—no opportunity of speaking to you
before—in demand, you know!
GERTRUDE.   I have no choice, I must be civil to him. (*Aside*) What were
you remarking, sir?
COUNT.   Miss Gertrude—charming Ger—aw—aw—I never found it so difficult to speak to a woman before. (*Aside*)
GERTRUDE.   Yes, a very charming ball—many beautiful faces here.
COUNT.   Only one!—aw—aw—one—the fact is—(*Talks to her in dumb
show*)
HOWARD.   What could old Trueman have meant by saying she fancied
that puppy of a Count—that paste-jewel thrust upon the little finger of
society.
COUNT.   Miss Gertrude—aw—'pon my honour— you don't understand—
really—aw—aw—will you dance the polka with me?

(*Gertrude bows and gives him her hand; he leads her to the set form-
ing; Howard remains looking after them.*)

HOWARD.   Going to dance with him, too! A few days ago she would
hardly bow to him civilly—could old Trueman have had reasons for what
he said? (*Retires*)

(*Dance, the polka; Seraphina, after having distributed her bouquet,
vinaigrette and fan amongst the gentlemen, dances with Snobson.*)

PRUDENCE.   (*Peeping in, as dance concludes*) I don't like dancing on Friday; something strange is always sure to happen! I'll be on the look out.

(*Remains peeping and concealing herself when any of the company
approach*)

GERTRUDE.   (*Advancing hastily to center*) They are preparing the supper
—now, if I can only dispose of Millinette while I unmask this insolent
pretender! (*Exit*)
PRUDENCE.   (*Peeping*) What's that she said? It's coming!

(*Reenter Gertrude, bearing a small basket filled with bouquets; approaches Mrs. Tiffany; they walk to the front of the stage.*)

GERTRUDE.   Excuse me, Madam—I believe this is just the hour at which you ordered supper?

MRS. TIFFANY.   Well, what's that to you! So, you've been dancing with the Count—how dare you dance with a nobleman—*you?*

GERTRUDE.   I will answer that question half an hour hence. At present I have something to propose, which I think will gratify you and please your guests. I have heard that at the most elegant balls in Paris, it is customary—

MRS. TIFFANY.   What? what?

GERTRUDE.   To station a servant at the door with a basket of flowers. A bouquet is then presented to every lady as she passes in—I prepared this basket a short time ago. As the company walk in to supper, might not the flowers be distributed to advantage?

MRS. TIFFANY.   How *distingué!* You are a good creature, Gertrude—there, run and hand the *bokettes* to them yourself! You shall have the whole credit of the thing.

GERTRUDE.   Caught in my own net! (*Aside*) But, Madam, I know so little of fashions—Millinette, being French, herself will do it with so much more grace. I am sure Millinette—

MRS. TIFFANY.   So am I. She will do it a thousand times better than you—there, go call her.

GERTRUDE.   (*Giving basket*) But, Madam, pray order Millinette not to leave her station till supper is ended—as the company pass out of the supper room she may find that some of the ladies have been overlooked.

MRS. TIFFANY.   That is true—very thoughtful of you, Gertrude. (*Exit Gertrude*) What a *recherché* idea!

(*Enter Millinette*)

Here, Millinette, take this basket. Place yourself there, (*Center*) and distribute these *bokettes* as the company pass in to supper; but remember not to stir from the spot until supper is over. It is a French fashion, you know, Millinette. I am so delighted to be the first to introduce it—it will be all the rage in the *bowmonde!*

MILLINETTE.   *Mon Dieu!* dis vill ruin all! (*Aside*) Madame, madame, let me tell you, Madame, dat in France, in Paris, it is de custom to present *les* bouquets ven everybody first come—long before de supper. Dis would be *outré! barbare!* not at all *la mode!* Ven dey do come in, dat is de fashion in Paris!

MRS. TIFFANY.   Dear me! Millinette, what is the difference? besides, I'd have you to know that Americans always improve upon French fashions! here, take the basket, and let me see that you do it in the most *you-nick* and genteel manner.

(*Millinette poutingly takes the basket and retires up stage. A march. Curtain hung at the further end of the room is drawn back, and discloses a room, in the center of which stands a supper-table, beautifully decorated and illuminated; the company promenade two by two into the supper room; Millinette presents bouquets as they pass; Count leads Mrs. Tiffany.*)

TRUEMAN. (*Encountering Fogg, who is hurrying alone to the supper room*) Mr. Fogg, never mind the supper, man! Ha, ha, ha! Of course you are indifferent to suppers!

FOGG. Indifferent! suppers—oh, ah—no, sir—suppers? no—no—I'm not indifferent to suppers. (*Hurries away towards table*)

TRUEMAN. Ha, ha, ha! Here's a new discovery I've made in the fashionable world! Fashion don't permit the critters to have *heads* or *hearts*, but it allows them stomachs! (*To Tiffany, who advances*) So, it's not fashionable to *feel*, but it's fashionable to *feed*, eh, Antony? Ha, ha, ha!

(*Trueman and Tiffany retire towards supper room.*)

(*Enter Gertrude, followed by Zeke*)

GERTRUDE. Zeke, go to the supper room instantly,—whisper to Count Jolimaitre that all is ready, and that he must keep his appointment without delay,—then watch him, and as he passes out of the room, place yourself in front of Millinette in such a manner, that the Count cannot see her nor she him. Be sure that they do not see each other—everything depends upon that. (*Crosses to right*)

ZEKE. Missy, consider dat business brought to a scientific conclusion. (*Exit into supper room. Exit Gertrude.*)

PRUDENCE. (*Who has been listening*) What can she want of the Count? I always suspected that Gertrude, because she is so merry and busy! Mr. Trueman thinks so much of her, too,—I'll tell him this! There's something wrong—but it all comes of giving a ball on a Friday! How astonished the dear old man will be when he finds out how much I know! (*Advances timidly towards the supper room*)

Scene 2

Housekeeper's room; dark stage; table, two chairs. Enter Gertrude, with a lighted candle in her hand.

GERTRUDE. So far the scheme prospers! and yet this imprudence—if I fail? Fail! to lack courage in a difficulty, or ingenuity in a dilemma, are not woman's failings!

(*Enter Zeke, with a napkin over his arm, and a bottle of champagne in his hand*)

Well, Zeke—Adolph!
ZEKE.   Dat's right, Missy; I feels just now as if dat was my legitimate title; dis here's de stuff to make a nigger feel like a gemman!
GERTRUDE.   But is he coming?
ZEKE.   He's coming! (*Sound of a champagne cork heard*) Do you hear dat, Missy? Don't it put you all in a froth, and make you feel as light as a cork? Dere's nothing like the *union brand*, to wake up de harmonies ob de heart. (*Drinks from bottle*)
GERTRUDE.   Remember to keep watch upon the outside—do not stir from the spot; when I call you, come in quickly with a light—now, will you be gone!
ZEKE.   I'm off, Missy, like a champagne cork wid de strings cut. (*Exit*)
GERTRUDE.   I think I hear the Count's step. (*Crosses left; stage dark; she blows out candle.*)Now, if I can but disguise my voice, and make the best of my French.

(*Enter Count*)

COUNT.   Millinette, where are you? How am I to see you in the dark?
GERTRUDE.   (*Imitating Millinette's voice in a whisper*) Hush! *parle bas.*
COUNT.   Come here and give me a kiss.
GERTRUDE.   Non—non—(*Retreating, alarmed; Count follows.*) make haste, I must know all.
COUNT.   You did not use to be so deuced particular.
ZEKE.   (*Without*) No admission, gemman! Box office closed, tickets stopped!
TRUEMAN.   (*Without*) Out of my way; do you want me to try if your head is as hard as my stick?
GERTRUDE.   What shall I do? Ruined, ruined!

(*She stands with her hands clasped in speechless despair.*)

COUNT.   Halloa! they are coming here, Millinette! Millinette, why don't you speak? Where can I hide myself? (*Running about stage, feeling for a door*) Where are all your closets? If I could only get out—or get in somewhere; may I be smothered in a clothes basket, if you ever catch me in such a scrape again! (*His hand accidentally touches the knob of a door opening into a closet.*) Fortune's favorite yet! I'm safe!

(*Gets into closet, and closes door. Enter Prudence, Trueman, Mrs. Tiffany, and Colonel Howard, followed by Zeke, bearing a light.*)

PRUDENCE.   Here they are, the Count and Gertrude! I told you so! (*Stops in surprise on seeing only Gertrude*)

TRUEMAN.   And you see what a lie you told!

MRS. TIFFANY.   Prudence, how dare you create this disturbance in my house? To suspect the Count, too—a nobleman!

HOWARD.   My sweet Gertrude, this foolish old woman would—

PRUDENCE.   Oh! you needn't talk—I heard her make the appointment—I know he's here—or he's been here. I wonder if she hasn't hid him away! (*Runs peeping about the room*)

TRUEMAN.   (*Following her angrily*) You're what I call a confounded—troublesome—meddling—old—prying—(*As he says the last word, Prudence opens closet where the Count is concealed.*) Thunder and lightning!

PRUDENCE.   I told you so!

(*They all stand aghast; Mrs. Tiffany, with her hands lifted in surprise and anger; Trueman, clutching his stick; Howard, looking with an expression of bewildered horror from the Count to Gertrude.*)

MRS. TIFFANY.   (*Shaking her fist at Gertrude*) You depraved little minx! this is the meaning of your dancing with the Count!

COUNT.   (*Stepping from the closet and advancing*) I don't know what to make of it! Millinette not here! Miss Gertrude—Oh! I see—a disguise—the girl's desperate about me—the way with them all. (*Aside*)

TRUEMAN.   I'm choking—I can't speak—Gertrude—no—no—it is some horrid mistake! (*Partly aside, changes his tone suddenly*) The villain! I'll hunt the truth out of him, if there's any in—(*Approaches Count threateningly*) Do you see this stick? You made its first acquaintance a few days ago; it is time you were better known to each other.

(*As Trueman attempts to seize him, Count escapes and shields himself behind Mrs. Tiffany, Trueman following.*)

COUNT.   You ruffian! would you strike a woman?—Madam—my dear Madam—keep off that barbarous old man, and I will explain! Madam, with—aw—your natural *bon gout*—aw—your fashionable refinement—aw—your—aw—your knowledge of *foreign customs*—

MRS. TIFFANY.   Oh! Count, I hope it ain't a *foreign custom* for the nobility to shut themselves up in the dark with young women? We think such things *dreadful* in *America*.

COUNT.   Demme—aw—hear what I have to say, Madam—I'll satisfy all sides—I am perfectly innocent in this affair—'pon my honour I am! That young lady shall inform you that I am so herself!—can't help it, sorry for her. Old matter-of-fact won't be convinced any other way,—that club of his is so particularly unpleasant! (*Aside*) Madam, I was summoned here *malgré moi*, and not knowing whom I was to meet—Miss Gertrude, favor this company by saying whether or not you directed—that—aw—aw—that coloured individual to conduct me here?

GERTRUDE.   Sir, you well know—

COUNT. A simple yes or no will suffice.

MRS. TIFFANY. Answer the Count's question instantly, Miss.

GERTRUDE. I did—but—

COUNT. You hear, Madam—

TRUEMAN. I won't believe it—I can't! Here, you nigger, stop rolling up your eyes, and let us know whether she told you to bring that critter here?

ZEKE. I'se refuse to gib ebidence; dat's de device ob de skillfullest counsels ob de day! Can't answer, Boss—neber git a word out ob dis child—Yah! yah! (*Exit*)

GERTRUDE. Mrs. Tiffany,—Mr. Trueman, if you will but have patience—

TRUEMAN. Patience! Oh, Gertrude, you've taken from an old man something better and dearer than his patience—the one bright hope of nineteen years of self-denial—of nineteen years of—

(*Throws himself upon a chair, his head leaning on table*)

MRS. TIFFANY. Get out of my house, you *ow*dacious—you ruined—you *abimé* young woman! You will corrupt all my family. Good gracious! don't touch me,—don't come near me. Never let me see your face after to-morrow. Pack. (*Goes up stage*)

HOWARD. Gertrude, I have striven to find some excuse for you—to doubt—to disbelieve—but this is beyond all endurance! (*Exit*)

(*Enter Millinette in haste*)

MILLINETTE. I could not come before—(*Stops in surprise at seeing the persons assembled*) Mon Dieu! Vat does dis mean?

COUNT. Hold your tongue, fool! You will ruin everything. I will explain to-morrow. (*Aside to her*) Mrs. Tiffany—Madam—my dear Madam, let me conduct you back to the ballroom. (*She takes his arm.*) You see I am quite innocent in this matter; a man of my standing, you know,—aw, aw—you comprehend the whole affair.

(*Exit Count leading Mrs. Tiffany*)

MILLINETTE. I vill say to him von vord, I vill! (*Exit*)

GERTRUDE. Mr. Trueman, I beseech you—I insist upon being heard,—I claim it as a right!

TRUEMAN. Right? How dare you have the face, girl, to talk of rights? (*Comes down stage*) You had more rights than you thought for, but you have forfeited them all! All right to love, respect, protection, and to not a little else that you don't dream of. Go, go! I'll start for Catteraugus to-morrow,—I've seen enough of what fashion can do! (*Exit*)

PRUDENCE. (*Wiping her eyes*) Dear old man, how he takes on! I'll go and console him! (*Exit*)

GERTRUDE.   This is too much! How heavy a penalty has my imprudence cost me!—his esteem, and that of one dearer—my home—my—(*Burst of lively music from ball-room*) They are dancing, and I—I should be weeping, if pride had not sealed up my tears.

(*She sinks into a chair. Band plays the polka behind till curtain falls.*)

ACT V

Mrs. Tiffany's Drawing-room—same scene as Act I. Gertrude seated at a table, with her head leaning on her hand; in the other hand she holds a pen. A sheet of paper and an inkstand before her.

GERTRUDE.   How shall I write to them? What shall I say? Prevaricate I cannot—(*Rises and comes forward*) and yet if I write the truth—simple souls! how can they comprehend the motives for my conduct? Nay—the truly pure see no imaginary evil in others! It is only vice, that reflecting its own image, suspects even the innocent. I have no time to lose—I must prepare them for my return. (*Resumes her seat and writes*) What a true pleasure there is in daring to be frank! (*After writing a few lines more, pauses*) Not so frank, either,—there is one name that I cannot mention. Ah! that he should suspect—should despise me. (*Writes*)

(*Enter Trueman*)

TRUEMAN.   There she is! If this girl's soul had only been as fair as her face,—yet she dared to speak the truth,—I'll not forget that! A woman who refuses to tell a lie has one spark of heaven in her still. (*Approaches her*) Gertrude, (*Gertrude starts and looks up.*) what are you writing there? Plotting more mischief, eh, girl?
GERTRUDE.   I was writing a few lines to some friends in Geneva.
TRUEMAN.   The Wilsons, eh?
GERTRUDE.   (*Surprised, rising*) Are you acquainted with them, sir?
TRUEMAN.   I shouldn't wonder if I was. I suppose you have taken good care not to mention the dark room—that foreign puppy in the closet— the pleasant surprise—and all that sort of thing, eh?
GERTRUDE.   I have no reason for concealment, sir! for I have done nothing of which I am ashamed!
TRUEMAN.   Then I can't say much for your modesty.
GERTRUDE.   I should not wish you to say more than I deserve.
TRUEMAN.   There's a bold minx! (*Aside*)
GERTRUDE.   Since my affairs seem to have excited your interest—I will not say *curiosity*,—perhaps you even feel a desire to inspect my correspondence? There, (*Handing the letter*) I pride myself upon my good nature,—you may like to take advantage of it?

TRUEMAN.　With what an air she carries it off! (*Aside*) Take advantage of it? So I will. (*Reads*) What's this? "French chambermaid—Count—impostor—infatuation—Seraphina—Millinette—disguised　myself—expose him." Thunder and lightning! I see it all! Come and kiss me, girl! (*Gertrude evinces surprise.*) No, no—I forgot—it won't do to come to that yet! She's a rare girl! I'm out of my senses with joy! I don't know what to do with myself! Tol, de rol, de rol, de ra! (*Capers and sings*)

GERTRUDE.　What a remarkable old man! (*Aside*) Then you do me justice, Mr. Trueman?

TRUEMAN.　I say I don't! Justice? You're above all dependence upon justice! Hurrah! I've found one true woman at last! *True?* (*Pauses thoughtfully*) Humph! I didn't think of that flaw! Plotting and manoeuvering—not much truth in that? An honest girl should be above stratagems!

GERTRUDE.　But my *motive*, sir, was good.

TRUEMAN.　That's not enough—your *actions* must be *good* as well as your *motives!* Why could you not tell the silly girl that the man was an impostor?

GERTRUDE.　I did inform her of my suspicions—she ridiculed them; the plan I chose was an imprudent one, but I could not devise—

TRUEMAN.　I hate devising! Give me a woman with the *firmness* to be *frank!* But no matter—I had no right to look for an angel out of Paradise; and I am as happy—as happy as a lord! that is, ten times happier than any lord ever was! Tol, de rol, de rol! Oh! you—you—I'll thrash every fellow that says a word against you!

GERTRUDE.　You will have plenty of employment then, sir, for I do not know of one just now who would speak in my favour!

TRUEMAN.　Not *one*, eh? Why, where's your dear Mr. Twinkle? I know all about it—can't say that I admire your choice of a husband! But there's no accounting for a girl's taste.

GERTRUDE.　Mr. Twinkle! Indeed you are quite mistaken!

TRUEMAN.　No—really? Then you're not taken with him, eh?

GERTRUDE.　Not even with his rhymes.

TRUEMAN.　Hang that old mother meddle-much! What a fool she has made of me. And so you're quite free, and I may choose a husband for you myself? Heart-whole, eh?

GERTRUDE.　I—I trust there is nothing *unsound* about my heart.

TRUEMAN.　There it is again. Don't prevaricate, girl! I tell you an *evasion* is a *lie in contemplation*, and I hate lying! Out with the truth! Is your heart *free* or not?

GERTRUDE.　Nay, sir, since you *demand* an answer, permit *me* to demand by what right you ask the question?

(*Enter Howard*)

Colonel Howard here!

TRUEMAN.　I'm out again! What's the Colonel to her? (*Retires up stage*)

HOWARD.　(*Crosses to her*) I have come, Gertrude, to bid you farewell.

To-morrow I resign my commission and leave this city, perhaps for ever. You, Gertrude, it is you who have exiled me! After last evening—

TRUEMAN. (*Coming forward to Howard*) What the plague have you got to say about last evening?

HOWARD. Mr. Trueman!

TRUEMAN. What have you got to say about last evening? and what have you to say to that little girl at all? It's Tiffany's precious daughter you're in love with.

HOWARD. Miss Tiffany? Never! I never had the slightest pretension—

TRUEMAN. That lying old woman! But I'm glad of it! Oh! Ah! Um! (*Looking significantly at Gertrude and then at Howard*) I see how it is. So you don't choose to marry Seraphina, eh? Well, now, whom do you choose to marry? (*Glancing at Gertrude*)

HOWARD. I shall not marry at all!

TRUEMAN. You won't? (*Looking at them both again*) Why, you don't mean to say that you don't like—(*Points with his thumb to Gertrude*)

GERTRUDE. Mr. Trueman, I may have been wrong to boast of my good nature, but do not presume too far upon it.

HOWARD. You like frankness, Mr. Trueman, therefore I will speak plainly. I have long cherished a dream from which I was last night rudely awakened.

TRUEMAN. And that's what you call speaking plainly? Well, I differ with you! But I can guess what you mean. Last night you suspected Gertrude there of—(*Angrily*) of what no man shall ever suspect her again while I'm above ground! You did her injustice,—it was a mistake! There, now that matter's settled. Go, and ask her to forgive you,—she's woman enough to do it! Go, go!

HOWARD. Mr. Trueman, you have forgotten to whom you dictate.

TRUEMAN. Then you won't do it? you won't ask her pardon?

HOWARD. Most undoubtedly I will not—not at any man's bidding. I must first know—

TRUEMAN. You won't do it? Then, if I don't give you a lesson in politeness—

HOWARD. It will be because you find me your *tutor* in the same science. I am not a man to brook an insult, Mr. Trueman! but we'll not quarrel in the presence of the lady. (*Crosses*)

TRUEMAN. Won't we? I don't know that—

GERTRUDE. Pray, Mr. Trueman—Colonel Howard, (*Crosses to center*) pray desist, Mr. Trueman, for my sake! (*Taking hold of his arm to hold him back*) Colonel Howard, if you will read this letter it will explain everything. (*Hands letter to Howard, who reads*)

TRUEMAN. He don't deserve an explanation! Didn't I tell him that it was a mistake? Refuse to beg your pardon! I'll teach him, I'll teach him!

HOWARD. (*After reading*) Gertrude, how I have wronged you!

TRUEMAN. Oh! you'll beg her pardon now? (*Between them*)

HOWARD. Hers, sir, and yours! Gertrude, I fear—

TRUEMAN. You needn't,—she'll forgive you. You don't know these women as well as I do,—they're always ready to pardon; it's their nature, and they can't help it. Come along, I left Antony and his wife in the dining-room; we'll go and find them. I've a story of my own to tell! As for you, Colonel, you may follow. Come along, come along! (*Leads out Gertrude, followed by Howard*)

(*Enter Mr. and Mrs. Tiffany. Mr. Tiffany with a bundle of bills in his hand.*)

MRS. TIFFANY. I beg you won't mention the subject again, Mr. Tiffany. Nothing is more plebeian than a discussion upon economy—nothing more *ungenteel* than looking over and fretting over one's bills!

TIFFANY. Then I suppose, my dear, it is quite as ungenteel to *pay* one's bills?

MRS. TIFFANY. Certainly! I hear the *ee-light* never condescend to do anything of the kind. The honour of their invaluable patronage is sufficient for the persons they employ!

TIFFANY. *Patronage* then is a newly invented food upon which the working-classes fatten? What convenient appetites poor people must have! Now listen to what I am going to say. As soon as my daughter marries Mr. Snobson—

(*Enter Prudence, a three-cornered note in her hand*)

PRUDENCE. Oh, dear! oh, dear! what shall we do! Such a misfortune! Such a disaster! Oh, dear! oh, dear!

MRS. TIFFANY. Prudence, you are the most tiresome creature! What *is* the matter?

PRUDENCE. (*Pacing up and down the stage*) Such a disgrace to the whole family! But I always expected it. Oh, dear! oh, dear!

MRS. TIFFANY. (*Following her up and down the stage*) What are you talking about, Prudence? Will you tell me what has happened?

PRUDENCE. (*Still pacing, Mrs. Tiffany following*) Oh! I can't, I can't! You'll feel so dreadfully! How could she do such a thing! But I expected nothing else! I never did, I never did!

MRS. TIFFANY. (*Still following*) Good gracious! what do you mean, Prudence? Tell me, will you tell me? I shall get into such a passion! What *is* the matter?

PRUDENCE. (*Still pacing*) Oh, Betsy, Betsy! That your daughter should have come to that! Dear me, dear me!

TIFFANY. Seraphina? Did you say Seraphina? What has happened to her? what has she done?

(*Following Prudence up and down the stage on the opposite side from Mrs. Tiffany*)

MRS. TIFFANY. (*Still following*) What *has* she done? What *has* she done?

PRUDENCE. Oh! Something dreadful—dreadful—shocking!

TIFFANY. (*Still following*) Speak quickly and plainly—you torture me by this delay,—Prudence, be calm, and speak! What is it?

PRUDENCE. (*Stopping*) Zeke just told me—he carried her travelling trunk himself—she gave him a whole dollar! Oh, my!

TIFFANY. Her trunk? where? where?

PRUDENCE. Round the corner!

MRS. TIFFANY. What did she want with her trunk? You are the most vexatious creature, Prudence! There is no bearing your ridiculous conduct!

PRUDENCE. Oh, you will have worse to bear—worse! Seraphina's gone!

TIFFANY. Gone! where?

PRUDENCE. Off!—eloped—eloped with the Count! Dear me, dear me! I always told you she would!

TIFFANY. Then I am ruined! (*Stands with his face buried in his hands*)

MRS. TIFFANY. Oh, what a ridiculous girl! And she might have had such a splendid wedding! What could have possessed her?

TIFFANY. The devil himself possessed her, for she has ruined me past all redemption! Gone, Prudence, did you say gone? Are you *sure* they are gone?

PRUDENCE. Didn't I tell you so! Just look at this note—one might know by the very fold of it—

TIFFANY. (*Snatching the note*) Let me see it! (*Opens the note and reads*) "My dear Ma,—When you receive this I shall be a *countess*! Isn't it a sweet title? The Count and I were forced to be married privately, for reasons which I will explain in my next. You must pacify Pa, and put him in a good humour before I come back, though now I'm to be a countess I suppose I shouldn't care!" Undutiful huzzy! "We are going to make a little excursion and will be back in a week. Your dutiful daughter—Seraphina." A man's curse is sure to spring up at his own hearth,—here is mine! The sole curb upon that villain gone, I am wholly in his power! Oh! the first downward step from honour—he who takes it cannot pause in his mad descent and is sure to be hurried on to ruin!

MRS. TIFFANY. Why, Mr. Tiffany, how you do take on! And I dare say to elope was the most fashionable way after all!

(*Enter Trueman, leading Gertrude, and followed by Howard*)

TRUEMAN. Where are all the folks? Here, Antony, you are the man I want. We've been hunting for you all over the house. Why—what's the matter? There's a face for a thriving city merchant! Ah! Antony, you never wore such a hang-dog look as that when you trotted about the country with your pack upon your back! Your shoulders are no broader now—but they've a heavier load to carry—that's plain!

MRS. TIFFANY.   Mr. Trueman, such allusions are highly improper! What would my daughter, *the Countess*, say!

GERTRUDE.   The Countess? Oh! Madam!

MRS. TIFFANY.   Yes, the Countess! My daughter Seraphina, the Countess *dee* Jolimaitre! What have you to say to that? No wonder you are surprised after your *recherché, abimé* conduct! I have told you already, Miss Gertrude, that you were not a proper person to enjoy the inestimable advantages of my patronage. You are dismissed—do you understand? Discharged!

TRUEMAN.   Have you done? Very well, it's my turn now. Antony, perhaps what I have to say don't concern you as much as some others—but I want you to listen to me. You remember, Antony, (*His tone becomes serious.*) a blue-eyed, smiling girl—

TIFFANY.   Your daughter, sir? I remember her well.

TRUEMAN.   None ever saw her to forget her! Give me your hand, man. There—that will do! Now let me go on. I never coveted wealth—yet twenty years ago I found myself the richest farmer in Catteraugus. This cursed money made my girl an object of speculation. Every idle fellow that wanted to feather his nest was sure to come courting Ruth. There was one—my heart misgave me the instant I laid eyes upon him—for he was a city chap, and not over-fond of the truth. But Ruth—ah! she was too pure herself to look for guile! His fine words and his fair looks—the old story—she was taken with him—I said, "no"—but the girl liked her own way better than her old father's—girls always do! and one morning—the rascal robbed me—not of my money,—he would have been welcome to that—but of the only treasure I cherished—my daughter!

TIFFANY.   But you forgave her!

TRUEMAN.   I did! I knew she would never forgive herself—that was punishment enough! The scoundrel thought he was marrying my gold with my daughter—he was mistaken! I took care that they should never want; but that was all. She loved him—what will not woman love? The villain broke her heart—mine was tougher, or it wouldn't have stood what it did. A year after they were married, he forsook her! She came back to her old home—her old father! It couldn't last long—she pined—and pined—and—then—she died! Don't think me an old fool—though I am one—for grieving won't bring her back. (*Bursts into tears*)

TIFFANY.   It was a heavy loss.

TRUEMAN.   So heavy that I should not have cared how soon I followed her, but for the child she left! As I pressed that child in my arms, I swore that my unlucky wealth should never curse it, as it had cursed its mother! It was all I had to love—but I sent it away—and the neighbors thought it was dead. The girl was brought up tenderly but humbly by my wife's relatives in Geneva. I had her taught true independence—she had hands—capacities—and should use them! Money should never buy her a husband! For I resolved not to claim her until she had made her choice, and found the man who was willing to take her for herself alone. She turned out a rare girl! and it's time her old grandfather claimed her. Here he is to do it! And there stands Ruth's child! Old Adam's heiress! Gertrude, Gertrude!—my child! (*Gertrude rushes into his arms.*)

PRUDENCE. (*After a pause*) Do tell; I want to know! But I knew it! I always said Gertrude would turn out somebody, after all!

MRS. TIFFANY. Dear me! Gertrude an heiress! My dear Gertrude, I always thought you a very charming girl—quite YOU-NICK—an heiress! I must give her a ball! I'll introduce her into society myself—of course an heiress must make a sensation! (*Aside*)

HOWARD. I am too bewildered even to wish her joy. Ah! there will be plenty to do that now—but the gulf between us is wider than ever. (*Aside*)

TRUEMAN. Step forward, young man, and let us know what you are muttering about. I said I would never claim her until she had found the man who loved her for herself. I *have* claimed her—yet I never break my word—I think I *have* found that man! and here he is. (*Strikes Howard on the shoulder*) Gertrude's yours! There—never say a word, man—don't bore me with your thanks—you can cancel all obligations by making that child happy! There—take her!—Well, girl, and what do you say?

GERTRUDE. That I rejoice too much at having found a parent for my first act to be one of disobedience! (*Gives her hand to Howard*)

TRUEMAN. How very dutiful! and how disinterested!

(*Tiffany retires—and paces the stage, exhibiting great agitation.*)

PRUDENCE. (*To Trueman*) All the *single folks* are getting married!

TRUEMAN. No they are not. You and I are single folks, and we're not likely to get married.

MRS. TIFFANY. My dear Mr. Trueman—my sweet Gertrude, when my daughter, the Countess, returns, she will be delighted to hear of this *deenooment!* I assure you that the Countess will be quite charmed!

GERTRUDE. The Countess? Pray, Madam, where *is* Seraphina?

MRS. TIFFANY. The Countess *dee* Jolimaitre, my dear, is at this moment on her way to—to Washington! Where, after visiting all the fashionable curiosities of the day—including the President—she will return to grace her native city!

GERTRUDE. I hope you are only jesting, Madam? Seraphina is not married?

MRS. TIFFANY. Excuse me, my dear, my daughter had this morning the honour of being united to the Count *dee* Jolimaitre!

GERTRUDE. Madam! He is an impostor!

MRS. TIFFANY. Good gracious! Gertrude, how can you talk in that disrespectful way of a man of rank? An heiress, my dear, should have better manners! The Count—

(*Enter Millinette, crying*)

MILLINETTE.   Oh! Madame! I will tell everything—oh! dat monstre! He break my heart!

MRS. TIFFANY.   Millinette, what is the matter?

MILLINETTE.   Oh! he promise to marry me—I love him much—and now Zeke say he run away vid Mademoiselle Seraphina!

MRS. TIFFANY.   What insolence! The girl is mad! Count Jolimaitre marry my *femmy de chamber!*

MILLINETTE.   Oh! Madame, he is not one Count, not at all! Dat is only de title he go by in dis country. De foreigners always take de large title ven dey do come here. His name *à Paris* vas Gustave Tread-mill. But he not one Frenchman at all, but he do live one long time *à Paris*. First he live vid Monsieur Vermicelle—dere he vas de head cook! Den he live vid Monsieur Tire-nez, de barber! After dat he live vid Monsieur le Comte Frippon-fin—and dere he vas le Comte's valet. Dere, now I tell everyting, I feel one great deal better!

MRS. TIFFANY.   Oh! good gracious! I shall faint! Not a Count! What will everybody say? It's no such thing! I say he *is* a Count! One can see the foreign *jenny says quoi* in his face! Don't you think I can tell a Count when I see one? I say he *is* a Count!

(Enter Snobson, his hat on—his hands thrust in his pocket—evidently a little intoxicated)

SNOBSON.   I won't stand it! I say I won't!

TIFFANY.   *(Rushing up to him)* Mr. Snobson, for heaven's sake—*(Aside)*

SNOBSON.   Keep off. I'm a hard customer to get the better of! You'll see if I don't come out strong!

TRUEMAN.   *(Quietly knocking off Snobson's hat with his stick)* Where are your manners, man?

SNOBSON.   My business ain't with you, Catteraugus; you've waked up the wrong passenger!—Now the way I'll put it into Tiff will be a caution. I'll make him wince! That extra mint julep has put the true pluck in me. Now for it! *(Aside)* Mr. Tiffany, sir—you needn't think to come over me, sir— you'll have to get up a little earlier in the morning before you do *that*, sir! I'd like to know, sir, how you came to assist your daughter in running away with that foreign loafer? It was a downright swindle, sir. After the conversation I and you had on that subject she wasn't your property, sir.

TRUEMAN.   What, Antony, is that the way your city clerk bullies his boss?

SNOBSON.   You're drunk, Catteraugus—don't expose yourself—you're drunk! Taken a little too much toddy, my old boy! Be quiet! I'll look after you, and they won't find it out. If you want to be busy, you may take care of my *hat*—I feel so deuced weak in the chest, I don't think I *could* pick it up myself.—Now to put the screws to Tiff. *(Aside)* Mr. Tiffany, sir—you have broken your word, as no virtuous individual—no honourable member—of-the—com-mu-ni-ty—

TIFFANY.   Have some pity, Mr. Snobson, I beseech you! I had nothing to do with my daughter's elopement! I will agree to anything you desire—your salary shall be doubled—trebled—(*Aside to him*)

SNOBSON.   (*Aloud*) No you don't. No bribery and corruption.

TIFFANY.   I implore you to be silent. You shall become partner of the concern, if you please—only do not speak. You are not yourself at this moment. (*Aside to him*)

SNOBSON.   Ain't I though. I feel *twice* myself. I feel like two Snobsons rolled into one, and I'm chock full of the spunk of a dozen! Now Mr. Tiffany, sir—

TIFFANY.   I shall go distracted! Mr. Snobson, if you have one spark of manly feeling—(*Aside to him*)

TRUEMAN.   Antony, why do you stand disputing with that drunken jack-ass? Where's your nigger? Let him kick the critter out, and be of use for once in his life.

SNOBSON.   Better be quiet, Catteraugus. This ain't your hash, so keep your spoon out of the dish. Don't expose yourself, old boy.

TRUEMAN.   Turn him out, Antony!

SNOBSON.   He daren't do it! Ain't I up to him? Ain't he in my power? Can't I knock him into a cocked hat with a word? And now he's got my steam up—I *will* do it!

TIFFANY.   (*Beseechingly*) Mr. Snobson—my friend—

SNOBSON.   It's no go—steam's up—and I don't stand at anything!

TRUEMAN.   You won't *stand* here long unless you mend your manners—you're not the first man I've *upset* because he didn't know his place.

SNOBSON.   I know where Tiff's place is, and that's in the *State's Prison!* It's bespoke already. He would have it! He wouldn't take pattern of me, and behave like a gentleman! He's a *forger*, sir!

(*Tiffany throws himself into a chair in an attitude of despair; the others stand transfixed with astonishment.*)

He's been forging Dick Anderson's endorsements of his notes these ten months. He's got a couple in the bank that will send him to the wall any-how—if he can't make a raise. I took them there myself! Now you know what he's worth. I said I'd expose him, and I have done it!

MRS. TIFFANY.   Get out of the house! You ugly, little, drunken brute, get out! It's not true. Mr. Trueman, put him out; you have got a stick—put him out!

(*Enter Seraphina, in her bonnet and shawl—a parasol in her hand*)

SERAPHINA.   I hope Zeke hasn't delivered my note. (*Stops in surprise at seeing the persons assembled*)

MRS. TIFFANY.   Oh, here is the Countess! (*Advances to embrace her*)

TIFFANY. (*Starting from his seat, and seizing Seraphina violently by the arm*) Are—you—married?

SERAPHINA. Goodness, Pa, how you frighten me! No, I'm not married, *quite.*

TIFFANY. Thank heaven.

MRS. TIFFANY. (*Drawing Seraphina aside*) What's the matter? Why did you come back?

SERAPHINA. The clergyman wasn't at home—I came back for my jewels—the Count said nobility couldn't get on without them.

TIFFANY. I may be saved yet! Seraphina, my child, you will not see me disgraced—ruined! I have been a kind father to you—at least I have tried to be one—although your mother's extravagance made a *madman* of me! The Count is an impostor—you seemed to like him—(*Pointing to Snobson*) Heaven forgive me! (*Aside*) Marry *him* and save *me.* You, Mr. Trueman, you will be my friend in this hour of extreme need—you will advance the sum which I require—I pledge myself to return it. My wife—my child—who will support them were I—the thought makes me frantic! You will aid me? You had a child yourself.

TRUEMAN. But I did not *sell* her—it was her own doings. Shame on you, Antony! Put a price on your own flesh and blood! Shame on such foul traffic!

TIFFANY. Save me—I conjure you—for my father's sake.

TRUEMAN. For your *father's* SON's sake I will *not* aid you in becoming a greater villain than you are!

GERTRUDE. Mr. Trueman,—Father, I should say—save him—do not embitter our happiness by permitting this calamity to fall upon another—

TRUEMAN. Enough—I did not need your voice, child. I am going to settle this matter my own way.

(*Goes up to Snobson—who has seated himself and fallen asleep—tilts him out of the chair*)

SNOBSON. (*Waking up*) Eh? Where's the fire? Oh! it's you, Catteraugus.

TRUEMAN. If I comprehend aright, you have been for some time aware of your principal's forgeries?

(*As he says this, he beckons to Howard, who advances as witness.*)

SNOBSON. You've hit the nail, Catteraugus! Old chap saw that I was up to him six months ago; left off throwing dust into my eyes—

TRUEMAN. Oh, he did!

SNOBSON. Made no bones of forging Anderson's name at my elbow.

TRUEMAN. Forged at your elbow? You saw him do it?

SNOBSON. I did.

TRUEMAN. Repeatedly?

SNOBSON. Re-pea-ted-ly.

TRUEMAN. Then you, Rattlesnake, if he goes to the State's Prison, you'll take up your quarters there too. You are an accomplice, an *accessory!*

(*Trueman walks away and seats himself. Howard rejoins Gertrude. Snobson stands for some time bewildered.*)

SNOBSON. The deuce, so I am! I never thought of that! I must make myself scarce. I'll be off. Tiff, I say Tiff! (*Going up to him and speaking confidentially*) that drunken old rip has got us in his power. Let's give him the slip and be off. They want men of genius at the West,—we're sure to get on! You—you can set up for a writing-master, and teach copying *signatures;* and I—I'll give lectures on *temperance!* You won't come, eh? Then I'm off without you. Good-bye Catteraugus! Which is the way to California? (*Steals off*)

TRUEMAN. There's one debt your city owes me. And now let us see what other nuisances we can abate. Antony, I'm not given to preaching, therefore I shall not say much about what you have done. Your face speaks for itself,—the crime has brought its punishment along with it.

TIFFANY. Indeed it has, sir! In *one year* I have lived a *century* of misery.

TRUEMAN. I believe you, and upon one condition I will assist you—

TIFFANY. My friend—my first, ever kind friend,—only name it!

TRUEMAN. You must sell your house and all these gew-gaws, and bundle your wife and daughter off to the country. There let them learn economy, true independence, and home virtues, instead of foreign follies. As for yourself, continue your business—but let moderation, in future, be your counsellor, and let *honesty* be your confidential clerk.

TIFFANY. Mr. Trueman, you have made existence once more precious to me! My wife and daughter shall quit the city to-morrow, and—

PRUDENCE. It's all coming right! It's all coming right! We'll go to the county of Catteraugus. (*Walking up to Trueman*)

TRUEMAN. No, you won't—I make that a stipulation, Antony; keep clear of Catteraugus. None of your fashionable examples there!

(*Jolimaitre appears in the Conservatory and peeps into the room unperceived.*)

COUNT. What can detain Seraphina? We ought to be off!

MILLINETTE. (*Turns round, perceives him, runs and forces him into the room*) Here he is! Ah, Gustave, *mon cher* Gustave! I have you now and we never part no more. Don't frown, Gustave, don't frown—

TRUEMAN. Come forward, Mr. Count! and for the edification of fashionable society confess that you're an imposter.

COUNT. An impostor? Why, you abominable old—

TRUEMAN. Oh, your feminine friend has told us all about it, the cook—

the valet—barber, and all that sort of thing. Come, confess, and something may be done for you.

COUNT. Well, then, I do confess I am no count; but really, ladies and gentlemen, I may recommend myself as the most capital cook.

MRS. TIFFANY. Oh, Seraphina!

SERAPHINA. Oh, Ma! (*They embrace and retire.*)

TRUEMAN. Promise me to call upon the whole circle of your fashionable acquaintances with your own advertisements and in your cook's attire, and I will set you up in business to-morrow. Better turn stomachs than turn heads!

MILLINETTE. But you will marry me?

COUNT. Give us your hand, Millinette! Sir, command me for the most delicate *paté*—the daintiest *croquette à la royale*—the most transcendent *omelette soufflé* that ever issued from a French pastry-cook's oven. I hope you will pardon my conduct, but I heard that in America, where you pay homage to titles while you profess to scorn them—where *Fashion* makes the basest coin current—where you have no kings, no princes, no *nobility*—

TRUEMAN. Stop there! I object to your use of that word. When justice is found only among lawyers—health among physicians—and patriotism among politicians, *then* may you say that there is no *nobility* where there are no titles! But we *have* kings, princes, and nobles in abundance—of *Nature's stamp*, if not of *Fashion's*—we have honest men, warm-hearted and brave, and we have women—gentle, fair, and true, to whom no *title* could add *nobility*.

Epilogue

PRUDENCE.   I told you so! And now you hear and see.
I told you *Fashion* would the fashion be!
TRUEMAN.   Then both its point and moral I distrust.
COUNT.   Sir, is that liberal?
HOWARD.   Or is it just?
TRUEMAN.   The guilty have escaped!
TIFFANY.   Is, therefore, sin
Made charming? Ah! there's punishment within!
Guilt ever carries his own scourge along.
GERTRUDE.   Virtue her own reward!
TRUEMAN.   You're right, I'm wrong.
MRS. TIFFANY.   How we have been deceived!
PRUDENCE.   I told you so.
SERAPHINA.   To lose at once a title and a beau!
COUNT.   A count no more, I'm no more of *account*.
TRUEMAN.   But to a nobler title you may mount,
And be in time—who knows?—an honest man!
COUNT.   Eh, Millinette?
MILLINETTE.   Oh, *oui*, I know you can!
GERTRUDE.   (*To audience*) But, ere we close the scene, a word with you,—
We charge you answer,—Is this picture true?
Some little mercy to our efforts show,
Then let the world your honest verdict know.
Here let it see portrayed its ruling passion,
And learn to prize at its just value—*Fashion*.

The End

THE OCTOROON

or

Life in Louisiana

by
Dion Boucicault

Introduction

Dion Boucicault (Dionysus Lardner Bourciquot) was born in Dublin and was educated in London. His early life is somewhat mysterious, and three different birthdates are cited for him, but December 26, 1820, seems most probable. He made his acting debut in 1838 under the name Lee Moreton. *London Assurance* (1841) established him as a successful playwright. Four years in Paris (1844-48) gave him a taste for spectacular melodrama that he never lost. After coming to America in 1853, he traveled widely throughout this country, returned several times to England, and in the mid-1880's toured Australia. His most productive year, 1859-60, was called the "Boucicault season" in New York because he had six successful plays running as house dramatist for the Winter Garden, which he had designed, and for Laura Keene's Theatre. In 1860 he returned to England to produce one of his greatest successes, *The Colleen Bawn*. By the 1870's popular taste had passed him by, and he struggled pathetically to duplicate his earlier successes. He made his last stage appearance in 1886, and until his death September 18, 1890, he served as an acting teacher and advisor for the producer A. M. Palmer. Boucicault was the most prolific and the most popular playwright of the mid-19th century in both England and America. He was not only a successful writer, adapter, and translator of innumerable plays but also a celebrated actor, stage manager, set designer, and acting teacher. *The Career of Dion Boucicault* (New York, 1915) by Townsend Walsh is the only book-length account of his busy and hectic life.

An accurate census of Boucicault's plays is an impossible undertaking. He is sometimes credited with 400, but less than half that number would seem nearer the truth. He sometimes issued a play anonymously and then if it succeeded, stepped forward to claim authorship. Many of his plays were produced under different titles. An example of the complex tangle in his bibliography is one of his greatest successes, *The Poor of New York* (1857), which was based on a French play, *Les Pauvres de Paris*. Although Boucicault copyrighted the play in his own name, he had three collaborators, whose contributions cannot be determined. The play attracted great attention because of its elaborate sets and the portrayal of a spectacular tenement fire. Boucicault later revised his script to fit new locales and produced it under such titles as *The Streets of London, The Poor of Liverpool, The Streets of Philadelphia,* and *The Money Panic of '57.*

Ingenious rather than truly original, aspiring to financial rather than artistic success, Boucicault introduced or popularized many changes in stage practices. He devised many spectacular stage effects, used the new box set as early as 1841, devised a wagon stage for rapid shifting of scenery, presented the first matinee performances in New York, and was the first designer to use fireproof curtains and scenery. He worked with George Henry Boker and others for passage of the first American dramatic copyright law in 1856. Though unsatisfactory because it stipulated that a dramatist lost his rights in a play if it was performed even once before being copyrighted, the new law gave playwrights some protection for their work. Loopholes in the law, incidentally, forced playwrights to guard their play scripts jealously and avoid publication if possible—the major reason that texts of many 19th century plays are difficut or impossible to locate today. Boucicault also was influential in developing the practice of paying a playwright royalties for the use of his work. Most theatres outside New York were dependent on a stock company—a permanent troupe of actors and other personnel, occasionally augmented by a touring star. Around 1860 Boucicault sent out the first touring company and thus received royalties from its performances on the road as well as from the New York run. As railroads facilitated travel, the use of touring companies became standard procedure, and by 1872 local stock companies no longer dominated theatres outside New York.

Another revolutionary change for which Boucicault was partly responsible was the custom of the traveling star. In 1865, at the request of Joseph Jefferson, he revised an earlier version of *Rip Van Winkle*, making it both more melodramatic and more sentimental. In part of Rip, Jefferson became the best-loved performer in the history of the American stage and is the chief example of the late 19th century tradition of the one-part actor. In 1881 he claimed to have played the role 2500 times.

Boucicault was also famous for his Irish plays. He once said, "When I wrote *The Colleen Bawn*, I invented the Irish Drama. It was original in form, in material, in treatment, and in dialogue." The most successful of these plays were *The Colleen Bawn* (1860), *Arrah-na-Pogue* (1864), *The O'Dowd* (1873), and *The Shaughraun* (1874). Highly sentimental and superficial in their portrayal of Irish life, the plays did much to create the stereotype of the stage Irishman. Not until the Dublin Abbey Theatre productions of playwrights like Synge and Yeats were characters individualized in plays about Ireland.

Like most of Boucicault's plays, *The Octoroon* was derivative. Its chief source was a novel by Mayne Reid, *The Quadroon*, published in New York in 1856 and dramatized in London in 1859. In the novel an Englishman, Edward Rutherford, rescues a Creole woman, Eugénie Besancon, from drowning when a river steamboat explodes. He falls in love with her quadroon slave, Aurore, who is put up for auction. Eugénie, disguised as a man, tries to save her but fails. Rutherford kidnaps Aurore; a mob pursue and capture him, but the sheriff saves him from being lynched. When he discovers that Aurore had been set free by her former owner, Rutherford marries her. Boucicault's changes make his plot only slightly more ridiculous than the original, but they all demonstrate his ability to satisfy popular taste. He reduced the slave woman's Negro inheritance by one half, probably to heighten the pathos of her hopeless love, and made her the illegitimate daughter of her former owner. He recognized that an American audience would not accept Zoe's marriage to George Peyton, but in a version of the play presented in England Zoe escaped in a canoe and the audience was informed that she and George would marry. Boucicault changed the hero from an Englishman to a Southerner who has lived in Paris. He transformed the Creole beauty, Eugénie, into a wholesome Southern belle, Dora Sunnyside. Boucicault added such spectacles as the burning steamboat and the lynching scene. Though a somewhat decrepit version of the noble savage, Wah-no-tee would appeal to any lingering interest in the Indian theme. Following the lead of Mrs. Stowe in *Uncle Tom's Cabin*, Boucicault made his villain a Northerner. To offset any resentment caused by this character, he added a kindly though inept Yankee, Salem Scudder.

Probably another source used by Boucicault was the first American play to treat miscegenation, *Neighbor Jackwood* (1857), J. T. Trowbridge's dramatization of his novel of the same name. The story concerns the tribulations of an octoroon slave, Camille, who escapes to the North. She is captured, but later the hero wins her freedom and marries her. The use of self-developing liquid to obtain an incriminating photograph Boucicault found in Albany Fonblanque's novel *The Filibuster* (1859). A similar device was used in a television western of the early 1960's.

December 6, 1859—four days after the execution of John Brown and the day Fernando B. Wood, a pro-Southern Democrat, was elected mayor of New York—would seem the worst possible time in history to produce a play about slavery. Boucicault conducted a publicity campaign to excite interest in the play before it opened at the Winter Garden and wrote himself anonymous threats, which he displayed to reporters. Nevertheless, the play was received enthusiastically and no great furor resulted. Boucicault balanced the views of Southern life in such a way that no one was offended. As Joseph Jefferson wrote in his autobiography: "The dialogue and characters of the play made one feel for the South, but the action proclaimed against slavery, and called for its abolition." That *The Octoroon* was not considered an anti-slavery play is indicated by the fact that revivals of the play were popular for the rest of the century. Today the outlandish Negro dialect, though no more absurd than the high-flown rhetoric of the white characters, seems offensive.

During the first week of performances Boucicault played Wah-no-tee, Agnes Robertson (Mrs. Boucicault) played Zoe, and Joseph Jefferson played Salem Scudder. Shortly before an evening performance, Boucicault announced that he and his wife would not appear because of the danger of rioting. He apparently hoped to force the management into paying him more money, but he had not realized that because the role of Wah-no-tee involved little dialogue it would be fairly easy for an actor to replace him. He was discharged from his position as stage manager-director at the Winter Garden and accepted a position at Laura Keene's Theatre, where in less than a month he produced *The Trial of*

Effie Deans, based on Scott's *Heart of Midlothian*. Boucicault sought a court injunction to stop performance of *The Octoroon*, but his suit was denied. With other actors in the Boucicaults' roles and with Jefferson as director, the play continued at the Winter Garden until January 21, 1860. Soon the play was showing at three other theatres in New York, and at Niblo's Concert Saloon Christy's Minstrels presented a burlesque version, *The Moctoroon*. The New York *Tribune* described the activity stimulated by the play as "Octorooning." It must be classed as one of the most popular American melodramas of the century.

Alan S. Downer has described melodrama as "the dramatic weed." Although the term is never used favorably, each generation enjoys its own brand of melodramatic entertainment. Melodrama implies violent action, thrilling suspense, and emotional language. The characters are extreme types, wholly virtuous or wholly evil—dastardly villains, noble heroes, and demurely innocent heroines. Stock situations are also associated with 19th century melodramas—the last-minute payment of a widow's mortgage, a deathbed surrounded by weeping servants and relatives, a shawl-covered maiden thrust into a snowstorm by her cruel father, a heroine tied to a railroad track. American audiences in the mid-19th century enjoyed sensational spectacles, particularly if they were superficially accurate in detail. Boucicault helped create this taste and catered to it, and most of his extant plays are more or less melodramatic. Other 19th century melodramas with which *The Octoroon* might be compared include *Uncle Tom's Cabin* (1852) as dramatized by George L. Aiken, *East Lynne* (1868), Clifton W. Tayleure's adaptation of the novel by Mrs. Henry Wood, *The White Slave* (1882) by Bartley Campbell, and *The Girl I Left Behind Me* (1893) by David Belasco and Franklyn Fyles.

Program picture of the steamboat Magnolia ablaze

(Harvard Theatre Collection)

WINTER
GARDEN

TO-NIGHT AND EVERY NIGHT

Will be performed, a new play, in five acts, illustrative of AMERICAN CHARACTER,
AMERICAN SCENES and SOUTHERN HOMES, called the

OCTOROON

Or Life in Louisiana.

The scene is laid in the Delta of the Mississippi River, on the Plantation of Terrebonne. The time—the present day.

CHARACTERS:

Mrs. Peyton, of Terrebonne Plantation, in the Attakapas, widow of the late
Judge Peyton ....Mrs. Blake
George Peyton, her orphew, educated in Europe, and just returned home.
....Mr. A. H. Davenport
Jacob M'Closkey, formerly overseer of Terrebonne, but now owner of one
half of the estate..Mr. T. B. Johnston
Salem Scudder, a Yankee from Massachusetts, now overseer of Terrebonne,
great on improvements and inventions, once a photographic operator,
and been a little of everything generally..................Mr. J. Jefferson
Pete, an "ole uncle," once the late Judge's body servant, but now "too ole
to work, sa"..Mr. G. Jamieson
(His first appearance in New York for many years.)
Zoe, an Octoroon girl, free, the natural child of the late Judge by a Quadroon
slave...Mrs. J. H. Allen
Sunnyside, a planter, neighbor and old friend of the Peytons. .Mr. G. Holland
Dora Sunnyside, his only daughter and heiress, a Southern Belle.
....Mrs. Stoddart
Lafouroche, a rich Planter...............................Mr. Stoddart
Wah-no-tee, an Indian Chief, of the Lepan Tribe ....Mr. Pearson
Paul, a yellow boy, a faverite of the late Judge's, and so allowed to do much
as he likes ....Miss Burke
Ratts, Mate of the Magnolia steamer.....................Mr. Harrison
Colonel Pointdexter, an Auctioneer and slave salesman ....Mr. Russell
Jules Thibodeaux, a young creole Planter ....Miss H. Secor
Caillou, an Overseer.....................................Mr. Peck
Jackson, a Planter......................................Mr. Tree
Ouatoroe, the auctioneer's Clerk.........................Mr. Pomiel
Gr-oe, a yellow girl, a slave............................Miss Gimber
Solon, a grief boy slave.................................Mr. Styles
Dido, the cook, a slave..................................Mrs. Dunn
Mrs. Claiborne..Miss Clinton
Minnie, a Quadroon slave................................Miss Walters
Planters, Slaves, Deck Hands and Ladies.

SCENE OF THE FIRST ACT.

The PLANTATION of TERREBONNE.

A Southern home under a Southern sun. The little darkie, "dem's was das Skeeters."
Pete, the old servant. George Peyton just arrived home. A Paris lion is a sunstreak;
Madame Peyton and the patriarchal home. The good old Judge. Salem Scudder's description
of Zoe, the Octoroon. The two overseers. A confession. The strange relation and affection
existing between Madam Peyton and her husband's natural daughter. Plantation life. Southern
ways and Northern thrift. Zoe, the Octoroon. The arrival of Sunnyside and Dora.
Dora Sunnyside a portrait. George cannot understand the social position of Zoe. M'Closkey
arrives. The hard customer. Paul, the yellow boy, and Wah-no-tee, the Indian hunter. The
strange affection between the savage and the boy slave, companions in the Swamp hunt. Paul
and the Indian start across the Red Cedar Swamp for the United States mail. Border United
States mail delivery. The foreclosure on Terrebonne. The plantation to be sold. The last
hope of recovering the estate. The Judge's desk. M'Closkey's love for the Octoroon. "I cannot marry you, but I can make you mistress of the richest estate in Louisiana." The two
overseers review the state of things. The live oak and the creeper. Two live Yankees, or
diamond cut diamond. Scudder's confession of his love for Zoe. M'Closkey discovers the free
papers of Zoe. The judgment. The dark hope. The resolve.

ACT THE SECOND.

THE LANDING ON THE ATCHAFALAYA.

The Lumber Shed.

Scudder returns to his old trade and takes a photograph. Paul wants his picture took.
Pete brings terrible news. Zoe confirms it. George's declaration of his love. "He does not
know what I am." The "eighth blood." M'Closkey's resolve. Wah-no-tee and Paul. The
apparatus at work. The daguerreotype portrait. Paul takes his own likeness, assisted by the
Indian. The savage's dread for the machine. Thinks it a deadly weapon. Paul sits for his
portrait. The attack. The murder. The letter and the fight. "Terrebonne will be sold, and
Zoe will be mine." The revenge of the Indian, and his grief for Paul.

ACT THE THIRD.

THE PARLOR AND HALL AT TERREBONNE.

Preparations for the sale. M'Closkey claims the pound of flesh. The slaves are to be sold.
Pete on the stump. His address to his "cullored breeders." Darkie enthusiasm.

THE SLAVE SALE.

Ratts, the mate of the Magnolia Grace, the yellow girl, and her children. " Buy me,
mas'r!" Pete on the stand. His indignation at going cheap. No. 4—The Octoroon girl,
Zoe. Consternation of the slaves. M'Closkey bids. The assault by George. Bowie knives
and revolvers. Does a revenge on Zoe, who has taken away her lover. The sale of the Octoroon

ACT THE FOURTH.

THE BOILER DECK OF THE MAGNOLIA

THE LANDING AND THE WOODPILE.

Ball on the boiler deck. Take her guards under. She is freighted down into the solid mud,
and can't float. No matter. "Wood up; bang on to the safety valve; she'll crawl off on her
paddles." Alarm! The Indian comes. Wah-no-tee, the murderer of Paul. Seizure of the
savage. Popular fury. Lynch him! Lynch him! Scudder protects him. Paul's grave discovered, and the missing mail bags brought to light. Evidence strong.

THE LYNCH TRIAL.

Counsellor Scudder defends the Indian. Scudder on Lynch. A new witness arrives very unexpectedly. An alteration of the entertainments for that evening. Scudder on M'Closkey. Improved and corrected Edition. M'Closkey in a fit. The verdict and the seizure of the prisoner.
M'Closkey's escape.

THE SHED ON FIRE.

Cut the ropes. Back her out. Clear away. The criminal away. His Indian destiny por-
sues him.

The Destruction of the Steamer Magnolia by Fire

ACT THE FIFTH.

Scene First.—The Negro Quarter—Night.

Zoe seeks her old nurse, Dido. The old Obi Doctress. The drink that cures the Red Fever.
The night after the sale. Life is so beautiful to one so young.

Scene Second.—The Cane Brake—Sunrise.

M'Closkey out of danger. His flight through the swamp. His escape. The dusky shadow
of death behind him. The Indian on the war path. The pursuit. The human bloodhound.

Scene Third.—The Red Cedar Swamp.

Scudder and Pete on their road home. The alarm. What's that in the bush, "A Bar or
a runaway Nigger." The man hunt. The wolf run down at last. The Indian and his victim.
Save us from the scalping knife of the savage. Judge revokes revision of the lynch verdict.
His decision. Pete's petition. Scudder refuses. His protection of the white man.

Scene Fourth, and Last.

The parlor at Terrebonne again. Zoe's adieu to her home before she leaves it for the house
of her new master. The glass of water. The arrival of scudder. The joyful news. Pete in a
bad way. Zoe's freedom. Free at last.

THE OCTOROON GOES HOME

THE VISION OF THE LANDING.

LITTLE PAUL'S GRAVE.

M'Closkey appeals to the highest tribunal. The last fearless move of the Indian Wah-no-tee.

During the winter season the doors will open at 6½. The entertainments will commence at 7¼
Families bringing children are informed that the entertainments conclude before 10½ o'clock.

Cast of Characters

GEORGE PEYTON

SALEM SCUDDER

MR. SUNNYSIDE

JACOB M'CLOSKY

WAHNOTEE

CAPTAIN RATTS

COLONEL POINDEXTER

JULES THIBODEAUX

JUDGE CAILLOU

LAFOUCHE

JACKSON

OLD PETE

PAUL (a boy slave)

SOLON

MRS. PEYTON

ZOE

DORA SUNNYSIDE

GRACE

MINNIE

DIDO

ACT I.

A view of the Plantation Terrebonne, in Louisiana.—A branch of the Mississippi is seen winding through the estate.—A low built, but extensive planter's dwelling, surrounded with a veranda, and raised a few feet from the ground, occupies the left side.—A table and chairs are at the right. Grace is discovered sitting at breakfast-table with children.

(Enter Solon from house)

SOLON.   Yah! you bomn'ble fry—git out—a gen'leman can't pass for you.
GRACE.   (*Seizing a fly whisk*) Hee ha! git out! (*Drives children away: in escaping they tumble against and trip up Solon, who falls with tray; the children steal the bananas and rolls that fall about.*)

(Enter Pete, he is lame; he carries a mop and pail.)

PETE.   Hey! laws a massey! why, clar out! drop dat banana! I'll murder this yer crowd. (*He chases children about; they leap over railing at back.*) (*Exit Solon*) Dem little niggers is a judgment upon dis generation.

(Enter George from house)

GEORGE.   What's the matter, Pete?
PETE.   It's dem black trash, Mas'r George; dis ere property wants claring; dem's getting too numerous round: when I gets time I'll kill some on 'em, sure!
GEORGE.   They don't seem to be scared by the threat.
PETE.   'Top, you varmin! 'top, till I get enough of you in one place.
GEORGE.   Were they all born on this estate?
PETE.   Guess they nebber was born—dem tings! what, dem?—get away! Born here—dem darkies? What, on Terrebonne! Don't b'lieve it, Mas'r George; dem black tings never was born at all; dey swarmed one mornin' on a sassafras tree in the swamp; I cotched 'em; dey ain't no'count. Don't b'lieve dey'll turn out niggers when dey're growed; dey'll come out sunthin' else.
GRACE.   Yes, Mas'r George, dey was born here; and old Pete is fonder on 'em dan he is of his fiddle on a Sunday.
PETE.   What? dem tings—dem?—get away. (*Makes blow at the children*) Born here! dem darkies! What, on Terrebonne? Don't b'lieve it, Mas'r George,—no. One morning dey swarmed on a sassafras tree in de swamp, and I cotched 'em all in a sieve,—dat's how dey come on top of dis yearth —git out, you,—ya, ya! (*Laughs. Exit Grace.*)

164

(Enter Mrs. Peyton from house)

MRS. PEYTON.   So, Pete, you are spoiling those children as usual!

PETE.   Dat's right, missus! gib it to ole Pete! he's allers in for it. Git away dere! Ya! if dey ain't all lighted, like coons, on dat snake fence, just out of shot. Look dar! Ya! ya! dem debils. Ya!

MRS. PEYTON.   Pete, do you hear?

PETE.   Git down dar! I'm arter you! *(Hobbles off)*

MRS. PEYTON.   You are out early this morning, George.

GEORGE.   I was up before daylight. We got the horses saddled, and galloped down the shell road over the Piney Patch; then coasting the Bayou Lake, we crossed the long swamps, by Paul's Path, and so came home again.

MRS. PEYTON.   *(Laughing)* You seem already familiar with the names of every spot on the estate.

(Enter Pete.—Arranges breakfast, etc.)

GEORGE.   Just one month ago I quitted Paris. I left that siren city as I would have left a beloved woman.

MRS. PEYTON.   No wonder! I dare say you left at least a dozen beloved women there, at the same time.

GEORGE.   I feel that I departed amid universal and sincere regret. I left my loves and my creditors equally inconsolable.

MRS. PEYTON.   George, you are incorrigible. Ah, you remind me so much of your uncle, the judge.

GEORGE.   Bless his dear old handwriting, it's all I ever saw of him. For ten years his letters came every quarter-day, with a remittance and a word of advice in his formal cavalier style; and then a joke in the postscript, that upset the dignity of the foregoing. Aunt, when he died, two years ago, I read over those letters of his, and if I didn't cry like a baby—

MRS. PEYTON.   No, George; say you wept like a man. And so you really kept those foolish letters?

GEORGE.   Yes; I kept the letters, and squandered the money.

MRS. PEYTON.   *(Embracing him)* Ah! why were you not my son—you are so like my dear husband.

(Enter Salem Scudder)

SCUDDER.   Ain't he! Yes—when I saw him and Miss Zoe galloping through the green sugar crop, and doing ten dollars' worth of damage at every stride, says I, how like his old uncle he do make the dirt fly.

GEORGE.   O, aunt! what a bright, gay creature she is!

SCUDDER.   What, Zoe! Guess that you didn't leave anything female in Europe that can lift an eyelash beside that gal. When she goes along, she just leaves a streak of love behind her. It's a good drink to see her come into the cotton fields—the niggers get fresh on the sight of her. If she ain't worth her weight in sunshine you may take one of my fingers off, and choose which you like.

MRS. PEYTON.   She need not keep us waiting breakfast, though. Pete, tell Miss Zoe that we are waiting.

PETE.   Yes, missus. Why, Minnie, why don't you run when you hear, you lazy crittur? (*Minnie runs off.*) Dat's de laziest nigger on dis yere property. (*Sits down*) Don't do nuffin.

MRS. PEYTON.   My dear George, you are left in your uncle's will heir to this estate.

GEORGE.   Subject to your life interest and an annuity to Zoe, is it not so?

MRS. PEYTON.   I fear that the property is so involved that the strictest economy will scarcely recover it. My dear husband never kept any accounts, and we scarcely know in what condition the estate really is.

SCUDDER.   Yes, we do, ma'am; it's in a darned bad condition. Ten years ago the judge took as overseer a bit of Connecticut hardware called M'Closky. The judge didn't understand accounts—the overseer did. For a year or two all went fine. The judge drew money like Bourbon whisky from a barrel, and never turned off the tap. But out it flew, free for everybody or anybody to beg, borrow, or steal. So it went, till one day the judge found the tap wouldn't run. He looked in to see what stopped it, and pulled out a big mortgage. "Sign that," says the overseer; "it's only a formality." "All right," says the judge, and away went a thousand acres; so at the end of eight years, Jacob M'Closky, Esquire, finds himself proprietor of the richest half of Terrebonne—

GEORGE.   But the other half is free.

SCUDDER.   No, it ain't; because, just then, what does the judge do, but hire another overseer—a Yankee—a Yankee named Salem Scudder.

MRS. PEYTON.   O, no, it was—

SCUDDER.   Hold on, now! I'm going to straighten this account clear out. What was this here Scudder? Well, he lived in New York by sittin' with his heels up in front of French's Hotel, and inventin'—

GEORGE.   Inventing what?

SCUDDER.   Improvements—anything, from a stay-lace to a fire-engine. Well, he cut that for the photographing line. He and his apparatus arrived here, took the judge's likeness and his fancy, who made him overseer right off. Well, sir, what does this Scudder do but introduces his inventions and improvements on this estate. His new cotton gins broke down, the steam sugar-mills burst up, until he finished off with his folly what Mr. M'Closky with his knavery began.

MRS. PEYTON.   O, Salem! how can you say so? Haven't you worked like a horse?

SCUDDER.   No, ma'am, I worked like an ass—an honest one, and that's all. Now, Mr. George, between the two overseers, you and that good old lady have come to the ground; that is the state of things, just as near as I can fix it. (*Zoe sings without.*)

GEORGE.   'Tis Zoe.

SCUDDER.   O, I have not spoiled that anyhow. I can't introduce any darned improvement there. Ain't that a cure for old age? It kinder lifts the heart up, don't it?

MRS. PEYTON.   Poor child! what will become of her when I am gone? If you haven't spoiled her, I fear I have. She has had the education of a lady.

GEORGE.   I have remarked that she is treated by the neighbors with a kind of familiar condescension that annoyed me.

SCUDDER.   Don't you know that she is the natural daughter of the judge, your uncle, and that old lady thar just adored anything her husband cared for; and this girl, that another woman would a hated, she loves as if she'd been her own child.

GEORGE.   Aunt, I am prouder and happier to be your nephew and heir to the ruins of Terrebonne, than I would have been to have had half Louisiana without you.

(*Enter Zoe from house*)

ZOE.   Am I late? Ah! Mr. Scudder, good morning.

SCUDDER.   Thank ye. I'm from fair to middlin', like a bamboo cane, much the same all the year round.

ZOE.   No; like a sugar cane; so dry outside, one would never think there was so much sweetness within.

SCUDDER.   Look here: I can't stand that gal! If I stop here, I shall hug her right off. (*Sees Pete, who has set his pail down up stage and goes to sleep on it*) If that old nigger ain't asleep, I'm blamed. Hillo! (*Kicks pail from under Pete and lets him down. Exit.*)

PETE.   Hi! Debbel's in de pail! Whar's breakfass?

(*Enter Solon and Dido with coffee-pot, dishes, etc.*)

DIDO.   Bless'ee, Missey Zoe, here it be. Dere's a dish of penpans—jess taste, Mas'r George—and here's fried bananas; smell 'em do, sa glosh.

PETE.   Hole yer tongue, Dido. Whar's de coffee? (*Pours out*) If it don't stain de cup, your wicked ole life's in danger, sure! dat right! black as nigger; clar as ice. You may drink dat, Mas'r George. (*Looks off*) Yah! here's Mas'r Sunnyside, and Missey Dora, jist drove up. Some of you niggers run and hole de hosses; and take dis, Dido. (*Gives her coffee-pot to hold and hobbles off, followed by Solon and Dido*)

(*Enter Sunnyside and Dora*)

SUNNYSIDE.   Good day, ma'am. (*Shakes hands with George*) I see we are just in time for breakfast. (*Sits*)

DORA.   O, none for me; I never eat. (*Sits*)

GEORGE.   (*Aside*) They do not notice Zoe.—(*Aloud*) You don't see Zoe, Mr. Sunnyside.

SUNNYSIDE.   Ah! Zoe, girl; are you there?

DORA.   Take my shawl, Zoe. (*Zoe helps her.*) What a good creature she is.

SUNNYSIDE.   I dare say, now, that in Europe you have never met any lady more beautiful in person, or more polished in manners, than that girl.

GEORGE.   You are right, sir; though I shrank from expressing that opinion in her presence, so bluntly.

SUNNYSIDE.   Why so?

GEORGE.   It may be considered offensive.

SUNNYSIDE.   (*Astonished*) What? I say, Zoe, do you hear that?

DORA.   Mr. Peyton is joking.

MRS. PEYTON.   My nephew is not acquainted with our customs in Louisiana, but he will soon understand.

GEORGE.   Never, aunt! I shall never understand how to wound the feelings of any lady; and, if that is the custom here, I shall never acquire it.

DORA.   Zoe, my dear, what does he mean?

ZOE.   I don't know.

GEORGE.   Excuse me, I'll light a cigar. (*Goes up stage*)

DORA.   (*Aside to Zoe*) Isn't he sweet! O, dear, Zoe, is he in love with anybody?

ZOE.   How can I tell?

DORA.   Ask him. I want to know; don't say I told you to inquire, but find out. Minnie, fan me, it is so nice—and his clothes are French, ain't they?

ZOE.   I think so; shall I ask him that too?

DORA.   No, dear. I wish he would make love to me. When he speaks to one he does it so easy, so gentle; it isn't bar-room style; love lined with drinks, sighs tinged with tobacco—and they say all the women in Paris were in love with him, which I feel I shall be: stop fanning me; what nice boots he wears.

SUNNYSIDE.   (*To Mrs. Peyton*) Yes, ma'am, I hold a mortgage over Terrebonne; mine's a ninth, and pretty near covers all the property, except the slaves. I believe Mr. M'Closky has a bill of sale on them. O, here he is.

(*Enter M'Closky*)

SUNNYSIDE.   Good morning, Mr. M'Closky.

M'CLOSKY.   Good morning, Mr. Sunnyside; Miss Dora, your servant.

DORA.   (*Seated*) Fan me, Minnie.—(*Aside*) I don't like that man.

M'CLOSKY.   (*Aside*) Insolent as usual.—(*Aloud*) You begged me to call this morning. I hope I'm not intruding.

MRS. PEYTON.   My nephew, Mr. Peyton.

M'CLOSKY.   O, how d'ye do, sir? (*Offers hand, George bows coldly.*) (*Aside*) A puppy; if he brings any of his European airs here we'll fix him—

(*Aloud*) Zoe, tell Pete to give my mare a feed, will ye?

GEORGE. (*Angrily*) Sir!

M'CLOSKY. Hillo! did I tread on ye?

MRS. PEYTON. What is the matter with George?

ZOE. (*Takes fan from Minnie*) Go, Minnie, tell Pete; run! (*Exit Minnie*)

MRS. PEYTON. Grace, attend to Mr. M'Closky.

M'CLOSKY. A julep, gal, that's my breakfast, and a bit of cheese.

GEORGE. (*Aside to Mrs. Peyton*) How can you ask that vulgar ruffian to your table!

MRS. PEYTON. Hospitality in Europe is a courtesy; here, it is an obligation. We tender food to a stranger, not because he is a gentleman, but because he is hungry.

GEORGE. Aunt, I will take my rifle down to the Atchafalaya. Paul has promised me a bear and a deer or two. I see my little Nimrod yonder, with his Indian companion. Excuse me, ladies. Ho! Paul! (*Enters house*)

PAUL. (*Outside*) I'ss, Mas'r George.

(*Enter Paul with Indian, who goes up*)

SUNNYSIDE. It's a shame to allow that young cub to run over the swamps and woods, hunting and fishing his life away instead of hoeing cane.

MRS. PEYTON. The child was a favorite of the judge, who encouraged his gambols. I couldn't bear to see him put to work.

GEORGE. (*Returning with rifle*) Come, Paul, are you ready?

PAUL. I'ss, Mas'r George. O, golly! ain't that a pooty gun.

M'CLOSKY. See here, you imp; if I catch you, and your redskin yonder, gunning in my swamps, I'll give you rats, mind; them vagabonds, when the game's about, shoot my pigs. (*Exit George into house*)

PAUL. You gib me rattan, Mas'r Clostry, but I guess you take a berry long stick to Wahnotee; ugh, he make bacon of you.

M'CLOSKY. Make bacon of me, you young whelp! Do you mean that I'm a pig? Hold on a bit. (*Seizes whip and holds Paul*)

ZOE. O, sir! don't, pray, don't.

M'CLOSKY. (*Slowly lowering his whip*) Darn you, redskin, I'll pay you off some day, both of ye. (*Returns to table and drinks*)

SUNNYSIDE. That Indian is a nuisance. Why don't he return to his nation out West?

M'CLOSKY. He's too fond of thieving and whiskey.

ZOE. No; Wahnotee is a gentle, honest creature, and remains here because he loves that boy with the tenderness of a woman. When Paul was taken down with the swamp fever the Indian sat outside the hut, and neither ate, slept, or spoke for five days, till the child could recognize and call him to his bedside. He who can love so well is honest—don't speak ill of poor Wahnotee.

MRS. PEYTON. Wahnotee, will you go back to your people?

WAHNOTEE. Sleugh.

PAUL.   He don't understand; he speaks a mash-up of Indian and Mexican. Wahnotee Patira na sepau assa wigiran?

WAHNOTEE.   Weal Omenee.

PAUL.   Says he'll go if I'll go with him. He calls me Omenee, the Pigeon, and Miss Zoe is Ninemoosha, the Sweetheart.

WAHNOTEE.   (*Pointing to Zoe*) Ninemoosha.

ZOE.   No, Wahnotee, we can't spare Paul.

PAUL.   If Omenee remain, Wahnotee will die in Terrebonne. (*During the dialogue Wahnotee has taken George's gun.*)

(*Enter George*)

GEORGE.   Now I'm ready. (*George tries to regain his gun; Wahnotee refuses to give it up; Paul quietly takes it from him and remonstrates with him.*)

DORA.   Zoe, he's going; I want him to stay and make love to me; that's what I came for to-day.

MRS. PEYTON.   George, I can't spare Paul for an hour or two; he must run over to the landing; the steamer from New Orleans passed up the river last night, and if there's a mail they have thrown it ashore.

SUNNYSIDE.   I saw the mail-bags lying in the shed this morning.

MRS. PEYTON.   I expect an important letter from Liverpool; away with you, Paul; bring the mail-bags here.

PAUL.   I'm 'most afraid to take Wahnotee to the shed, there's rum there.

WAHNOTEE.   Rum!

PAUL.   Come, then, but if I catch you drinkin', O, laws a mussey, you'll get snakes! I'll gib it you! now mind. (*Exit with Indian*)

GEORGE.   Come, Miss Dora, let me offer you my arm.

DORA.   Mr. George, I am afraid, if all we hear is true, you have led a dreadful life in Europe.

GEORGE.   That's a challenge to begin a description of my feminine adventures.

DORA.   You have been in love, then?

GEORGE.   Two hundred and forty-nine times! Let me relate you the worst cases.

DORA.   No! no!

GEORGE.   I'll put the naughty parts in French.

DORA.   I won't hear a word! O, you horrible man! go on.

(*Exit George and Dora to house*)

M'CLOSKY.   Now, ma'am, I'd like a little business, if agreeable. I bring you news; your banker, old LaFouche, of New Orleans, is dead; the executors are winding up his affairs, and have foreclosed on all overdue mortgages, so Terrebonne is for sale. Here's the *Picayune* (*producing paper*) with the advertisement.

ZOE.   Terrebonne for sale!

MRS. PEYTON. Terrebonne for sale, and you, sir, will doubtless become its purchaser.

M'CLOSKY. Well, Ma'am, I spose there's no law agin my bidding for it. The more bidders, the better for you. You'll take care, I guess, it don't go too cheap.

MRS. PEYTON. O, sir, I don't value the place for its price, but for the many happy days I've spent here; that landscape, flat and uninteresting though it may be, is full of charm for me; those poor people, born around me, growing up about my heart, have bounded my view of life; and now to lose that homely scene, lose their black, ungainly faces! O, sir, perhaps you should be as old as I am, to feel as I do, when my past life is torn away from me.

M'CLOSKY. I'd be darned glad if somebody would tear my past life away from *me*. Sorry I can't help you, but the fact is, you're in such an all-fired mess that you couldn't be pulled out without a derrick.

MRS. PEYTON. Yes, there is a hope left yet, and I cling to it. The house of Mason Brothers, of Liverpool, failed some twenty years ago in my husband's debt.

M'CLOSKY. They owed him over fifty thousand dollars.

MRS. PEYTON. I cannot find the entry in my husband's accounts; but you, Mr. M'Closky, can doubtless detect it. Zoe, bring here the judge's old desk; it is in the library. (*Exit Zoe to house*)

M'CLOSKY. You don't expect to recover any of this old debt, do you?

MRS. PEYTON. Yes; the firm has recovered itself, and I received a notice two months ago that some settlement might be anticipated.

SUNNYSIDE. Why, with principal and interest this debt has been more than doubled in twenty years.

MRS. PEYTON. But it may be years yet before it will be paid off, if ever.

SUNNYSIDE. If there's a chance of it, there's not a planter round here who wouldn't lend you the whole cash, to keep your name and blood amongst us. Come, cheer up, old friend.

MRS. PEYTON. Ah! Sunnyside, how good you are; so like my poor Peyton. (*Exit Mrs. Peyton and Sunnyside to house*)

M'CLOSKY. Curse their old families—they cut me—a bilious, conceited, thin lot of dried up aristocracy. I hate 'm. Just because my grandfather wasn't some broken-down Virginia transplant, or a stingy old Creole, I ain't fit to sit down to the same meat with them. It makes my blood so hot I feel my heart hiss. I'll sweep these Peytons from this section of the country. Their presence keeps alive the reproach against me that I ruined them; yet, if this money should come. Bah! There's no chance of it. Then, if they go, they'll take Zoe—she'll follow them. Darn that girl; she makes me quiver when I think of her; she's took me for all I'm worth. (*Enter Zoe from house with the desk*) O, here, do you know what the annuity the old judge left you is worth today? Not a picayune.

ZOE. It's surely worth the love that dictated it; here are the papers and accounts. (*Putting it on the table*)

M'CLOSKY. Stop, Zoe; come here! How would you like to rule the house

of the richest planter on Atchapalaga—eh? or say the word, and I'll buy
this old barrack, and you shall be mistress of Terrebonne.

ZOE.   O, sir, do not speak so to me!

M'CLOSKY.   Why not! Look here, these Peytons are bust; cut 'em; I am
rich, jine me; I'll set you up grand, and we'll give these first families here
our dust, until you'll see their white skins shrivel up with hate and rage;
what d'ye say?

ZOE.   Let me pass! O, pray, let me go!

M'CLOSKY.   What, you won't, won't ye? If young George Peyton was to
make you the same offer, you'd jump at it pretty darned quick, I guess.
Come, Zoe, don't be a fool; I'd marry you if I could, but you know I
can't; so just say what you want. Here, then, I'll put back these Peytons
in Terrebonne, and they shall know you done it; yes, they'll have you to
thank for saving them from ruin.

ZOE.   Do you think they would live here on such terms?

M'CLOSKY.   Why not? We'll hire out our slaves, and live on their wages.

ZOE.   But I'm not a slave.

M'CLOSKY.   No; if you were I'd buy you, if you cost all I'm worth.

ZOE.   Let me pass!

M'CLOSKY.   Stop.

(Enter Scudder)

SCUDDER.   Let her pass.

M'CLOSKY.   Eh?

SCUDDER.   Let her pass! *(Takes out his knife. Exit Zoe to house.)*

M'CLOSKY.   Is that you, Mr. Overseer? *(Examines paper)*

SCUDDER.   Yes, I'm here, somewhere, interferin'.

M'CLOSKY.   *(Sitting)* A pretty mess you've got this estate in—

SCUDDER.   Yes—me and Co.—we done it; but, as you were senior partner
in the concern, I reckon you got the big lick.

M'CLOSKY.   What d'ye mean?

SCUDDER.   Let me proceed by illustration. *(Sits)* Look thar! *(Points with
knife)* D'ye see that tree?—it's called a live oak, and is a native here; beside it grows a creeper; year after year that creeper twines its long arms
round and round the tree—sucking the earth dry all about its roots—living
on its life—overrunning its branches, until at last the live oak withers
and dies out. Do you know what the niggers round here call that sight?
they call it the Yankee hugging the Creole. *(Sits)*

M'CLOSKY.   Mr. Scudder, I've listened to a great many of your insinua-
tions, and now I'd like to come to an understanding what they mean. If
you want a quarrel—

SCUDDER.   No, I'm the skurriest crittur at a fight you ever see; my legs
have been too well brought up to stand and see my body abused; I take
good care of myself, I can tell you.

M'CLOSKY.   Because I heard that you had traduced my character.

SCUDDER. Traduced! Whoever said so lied. I always said you were the darndest thief that ever escaped a white jail to misrepresent the North to the South.

M'CLOSKY. (*Raises hand to back of his neck*) What!

SCUDDER. Take your hand down—take it down. (*M'Closky lowers his hand.*) Whenever I gets into company like yours, I always start with the advantage on my side.

M'CLOSKY. What d'ye mean?

SCUDDER. I mean that before you could draw that bowie-knife, you wear down your back, I'd cut you into shingles. Keep quiet, and let's talk sense. You wanted to come to an understanding, and I'm coming thar as quick as I can. Now, Jacob McClosky, you despise me because you think I'm a fool; I despise you because I know you to be a knave. Between us we've ruined these Peytons; you fired the judge, and I finished off the widow. Now, I feel bad about my share in the business. I'd give half the balance of my life to wipe out my part of the work. Many a night I've laid awake and thought how to pull them through, till I've cried like a child over the sum I couldn't do; and you know how darned hard 'tis to make a Yankee cry.

M'CLOSKY. Well, what's that to me?

SCUDDER. Hold on, Jacob, I'm coming to that—I tell ye, I'm such a fool—I can't bear the feeling, it keeps at me like a skin complaint, and if this family is sold up—

M'CLOSKY. What then?

SCUDDER. (*Rising*) I'd cut my throat—or yours—yours I'd prefer.

M'CLOSKY. Would you now? why don't you do it?

SCUDDER. 'Cos I's skeered to try! I never killed a man in my life—and civilization is so strong in me I guess I couldn't do it—I'd like to, though!

M'CLOSKY. And all for the sake of that old woman and that young puppy —eh? No other cause to hate—to envy me—to be jealous of me—eh?

SCUDDER. Jealous? what for?

M'CLOSKY. Ask the color in your face: d'ye think I can't read you, like a book? With your New England hypocrisy, you would persuade yourself that it was this family alone you cared for; it ain't—you know it ain't— 'tis the "Octoroon"; and you love her as I do; and you hate me because I'm your rival—that's where the tears come from, Salem Scudder, if you ever shed any—that's where the shoe pinches.

SCUDDER. Wal, I do like the gal; she's a—

M'CLOSKY. She's in love with young Peyton; it made me curse whar it made you cry, as it does now; I see the tears on your cheeks now.

SCUDDER. Look at 'em, Jacob, for they are honest water from the well of truth. I ain't ashamed of it—I do love the gal; but I ain't jealous of you, because I believe the only sincere feeling about you is your love for Zoe, and it does your heart good to have her image thar; but I believe you put it thar to spile. By fair means I don't think you can get her, and don't you try foul with her, 'cause if you do, Jacob, civilization be darned, I'm on you like a painter, and when I'm drawed out I'm pizin. (*Exit Scudder to house*)

M'CLOSKY.   Fair or foul, I'll have her—take that home with you! (*Opens desk*) What's here—judgments? yes, plenty of em; bill of costs; account with Citizens' Bank—what's this? "Judgment, $40,000, 'Thibodeaux against Peyton,'"—surely, that is the judgment under which this estate is now advertised for sale—(*Takes up paper and examines it*) yes, "Thibodeaux against Peyton, 1838." Hold on! whew! this is worth taking to—in this desk the judge used to keep one paper I want—this should be it. (*Reads*) "The free papers of my daughter Zoe, registered February 4th, 1841." Why, judge, wasn't you lawyer enough to know that while a judgment stood against you it was a lien on your slaves? Zoe is your child by a quadroon slave, and you didn't free her; blood! if this is so, she's mine! this old Liverpool debt—that may cross me—if it only arrive too late—if it don't come by this mail—Hold on! this letter the old lady expects—that's it; let me only head off that letter, and Terrebonne will be sold before they can recover it. That boy and the Indian have gone down to the landing for the postbags; they'll idle on the way as usual; my mare will take me across the swamp, and before they can reach the shed, I'll have purified them bags—ne'er a letter shall show this mail. Ha, ha!—(*Calls*) Pete, you old turkey-buzzard, saddle my mare. Then, if I sink every dollar I'm worth in her purchase, I'll own that Octoroon. (*Stands with his hands extended towards the house, and tableau*)

END OF THE FIRST ACT.

ACT II.

The Wharf—goods, boxes, and bales scattered about—a camera on a stand. Scudder, Dora, George and Paul discovered; Dora being photographed by Scudder, who is arranging photographic apparatus, George and Paul looking on at back.

SCUDDER.   Just turn your face a leetle this way—fix your—let's see—look here.

DORA.   So?

SCUDDER.   That's right. (*Puts his head under the darkening apron*) It's such a long time since I did this sort of thing, and this old machine has got so dirty and stiff, I'm afraid it won't operate. That's about right. Now don't stir.

PAUL.   Ugh! she looks as though she war gwine to have a tooth drawed!

SCUDDER.   I've got four plates ready, in case we miss the first shot. One of them is prepared with a self-developing liquid that I've invented. I hope it will turn out better than most of my notions. Now fix yourself. Are you ready?

DORA. Ready!

SCUDDER. Fire!—one, two, three. (*Scudder takes out watch.*)

PAUL. Now it's cooking; laws mussey! I feel it all inside, as if I was at a lottery.

SCUDDER. So! (*Throws down apron*) That's enough. (*Withdraws slide, turns and sees Paul*) What! what are you doing there, you young varmint! Ain't you took them bags to the house yet?

PAUL. Now, it ain't no use trying to get mad, Mas'r Scudder. I'm gwine! I only come back to find Wahnotee; whar is dat ign'ant Ingiun?

SCUDDER. You'll find him scenting round the rum store, hitched up by the nose. (*Exit into room*)

PAUL. (*Calling at door*) Say, Mas'r Scudder, take me in dat telescope?

SCUDDER. (*Inside room*) Get out, you cub! clar out!

PAUL. You got four of dem dishes ready. Gosh, wouldn't I like to hab myself took! What's de charge, Mas'r Scudder? (*Runs off*)

(*Enter Scudder from room*)

SCUDDER. Job had none of them critters on his plantation, else he'd never ha' stood through so many chapters. Well, that has come out clear, ain't it? (*Shows plate*)

DORA. O, beautiful! Look, Mr. Peyton.

GEORGE. (*Looking*) Yes, very fine!

SCUDDER. The apparatus can't mistake. When I travelled round with this machine, the homely folks used to sing out, "Hillo, mister, this ain't like me!" "Ma'am," says I, "the apparatus can't mistake." "But, mister, that ain't my nose." "Ma'am, your nose drawed it. The machine can't err— you may mistake your phiz but the apparatus don't." "But, sir, it ain't agreeable." "No, ma'am, the truth seldom is."

(*Enter Pete, puffing*)

PETE. Mas'r Scudder! Mas'r Scudder!

SCUDDER. Hillo! what are you blowing about like a steamboat with one wheel for?

PETE. *You* blow, Mas'r Scudder, when I tole you: dere's a man from Noo Aleens just arriv' at de house, and he's stuck up two papers on de gates: "For sale—dis yer property," and a heap of oder tings—and he seen missus, and arter he shown some papers she burst out crying—I yelled; den de corious of little niggers dey set up, den de hull plantation children—de live stock reared up and created a purpiration of lamentation as did de ole heart good to har.

DORA. What's the matter?

SCUDDER.   He's come.

PETE.   Dass it—I saw 'm!

SCUDDER.   The sheriff from New Orleans has taken possession—Terrebonne is in the hands of the law.

(Enter Zoe)

ZOE.   O, Mr. Scudder! Dora! Mr. Peyton! come home—there are strangers in the house.

DORA.   Stay, Mr. Peyton: Zoe, a word! *(Leads her forward—Aside)* Zoe, the more I see of George Peyton the better I like him; but he is too modest —that is a very impertinent virtue in a man.

ZOE.   I'm no judge, dear.

DORA.   Of course not, you little fool; no one ever made love to you, and you can't understand; I mean, that George knows I am an heiress; my fortune would release this estate from debt.

ZOE.   O, I see!

DORA.   If he would only propose to marry me I would accept him, but he don't know that, and he will go on fooling, in his slow European way, until it is too late.

ZOE.   What's to be done?

DORA.   You tell him.

ZOE.   What? that he isn't to go on fooling in his slow—

DORA.   No, you goose! twit him on his silence and abstraction—I'm sure it's plain enough, for he has not spoken two words to me all the day; then joke round the subject, and at last speak out.

SCUDDER.   Pete, as you came here, did you pass Paul and the Indian with the letter-bags?

PETE.   No, sar; but dem vagabonds neber take the 'spectable straight road, dey goes by de swamp. *(Exit up path)*

SCUDDER.   Come, sir!

DORA.   *(To Zoe)* Now's your time.—*(Aloud)* Mr. Scudder, take us with you—Mr. Peyton is so slow, there's no getting him on. *(Exit Dora and Scudder)*

ZOE.   They are gone!—*(Glancing at George)* Poor fellow, he has lost all.

GEORGE.   Poor child! how sad she looks now she has no resource.

ZOE.   How shall I ask him to stay?

GEORGE.   Zoe, will you remain here? I wish to speak to you.

ZOE.   *(Aside)* Well, that saves trouble.

GEORGE.   By our ruin you lose all.

ZOE.   O, I'm nothing; think of yourself.

GEORGE.   I can think of nothing but the image that remains face to face with me; so beautiful, so simple, so confiding, that I dare not express the feelings that have grown up so rapidly in my heart.

ZOE.   *(Aside)* He means Dora.

GEORGE. If I dared to speak!

ZOE. That's just what you must do, and do it at once, or it will be too late.

GEORGE. Has my love been divined?

ZOE. It has been more than suspected.

GEORGE. Zoe, listen to me, then. I shall see this estate pass from me without a sigh, for it possesses no charm for me; the wealth I covet is the love of those around me—eyes that are rich in fond looks, lips that breathe endearing words; the only estate I value is the heart of one true woman, and the slaves I'd have are her thoughts.

ZOE. George, George, your words take away my breath!

GEORGE. The world, Zoe, the free struggle of minds and hands, is before me; the education bestowed on me by my dear uncle is a noble heritage which no sheriff can seize; with that I can build up a fortune, spread a roof over the heads I love, and place before them the food I have earned; I will work—

ZOE. Work! I thought none but colored people worked.

GEORGE. Work, Zoe, is the salt that gives savor to life.

ZOE. Dora said you were slow; if she could hear you now—

GEORGE. Zoe, you are young; your mirror must have told you that you are beautiful. Is your heart free?

ZOE. Free? of course it is!

GEORGE. We have known each other but a few days, but to me those days have been worth all the rest of my life. Zoe, you have suspected the feeling that now commands an utterance—you have seen that I love you.

ZOE. Me! you love *me?*

GEORGE. As my wife,—the sharer of my hopes, my ambitions, and my sorrows; under the shelter of your love I could watch the storms of fortune pass unheeded by.

ZOE. *My* love! *My* love? George, you know not what you say! *I* the sharer of your sorrows—your wife! Do you know what I am?

GEORGE. Your birth—I know it. Has not my dear aunt forgotten it—she who had the most right to remember it? You are illegitimate, but love knows no prejudice.

ZOE. (*Aside*) Alas! he does not know, he does not know! and will despise me, spurn me, loathe me, when he learns who, what, he has so loved.— (*Aloud*) George, O, forgive me? Yes, I love you—I did not know it until your words showed me what has been in my heart; each of them awoke a new sense, and now I know how unhappy—how very unhappy—how very unhappy I am.

GEORGE. Zoe, what have I said to wound you?

ZOE. Nothing; but you must learn what I thought you already knew. George, you cannot marry me; the laws forbid it!

GEORGE. Forbid it?

ZOE. There is a gulf between us, as wide as your love, as deep as my despair; but, O, tell me, say you will pity me! that you will not throw me from you like a poisoned thing!

GEORGE. Zoe, explain yourself—your language fills me with shapeless fears.

ZOE. And what shall I say? I—my mother was—no, no—not her! Why should I refer the blame to her? George, do you see that hand you hold? look at these fingers; do you see the nails are of a bluish tinge?

GEORGE. Yes, near the quick there is a faint blue mark.

ZOE. Look in my eyes; is not the same color in the white?

GEORGE. It is their beauty.

ZOE. Could you see the roots of my hair you would see the same dark, fatal mark. Do you know what that is?

GEORGE. No.

ZOE. That is the ineffaceable curse of Cain. Of the blood that feeds my heart, one drop in eight is black—bright red as the rest may be, that one drop poisons all the flood; those seven bright drops give me love like yours—hope like yours—ambition like yours—life hung with passions like dew-drops on the morning flowers; but the one black drop gives me despair, for I'm an unclean thing—forbidden by the laws—I'm an Octoroon!

GEORGE. Zoe, I love you none the less; this knowledge brings no revolt to my heart, and I can overcome the obstacle.

ZOE. But *I* cannot.

GEORGE. We can leave this country, and go far away where none can know.

ZOE. And your mother, she who from infancy treated me with such fondness, she who, as you said, has most reason to spurn me, can she forget what I am? Will she gladly see you wedded to the child of her husband's slave? No! she would revolt from it, as all but you would; and if I consented to hear the cries of my heart, if I did not crush out my infant love, what would she say to the poor girl on whom she had bestowed so much? No, no!

GEORGE. Zoe, must we immolate our lives on her prejudice?

ZOE. Yes, for I'd rather be black than ungrateful! Ah, George, our race has at least one virtue—it knows how to suffer!

GEORGE. Each word you utter makes my love sink deeper into my heart.

ZOE. And I remained here to induce you to offer that heart to Dora!

GEORGE. If you bid me do so I will obey you—

ZOE. No, no! if you cannot be mine, O, let me not blush when I think of you.

GEORGE. Dearest Zoe! (*Exit George and Zoe*)

(*As they exit, M'Closky rises from behind rock and looks after them.*)

M'CLOSKY. She loves him! I felt it—and how she can love! (*Advances*) That one black drop of blood burns in her veins and lights up her heart like a foggy sun. O, how I lapped up her words, like a thirsty blood-hound! I'll have her, if it costs me my life! Yonder the boy still lurks with those mail-bags; the devil still keeps him here to tempt me, darn his yellow skin! I arrived just too late, he had grabbed the prize as I came up. Hillo! he's coming this way, fighting with his Injiun. (*Conceals himself*)

(*Enter Paul, wrestling with Wahnotee*)

PAUL. It ain't no use now: you got to gib it up!

WAHNOTEE. Ugh!

PAUL. It won't do! You got dat bottle of rum hid under your blanket—gib it up now, you—. Yar! (*Wrenches it from him*) You nasty, lying Injiun! It's no use you putting on airs; I ain't gwine to sit up wid you all night and you drunk. Hillo! war's de crowd gone? And dars de 'paratus—O, gosh, if I could take a likeness ob dis child! Uh—uh, let's have a peep. (*Looks through camera*) O, golly! yar, you Wahnotee! you stan' dar, I see you. Ta demine usti. (*Looks at Wahnotee through the camera; Wahnotee springs back with an expression of alarm.*)

WAHNOTEE. No tue Wahnotee.

PAUL. Ha, ha! he tinks it's a gun. You ign'ant Injiun, it can't hurt you! Stop, here's dem dishes—plates—dat's what he call 'em, all fix: I see Mas'r Scudder do it often—tink I can take likeness—stay dere, Wahnotee.

WAHNOTEE. No, carabine tue.

PAUL. I must operate and take my own likeness too—how debbel I do dat? Can't be ober dar an' here too—I ain't twins. Ugh! ach! 'Top; you look, you Wahnotee; you see dis rag, eh? Well, when I say go, den lift dis rag like dis, see! den run to dat pine tree up dar (*Points*) and back agin, and den pull down de rag so, d'ye see?

WAHNOTEE. Hugh!

PAUL. Den you hab glass ob rum.

WAHNOTEE. Rum!

PAUL. Dat wakes him up. Coute Wahnotee in omenee dit go Wahnotee, poina la fa, comb a pine tree, la revieut sala, la fa.

WAHNOTEE. Fire-water!

PAUL. Yes, den a glass ob fire-water; now den. (*Throws mail-bags down and sits on them*) Pret, now, den go. (*Wahnotee raises apron and runs off. Paul sits for his picture—M'Closky appears.*)

M'CLOSKY. Where are they? Ah, yonder goes the Indian!

PAUL. De time he gone just 'bout enough to cook dat dish plate.

M'CLOSKY. Yonder is the boy—now is my time! What's he doing; is he asleep? (*Advances*) He is sitting on my prize! darn his carcass! I'll clear him off there—he'll never know what stunned him. (*Takes Indian's tomahawk and steals to Paul*)

PAUL. Dam dat Injiun! is dat him creeping dar? I daren't move fear to spile myself. (*M'Closky strikes him on the head—he falls dead.*)

M'CLOSKY.   Hooraw! the bags are mine—now for it!—(*Opens mail-bags*)
What's here? Sunnyside, Pointdexter, Jackson, Peyton; here it is—the
Liverpool postmark, sure enough!—(*Opens letter—reads*) "Madam, we
are instructed by the firm of Mason and Co., to inform you that a dividend
of forty per cent. is payable on the 1st proximo, this amount in consideration of position, they send herewith, and you will find enclosed by draft
to your order, on the Bank of Louisiana which please acknowledge—the
balance will be paid in full, with interest, in three, six, and nine months—
your drafts on Mason Brothers at those dates will be accepted by La
Palisse and Compagnie, N.O., so that you may command immediate use
of the whole amount at once, if required. Yours, etc., James Brown."
What a find! this infernal letter would have saved all. (*During the reading of letter he remains nearly motionless under the focus of the camera.*)
But now I guess it will arrive too late—these darned U.S. mails are to
blame. The injiun! he must not see me. (*Exit rapidly*)

(*Wahnotee runs on, pulls down apron—sees Paul, lying on ground—
speaks to him—thinks he's shamming sleep—gesticulates and jab-
bers—goes to him—moves him with feet, then kneels down to rouse
him—to his horror finds him dead—expresses great grief—raises his
eyes—they fall upon the camera—rises with savage growl, seizes tomahawk and smashes camera to pieces, then goes to Paul—expresses
grief, sorrow, and fondness, and takes him in his arms to carry him
away.—Tableau.*)

END OF THE SECOND ACT.

ACT III.

*A Room in Mrs. Peyton's house.—An auction bill is stuck up at the
entrance.—Solon and Grace discovered.*

PETE.   (*Outside*) Dis way—dis way.

(*Enter Pete, Pointdexter, Jackson, Lafouche, and Caillou*)

PETE.   Dis way, gen'l'men; now, Solon—Grace—dey's hot and tirsty—
sangaree, brandy, rum.
JACKSON.   Well, what d'ye say, Lafouche—d'ye smile?

(*Enter Thibodeaux and Sunnyside*)

THIBODEAUX.   I hope we don't intrude on the family.

PETE.   You see dat hole in dar, sar? I was raised on dis yar plantation—nebber see no door in it—always open, sar, for stranger to walk in.

SUNNYSIDE.   And for substance to walk out.

(*Enter Ratts*)

RATTS.   Fine southern style that, eh!

LAFOUCHE.   (*Reading bill*) "A fine, well-built old family mansion, replete with every comfort."

RATTS.   There's one name on the list of slaves scratched, I see.

LAFOUCHE.   Yes; No. 49, Paul, a quadroon boy, aged thirteen.

SUNNYSIDE.   He's missing.

POINTDEXTER.   Run away, I suppose.

PETE.   (*Indignantly*) No, sar; nigger neber cut stick on Terrebonne; dat boy's dead, sure.

RATTS.   What, Picayune Paul, as we called him, that used to come aboard my boat?—poor little darkey, I hope not; many a picayune he picked up for his dance and nigger songs, and he supplied our table with fish and game from the Bayous.

PETE.   Nebber supply no more, sar—nebber dance again. Mas'r Ratts, you hard him sing about de place where de good niggers go, de last time.

RATTS.   Well!

PETE.   Well, he gone dar hisself; why I tink so—'cause we missed Paul for some days, but nebber tout nothin' til one night dat Injiun Wahnotee suddenly stood right dar 'mongst us—was in his war paint, and mighty cold and grave—he sit down by de fire. "Whar's Paul?" I say—he smoke and smoke, but nebber look out ob de fire; well, knowing dem critters, I wait a long time—den he say, "Wahnotee great chief"; den I say nothing —smoke anoder time—last, rising to go, he turn round at door, and say berry low—O, like a woman's voice he say, "Omenee Pangeuk,"—dat is, Paul is dead—nebber see him since.

RATTS.   That red-skin killed him.

SUNNYSIDE.   So we believe; and so mad are the folks around, if they catch the red-skin they'll lynch him sure.

RATTS.   Lynch him! Darn his copper carcass, I've got a set of Irish deck-hands aboard that just loved that child; and after I tell them this, let them get a sight of the red-skin, I believe they would eat him, tomahawk and all. Poor little Paul!

THIBODEAUX.   What was he worth?

RATTS.   Well, near on five hundred dollars.

PETE.   (*Scandalized*) What, sar! You p'tend to be sorry for Paul, and prize him like dat! Five hundred dollars!—(*To Thibodeaux*) Thousand dollars, Massa Thibodeaux.

(*Enter Scudder*)

SCUDDER.　Gentlemen, the sale takes place at three. Good morning, Colonel. It's near that now, and there's still the sugar-houses to be inspected. Good day, Mr. Thibodeaux—shall we drive down that way? Mr. Lafouche, why, how do you do, sir? you're looking well.

LAFOUCHE.　Sorry I can't return the compliment.

RATTS.　Salem's looking a kinder hollowed out.

SCUDDER.　What, Mr. Ratts, are you going to invest in swamps?

RATTS.　No; I want a nigger.

SCUDDER.　Hush.

PETE.　Eh! wass dat?

SCUDDER.　Mr. Sunnyside, I can't do this job of showin' round the folks; my stomach goes agin it. I want Pete here a minute.

SUNNYSIDE.　I'll accompany them certainly.

SCUDDER.　(*Eagerly*) Will ye? Thank ye; thank ye.

SUNNYSIDE.　We must excuse Scudder, friends. I'll see you round the estate.

(*Enter George and Mrs. Peyton*)

LAFOUCHE.　Good morning, Mrs. Peyton. (*All salute.*)

SUNNYSIDE.　This way, gentlemen.

RATTS.　(*Aside to Sunnyside*) I say, I'd like to say summit soft to the old woman; perhaps it wouldn't go well, would it?

THIBODEAUX.　No, leave it alone.

RATTS.　Darn it, when I see a woman in trouble, I feel like selling the skin off my back. (*Exit Thibodeaux, Sunnyside, Ratts, Pointdexter, Grace, Jackson, Lafouche, Caillou, Solon*)

SCUDDER.　(*Aside to Pete*) Go outside there; listen to what you hear, then go down to the quarters and tell the boys, for I can't do it. O, get out.

PETE.　He said I wan't a nigger. Laws, mussey! What am goin' to cum ob us! (*Exit slowly, as if concealing himself*)

GEORGE.　My dear aunt, why do you not move from this painful scene? Go with Dora to Sunnyside.

MRS. PEYTON.　No, George; your uncle said to me with his dying breath, "Nellie, never leave Terrebonne," and I never *will* leave it, till the law compels me.

SCUDDER.　Mr. George, I'm going to say somethin' that has been chokin' me for some time. I know you'll excuse it. Thar's Miss Dora—that girl's in love with you; yes, sir; her eyes are startin' out of her head with it: now her fortune would redeem a good part of this estate.

MRS. PEYTON.　Why, George, I never suspected this!

GEORGE.　I did, aunt, I confess, but—

MRS. PEYTON.　And you hesitated from motives of delicacy?

SCUDDER.　No, ma'am; here's the plan of it. Mr. George is in love with Zoe.

GEORGE.　Scudder!

MRS. PEYTON. George!

SCUDDER. Hold on, now! things have got so jammed in on top of us, we ain't got time to put kid gloves on to handle them. He loves Zoe, and has found out that she loves him. (*Sighing*) Well, that's all right; but as he can't marry her, and as Miss Dora would jump at him—

MRS. PEYTON. Why didn't you mention this before?

SCUDDER. Why, because I love Zoe, too, and I couldn't take that young feller from her; and she's just living on the sight of him, as I saw her do; and they so happy in spite of this yer misery around them, and they reproachin' themselves with not feeling as they ought. I've seen it, I tell you; and darn it, ma'am, can't you see that's what's been a hollowing me out so—I beg your pardon.

MRS. PEYTON. O, George,—my son, let me call you,—I do not speak for my own sake, nor for the loss of the estate, but for the poor people here: they will be sold, divided, and taken away—they have been born here. Heaven has denied me children; so all the strings of my heart have grown around and amongst them, like the fibres and roots of an old tree in its native earth. O, let all go, but save them! With them around us, if we have not wealth, we shall at least have the home that they alone can make—

GEORGE. My dear mother—Mr. Scudder—you teach me what I ought to do; if Miss Sunnyside will accept me as I am, Terrebonne shall be saved: I will sell myself, but the slaves shall be protected.

MRS. PEYTON. *Sell* yourself, George! Is not Dora worth any man's—

SCUDDER. Don't say that, ma'am; don't say that to a man that loves another gal. He' going to do an heroic act; don't spile it.

MRS. PEYTON. But Zoe is only an Octoroon.

SCUDDER. She's won this race agin the white, anyhow; it's too late now to start her pedigree. (*Seeing Dora*) Come, Mrs. Peyton, take my arm. Hush! here's the other one; she's a little too thoroughbred—too much of the greyhound; but the heart's there, I believe. (*Exit Scudder and Mrs. Peyton*)

DORA. Poor Mrs. Peyton.

GEORGE. Miss Sunnyside, permit me a word: a feeling of delicacy has suspended upon my lips an avowal, which—

DORA. (*Aside*) O, dear, has he suddenly come to his senses?

(*Enter Zoe; she stops at back.*)

GEORGE. In a word, I have seen and admired you!

DORA. (*Aside*) He has a strange way of showing it. European, I suppose.

GEORGE. If you would pardon the abruptness of the question, I would ask you, Do you think the sincere devotion of my life to make yours happy would succeed?

DORA. (*Aside*) Well, he has the oddest way of making love.

GEORGE. You are silent?

DORA. Mr. Peyton, I presume you have hesitated to make this avowal because you feared, in the present condition of affairs here, your object might be misconstrued, and that your attention was rather to my fortune than myself. (*A pause*) Why don't he speak?—I mean, you feared I might not give you credit for sincere and pure feelings. Well, you wrong me. I don't think you capable of anything else but—

GEORGE. No, I hesitated because an attachment I had formed before I had the pleasure of seeing you had not altogether died out.

DORA. (*Smiling*) Some of those sirens of Paris, I presume. (*Pause*) I shall endeavor not to be jealous of the past; perhaps I have no right to be. (*Pause*) But now that vagrant love is—eh? faded—is it not? Why don't you speak, sir?

GEORGE. Because, Miss Sunnyside, I have not learned to lie.

DORA. Good gracious—who wants you to?

GEORGE. I do, but I can't do it. No, the love I speak of is not such as you suppose,—it is a passion that has grown up here since I arrived; but it is a hopeless, mad, wild feeling, that must perish.

DORA. Here! since you arrived! Impossible: you have seen no one; whom can you mean?

ZOE. (*Advancing*) Me.

GEORGE. Zoe!

DORA. You!

ZOE. Forgive him, Dora; for he knew no better until I told him. Dora, you are right. He is incapable of any but sincere and pure feelings—so are you. He loves me—what of that? You know you can't be jealous of a poor creature like me. If he caught the fever, were stung by a snake, or possessed of any other poisonous or unclean thing, you could pity, tend, love him through it, and for your gentle care he would love you in return. Well, is he not thus afflicted now? I am his love—he loves an Octoroon.

GEORGE. O, Zoe, you break my heart!

DORA. At college they said I was a fool—I must be. At New Orleans, they said, "She's pretty, very pretty, but no brains." I'm afraid they must be right; I can't understand a word of all this.

ZOE. Dear Dora, try to understand it with your heart. You love George; you love him dearly; I know it; and you deserve to be loved by him. He will love you—he must. His love for me will pass away—it shall. You heard him say it was hopeless. O, forgive him and me!

DORA. (*Weeping*) O, why did he speak to me at all then? You've made me cry, then, and I hate you both! (*Exit through room*)

(*Enter Mrs. Peyton and Scudder, M'Closky and Pointdexter*)

M'CLOSKY. I'm sorry to intrude, but the business I came upon will excuse me.

MRS. PEYTON. Here is my nephew, sir.

ZOE. Perhaps I had better go.

M'CLOSKY. Wal, as it consarns you, perhaps you better had.

SCUDDER. Consarns Zoe?

M'CLOSKY. I don't know; she may as well hear the hull of it. Go on, Colonel—Colonel Pointdexter, ma'am—the mortgagee, auctioneer, and general agent.

POINTDEXTER. Pardon me, madam, but do you know these papers? (*Hands papers to Mrs. Peyton*)

MRS. PEYTON. (*Takes them*) Yes, sir; they were the free papers of the girl Zoe; but they were in my husband's secretary. How came they in your possession?

M'CLOSKY. I—I found them.

GEORGE. And you purloined them?

M'CLOSKY. Hold on, you'll see. Go on, Colonel.

POINTDEXTER. The list of your slaves is incomplete—it wants one.

SCUDDER. The boy Paul—we know it.

POINTDEXTER. No, sir; you have omitted the Octoroon girl, Zoe.

MRS. PEYTON. ⎱ Zoe!
ZOE. ⎰ Me!

POINTDEXTER. At the time the judge executed those free papers to his infant slave, a judgment stood recorded against him; while that was on record he had no right to make away with his property. That judgment still exists: under it and others this estate is sold today. Those free papers ain't worth the sand that's on 'em.

MRS. PEYTON. Zoe a slave! It is impossible!

POINTDEXTER. It is certain, madam: the judge was negligent, and doubtless forgot this small formality.

SCUDDER. But the creditors will not claim the gal?

M'CLOSKY. Excuse me; one of the principal mortgagees has made the demand. (*Exit M'Closky and Pointdexter*)

SCUDDER. Hold on yere, George Peyton; you sit down there. You're trembling so, you'll fall down directly. This blow has staggered me some.

MRS. PEYTON. O, Zoe, my child! don't think too hardly of your poor father.

ZOE. I shall do so if you weep. See, I'm calm.

SCUDDER. Calm as a tombstone, and with about as much life. I see it in your face.

GEORGE. It cannot be! It shall not be!

SCUDDER. Hold your tongue—it must. Be calm—darn the things; the proceeds of this sale won't cover the debts of the estate. Consarn those Liverpool English fellers, why couldn't they send something by the last mail? Even a letter, promising something—such is the feeling round amongst the planters. Darn me, if I couldn't raise thirty thousand on the envelope alone, and ten thousand more on the postmark.

GEORGE. Zoe, they shall not take you from us while I live.

SCUDDER. Don't be a fool; they'd kill you, and then take her, just as soon as—stop: old Sunnyside, he'll buy her! that'll save her.

ZOE.   No, it won't; we have confessed to Dora that we love each other. How can she then ask her father to free me?
SCUDDER.   What in thunder made you do that?
ZOE.   Because it was the truth; and I had rather be a slave with a free soul, than remain free with a slavish, deceitful heart. My father gives me freedom—at least he thought so. May Heaven bless him for the thought, bless him for the happiness he spread around my life. You say the proceeds of the sale will not cover his debts. Let me be sold then, that I may free his name. I give him back the liberty he bestowed upon me; for I can never repay him the love he bore his poor Octoroon child, on whose breast his last sigh was drawn, into whose eyes he looked with the last ·gaze of affection.
MRS. PEYTON.   O, my husband! I thank Heaven you have not lived to see this day.
ZOE.   George, leave me! I would be alone a little while.
GEORGE.   Zoe! (*Turns away overpowered*)
ZOE.   Do not weep, George. Dear George, you now see what a miserable thing I am.
GEORGE.   Zoe!
SCUDDER.   I wish they could sell *me*! I brought half this ruin on this family, with my all-fired improvements. I deserve to be a nigger this day— I feel like one, inside. (*Exit Scudder*)
ZOE.   Go now, George—leave me—take her with you. (*Exit Mrs. Peyton and George*) A slave! a slave! Is this a dream—for my brain reels with the blow? He said so. What! then I shall be sold!—sold! and my master— O! (*Falls on her knees, with her face in her hands*) no—no master but one. George—George—hush—they come! save me! No, (*Looks off*) 'tis Pete and the servants—they come this way. (*Enters inner room*)

(*Enter Pete, Grace, Minnie, Solon, Dido, and all slaves*)

PETE.   Cum yer now—stand round, 'cause I've got to talk to you darkies— keep dem chil'n quiet—don't make no noise, de missus up dar har us.
SOLON.   Go on, Pete.
PETE.   Gen'l'men, my colored frens and ladies, dar's mighty bad news gone round. Dis yer prop'ty to be sold—old Terrebonne—whar we all been raised, is gwine—dey's gwine to tak it away—can't stop here nohow.
OMNES.   O-o!—O-o!
PETE.   Hold quiet, you trash o' niggers! tink anybody wants you to cry? Who's you to set up screeching?—be quiet! But dis ain't all. Now, my cullud brethren, gird up your lines, and listen—hold on yer bref—it's a comin'. We tought dat de niggers would belong to de ole missus, and if she lost Terrebonne, we must live dere allers, and we would hire out, and bring our wages to Ole Missus Peyton.
OMNES.   Ya! ya! Well—

PETE. Hush! I tell ye, 'tain't so—we can't do it—we've got to be sold—
OMNES. Sold!
PETE. Will you hush? she will har you. Yes! I listen dar jess now—was ole lady cryin'—Mas'r George—ah! you seen dem big tears in his eyes. O, Mas'r Scudder, he didn't cry zackly; both ob his eyes and cheek look like de bad Bayou in low season—so dry dat I cry for him. (*Raising his voice*) Den say de missus, "'Tain't for de land I keer, but for dem poor niggers—dey'll be sold—dat wot stagger me." "No," say Mas'r George, "I'd rather sell myself fuss; but dey shan't suffer nohow,—I see 'em dam fuss."
OMNES. O, bless 'um! Bless Mas'r George.
PETE. Hole yer tongues. Yes, for you, for me, for dem little ones, dem folks cried. Now, den, if Grace dere wid her chil'n were all sold, she'll begin screechin' like a cat. She didn't mind how kind old judge was to her; and Solon, too, he'll holler, and break de ole lady's heart.
GRACE. No, Pete; no, I won't. I'll bear it.
PETE. I don't tink you will any more, but dis here will; 'cause de family spile Dido, dey has. She nebber was worth much a' dat nigger.
DIDO. How dar you say dat, you black nigger, you? I fetch as much as any odder cook in Louisiana.
PETE. What's the use of your takin' it kind, and comfortin' de missus' heart, if Minnie dere, and Louise, and Marie, and Julie is to spile it?
MINNIE. We won't, Pete; we won't.
PETE. (*To the men*) Dar, do ye hear dat, ye mis'able darkies; dem gals is worth a boat load of kinder men dem is. Cum, for de pride of de family, let every darky look his best for the judge's sake—dat ole man so good to us, and dat ole woman—so dem strangers from New Orleans shall say, Dem's happy darkies, dem's a fine set of niggers; every one say when he's sold, "Lor' bless dis yer family I'm gwine out of, and send me as good a home."
OMNES. We'll do it, Pete; we'll do it.
PETE. Hush! hark! I tell ye dar's somebody in dar. Who is it?
GRACE. It's Missy Zoe. See! see!
PETE. Come along; she har what we say, and she's cryin' for us. None o' ye ign'rant niggers could cry for yerselves like dat. Come here quite: now quite. (*Exit Pete and all the Negroes slowly*)

(*Enter Zoe, supposed to have overheard the last scene*)

ZOE. O! must I learn from these poor wretches how much I owe, and how I ought to pay the debt? Have I slept upon the benefits I received, and never saw, never felt, never knew that I was forgetful and ungrateful? O, my father! my dear, dear father! forgive your poor child. You made her life too happy, and now these tears will flow. Let me hide them till I teach my heart. O, my—my heart! (*Exit, with a low, wailing, suffocating cry*)

(Enter M'Closky, Lafouche, Jackson, Sunnyside and Pointdexter)

POINTDEXTER. *(Looking at watch)* Come, the hour is past. I think we may begin business. Where is Mr. Scudder?
JACKSON. I want to get to Ophelensis to-night.

(Enter Dora)

DORA. Father, come here.
SUNNYSIDE. Why, Dora, what's the matter? Your eyes are red.
DORA. Are they? thank you. I don't care, they were blue this morning, but it don't signify now.
SUNNYSIDE. My darling! who has been teasing you?
DORA. Never mind. I want you to buy Terrebonne.
SUNNYSIDE. Buy Terrebonne! What for?
DORA. No matter—buy it!
SUNNYSIDE. It will cost me all I'm worth. This is folly, Dora.
DORA. Is my plantation at Comptableau worth this?
SUNNYSIDE. Nearly—perhaps.
DORA. Sell it, then, and buy this.
SUNNYSIDE. Are you mad, my love?
DORA. Do you want *me* to stop here and *bid* for it?
SUNNYSIDE. Good gracious, no!
DORA. Then I'll do it if you don't.
SUNNYSIDE. I will! I will! But for Heaven's sake go—here comes the crowd. *(Exit Dora)* What on earth does that child mean or want?

(Enter Scudder, George, Ratts, Caillou, Pete, Grace, Minnie, and all the Negroes. A large table is in the center at back. Pointdexter mounts the table with his hammer; his clerk sits at his feet. The Negro mounts the table from behind. The company sit.)

POINTDEXTER. Now, gentlemen, we shall proceed to business. It ain't necessary for me to dilate, describe or enumerate; Terrebonne is known to you as one of the richest bits of sile in Louisiana, and its condition reflects credit on them as had to keep it. I'll trouble you for that piece of baccy, Judge—thank you—so gentlemen, as life is short, we'll start right off. The first lot on here is the estate in block, with its sugar-houses, stock machines, implements, good dwelling-houses and furniture. If there is no bid for the estate and stuff, we'll sell it in smaller lots. Come, Mr. Thibodeaux, a man has a chance once in his life—here's yours.
THIBODEAUX. Go on. What's the reserve bid?
POINTDEXTER. The first mortgagee bids forty thousand dollars.
THIBODEAUX. Forty-five thousand.
SUNNYSIDE. Fifty thousand.
POINTDEXTER. When you have done joking, gentlemen, you'll say one hundred and twenty thousand. It carried that easy on mortgage.

LAFOUCHE.   Then why don't you buy it yourself, Colonel?

POINTDEXTER.   I'm waiting on your fifty thousand bid.

CAILLOU.   Eighty thousand.

POINTDEXTER.   Don't be afraid; it ain't going for that, Judge.

SUNNYSIDE.   Ninety thousand.

POINTDEXTER.   We're getting on.

THIBODEAUX.   One hundred—

POINTDEXTER.   One hundred thousand bid for this mag—

CAILLOU.   One hundred and ten thousand—

POINTDEXTER.   Good again—one hundred and—

SUNNYSIDE.   Twenty.

POINTDEXTER.   And twenty thousand bid. Squire Sunnyside is going to sell this at fifty thousand advance to-morrow.—(*Looks round*) Where's that man from Mobile that wanted to give one hundred and eighty thousand?

THIBODEAUX.   I guess he ain't left home yet, Colonel.

POINTDEXTER.   I shall knock it down to the Squire—going—gone—for one hundred and twenty thousand dollars. (*Raises hammer*) Judge, you can raise the hull on mortgage—going for half its value. (*Knocks*) Squire Sunnyside, you've got a pretty bit o' land, Squire. Hillo, darkey, hand me a smash dar.

SUNNYSIDE.   I got more than I can work now.

POINTDEXTER.   Then buy the hands along with the property. Now, gentlemen, I'm proud to submit to you the finest lot of field hands and house servants that was ever offered for competition: they speak for themselves, and do credit to their owners.—(*Reads*) "No. 1, Solon, a guest boy, and good waiter."

PETE.   That's my son—buy him, Mas'r Ratts; he's sure to sarve you well.

POINTDEXTER.   Hold your tongue!

RATTS.   Let the old darkey alone—eight hundred for that boy.

CAILLOU.   Nine.

RATTS.   A thousand.

SOLON.   Thank you, Mas'r Ratts: I die for you, sar; hold up for me, sar.

RATTS.   Look here, the boy knows and likes me, Judge; let him come my way?

CAILLOU.   Go on—I'm dumb.

POINTDEXTER.   One thousand bid. (*Knocks*) He's yours, Captain Ratts, Magnolia steamer. (*Solon goes down and stands behind Ratts.*) "No. 2, the yellow girl Grace, with two children—Saul, aged four, and Victoria five." (*They get on table.*)

SCUDDER.   That's Solon's wife and children, Judge.

GRACE.   (*To Ratts*) Buy me, Mas'r Ratts, do buy me, sar?

RATTS.   What in thunder should I do with you and those devils on board my boat?

GRACE.   Wash, sar—cook, sar—anyting.

RATTS.   Eight hundred agin, then—I'll go it.

JACKSON.   Nine.

RATTS. I'm broke, Solon—I can't stop the Judge.

THIBODEAUX. What's the matter, Ratts? I'll lend you all you want. Go it, if you're a mind to.

RATTS. Eleven.

JACKSON. Twelve.

SUNNYSIDE. O, O!

SCUDDER. (*To Jackson*) Judge, my friend. The Judge is a little deaf. Hello! (*Speaking in his ear-trumpet*) This gal and them children belong to that boy Solon there. You're bidding to separate them, Judge.

JACKSON. The devil I am! (*Rises*) I'll take back my bid, Colonel.

POINTDEXTER. All right, Judge; I thought there was a mistake. I must keep you, Captain, to the eleven hundred.

RATTS. Go it.

POINTDEXTER. Eleven hundred—going—going—sold! "No. 3, Pete, a house servant."

PETE. Dat's me—yer, I'm comin'—stand around dar. (*Tumbles upon the table*)

POINTDEXTER. Aged seventy-two.

PETE. What's dat? A mistake, sar—forty-six.

POINTDEXTER. Lame.

PETE. But don't mount to nuffin—kin work cannel. Come, Judge, pick up. Now's your time, sar.

JACKSON. One hundred dollars.

PETE. What, sar? me! for me—look ye here! (*Dances*)

GEORGE. Five hundred.

PETE. Mas'r George—ah, no, sar—don't buy me—keep your money for some udder dat is to be sold. I ain't no 'count, sar.

POINTDEXTER. Five hundred bid—it's a good price. (*Knocks*) He's yours, Mr. George Peyton. (*Pete goes down.*) "No. 4, the Octoroon girl, Zoe."

(*Enter Zoe, very pale, and stands on table.—M'Closky hitherto has taken no interest in the sale, now turns his chair.*)

SUNNYSIDE. (*Rising*) Gentlemen, we are all acquainted with the circumstances of this girl's position, and I feel sure that no one here will oppose the family who desires to redeem the child of our esteemed and noble friend, the late Judge Peyton.

OMNES. Hear! bravo! hear!

POINTDEXTER. While the proceeds of this sale promises to realize less than the debts upon it, it is my duty to prevent any collusion for the depreciation of the property.

RATTS. Darn ye! You're a man as well as an auctioneer, ain't ye!

POINTDEXTER. What is offered for this slave?

SUNNYSIDE. One thousand dollars.

M'CLOSKY. Two thousand.

SUNNYSIDE. Three thousand.

M'CLOSKY.   Five thousand.

GEORGE.   Demon!

SUNNYSIDE.   I bid seven thousand, which is the last dollar this family possesses.

M'CLOSKY.   Eight.

THIBODEAUX.   Nine.

OMNES.   Bravo!

M'CLOSKY.   Ten. It's no use, Squire.

SCUDDER.   Jacob M'Closky, you shan't have that girl. Now, take care what you do. Twelve thousand.

M'CLOSKY.   Shan't I! Fifteen thousand. Beat that any of ye.

POINTDEXTER.   Fifteen thousand bid for the Octoroon.

(Enter Dora)

DORA.   Twenty thousand.

OMNES.   Bravo!

M'CLOSKY.   Twenty-five thousand.

OMNES.   *(Groan)* O! O!

GEORGE.   Yelping hound—take that. *(Rushes on M'Closky—M'Closky draws his knife.)*

SCUDDER.   *(Darts between them)* Hold on, George Peyton—stand back. This is your own house; we are under your uncle's roof; recollect yourself. And, strangers, ain't we forgetting there's a lady present? *(The knives disappear.)* If we can't behave like Christians, let's try and act like gentlemen. Go on, Colonel.

LAFOUCHE.   He didn't ought to bid against a lady.

M'CLOSKY.   O, that's it, is it? Then I'd like to hire a lady to go to auction and buy my hands.

POINTDEXTER.   Gentlemen, I believe none of us have two feelings about the conduct of that man; but he has the law on his side—we may regret, but we must respect it. Mr. M'Closky has bid twenty-five thousand dollars for the Octoroon. Is there any other bid? For the first time, twenty-five thousand—last time! *(Brings hammer down)* To Jacob M'Closky, the Octoroon girl, Zoe, twenty-five thousand dollars. *(Tableau)*

END OF ACT THIRD.

ACT IV.

Scene, The Wharf. The Steamer "Magnolia" alongside; a bluff rock; Ratts discovered, superintending the loading of the ship. Enter Lafouche and Jackson.

JACKSON. How long before we start, captain?

RATTS. Just as soon as we put this cotton on board.

(*Enter Pete, with lantern, and Scudder, with note book*)

SCUDDER. One hundred and forty-nine bales. Can you take any more?

RATTS. Not a bale. I've got engaged eight hundred bales at the next landing, and one hundred hogsheads of sugar at Patten's Slide—that'll take my guards under—hurry up thar.

VOICE. (*Outside*) Wood's aboard.

RATTS. All aboard then.

(*Enter M'Closky*)

SCUDDER. Sign that receipt, captain, and save me going up to the clerk.

M'CLOSKY. See here—there's a small freight of turpentine in the fore hold there, and one of the barrels leaks; a spark from your engines might set the ship on fire, and you'll go with it.

RATTS. You be darned! Go and try it, if you've a mind to.

LAFOUCHE. Captain, you've loaded up here until the boat is sunk so deep in the mud she won't float.

RATTS. (*Calls off*) Wood up thar, you Pollo—hang on to the safety valve —guess she'll crawl off on her paddles. (*Shouts heard*)

JACKSON. What's the matter?

(*Enter Solon*)

SOLON. We got him!

SCUDDER. Who?

SOLON. The Injiun!

SCUDDER. Wahnotee? Where is he? D'ye call running away from a fellow catching him?

RATTS. Here he comes.

OMNES. Where? Where?

(*Enter Wahnotee; they are all about to rush on him.*)

SCUDDER. Hold on! stan' round thar! no violence—the critter don't know what we mean.

JACKSON. Let him answer for the boy then.

M'CLOSKY. Down with him—lynch him.

OMNES. Lynch him! (*Exit Lafouche*)

SCUDDER. Stan' back, I say! I'll nip the first that lays a finger on him. Pete, speak to the red-skin.

PETE. Whar's Paul, Wahnotee? What's come ob de child?

WAHNOTEE. Paul wunce—Paul pangeuk.

PETE. Pangeuk—dead!

WAHNOTEE. Mort!

M'CLOSKY. And you killed him? (*They approach again.*)

SCUDDER. Hold on!

PETE. Um, Paul reste?

WAHNOTEE. Hugh vieu. Paul reste ci!

SCUDDER. Here, stay! (*Examines the ground*) The earth has been stirred here lately.

WAHNOTEE. Weenee Paul. (*Points down, and shows by pantomime how he buried Paul*)

SCUDDER. The Injiun means that he buried him there! Stop! here's a bit of leather; (*Draws out mail-bags*) the mail-bags that were lost! (*Sees tomahawk in Wahnotee's belt—draws it out and examines it*) Look! here are marks of blood—look thar, red-skin, what's that?

WAHNOTEE. Paul! (*Makes sign that Paul was killed by a blow on the head*)

M'CLOSKY. He confesses it; the Indian got drunk, quarrelled with him, and killed him.

(*Re-enter Lafouche with smashed apparatus*)

LAFOUCHE. Here are evidences of the crime; this rum-bottle half emptied—this photographic apparatus smashed—and there are marks of blood and footsteps around the shed.

M'CLOSKY. What more d'ye want—ain't that proof enough? Lynch him!

OMNES. Lynch him! Lynch him!

SCUDDER. Stan' back, boys! He's an Injiun—fair play.

JACKSON. Try him, then—try him on the spot of his crime.

OMNES. Try him! Try him!

LAFOUCHE. Don't let him escape!

RATTS. I'll see to that (*Draws revolver*) If he stirs, I'll put a bullet through his skull, mighty quick.

M'CLOSKY. Come, form a court then, choose a jury—we'll fix this varmin.

(*Enter Thibodeaux and Caillou*)

THIBODEAUX. What's the matter?

LAFOUCHE. We've caught this murdering Injiun, and are going to try him. (*Wahnotee sits, rolled in blanket.*)

PETE. Poor little Paul—poor little nigger!

SCUDDER. This business goes agin me, Ratts—'tain't right.

LAFOUCHE. We're ready; the jury's impanelled—go ahead—who'll be accuser?

RATTS. M'Closky.

M'CLOSKY. Me?

RATTS. Yes; you was the first to hail Judge Lynch.

M'CLOSKY. Well, what's the use of argument whar guilt sticks out so plain; the boy and Injiun were alone when last seen.

SCUDDER.　Who says that?

M'CLOSKY.　Everybody—that is, I heard so.

SCUDDER.　Say what you know—not what you heard.

M'CLOSKY.　I know then that the boy was killed with that tomahawk—the redskin owns it—the signs of violence are all round the shed—this apparatus smashed—ain't it plain that in a drunken fit he slew the boy, and when sober concealed the body yonder?

OMNES.　That's it—that's it.

RATTS.　Who defends the Injiun?

SCUDDER.　I will; for it is agin my natur' to b'lieve him guilty; and if he be, this ain't the place, nor you the authority to try him. How are we sure the boy is dead at all? There are no witnesses but a rum bottle and an old machine. Is it on such evidence you'd hang a human being?

RATTS.　His own confession.

SCUDDER.　I appeal against your usurped authority. This lynch law is a wild and lawless proceeding. Here's a pictur' for a civilized community to afford; yonder, a poor, ignorant savage, and round him a circle of hearts, white with revenge and hate, thirsting for his blood: you call yourself judges—you ain't—you're a jury of executioners. It is such scenes as these that bring disgrace upon our Western life.

M'CLOSKY.　Evidence! Evidence! Give us evidence. We've had talk enough; now for proof.

OMNES.　Yes, yes! Proof, proof!

SCUDDER.　Where am I to get it? The proof is here, in my heart.

PETE.　(*Who has been looking about the camera*) 'Top, sar! 'Top a bit! O, laws-a-mussey, see dis! here's a pictur' I found stickin' in that yar telescope machine, sar! look sar!

SCUDDER.　A photographic plate. (*Pete holds lantern up.*) What's this, eh? two forms! The child—'tis he! dead—and above him—Ah! ah! Jacob M'Closky, 'twas you murdered that boy!

M'CLOSKY.　Me?

SCUDDER.　You! You slew him with that tomahawk; and as you stood over his body with the letter in your hand, you thought that no witness saw the deed, that no eye was on you—but there was, Jacob M'Closky, there was. The eye of the Eternal was on you—the blessed sun in heaven, that looking down, struck upon this plate the image of the deed. Here you are, in the very attitude of your crime!

M'CLOSKY.　'Tis false!

SCUDDER.　'Tis true! the apparatus can't lie. Look there, jurymen. (*Shows plate to jury*) Look there. O, you wanted evidence—you called for proof—Heaven has answered and convicted you.

M'CLOSKY.　What court of law would receive such evidence? (*Going*)

RATTS.　Stop! *this* would! You called it yourself; you wanted to make us murder that Injiun; and since we've got our hands in for justice, we'll try it on *you*. What say ye? shall we have one law for the red-skin and another for the white?

OMNES.　Try him! Try him!

RATTS. Who'll be accuser?

SCUDDER. I will! Fellow-citizens, you are convened and assembled here under a higher power than the law. What's the law? When the ship's abroad on the ocean, when the army is before the enemy, where in thunder's the law? It is in the hearts of brave men, who can tell right from wrong, and from whom justice can't be bought. So it is here, in the wilds of the West, where our hatred of crime is measured by the speed of our executions—where necessity is law! I say, then, air you honest men? air you true? Put your hands on your naked breasts, and let every man as don't feel a real American heart there, bustin' up with freedom, truth, and right, let that man step out—that's the oath I put to ye—and then say, Darn ye, go it!

OMNES. Go on! Go on!

SCUDDER. No! I won't go on; that man's down. I won't strike him, even with words. Jacob, your accuser is that picter of the crime—let that speak —defend yourself.

M'CLOSKY. (*Draws knife*) I will, quicker than lightning.

RATTS. Seize him, then! (*They rush on M'Closky, and disarm him.*) He can fight though he's a painter: claws all over.

SCUDDER. Stop! Search him, we may find more evidence.

M'CLOSKY. Would you rob me first, and murder me afterwards?

RATTS. (*Searching him*) That's his programme—here's a pocket-book.

SCUDDER. (*Opens it*) What's here? Letters! Hello! To "Mrs. Peyton, Terrebonne, Louisiana, United States." Liverpool postmark. Ho! I've got hold of the tail of a rat—come out. (*Reads*) What's this? A draft for eighty-five thousand dollars, and credit on Palisse and Co., of New Orleans, for the balance. Hi! the rat's out. You killed the boy to steal this letter from the mail-bags—you stole this letter, that the money should not arrive in time to save the Octoroon; had it done so, the lien on the estate would have ceased, and Zoe be free.

OMNES. Lynch him! Lynch him! Down with him!

SCUDDER. Silence in the court; stand back, let the gentlemen of the jury retire, consult, and return their verdict.

RATTS. I'm responsible for the crittur—go on.

PETE. (*To Wahnotee*) See Injiun; look dar, (*Shows him plate*) see dat innocent; look, dar's de murderer of poor Paul.

WAHNOTEE. Ugh! (*Examines plate*)

PETE. Ya! as he? Closky tue Paul—kill de child with your tomahawk dar: 'twasn't you, no—ole Pete allus say so. Poor Injiun lub our little Paul. (*Wahnotee rises and looks at M'Closky—he is in his war paint and fully armed.*)

SCUDDER. What say ye, gentlemen? Is the prisoner guilty, or is he not guilty?

OMNES. Guilty!

SCUDDER. And what is to be his punishment?

OMNES. Death! (*All advance.*)

WAHNOTEE. (*Crosses to M'Closky*) Ugh!

SCUDDER. No, Injiun; we deal out justice here, not revenge. 'Tain't you he has injured, 'tis the white man, whose laws he has offended.

RATTS. Away with him—put him down the aft hatch, till we rig his funeral.

M'CLOSKY. Fifty against one! O! if I had you one by one, alone in the swamp, I'd rip ye all. (*He is borne off in boat struggling.*)

SCUDDER. Now, then, to business.

PETE. (*Re-enters from boat*) O, law, sir, dat debil Closky, he tore hisself from de gen'lam, knock me down, take my light, and trows it on de turpentine barrels, and de shed's all afire! (*Fire seen*)

JACKSON. (*Re-entering*) We are catching fire forward: quick, cut free from the shore.

RATTS. All hands aboard there—cut the starn ropes—give her headway!

ALL. Ay, ay! (*Cry of "fire" heard—Engine bells heard—Steam whistle noise*)

RATTS. Cut all away for'ard—overboard with every bale afire. (*The steamer moves off—fire kept up—M'Closky re-enters, swimming on.*)

M'CLOSKY. Ha! have I fixed ye? Burn! burn! that's right. You thought you had cornered me, did ye? As I swam down, I thought I heard something in the water, as if pursuing me—one of them darned alligators, I suppose—they swarm hereabout—may they crunch every limb of ye. (*Exit*)

(*Wahnotee swims on—finds trail—follows him. The steamer floats on at back, burning. Tableau.*)

END OF ACT FOURTH.

ACT V.

Scene I

Negroes' Quarters. Enter Zoe.

ZOE. It wants an hour yet to daylight—here is Pete's hut—(*Knocks*) He sleeps—no; I see a light.

DIDO. (*Enters from hut*) Who dat?

ZOE. Hush, aunty! 'Tis I—Zoe.

DIDO. Missey Zoe? Why you out in de swamp dis time ob night; you catch de fever sure—you is all wet.

ZOE. Where's Pete?

DIDO. He gone down to de landing last night wid Mas'r Scudder; not come back since—kint make it out.

ZOE. Aunty, there is sickness up at the house; I have been up all night beside one who suffers, and I remembered that when I had the fever you gave me a drink, a bitter drink, that made me sleep—do you remember it?

DIDO. Didn't I? Dem doctors ain't no 'count; dey don't know nuffin.

ZOE. No; but you, aunty, you are wise—you know every plant, don't you, and what it is good for?

DIDO. Dat you drink is fust rate for red fever. Is de folks' head bad?

ZOE. Very bad, aunty; and the heart aches worse, so they can get no rest.

DIDO. Hold on a bit, I get you de bottle. (*Exit*)

ZOE. In a few hours that man, my master, will come for me: he has paid my price, and he only consented to let me remain here this one night, because Mrs. Peyton promised to give me up to him to-day.

DIDO. (*Re-enters with phial*) Here 'tis—now you give one timble-full—dat's nuff.

ZOE. All there is there would kill one, wouldn't it?

DIDO. Guess it kill a dozen—nebber try.

ZOE. It's not a painful death, aunty, is it? You told me it produced a long, long sleep.

DIDO. Why you tremble so? Why you speak so wild? What you's gwine to do, missey?

ZOE. Give me the drink.

DIDO. No. Who dat sick at de house?

ZOE. Give it to me.

DIDO. No. You want to hurt yourself. O, Miss Zoe, why you ask ole Dido for dis pizen?

ZOE. Listen to me. I love one who is here, and he loves me—George. I sat outside his door all night—I heard his sighs—his agony—torn from him by my coming fate; and he said, "I'd rather see her dead than his!"

DIDO. Dead!

ZOE. He said so—then I rose up, and stole from the house, and ran down to the bayou; but its cold, black, silent stream terrified me—drowning must be so horrible a death. I could not do it. Then, as I knelt there, weeping for courage, a snake rattled beside me. I shrunk from it and fled. Death was there beside me, and I dared not take it. O! I'm afraid to die; yet I am more afraid to live.

DIDO. Die!

ZOE. So I came here to you; to you, my own dear nurse; to you, who so often hushed me to sleep when I was a child; who dried my eyes and put your little Zoe to rest. Ah! give me the rest that no master but One can disturb—the sleep from which I shall awake free! You can protect me from that man—do let me die without pain. (*Music*)

DIDO. No, no—life is good for young ting like you.

ZOE. O! good, good nurse: you will, you will.

DIDO. No—g'way.

ZOE. Then I shall never leave Terrebonne—the drink, nurse; the drink; that I may never leave my home—my dear, dear home. You will not give

me to that man? Your own Zoe, that loves you, aunty, so much, so much.—
(*Gets phial*) Ah! I have it.
DIDO.   No, missey. O! no—don't.
ZOE.   Hush! (*Runs off*)
DIDO.   Here, Solon, Minnie, Grace.

(*They enter*)

ALL.   Was de matter?
DIDO.   Miss Zoe got de pizen. (*Exit*)
ALL.   O! O!

(*Exeunt*)

Scene II

*Cane-brake bayou,—Fire in the background. M'Closky discovered
asleep on a bank, a canoe nearby.*

M'CLOSKY.   Burn, burn! blaze away! How the flames crack. I'm not guilty;
would ye murder me? Cut, cut the rope—I choke—choke!—Ah! (*Wakes*)
Hello! where am I? Why, I was dreaming—curse it! I can never sleep
now without dreaming. Hush! I thought I heard the sound of a paddle
in the water. All night, as I fled through the cane-brake, I heard footsteps
behind me. I lost them in the cedar swamp—again they haunted my path
down the bayou, moving as I moved, resting when I rested—hush! there
again!—no; it was only the wind over the canes. The sun is rising. I must
launch my dug-out, and put for the bay, and in a few hours I shall be
safe from pursuit on board of one of the coasting schooners that run from
Galveston to Matagorda. In a little time this darned business will blow
over, and I can show again. Hark! there's that noise again! If it was the
ghost of that murdered boy haunting me! Well—I didn't mean to kill him,
did I? Well, then, what has my all-cowardly heart got to skeer me so
for? (*Music. Gets in canoe and rows off.—Wahnotee paddles canoe on—
gets out and finds trail—paddles off after him.*)

Scene III

Cedar swamp. Enter Scudder and Pete.

SCUDDER.   Come on, Pete, we shan't reach the house before mid-day.
PETE.   Nebber mind, sa, we bring good news—it won't spile for de keeping.

SCUDDER. Ten miles we've had to walk, because some blamed varmin onhitched our dug-out. I left it last night all safe.

PETE. P'r'aps it floated away itself.

SCUDDER. No; the hitching line was cut with a knife.

PETE. Say, Mas'r Scudder, s'pose we go in round by de quarters and raise de darkies, den dey cum long wid us, and we 'proach dat ole house like Gin'ral Jackson when he took London out dar.

SCUDDER. Hello, Pete, I never heard of that affair.

PETE. I tell you, sa—hush!

SCUDDER. What? (*Music*)

PETE. Was dat?—a cry out dar in the swamp—dar agin!

SCUDDER. So it is. Something forcing its way through the undergrowth— it comes this way—it's either a bear or a runaway nigger. (*Draws pistol— M'Closky rushes on and falls at Scudder's feet.*)

SCUDDER. Stand off—what are ye?

PETE. Mas'r Clusky.

M'CLOSKY. Save me—save me! I can go no farther. I heard voices.

SCUDDER. Who's after you?

M'CLOSKY. I don't know, but I feel it's death! In some form, human, or wild beast, or ghost, it has tracked me through the night. I fled; it followed. Hark! there it comes—it comes—don't you hear a footstep on the dry leaves!

SCUDDER. Your crime has driven you mad.

M'CLOSKY. D'ye hear it—nearer—nearer—ah! (*Wahnotee rushes on and at M'Closky.*)

SCUDDER. The Injiun! by thunder.

PETE. You'se a dead man, Mas'r Clusky—you got to b'lieve dat.

M'CLOSKY. No—no. If I must die, give me up to the law; but save me from the tomahawk. You are a white man; you'll not leave one of your own blood to be butchered by the redskin?

SCUDDER. Hold on now, Jacob; we've got to figure on that—let us look straight at the thing. Here we are on the selvage of civilization. It ain't our side, I believe, rightly; but Nature has said that where the white man sets his foot, the red man and the black man shall up sticks and stand around. But what do we pay for that possession? In cash? No—in kind— that is, in protection, forbearance, gentleness, in all them goods that show the critters the difference between the Christian and the savage. Now, what have you done to show them the distinction? for, darn me, if I can find out.

M'CLOSKY. For what I have done, let me be tried.

SCUDDER. You have been tried—honestly tried and convicted. Providence has chosen your executioner. I shan't interfere.

PETE. O, no; Mas'r Scudder, don't leave Mas'r Closky like dat—don't, sa— 'tain't what good Christian should do.

SCUDDER. D'ye hear that, Jacob? This old nigger, the grandfather of the boy you murdered, speaks for you—don't that go through you? D'ye feel it? Go on, Pete, you've waked up the Christian here, and the old hoss responds. (*Throws bowie-knife to M'Closky.*) Take that, and defend yourself. (*Exit Scudder and Pete—Wahnotee faces him.—Fight.—M'Closky runs off.—Wahnotee follows him.—Screams outside.*)

Scene IV

Parlor at Terrebonne. Enter Zoe. Music.

ZOE.   My home, my home! I must see you no more. Those little flowers can live, but I cannot. To-morrow they'll bloom the same—all will be here as now, and I shall be cold. O! my life, my happy life, why has it been so bright?

(Enter Mrs. Peyton and Dora)

DORA.   Zoe, where have you been?
MRS. PEYTON.   We felt quite uneasy about you.
ZOE.   I've been to the negro quarters. I suppose I shall go before long, and I wished to visit all the places, once again, to see the poor people.
MRS. PEYTON.   Zoe, dear, I'm glad to see you more calm this morning.
DORA.   But how pale she looks, and she trembles so.
ZOE.   Do I? (*Enter George*) Ah! he is here.
DORA.   George, here she is.
ZOE.   I have come to say good-by, sir; two hard words—so hard, they might break many a heart; mightn't they?
GEORGE.   O, Zoe! can you smile at this moment?
ZOE.   You see how easily I have become reconciled to my fate—so it will be with you. You will not forget poor Zoe! but her image will pass away like a little cloud that obscured your happiness a while—you will love each other; you are both too good not to join your hearts. Brightness will return amongst you. Dora, I once made you weep; those were the only tears I caused anybody. Will you forgive me?
DORA.   Forgive you—(*Kisses her*)
ZOE.   I feel you do, George.
GEORGE.   Zoe, you are pale. Zoe!—she faints!
ZOE.   No; a weakness, that's all—a little water. (*Dora gets water.*) I have a restorative here—will you pour it in the glass? (*Dora attempts to take it.*) No; not you—George. (*George pours contents of phial in glass.*) Now, give it to me. George, dear George, do you love me?
GEORGE.   Do you doubt it, Zoe?
ZOE.   No! (*Drinks*)
DORA.   Zoe, if all I possess would buy your freedom, I would gladly give it.

ZOE.   I am free! I had but one Master on earth, and he has given me my freedom!

DORA.   Alas! but the deed that freed you was not lawful.

ZOE.   Not lawful—no—but I am going to where there is no law—where there is only justice.

GEORGE.   Zoe, you are suffering—your lips are white—your cheeks are flushed.

ZOE.   I must be going—it is late. Farewell, Dora. (*Retires*)

PETE.   (*Outside*) Whar's Missus—whar's Mas'r George?

GEORGE.   They come.

(*Enter Scudder*)

SCUDDER.   Stand around and let me pass—room thar! I feel so big with joy, creation ain't wide enough to hold me. Mrs. Peyton, George Peyton, Terrebonne is yours. It was that rascal M'Closky—but he got rats, I swow —he killed the boy, Paul, to rob this letter from the mail-bags—the letter from Liverpool you know—he sot fire to the shed—that was how the steamboat got burned up.

MRS. PEYTON.   What d'ye mean?

SCUDDER.   Read—read that. (*Gives letter*)

GEORGE.   Explain yourself.

(*Enter Sunnyside*)

SUNNYSIDE.   Is it true?

SCUDDER.   Every word of it, Squire. Here, you tell it, since you know it. If I was to try, I'd bust.

MRS. PEYTON.   Read, George. Terrebonne is yours.

(*Enter Pete, Dido, Solon, Minnie, and Grace*)

PETE.   Whar is she—whar is Miss Zoe?

SCUDDER.   What's the matter?

PETE.   Don't ax me. Whar's de gal? I say.

SCUDDER.   Here she is—Zoe!—water—she faints.

PETE.   No—no. 'Tain't no faint—she's a dying, sa: she got pizen from old Dido here this mornin'.

GEORGE.   Zoe!

SCUDDER.   Zoe! is this true?—no, it ain't—darn it, say it ain't. Look here, you're free, you know; nary a master to hurt you now: you will stop here as long as you're a mind to, only don't look so.

DORA.   Her eyes have changed color.

PETE.   Dat's what her soul's gwine to do. It's going up dar, whar dere's no line atween folks.

GEORGE.   She revives.

ZOE. (*On sofa*) George—where—where—

GEORGE.   O, Zoe! what have you done?

ZOE.   Last night I overheard you weeping in your room, and you said, "I'd rather see her dead than so!"

GEORGE.   Have I then prompted you to this?

ZOE.   No; but I loved you so, I could not bear my fate; and then I stood between your heart and hers. When I am dead she will not be jealous of your love for me, no laws will stand between us. Lift me; so—(*George raises her head.*)—let me look at you, that your face may be the last I see of this world. O! George, you may, without a blush, confess your love for the Octoroon! (*Dies—George lowers her head gently.—Kneels.—Others form picture.*)

(*Darken front of house and stage.*)

(*Light fires.—Draw flats and discover Paul's grave.—M'Closky dead on it.—Wahnotee standing triumphantly over him.*)

SLOW CURTAIN.

SHENANDOAH

a

Military Comedy in Four Acts

by

Bronson Howard

Introduction

Bronson Howard was born October 7, 1842, in Detroit, Michigan. The son of a prominent merchant, he attended Russell's Institute, New Haven, Connecticut, to prepare for Yale, but he did not complete his college course because of an eye defect, which also prevented him from serving in the Civil War. His first attempt at playwriting, *Fantine*, a dramatization of episodes from Victor Hugo's *Les Miserables*, was produced in Detroit in 1864 while he was a reporter for the Detroit *Free Press*. The next year he moved to New York, where he worked on the *Tribune* and the *Post*. Soon after the success of *Saratoga* in 1870, he was able to devote all his energies to playwriting and became the first American dramatist whose writing was not adjunctive to another career such as acting, directing, or producing. Later called the "Dean of American Drama," Howard fought for the recognition of American playwrights at a time when many managers preferred translations and adaptations of foreign plays. He founded the American Dramatists Club in 1891 and worked for copyright laws to protect the rights of dramatists. *Shenandoah* brought him to the attention of Charles Frohman, soon to become the dominant member of the Klaw-Erlanger Syndicate, and his subsequent plays were produced under the auspices of the Syndicate, whose conservative policies and preference for "safe" subjects and happy endings may have prevented him from fulfilling his full potential as a serious playwright. He was not an innovator or a rebel, however, and perhaps would have conformed to popular taste even if he had not worked under the aegis of the Syndicate. He died at Avon-by-the-Sea, New Jersey, August 4, 1908. *In Memoriam: Bronson Howard* (New York, 1910), a collection of tributes delivered at a memorial service conducted by the American Dramatists Club on October 18, 1908, at the Lyceum Theatre, New York, is as yet the only book-length account of his career.

A contemporary of William Dean Howells and Henry James, Howard often used similar themes and situations, but his work lacks the serious artistic purpose and the subtlety of analysis found in their novels. His innocent, wholesome, outspoken heroines somewhat resemble those of Howells and James, and he also concerned himself with contrasts between Old World and New World cultures and with the rise of the businessman to a dominant position in American life. He believed that America needed "plays that laud virtue and denounce vice," and Theodore Roosevelt praised his work as "clean and healthy." The limitations of Howard's brand of antiseptic realism are suggested by a statement that he made at Harvard in 1886: "The wife who has once taken the step from purity to impurity can never reinstate herself in the world of art on this side of the grave; and so an audience looks with complacent tears on the death of an erring woman." Howard's belief that a playwright's first function is to entertain the public led him to resist the "sombreness" of Ibsen, and his plays can be called realistic only with respect to their surface authenticity of detail. He firmly believed, too, that drama should be separated altogether from literary or esthetic considerations, and he discouraged the publication of his plays. He was, however, a careful student of dramatic structure who contrived clever stage effects; and his farces, social comedies, and melodramas act far more effectively than they read.

Howard's most successful play, *Shenandoah*, with the significant subtitle *A Military Comedy*, was first produced at the Boston Museum on November 19, 1888. It was based on an earlier effort, *Drum-Taps*, which he had written about twenty years before. According to legend, after a production of *Drum-Taps* in Louisville, Kentucky, Howard showed the script to a New York manager, who suggested that he change the setting to the Crimean War. Although this episode suggests accurately enough the attitude of leading managers like Lester Wallack and A. M. Palmer, it may be apocryphal because, contrary to widespread opinion, there was no dearth of Civil War plays from 1861 until the end of the century. Most of the plays of the 1860's and 1870's, however, were at best second-rate melodramas, pageants or farces. The first serious Civil War play, *Held by the Enemy* (1886) by William Gillette, may have influenced Howard.

In the published edition of *Shenandoah*, among the suggested program notes is a quotation from Grant's *Memoirs* which expresses the dominant theme of the play: "I feel that we are on the eve of a new era, when there is to be great harmony between the Federal and Confederate." The achievement of sectional harmony began with the removal of Federal troops from the South in 1877, and the desire for reconciliation between North and South predominates in Civil War plays and fiction of the period. The Old South is pictured sympathetically, and the valor of the Southern soldier in fighting for a lost cause against overwhelming odds is acknowledged. Slavery as a social evil or as a cause of the war is minimized. Melodramatic exploits of espionage agents are stressed more than actual battles, which might have aroused harsh memories. The struggle within an individual torn between conflicting loyalties is emphasized more than the struggle between sections. The pathos of friends, kinsmen, or lovers separated by the war is a favorite theme. Costume romance in the cloak-and-dagger tradition rather than authentic portrayal of war resulted from this trend toward reunion of North and South.

Impetus for serious treatment of the war came from a series of articles by actual participants published by *Century Magazine*. Later collected in four volumes as *Battles and Leaders of the Civil War* (1884-87), these first-hand accounts are still valuable source-books. Howard, it seems clear, used the descriptions in *Battles and Leaders* of the bombardment of Fort Sumter and the Battle of Cedar Creek.

Because *Shenandoah* was not written from a partisan or sectional point of view, neither side is judged harshly. Howard contrasts Ellingham's loyalty to Virginia with Kerchival West's loyalty to the Union, but he does not condemn or advocate either attitude. The characters are all too civilized to let the war break up their friendships or their love affairs. Rather than military, political, or social questions, Howard's theme is the effect of the war on human relationships. To dramatize this theme, he centers his play on five love stories, and his technical skill is suggested by the way in which he correlates this inordinate number of subplots. At the close of each act, he focuses the attention of the audience on his central characters, Kerchival West and Gertrude Ellingham, and on the way military events have affected their relationship. Two of the love stories involve the rather trite "hearts divided" situation, which was well suited to the popular theme of reconciliation.

After the first production of *Shenandoah* in Boston, Charles Frohman, the most astute producer of the period, suggested some revisions. The revised play opened at the Star Theatre, New York, on September 9, 1889. It passed its acid test when General Sherman, then living in retirement in New York, expressed his approval, and the play became a favorite occasion for sentimental reunions of veterans of both armies. It was an enormous success and made both Howard and Frohman wealthy.

Frohman's most important suggestion was that more emphasis should be given Sheridan's ride, the climactic scene in Act III. Although historians differ as to the importance of this incident and Sheridan himself once remarked that his troops would have rallied without his dramatic appearance, circumstances made it one of the best known events of the war. Howard's presentation is generally accurate. Sheridan had been sent into the Shenandoah Valley in August, 1864, to destroy crops and livestock that had been supplying the Confederacy and to end Southern troop movements along this north-south corridor. Early on the morning of October 19, Sheridan was at Winchester on his way back from a conference in Washington. After hearing the booming of artillery, he galloped fourteen miles down the Valley Pike to Cedar Creek, where his troops had been surprised by a dawn attack. He rallied the retreating soldiers and turned defeat into victory.

The public knew of this dramatic exploit through a picture and a poem, not from historical records. After the battle *Harper's Weekly* carried a drawing of Sheridan's ride by Sol Eytinge. Thomas Buchanan Read, a poet and painter, was probably inspired by this drawing to write his stirring poem "Sheridan's Ride." It was first recited at Pike's Opera House, Cincinnati, by the actor James E. Murdoch and for many years remained a popular piece for declamation on patriotic occasions. Read later painted a picture of Sheridan dashing toward the battle. The poem's vivid description of the ride and its emotional language ("Hurrah! hurrah for horse and man!") made Sheridan's horse, Rienzi, almost as famous as the general himself. Howard's portrayal of Gertrude Ellingham cheering the general as he gallops past on *her* horse is, of course, a distortion of fact to emphasize the reconciliation theme.

Other Civil War plays of the 19th century include *Belle Lamar* (1874) by Dion Boucicault, *Held by the Enemy* (1886) and *Secret Service* (1895) by William Gillette, *May Blossom* (1884) and *The Heart of Maryland* (1895) by David Belasco, *The Reverend Griffith Davenport* (1899) by James A. Herne, and *Barbara Freitchie* (1899) by Clyde Fitch. Although innumerable novels and moving pictures since 1900 have dealt with the Civil War, it has not been a popular subject on the modern stage.

"Sheridan's Ride" by Sol Eytinge

(From *Harper's Weekly*, November 5, 1864)

(Harvard Theatre Collection)

Cast of Characters

GENERAL HAVERILL
COLONEL KERCHIVAL WEST
CAPTAIN HEARTSEASE
LIEUTENANT FRANK BEDLOE } Officers of Sheridan's Cavalry

MAJOR-GENERAL FRANCIS BUCKTHORN, Commander of the 19th Army Corps

SERGEANT BARKET

COLONEL ROBERT ELLINGHAM, 10th Virginia

CAPTAIN THORNTON, Secret Service C. S. A.

LIEUTENANT OF SIGNAL CORPS

LIEUTENANT OF INFANTRY

MRS. CONSTANCE HAVERILL

GERTRUDE ELLINGHAM

MADELINE WEST

JENNY BUCKTHORN, U. S. A.

MRS. EDITH HAVERILL

HARDWICK (SURGEON)

CAPTAIN LOCKWOOD, U. S. Signal Corps

CORPORAL DUNN

BENSON

OLD MARGERY

JANNETTE

ACT I

Charleston Harbor in 1861. "After the Ball."

Scene, A Southern residence on the shore of Charleston Harbor. Large double doors at the rear of the stage are open. Large, wide window, with low sill, extending down the right side. Veranda beyond the doors extending beyond window. A wide opening at the rear with corridor beyond. Furniture and appointments quaint and old-fashioned, but an air of brightness and of light; the general tone of the walls and upholstery that of the old Colonial period in its more ornamental and decorative phase, as shown in the early days of Charleston. Old candlesticks and candelabra, with lighted candles nearly burned down.

Beyond the central doors and the window there is a lawn with southern foliage extending down to the shores of the harbor. A part of the bay lies in the distance with low-lying land beyond. The lights of Charleston are seen over the water along the shore. Moonlight. The gray twilight of early morning gradually steals over the scene as the Act progresses. As the curtain rises, Kerchival West is sitting in a chair, his feet extended and his head thrown back, a handkerchief over his face. Robert Ellingham strolls in on veranda, smoking. He looks to the right, starts, and moves to window; leans against the upper side of the window and looks across.

ELLINGHAM.   Kerchival!
KERCHIVAL.   (*Under handkerchief*) Eh? H'm!
ELLINGHAM.   Can you sleep at a time like this? My own nerves are on fire.
KERCHIVAL.   Fire? Oh—yes—I remember. Any more fireworks, Bob?
ELLINGHAM.   A signal rocket from one of the batteries, now and then. (*Exit beyond window. Kerchival arouses himself, taking handkerchief from his eyes.*)
KERCHIVAL.   What a preposterous hour to be up. The ball was over an hour ago, all the guests are gone, and it's nearly four o'clock. (*Looks at his watch*) Exactly ten minutes of four. (*Takes out a cigar*) Our Southern friends assure us that General Beauregard is to open fire on Fort Sumter this morning. I don't believe it. (*Lighting cigar and rising, looks out through window*) There lies the old fort—solemn and grim as ever, and the flagstaff stands above it, like a warning finger. If they do fire upon it— (*Shutting his teeth for a moment and looking down at the cigar in his hand*)—the echo of that first shot will be heard above their graves, and Heaven knows how many of our own, also; but the flag will still float!— over the graves of both sides.

212

(Ellingham enters from the central door.)

Are you Southerners all mad, Robert?

ELLINGHAM.   Are you Northerners all blind? *(Kerchival sits down.)* We Virginians would prevent a war if we could. But your people in the North do not believe that one is coming. You do not understand the determined frenzy of my fellow Southerners. Look! *(Pointing)* Do you see the lights of the city, over the water? The inhabitants of Charleston are gathering, even now, in the gray, morning twilight, to witness the long-promised bombardment of Fort Sumter. It is to be a gala day for them. They have talked and dreamed of nothing else for weeks. The preparations have become a part of their social life—of their amusement—their gayeties. This very night at the ball—here—in the house of my own relatives—what was their talk? What were the jests they laughed at? Sumter! War! Ladies were betting bonbons that the United States would not dare to fire a shot in return, and pinning ribbons on the breasts of their "heroes." There was a signal rocket from one of the forts, and the young men who were dancing here left their partners standing on the floor to return to the batteries—as if it were the night before another Waterloo. The ladies themselves hurried away to watch the "spectacle" from their own verandas. You won't see the truth! I tell you, Kerchival, a war between the North and South is inevitable!

KERCHIVAL.   And if it does come, you Virginians will join the rest.

ELLINGHAM.   Our State will be the battle ground, I fear. But every loyal son of Virginia will follow her flag. It is our religion!

KERCHIVAL.   My State is New York. If New York should go against the old flag, New York might go to the devil. That is my religion.

ELLINGHAM.   So differently have we been taught what the word "patriotism" means!

KERCHIVAL.   You and I are officers in the same regiment of the United States Regular Army, Robert; we were classmates at West Point, and we have fought side by side on the plains. You saved my scalp once; I'd have to wear a wig, now, if you hadn't. I say, old boy, are we to be enemies?

ELLINGHAM.   *(Laying his hand over his shoulder)* My dear old comrade, whatever else comes, our friendship shall be unbroken!

KERCHIVAL.   Bob! *(Looking up at him)* I only hope that we shall never meet in battle!

ELLINGHAM.   In battle? *(Stepping down front)* The idea is horrible!

KERCHIVAL.   *(Rising and crossing to him)* My dear old comrade, one of us will be wrong in this great fight, but we shall both be honest in it. *(Gives hand; Ellingham grasps it warmly, then turns away.)*

ELLINGHAM.   Colonel Haverill is watching the forts, also; he has been as sad tonight as we have. Next to leaving you, my greatest regret is that I must resign from his regiment.

KERCHIVAL.   You are his favorite officer.

ELLINGHAM.   Naturally, perhaps; he was my guardian.

(Enter Haverill)

HAVERILL.   Kerchival! I secured the necessary passports to the North yesterday afternoon; this one is yours; I brought it down for you early in the evening. *(Kerchival takes paper, goes to window.)* I am ordered direct to Washington at once, and shall start with Mrs. Haverill this forenoon. You will report to Capt. Lyon, of the Second Regiment, in St. Louis. Robert! I have hoped for peace to the last, but it is hoping against hope. I feel certain, now, that the fatal blow will be struck this morning. Our old regiment is already broken up, and you, also, will now resign, I suppose, like nearly all your fellow Southerners in the service.

ELLINGHAM.   You know how sorry I am to leave your command, Colonel!

HAVERILL.   I served under your father in Mexico; he left me, at his death, the guardian of you and your sister, Gertrude. Ever since you became of age, I have felt that I stood in his place. But you must be your sister's only guardian now. Your father fell in battle, fighting for our common country, but you—

ELLINGHAM.   He would have done as I shall do, had he lived. He was a Virginian!

HAVERILL.   I am glad, Robert, that he was never called upon to decide between two flags. He never knew but one, and we fought under it together. *(Exit)*

ELLINGHAM.   Kerchival! Something occurred in this house tonight which —which I shouldn't mention under ordinary circumstances, but I—I feel that it may require my further attention, and you, perhaps, can be of service to me. Mrs. Haverill, the wife of the Colonel—

KERCHIVAL.   Fainted away in her room.

ELLINGHAM.   You know?

KERCHIVAL.   I was one of the actors in the little drama.

ELLINGHAM.   Indeed!

KERCHIVAL.   About half-past nine this evening, while the ladies were dressing for the ball, I was going upstairs; I heard a quick, sharp cry, sprang forward, found myself at an open door. Mrs. Haverill lay on the floor inside, as if she had just reached the door to cry for help, when she fell. After doing all the unnecessary and useless things I could think of, I rushed out of the room to tell your sister, Gertrude, and my own sister, Madeline, to go and take care of the lady. Within less than twenty minutes afterwards, I saw Mrs. Haverill sail into the drawing-room, a thing of beauty, and with the glow of perfect health on her cheek. It was an immense relief to me when I saw her. Up to that time I have a vague idea that I had committed a murder.

ELLINGHAM.   Murder!

KERCHIVAL.   M—m. A guilty conscience. Every man, of course, does exactly the wrong thing when a woman faints. When I rushed out of Mrs. Haverill's room, I left my handkerchief soaked with water upon her face. I must ask her for it, it's a silk one. Luckily, the girls got there in time to take it off; she wouldn't have come to if they hadn't. It never occurred to me that she'd need to breathe in my absence. That's all I know about the matter. What troubles you? I suppose every woman has a right to faint whenever she chooses. The scream that I heard was so sharp, quick and intense that—

ELLINGHAM. That the cause must have been a serious one.

KERCHIVAL. Yes! So I thought. It must have been a mouse.

ELLINGHAM. Mr. Edward Thornton has occupied the next room to that of Mrs. Haverill tonight.

KERCHIVAL. (*Quickly*) What do you mean?

ELLINGHAM. During the past month or .more he has been pressing, not to say insolent, in his attentions to Mrs. Haverill.

KERCHIVAL. I've noticed that myself.

ELLINGHAM. And he is an utterly unscrupulous man; it is no fault of mine that he was asked to be a guest at this house tonight. He came to Charleston, some years ago, from the North, but if there are any vices and passions peculiarly strong in the South, he has carried them all to the extreme. In one of the many scandals connected with Edward Thornton's name, it was more than whispered that he entered a lady's room unexpectedly at night. But, as he killed the lady's husband in a duel a few days afterwards, the scandal dropped.

KERCHIVAL. Of course; the gentleman received ample satisfaction as an outraged husband, and Mr. Thornton apologized, I suppose, to his widow.

ELLINGHAM. He has repeated the adventure.

KERCHIVAL. Do—you—think—that?

ELLINGHAM. I was smoking on the lawn, and glanced up at the window; my eyes may have deceived me, and I must move cautiously in the matter; but it couldn't have been imagination; the shadow of Edward Thornton's face and head appeared upon the curtain.

KERCHIVAL. Whew! The devil!

ELLINGHAM. Just at that moment I, too, heard the stifled scream.

(*Enter Edward Thornton*)

THORNTON. Gentlemen!

ELLINGHAM. Your name was just on my tongue, Mr. Thornton.

THORNTON. I thought I heard it, but you are welcome to it. Miss Gertrude has asked me to ride over to Mrs. Pinckney's with her, to learn if there is any further news from the batteries. I am very glad the time to attack Fort Sumter has come at last!

ELLINGHAM. I do not share your pleasure.

THORNTON. You are a Southern gentleman.

ELLINGHAM. And you are a Northern "gentleman."

THORNTON. A Southerner by choice; I shall join the cause.

ELLINGHAM. We native Southerners will defend our own rights, sir; you may leave them in our keeping. It is my wish, Mr. Thornton, that you do not accompany my sister.

THORNTON.   Indeed!

ELLINGHAM.   Her groom, alone, will be sufficient.

THORNTON.   As you please, sir. Kindly offer my excuses to Miss Gertrude. You and I can chat over the subject later in the day, when we are alone. (*Moving up stage*)

ELLINGHAM.   By all means, and another subject, also, perhaps.

THORNTON.   I shall be entirely at your service. (*Exit on veranda*)

ELLINGHAM.   Kerchival, I shall learn the whole truth, if possible, today. If it is what I suspect—what I almost know—I will settle with him myself. He has insulted our Colonel's wife and outraged the hospitality of my friends.

KERCHIVAL.   I think it ought to be my quarrel. I'm sure I'm mixed up in it enough.

MADELINE.   (*Without, calling*) Kerchival!

ELLINGHAM.   Madeline. (*Aside, starting, Kerchival looks across at him sharply.*)

KERCHIVAL.   (*Aside*) I distinctly saw Bob give a start when he heard Madeline. Now, what can there be about my sister's voice to make a man jump like that?

GERTRUDE.   (*Without*) Brother Robert!

KERCHIVAL.   Gertrude! (*Aside, starting, Ellingham looks at him sharply.*) How the tones of a woman's voice thrill through a man's soul!

(*Enter Madeline*)

MADELINE.   Oh, Kerchival—here you are.

(*Enter Gertrude, from apartment, in a riding habit, with whip, etc.*)

GERTRUDE.   Robert, dear! (*Coming down to Robert; they converse in dumb show.*)

MADELINE.   Where are your field glasses? I've been rummaging all through your clothes, and swords, and sashes, and things. I've turned everything in your room upside down.

KERCHIVAL.   Have you?

MADELINE.   I can't find your glasses anywhere. I want to look at the forts. Another rocket went up just now. (*Runs and stands on piazza looking off*)

KERCHIVAL.   A sister has all the privileges of a wife to upset a man's things, without her legal obligation to put them straight again. (*Glances at Gertrude*) I wish Bob's sister had the same privileges in my room that my own has.

GERTRUDE.   Mr. Thornton isn't going with me, you say?

ELLINGHAM.   He requested me to offer you his apologies.

KERCHIVAL. May *I* accompany you? (*Ellingham turns to window.*)

GERTRUDE. My groom, old Pete, will be with me, of course; there's no particular need of anyone else. But you may go along, if you like. I've got my hands full of sugar plums for Jack. Dear old Jack—he always has his share when we have company. I'm going over to Mrs. Pinckney's to see if she's had any more news from General Beauregard; her son is on the General's staff.

MADELINE. (*Looking off to the right*) There's another rocket from Fort Johnson; and it is answered from Fort Moultrie. Ah! (*Angrily*) General Beauregard is a bad, wicked man! (*Coming down*)

GERTRUDE. Oh! Madeline! You are a bad, wicked Northern girl to say such a thing.

MADELINE. I *am* a Northern girl.

GERTRUDE. And I am a Southern girl. (*They face each other.*)

KERCHIVAL. The war has begun. (*Dropping into chair; Ellingham has turned from window; he strolls across the stage, watching the girls.*)

GERTRUDE. General Beauregard is a patriot.

MADELINE. He is a Rebel.

GERTRUDE. So am I.

MADELINE. Gertrude!—You—you——

GERTRUDE. Madeline!—You——

MADELINE. I—I——

GERTRUDE. I——

BOTH. O—O-h! (*Bursting into tears and rushing into each other's arms, sobbing, then suddenly kissing each other vigorously*)

KERCHIVAL. I say, Bob, if the North and South do fight, that will be the end of it.

GERTRUDE. I've got something to say to you, Madeline, dear. (*Confidentially, and turning with her arms about her waist. The girls sit, talking earnestly.*)

ELLINGHAM. Kerchival, old boy! There's—there's something I'd like to say to you before we part today.

KERCHIVAL. I'd like a word with you, also!

MADELINE. You don't really mean that, Gertrude—with me?

ELLINGHAM. I'm in love with your sister, Madeline.

KERCHIVAL. The devil you are!

ELLINGHAM. I never suspected such a thing until last night.

GERTRUDE. Robert was in love with you six weeks ago. (*Madeline kisses her.*)

KERCHIVAL. *I've* made a discovery, too, Bob.

MADELINE. *I've* got something to say to *you*, Gertrude.

KERCHIVAL. I'm in love with *your* sister.

ELLINGHAM. (*Astonished*) You are?

MADELINE. Kerchival has been in love with you for the last three months. (*Gertrude offers her lips—they kiss.*)

KERCHIVAL. I fell in love with her the day before yesterday. (*The two gentlemen grasp each other's hand warmly.*)

ELLINGHAM.   We understand each other, Kerchival. (*He turns, stops at door.*) Miss Madeline, you said just now that you wished to watch the forts. Would you like to walk down to the shore?

MADELINE.   Yes! (*Rising and going up to him. He takes one of her hands in his own and looks at her earnestly.*)

ELLINGHAM.   This will be the last day that we shall be together, for the present. But we shall meet again—sometime—if we both live.

MADELINE.   If we both live! You mean—if *you* live. You must go into this dreadful war, if it comes.

ELLINGHAM.   Yes, Madeline, I must. Come let us watch for our fate. (*Exeunt to veranda*)

KERCHIVAL.   (*Aside*) I must leave Charleston today. (*Sighs*) Does she love me?

GERTRUDE.   I am ready to start, Mr. West, when you are.

KERCHIVAL.   Oh! Of course, I forgot. (*Rising*) I shall be delighted to ride at your side.

GERTRUDE.   At my side! (*Rising*) There isn't a horse in America that can keep by the side of my Jack, when I give him his head, and I'm sure to do it. You may follow us. But you can hardly ride in that costume; while you are changing it, I'll give Jack his bonbons. (*Turning to window*) There he is, bless him! Pawing the ground, and impatient for me to be on his back. Let him come, Pete. (*Holding up bonbons at window*) I love you.

KERCHIVAL.   Eh? (*Turning suddenly*)

GERTRUDE.   (*Looking at him*) What?

KERCHIVAL.   You were saying——

GERTRUDE.   Jack! (*Looking out. The head of a large black horse appears through the window.*) You dear old fellow! (*Feeds with bonbons*) Jack has been my boy ever since he was a little colt. I brought you up, didn't I, Jack? He's the truest, and kindest, and best of friends; I wouldn't be parted from him for the world, and I'm the only woman he'll allow to be near him.

KERCHIVAL.   (*Earnestly*) You are the only woman, Miss Gertrude, that I——

GERTRUDE.   Dear Jack!

KERCHIVAL.   (*Aside*) Jack embarrasses me. He's a third party.

GERTRUDE.   There! That will do for the present, Jack. Now go along with Pete! If you are a very good boy, and don't let Lieutenant Kerchival West come within a quarter of a mile of me, after the first three minutes; you shall have some more sugar plums when we get to Mrs. Pinckney's. (*An old negro leads the horse away. Gertrude looks around at Kerchival.*) You haven't gone to dress yet; we shall be late. Mrs. Pinckney asked a party of friends to witness the bombardment this morning, and breakfast together on the piazza while they are looking at it. We can remain and join them, if you like.

KERCHIVAL. I hope they won't wait for breakfast until the bombardment begins.

GERTRUDE. I'll bet you an embroidered cigar-case, Lieutenant, against a box of gloves that it will begin in less than an hour.

KERCHIVAL. Done! You will lose the bet. But you shall have the gloves; and one of the hands that go inside them shall be——(*Taking one of her hands; she withdraws it.*)

GERTRUDE. My own—until someone wins it. You don't believe that General Beauregard will open fire on Fort Sumter this morning?

KERCHIVAL. No; I don't.

GERTRUDE. Everything is ready.

KERCHIVAL. It's so much easier to get everything ready to do a thing than it is to do it. I have been ready a dozen times, this very night, to say to you, Miss Gertrude, that I—that I—(*Pauses*)

GERTRUDE. (*Looking down and tapping skirt with her whip*) Well?

KERCHIVAL. But I didn't.

GERTRUDE. (*Glancing up at him suddenly*) I dare say, General Beauregard has more nerve than you have.

KERCHIVAL. It is easy enough to set the batteries around Charleston Harbor, but the man who fires the first shot at a woman——

GERTRUDE. Woman!

KERCHIVAL. At the American flag—must have nerves of steel.

GERTRUDE. You Northern men are so slow, to——

KERCHIVAL. I have been slow; but I assure you, Miss Gertrude, that my heart——

GERTRUDE. What subject are we on now?

KERCHIVAL. You were complaining because I was too slow.

GERTRUDE. I was doing nothing of the kind, sir!—let me finish, please. You Northern men are so slow, to believe that our Southern heroes— Northern *men* and Southern *heroes*—you recognize the distinction I make—you won't believe that they will keep their promises. They have sworn to attack Fort Sumter this morning, and—they—will do it. This "American Flag" you talk of is no longer our flag: it is foreign to us!—It is the flag of an enemy!

KERCHIVAL. (*Tenderly and earnestly*) Am I your enemy?

GERTRUDE. You have told me that you will return to the North, and take the field.

KERCHIVAL. Yes, I will. (*Decisively*)

GERTRUDE. You will be fighting against my friends, against my own brother, against me. We *shall* be enemies.

KERCHIVAL. (*Firmly*) Even that, Gertrude—(*She looks around at him, he looks squarely into her eyes as he proceeds.*)—if you will have it so. If my country needs my services, I shall not refuse them, though it makes us enemies! (*She wavers a moment, under strong emotion, and turns away; sinks upon the seat, her elbow on the back of it, and her tightly-clenched fist against her cheek, looking away from him.*)

GERTRUDE. I will have it so! I am a Southern woman!

KERCHIVAL. We have more at stake between us, this morning, than a cigar-case and a box of gloves. (*Turning up stage*)

(*Enter Mrs. Haverill from apartment*)

MRS. HAVERILL. Mr. West! I've been looking for you. I have a favor to ask.

KERCHIVAL. Of me?—with pleasure.

MRS. HAVERILL. But I am sorry to have interrupted you and Gertrude. (*Passing down stage, Kerchival moves up, Gertrude rises.*) (*Apart*) There are tears in your eyes, Gertrude, dear!

GERTRUDE. (*Apart*) They have no right there.

MRS. HAVERILL. (*Apart*) I'm afraid I know what has happened. A quarrel! and you are to part with each other so soon. Do not let a girl's coquetry trifle with her heart until it is too late. You remember the confession you made to me last night?

GERTRUDE. (*Apart*) Constance! (*Starting*) That is my secret; more a secret now than ever.

MRS. HAVERILL. (*Apart*) Yes, dear; but you do love him. (*Gertrude moves up the stage.*)

GERTRUDE. You need not ride over with me, Mr. West.

KERCHIVAL. I can be ready in one moment.

GERTRUDE. I choose to go alone! Old Pete will be with me; and Jack, himself, is a charming companion.

KERCHIVAL. If you prefer Jack's company to mine—

GERTRUDE. I do. (*Exit on veranda*)

KERCHIVAL. Damn Jack! But you will let me assist you to mount. (*Exit after her*)

MRS. HAVERILL. We leave for the North before noon, but every hour seems a month. If my husband should learn what happened in my room tonight, he would kill that man. What encouragement could I have given him? Innocence is never on its guard—but, (*Drawing up*) the last I remember before I fell unconscious, he was crouching before me like a whipped cur! (*Starts as she looks out of the window*) There is Mr. Thornton now—Ah! (*Angrily*) No—I must control my own indignation. I must keep him and Colonel Haverill from meeting before we leave Charleston. Edward Thornton would shoot my husband down without remorse. But poor Frank! I must not forget him, in my own trouble. I have but little time left to care for his welfare.

(*Re-enter Kerchival*)

KERCHIVAL. You said I could do you a favor, Mrs. Haverill?

MRS. HAVERILL. Yes, I wanted to speak with you about General Haverill's son, Frank. I should like you to carry a message to Charleston for me, as soon as it is light. It is a sad errand. You know too well the great misfortune that has fallen upon my husband in New York.

KERCHIVAL. His only son has brought disgrace upon his family name, and tarnished the reputation of a proud soldier. Colonel Haverill's fellow officers sympathize with him most deeply.

MRS. HAVERILL. And poor young Frank! I could hardly have loved the boy more if he had been my own son. If he had not himself confessed the crime against the bank, I could not have believed him guilty. He has escaped from arrest. He is in the City of Charleston. I am the only one in all the world he could turn to. He was only a lad of fourteen when his father and I were married, six years ago; and the boy has loved me from the first. His father is stern and bitter now in his humiliation. This note from Frank was handed to me while the company were here last evening. I want you to find him and arrange for me to meet him, if you can do it with safety. I shall give you a letter for him.

KERCHIVAL. I'll get ready at once; and I will do all I can for the boy.

MRS. HAVERILL. And—Mr. West! Gertrude and Madeline have told me that—that—I was under obligations to you last evening.

KERCHIVAL. Don't mention it. I merely ran for them, and I—I'm very glad you didn't choke—before they reached you. I trust you are quite well now?

MRS. HAVERILL. I am entirely recovered, thank you. And I will ask another favor of you, for we are old friends. I desire very much that General Haverill should not know that—that any accident occurred to me tonight—or that my health has not been perfect.

KERCHIVAL. Certainly, madam!

MRS. HAVERILL. It would render him anxious without cause.

KERCHIVAL. (*Aside*) It looks as if Robert was right; she doesn't want the two men to meet.

(*Enter Haverill, a white silk handkerchief in his hand.*)

HAVERILL. Constance, my dear, I've been all over the place looking for you. I thought you were in your room. But—by the way, Kerchival, this is your handkerchief; your initials are on it. (*Kerchival turns and stares at him a second. Mrs. Haverill starts slightly and turns front. Haverill glances quickly from one to the other, then extends his hands toward Kerchival, with the handkerchief. Kerchival moves to him and takes it. Mrs. Haverill drops into chair.*)

KERCHIVAL. Thank you. (*He walks up and exits with a quick glance back. Haverill looks at Mrs. Haverill, who sits nervously, looking away. He then glances after Kerchival. A cloud comes over his face and he stands a second in thought. Then, with a movement as if brushing away a passing suspicion, he smiles pleasantly and approaches Mrs. Haverill; leans over her.*)

HAVERILL. My fair Desdemona! (*Smiling*) I found Cassio's handkerchief in your room. Have you a kiss for me? (*She looks up, he raises her chin with a finger and kisses her.*) That's the way I shall smother you.

MRS. HAVERILL. (*Rising and dropping her head upon his breast*) Husband!

HAVERILL. But what is this they have been telling me?

MRS. HAVERILL. What have they said to you?

HAVERILL. There was something wrong with you in the early part of the evening; you are trembling and excited, my girl!

MRS. HAVERILL. It was nothing, John; I—I—was ill, for a few moments, but I am well now.

HAVERILL. You said nothing about it to me.

MRS. HAVERILL. Do not give it another thought.

HAVERILL. Was there anything besides your health involved in the affair? There was. (*Aside*) How came this handkerchief in her room?

MRS. HAVERILL. My husband! I do not want to say anything more—at—at present—about what happened tonight. There has never been a shadow between us—will you not trust me?

HAVERILL. Shadow! You stand in a bright light of your own, my wife; it shines upon my whole life—there can be no shadow there. Tell me as much or as little as you like, and in your own time. I am sure you will conceal nothing from me that I ought to know. I trust my honor and my happiness to you, absolutely.

MRS. HAVERILL. They will both be safe, John, in my keeping. But there is something else that I wish to speak with you about; something very near to your heart—your son!

HAVERILL. My son!

MRS. HAVERILL. He is in Charleston.

HAVERILL. And not—in prison? To me he is nowhere. I am childless.

MRS. HAVERILL. I hope to see him today; may I not take him some kind word from you?

HAVERILL. My lawyers in New York had instructions to provide him with whatever he needed.

MRS. HAVERILL. They have done so, and he wants for nothing; he asks for nothing except that I will seek out the poor young wife—only a girl herself—whom he is obliged to desert, in New York.

HAVERILL. His marriage was a piece of reckless folly, but I forgave him that.

MRS. HAVERILL. I am sure that it was only after another was dependent on him that the debts of a mere spendthrift were changed to fraud—and crime.

HAVERILL. You may tell him that I will provide for her.

MRS. HAVERILL. And may I take him no warmer message from his father?

HAVERILL. I am an officer of the United States Army. The name which my son bears came to me from men who had borne it with honor, and I transmitted it to him without a blot. He has disgraced it, by his own confession.

MRS. HAVERILL. *I* cannot forget the poor mother who died when he was born; her whose place I have tried to fill, to both Frank and to you. I never saw her, and she is sleeping in the old graveyard at home. But I am doing what she would do today, if she were living. No pride—no disgrace—could have turned her face from him. The care and the love of her son has been to me the most sacred duty which one woman can assume for another.

HAVERILL. You have fulfilled that duty, Constance. Go to my son! I would go with you, but he is a man now; he could not look into my eyes, and I could not trust myself. But I will send him something which a man will understand. Frank loves you as if you were his own mother; and I— I would like him to—to think tenderly of me, also. He will do it when he looks at this picture. (*Taking a miniature from his pocket*)

MRS. HAVERILL. Of me!

HAVERILL. I have never been without it one hour, before, since we were married. He will recognize it as the one that I have carried through every campaign, in every scene of danger on the Plains; the one that has always been with me. He is a fugitive from justice. At times, when despair might overcome him, this may give him nerve to meet his future life manfully. It has often nerved me, when I might have failed without it. Give it to him, and tell him that I send it. (*Giving her the miniature*) I could not send a kinder message, and he will understand it. (*Turning, he stands a moment in thought. Thornton appears at window, looking at them quietly over his shoulder, a cigar in his hand. Mrs. Haverill sees him and starts with a suppressed breath, then looks at Haverill, who moves away.*) (*Aside*) My son! My son! We shall never meet again! (*Exit in thought*) (*Mrs. Haverill looks after him earnestly, then turns and looks at Thornton, drawing up to her full height. Thornton moves up stage, beyond window.*)

MRS. HAVERILL. Will he dare to speak to me again? (*Enter Thornton; he comes down the stage quietly. He has thrown away cigar.*)

THORNTON. Mrs. Haverill! I wish to offer you an apology.

MRS. HAVERILL. I have not asked for one, sir!

THORNTON. Do you mean by that, that you will not accept one?

MRS. HAVERILL. (*Aside*) What can I say? (*Aloud*) Oh, Mr. Thornton!— for my husband's sake, I——

THORNTON. Ah! You are afraid that your husband may become involved in an unpleasant affair. Your solicitude for his safety, madame, makes me feel that my offense tonight was indeed unpardonable. No gentleman can excuse himself for making such a mistake as I have made. I had supposed that it was Lieutenant Kerchival West, who——

MRS. HAVERILL. What do you mean, sir?

THORNTON. But if it is your husband that stands between us——

MRS. HAVERILL. Let me say this, sir: whatever I may fear for my husband, he fears nothing for himself.

THORNTON. He knows? (*Looking at her keenly*)

(*Enter Kerchival Wèst, now in riding suit*)

(*He stops, looking at them.*) You are silent. Your husband does know what occurred tonight; that relieves my conscience. (*Lightly*) Colonel Haverill and I can now settle it between us.

MRS. HAVERILL.   No, Mr. Thornton! My husband knows nothing, and, I beg of you, do not let this horrible affair go further. (*Sees Kerchival*)

KERCHIVAL.   Pardon me. (*Stepping forward*) I hope I am not interrupting you. (*Aside*) It *was* Thornton. (*Aloud*) You said you would have a letter for me to carry, Mrs. Haverill.

MRS. HAVERILL.   Yes, I—I will go up and write it at once. (*Stops and looks back*) (*Aside*) I wonder how much he overheard.

KERCHIVAL.   (*Quietly*) I suppose eight o'clock will be time enough for me to go?

MRS. HAVERILL.   Oh, yes! (*Glancing at him a moment*)—quite. (*Exit through apartment*)

KERCHIVAL.   (*Quietly*) Mr. Thornton! you are a scoundrel! Do I make myself plain?

THORNTON.   You make the fact that you desire to pick a quarrel with me quite plain, sir; but I choose my own quarrels and my own enemies.

KERCHIVAL.   Colonel Haverill is my commander, and he is beloved by every officer in the regiment.

THORNTON.   On what authority, may I ask, do you—

KERCHIVAL.   The honor of Colonel Haverill's wife is under our protection.

THORNTON.   Under your protection? You have a better claim than that, perhaps, to act as her champion. Lieutenant Kerchival West is Mrs. Haverill's favorite officer in the regiment.

KERCHIVAL.   (*Approaching him*) You dare to suggest that I—

THORNTON.   If I accept your challenge, I shall do so not because you are her protector, but my rival.

KERCHIVAL.   Bah! (*Striking him sharply on the cheek with glove. The two men stand facing each other a moment.*) Is it my quarrel now?

THORNTON.   I think you are entitled to my attention, sir.

KERCHIVAL.   My time here is limited.

THORNTON.   We need not delay. The Bayou La Forge is convenient to this place.

KERCHIVAL.   I'll meet you there, with a friend, at once.

THORNTON.   It will be light enough to see the sights of our weapons in about one hour. (*They bow to each other, and Thornton goes out.*)

KERCHIVAL.   I've got ahead of Bob.

GERTRUDE.   (*Without*) Whoa! Jack! Old boy! Steady, now—that's a good fellow.

KERCHIVAL.   She has returned. I *must* know whether Gertrude Ellingham loves me—before Thornton and I meet. He is a good shot.

GERTRUDE.   (*Without, calling*) O-h! Pete! You may take Jack to the stable.

Ha—ha—ha! (*Appears at window: to Kerchival*) Old Pete, on the bay horse, has been doing his best to keep up with us; but Jack and I have led him such a race! Ha—ha—ha—ha! (*Disappearing beyond the window*)
KERCHIVAL.   Does she love me?
GERTRUDE.   I have the very latest news from the headquarters of the Confederate Army in South Carolina. At twenty minutes after three this morning General Beauregard sent this message to Major Anderson in Fort Sumter: "I shall open fire in one hour!" The time is up!—and he will keep his word! (*Turning and looking out of the window. Kerchival moves across to her.*)
KERCHIVAL.   Gertrude! I must speak to you; we may never meet again; but I must know the truth. I love you. (*Seizing her hand*) Do you love me? (*She looks around at him as if about to speak; hesitates.*) Answer me! (*She looks down with a coquettish smile, tapping her skirt with her riding whip.*) Well? (*A distant report of a cannon, and low rumbling reverberations over the harbor. Gertrude turns suddenly, looking out. Kerchival draws up, also looking off.*)
GERTRUDE.   A low—bright—line of fire—in the sky! It is a shell. (*A second's pause; she starts slightly.*) It has burst upon the fort. (*Looks over her shoulder at Kerchival, drawing up to her full height*) Now!—do you believe that we Southerners are in deadly earnest?
KERCHIVAL.   We Northerners are in deadly earnest, too. I have received my answer. (*He crosses quickly; turns.*) We are—enemies! (*They look at each other for a moment.*)   (*Exit Kerchival*)
GERTRUDE.   Kerchival! (*Moving quickly half across stage, looking after him eagerly; stops*) Enemies! (*She drops into chair, sobbing bitterly. Another distant report, and low, long reverberations as the curtain descends.*)

CURTAIN

ACT II

Scene, *The Ellingham Homestead in the Shenandoah Valley. Exterior. Three Top Mountain in the distance. A corner of the house with projecting end of veranda. Low wall extending up from veranda. A wide opening in the wall with a low, heavy stone post, with a flat top on each side. Beyond the wall and opening, a road runs across stage. At the back of this road, elevation of rock and turf. This slopes up behind wood. It is level on the top about twelve feet; slopes down to road and also out behind wood at the right. The level part in the center rises to about four feet above the stage. Beyond this elevation the distance is a broad valley, with Three Top Mountain rising on*

*the right. Foliage appropriate to Northern Virginia—walnut, cotton-
wood, etc. Rustic seats and table near veranda. A low rock near the
stone post. Sunset when curtain rises. As the act proceeds this fades
into twilight and then bright moonlight. At rise of curtain, a Trumpet
Signal is heard, very distant. Gertrude and Madeline are discovered
on elevation. Gertrude is shading her eyes with her hand and looking
off to the left. Madeline stands a little below her on the incline, resting her arm about Gertrude's waist, also looking off.*

GERTRUDE.   It is a regiment of Union Cavalry. The Federal troops now
have their lines three miles beyond us, and only a month ago the Confederate Army was north of Winchester. One army or the other has been
marching up and down the Shenandoah Valley for three years. I wonder
what the next change will be. We in Virginia have had more than our
share of the war. (*Looking off*)

MADELINE.   You have, indeed, Gertrude. (*Walking down to seat*) And we
at home in Washington have pitied you so much. But everybody says
that there will be peace in the valley after this. (*Dropping into seat*)

GERTRUDE.   Peace! (*Coming down*) That word means something very
different to us poor Southerners from what it means to you.

MADELINE.   I know, dear; and we in the North know how you have suffered, too. We were very glad when General Buckthorn was appointed to
the command of the Nineteenth Army Corps, so that Jenny could get
permission for herself and me to come and visit you.

GERTRUDE.   The old General will do anything for Jenny, I suppose.

MADELINE.   Yes. (*Laughing*) We say in Washington that Jenny is in
command of the Nineteenth Army Corps herself.

GERTRUDE.   I was never more astonished or delighted in my life than
when you and Jenny Buckthorn rode up this morning with a guard from
Winchester; and Madeline, dear, I—I only wish that my brother Robert
could be here, too. Do you remember in Charleston, darling—that morning—when I told you that—that Robert loved you?

MADELINE.   He—(*Looking down*)—he told me so himself only a little
while afterwards, and while we were standing there, on the shore of the
bay—the—the shot was fired which compelled him to enter this awful
war—and me to return to my home in the North.

GERTRUDE.   I was watching for that shot, too. (*Turning*)

MADELINE.   Yes—(*Rising*)—you and brother, Kerchival——

GERTRUDE.   We won't talk about that, my dear. We were speaking of
Robert. As I told you this morning, I have not heard from him since the
battle of Winchester, a month ago. Oh, Madeline! the many, many long
weeks like these we have suffered, after some terrible battle in which he
has been engaged. I do not know, now, whether he is living or dead.

MADELINE.   The whole war has been one long suspense to me. (*Dropping
her face into her hands*)

GERTRUDE.   My dear sister! (*Placing her arm about her waist and moving to the left)* You are a Northern girl, and I am a Rebel—but we are sisters. *(They go up to the veranda and out. An old countryman comes in on a cane. He stops and glances back, raises a broken portion of the capstone of the post, and places a letter under it. Gertrude has stepped back on the veranda and is watching him. He raises his head sharply, looking at her and bringing his finger to his lips. He drops his head again, as with age, and goes out. Gertrude moves down stage and up to the road, looks right and left, raises the broken stone, glancing back as she does so; takes letter and moves down.)* Robert is alive! It is his handwriting! *(Tears open the wrapper)* Only a line from him! And this—a dispatch—and also a letter to me! Why, it is from Mrs. Haverill—from Washington—with a United States postmark. *(Reads from a scrap of paper)*

"The enclosed dispatch must be in the hands of Captain Edward Thornton before eight o'clock tonight. We have signaled to him from Three Top Mountain, and he is waiting for it at the bend in Oak Run. Our trusty scout at the Old Forge will carry it if you will put it in his hands."

The scout is not there, now; I will carry it to Captain Thornton myself. I—I haven't my own dear horse to depend on now; Jack knew every foot of the way through the woods about here; he could have carried a dispatch himself. I can't bear to think of Jack; it's two years since he was captured by the enemy—and if he is still living—I—I suppose he is carrying one of their officers. No! Jack wouldn't fight on that side. He was a Rebel—as I am. He was one of the Black Horse Cavalry—his eyes always flashed towards the North. Poor Jack! my pet. *(Brushing her eyes)* But this is no time for tears. I must do the best I can with the gray horse. Captain Thornton shall have the dispatch. *(Reads from note)*

"I also inclose a letter for you. I found it in a United States mail-bag which we captured from the enemy."

Oh—that's the way Mrs. Haverill's letter came—Ha-ha-ha—by way of the Rebel army! *(Opens it; reads)*

"My Darling Gertrude: When Colonel Kerchival West was in Washington last week, on his way from Chattanooga, to serve under Sheridan in the Shenandoah Valley, he called upon me. It was the first time I had seen him since the opening of the war. I am certain that he still loves you, dear." *(She kisses the letter eagerly, then draws up.)* It is quite immaterial to me whether Kerchival West still loves me or not. *(Reads)*

"I have kept your secret, my darling."—Ah! My secret!—"but I was sorely tempted to betray the confidence you reposed in me at Charleston. If Kerchival West had heard you say, as I did, when your face was hidden in my bosom, that night, that you loved him with your whole heart—" Oh! I could bite my tongue out now for making that confession— *(Looks down at letter with a smile)* "I am certain that he still loves you." *(Trumpet Signal. Kisses the letter repeatedly. Trumpet Signal louder than at first. She starts, listening.)*

(Jenny Buckthorn runs in on the veranda.)

JENNY.   Do you hear, Gertrude, they are going to pass this very house.
(*Military band. "John Brown" playing in the distance. Chorus of Soldiers.*)
I've been watching them through my glass; it is Colonel Kerchival West's
regiment.

GERTRUDE.   (*Eagerly, then coldly*) Colonel West's! It is perfectly indifferent to me whose regiment it is.

JENNY.   Oh! Of course. (*Coming down*) It is equally indifferent to me;
Captain Heartsease is in command of the first troop. (*Trumpet Signal*)
Column right! (*She runs up to road. Looks to the left.*) They are coming
up the hill.

GERTRUDE.   At my very door! And Kerchival West in command! I will
not stand here and see them pass. The dispatch for Captain Thornton!
I will carry it to him as soon as they are gone. (*Exit up veranda, the band
and chorus increasing in volume*)

JENNY.   Cavalry! That's the branch of the service I was born in; I was
in a fort at the time—on the Plains. Sergeant Barket always said that my
first baby squall was a command to the garrison; if any officer or soldier,
from my father down, failed to obey my orders, I court-martialed him on
the spot. I'll make 'em pass in review. (*Jumping up on the rustic seat*)
Yes! (*Looking off to the left*) There's Captain Heartsease himself, at the
head of the first troop. Draw sabre! (*With parasol*) Present! (*Imitating
the action. Music. The band and chorus·now full and loud; she swings
parasol in time. Trumpet Signal. Band and chorus suddenly cease.*) Halt!
Why, they are stopping here. (*Trumpet Signal*) Dismount! I—I wonder if
they are going to—I do believe—(*Looking eagerly. Trumpet Signal.*) As-
sembly of Guard Details! As sure as fate, they are going into camp here.
We girls will have a jolly time. (*Jumping down*) Ha—ha—ha—ha! Let me
see. How shall I receive Captain Heartsease? He deserves a court-martial,
for he stole my lace handerchief—at Mrs. Grayson's reception—in Washington. He was called away by orders to the West that very night, and
we haven't met since. (*Sighs*) He's been in lots of battles since then; I
suppose he's forgotten all about the handkerchief. We girls at home don't
forget such things. We aren't in battles. All we do is to—to scrape lint and
flirt with other officers.

(*Enter Captain Heartsease, followed by Colonel Robert Ellingham;
stops at gate*)

HEARTSEASE.   This way, Colonel Ellingham. (*They enter. As they come
down, Heartsease stops suddenly, looking at Jenny; puts up his glasses.*)
Miss Buckthorn!

JENNY.   Captain Heartsease!

HEARTSEASE.   (*Very quietly and with perfect composure*) I am thunder-
struck. The unexpected sight of you has thrown me into a fever of excitement.

JENNY.   Has it? (*Aside*) If he gets so excited as that in battle it must be awful. (*Aloud*) Colonel Ellingham!

ELLINGHAM.   Miss Buckthorn! You are visiting my sister? I am what may be called a visitor—by force—myself.

JENNY.   Oh! You're a prisoner!

ELLINGHAM.   I ventured too far within the Union lines tonight, and they have picked me up. But Major Wilson has kindly accepted my parole, and I shall make the best of it.

JENNY.   Is Major Wilson in command of the regiment?

HEARTSEASE.   Yes, Colonel West is to join us at this point, during the evening.

ELLINGHAM.   I am very glad you are here, Miss Buckthorn, with Gertrude.

JENNY.   Somebody here will be delighted to see you, Colonel.

ELLINGHAM.   My sister can hardly be pleased to see me as a prisoner.

JENNY.   Not your sister. (*Passing him and crossing to veranda, turns and beckons to him. She motions with her thumb, over her shoulder. He goes up the steps of the veranda and turns.*)

ELLINGHAM.   What do you mean?

JENNY.   I mean this—(*Reaching up her face. He leans down, placing his ear near her lips.*)—somebody else's sister! When she first sees you, be near enough to catch her.

ELLINGHAM.   I understand you! Madeline! (*Exit on to the veranda. Jenny runs up steps after him, stops and looks back at Heartsease over the railing. Heartsease takes a lace handkerchief from his pocket.*)

JENNY.   I do believe that's my handkerchief. (*A guard of sentries marches in and across stage in road. The corporal in command orders halt and a sentry to post, then marches guard out. The sentry stands with his back to audience, afterwards moving out and in, appearing and disappearing during the act.*)

HEARTSEASE.   Miss Buckthorn! I owe you an apology. After I left your side, the last time we met, I found your handkerchief in my possession. I assure you, it was an accident.

JENNY.   (*Aside, pouting*) I thought he *intended* to steal it. (*Aloud*) That was more than a year ago. (*Then brightly*) Do you always carry it with you?

HEARTSEASE.   Always; there. (*Indicating his left breast pocket*)

JENNY.   Next to his heart!

HEARTSEASE.   Shall I return it to you?

JENNY.   Oh, if a lace handkerchief can be of any use to you, Captain, during the hardships of a campaign—you—you may keep that one. You soldiers have so few comforts—and it's real lace.

HEARTSEASE.   Thank you. (*Returning handkerchief to his pocket*) Miss Buckthorn, your papa is in command of the Nineteenth Army Corps. He doesn't like me.

JENNY.   I know it.

HEARTSEASE.   But you are in command of him.

JENNY.   Yes; I always have been.

HEARTSEASE.   If ever you decide to assume command of any other man, I—I trust you will give *me* your orders.

JENNY.   (*Aside, starting back*) If that was intended for a proposal, it's the queerest-shaped one I ever heard of. (*Aloud*) Do you mean, Captain, that—that you—I must command myself now. (*Shouldering her parasol*) 'Bout—face! March! (*Turning squarely around, marching out on the veranda*)

HEARTSEASE.   I have been placed on waiting orders. (*Stepping up the stage and looking after her; then very quietly and without emotion*) I am in an agony of suspense. The sight of that girl always arouses the strongest emotions of my nature. (*Enter Colonel Kerchival West, looking at paper in his hand. The Sentinel in the road comes to a salute.*) Colonel West!

KERCHIVAL.   Captain!

HEARTSEASE.   You have rejoined the regiment sooner than we expected.

KERCHIVAL.   (*Looking at paper*) Yes; General Haverill is to meet me here at seven o'clock. Major Wilson tells me that some of your company captured Colonel Robert Ellingham, of the Tenth Virginia.

HEARTSEASE.   He is here under parole.

KERCHIVAL.   And this is the old Ellingham homestead. (*Aside*) Gertrude herself is here, I suppose; almost a prisoner to me, like her brother, and my troops surround their home. She must, indeed, feel that I am her enemy now. Ah, well, war is war. (*Aloud*) By the bye, Heartsease, a young Lieutenant, Frank Bedloe, has joined our troop?

HEARTSEASE.   Yes; an excellent young officer.

KERCHIVAL.   I sent for him as I came through the camp. Lieutenant Frank "Bedloe" is the son of General Haverill.

HEARTSEASE.   Indeed! Under an assumed name!

KERCHIVAL.   He was supposed to have been killed in New Orleans more than a year ago; but he was taken prisoner instead.

HEARTSEASE.   He is here.

KERCHIVAL.   I should never have known him; with his full beard and bronzed face. His face was as smooth as a boy's when I last met him in Charleston.

(*Enter Lieutenant Frank Bedloe. He stops, saluting.*)

FRANK.   You wished me to report to you, Colonel?

KERCHIVAL.   You have been assigned to the regiment during my absence.

FRANK.   Yes, sir. (*Kerchival moves to him and grasps his hand; looks into his eyes a moment before speaking.*)

KERCHIVAL.   Frank Haverill.

FRANK.   You—you know me, sir?

KERCHIVAL.   I saw Mrs. Haverill while I was passing through Washington on Saturday. She told me that you had escaped from prison in Richmond, and had re-entered the service. She did not know then that you had been assigned to my regiment. I received a letter from her in Winchester this morning, informing me of the fact, and asking for my good offices in your behalf. But here is the letter. (*Taking letter from wallet and giving it to him*) It is for you rather than for me. I shall do everything I can for you, my dear fellow.

FRANK.   Thank you, sir. (*Opens letter, dropping the envelope upon the table*) Kind, thoughtful and gentle to my faults, as ever—(*Looking at the letter*)—and always thinking of my welfare. My poor little wife, too, is under her protection. Gentlemen, I beg of you not to reveal my secret to my father.

KERCHIVAL.   General Haverill shall know nothing from us, my boy, you have my word for that.

HEARTSEASE.   Nothing.

KERCHIVAL.   And he cannot possibly recognize you. What with your full beard, and thinking as he does, that you are—

FRANK.   That I am dead. I am dead to him. It would have been better if I had died. Nothing but my death—not even that—can wipe out the disgrace which I brought upon his name.

HEARTSEASE.   General Haverill has arrived.

(*Enter General Haverill with a Staff Officer*)

FRANK.   (*Moving down*) My father!

HAVERILL.   (*Exchanging salutes with the three officers. He turns to the Staff Officer, giving him a paper and brief instructions in dumb show. The Officer goes out over the incline. Another Staff Officer enters, salutes and hands him a paper, then stands up.*) Ah! The men are ready. (*Looking at the paper, then to Kerchival*) Colonel! I have a very important matter to arrange with you; there is not a moment to be lost. I will ask Captain Heartsease to remain. (*Frank salutes and starts up stage; Haverill looks at him, starting slightly; raises his hand to detain him.*) One moment; your name!

HEARTSEASE.   Lieutenant Bedloe, General, of my own troop, and one of our best officers. (*Haverill steps to Frank, looking into his face a moment.*)

HAVERILL.   Pardon me! (*Stepping down stage, Frank moves up, stops and looks back at him. Haverill stands up a moment in thought, covers his face with one hand, then draws up.*) Colonel West! We have a most dangerous piece of work for a young officer—(*Frank starts joyfully.*)—to lead a party of men, whom I have already selected. I cannot *order* an officer to undertake anything so nearly hopeless; he must be a volunteer.

FRANK.   Oh, sir, General! Let me be their leader.

HAVERILL.   I thought you had passed on.

FRANK.   Do not refuse me, sir. (*Haverill looks at him a moment. Heartsease and Kerchival exchange glances.*)

HAVERILL.   You are the man we need, my young friend. You shall go. Listen! We wish to secure a key to the cipher dispatches, which the enemy are now sending from their signal station on Three Top Mountain. There is another Confederate Signal Station in the valley, just beyond Buckton's Ford. (*Pointing*) Your duty will be this: First, to get inside the enemy's line; then to follow a path through the woods, with one of our scouts as your guide; attack the Station suddenly, and secure their code, if possible. I have this moment received word that the scout and the men are at the fort, now awaiting their leader. Major McCandless, of my staff, will take you to the place. (*Indicating the Staff Officer. Frank exchanges salutes with him.*) My young friend! I do not conceal from you the dangerous nature of the work on which I am sending you. If—if you do not return, I—I will write, myself, to your friends. (*Taking out note book*) Have you a father living?

FRANK.   My—father—is—is—he is—

HAVERILL.   I understand you. A mother? Or—

KERCHIVAL.   I have the address of Lieutenant Bedloe's friends, General.

HAVERILL.   I will ask you to give it to me if necessary. (*Extends his hand*) Good-bye, my lad. (*Frank moves to him. Haverill grasps his hand warmly.*) Keep a brave heart and come back to us. (*Frank moves up stage. Exit Staff Officer.*)

FRANK.   He is my father still. (*Exit*)

HAVERILL.   My dead boy's face! (*Dropping his face into both hands*)

HEARTSEASE.   (*Apart to Kerchival*) He shall not go alone. (*Aloud*) General! Will you kindly give me leave of absence from the command?

HAVERILL.   Leave of absence! To an officer in active service—and in the presence of the enemy?

KERCHIVAL.   (*Taking his hand. Apart.*) God bless you, old fellow! Look after the boy.

HAVERILL.   A—h—(*With a sudden thought, turns*) I think I understand you, Captain Heartsease. Yes; you may have leave of absence.

HEARTSEASE.   Thank you. (*Salutes. Haverill and Kerchival salute. Exit Heartsease.*)

KERCHIVAL.   Have you any further orders for me, General?

HAVERILL.   I wish you to understand the great importance of the duty to which I have just assigned this young officer. General Sheridan started for Washington this noon, by way of Front Royal. Since his departure, we have had reason to believe that the enemy are about to move, and we must be able to read their signal dispatches, if possible. (*Sitting*) I have ordered Captain Lockwood, of our own Signal Corps, to report to you here with officers and men. (*Takes up the empty envelope on table, unconsciously, as he speaks, tapping it on the table*) If Lieutenant Bedloe succeeds in getting the key to the enemy's cipher, we can signal from this point—(*Pointing to elevation*)—to our station at Front Royal. Men and horses are waiting there now, to carry forward a message, if necessary, to General Sheridan himself. (*He starts suddenly, looking at the envelope in his hand; reads address. Aside.*) "Colonel Kerchival West"—in my wife's handwriting!

KERCHIVAL.   I'll attend to your orders.

HAVERILL.   Postmarked at Washington, yesterday. (*Reads*) "Private and confidential." (*Aloud*) Colonel West! I found a paragraph, today, in a paper published in Richmond taken from a prisoner. I will read it to you. (*Takes newspaper slip from his wallet and reads*) "From the Charleston Mercury. Captain Edward Thornton, of the Confederate Secret Service, has been assigned to duty in the Shenandoah Valley. Our gallant Captain still bears upon his face the mark of his meeting, in 1861, with Lieutenant, now Colonel Kerchival West, who is also to serve in the valley with Sheridan's Army. Another meeting between these two men would be one of the strange coincidences of the war, as they were at one time, if not indeed at present, interested in the same beautiful woman." (*Rises*) I will ask you to read the last few lines, yourself. (*Crossing, he hands Kerchival the slip.*)

KERCHIVAL.   (*Reading*) "The scandal connected with the lovely wife of a Northern officer, at the opening of the war, was overshadowed, of course, by the attack on Fort Sumter; but many Charlestonians will remember it. The lady in defense of whose good name Captain Thornton fought the duel"—He defending her good name!—"is the wife of General Haverill, who will be Colonel West's immediate commander." (*He pauses a moment, then hands back the slip.*) General! I struck Mr. Thornton after a personal quarrel.

HAVERILL.   And the cause of the blow? There is much more in this than I have ever known of. I need hardly say that I do not accept the statement of this scandalous paragraph as correct. I will ask you to tell me the whole story, frankly, as man to man.

KERCHIVAL.   (*After a moment's thought*) I will tell you all—frankly, General.

(*Enter Sergeant Barket*)

BARKET.   Colonel Wist? Adjutant Rollins wishes to report—a prisoner—just captured.

HAVERILL.   We will meet again later, tonight, when the camp is at rest. We are both soldiers, and have duties before us at once. For the present, Colonel, be on the alert; we must watch the enemy. (*He moves up the stage. Barket salutes. Haverill stops and looks at envelope in his hands, reading.*) "Private and confidential." (*Exit*)

KERCHIVAL.   Sergeant Barket! Lieutenant Bedloe has crossed the enemy's line at Buckton's Ford with a party of men. I wish you to ride to the ford yourself, and remain there, with your horse in readiness and fresh. As soon as any survivor of the party returns, ride back with the first news at full speed.

BARKET.   Yes, sir. (*Starting*)

KERCHIVAL.   You say a prisoner has been captured? Is it a spy?

BARKET.   Worse—a petticoat.

KERCHIVAL.   A female prisoner! (*Dropping into seat*)

BARKET.   I towld the byes your honor wouldn't thank us fer the catchin' of her. The worst of it is she's a lady; and what's worse still, it's a purty one.

KERCHIVAL.   Tell Major Wilson, for me, to let her take the oath, and everything else she wants. The Government of the United States will send her an apology and a new bonnet.

BARKET.   The young lady is to take the oath, is it? She says she'll see us damned first.

KERCHIVAL.   A lady, Barket?

BARKET.   Well! she didn't use thim exact words. That's the way I understand her emphasis. Ivery time she looks at me, I feel like getting under a boom-proof. She was dashing through the woods on a gray horse, sur; and we had the divil's own chase. But we came up wid her, at last, down by the bend in Oak Run. Just at that moment we saw the figure of a Confederate officer, disappearing among the trays on the ither side.

KERCHIVAL.   A—h!

BARKET.   Two of us rayturned wid the girl; and the rist wint after the officer. Nothing has been heard of thim yet.

KERCHIVAL.   Have you found any dispatches on the prisoner?

BARKET.   Well!—yer honor, I'm a bachelor, meself; and I'm not familiar with the jayography of the sex. We byes are in mortal terror for fear somebody might order us to go on an exploring expedition.

KERCHIVAL.   Tell them to send the prisoner here, Barket, and hurry to Buckton's Ford yourself, at once.

BARKET.   As fast as me horse can carry me, sir, and it's a good one. (*Exit*)

KERCHIVAL.   I'd rather deal with half the Confederate army than with one woman, but I must question her. They captured her down by the Bend in Oak Run. (*Taking out map; looks at it*) I see. She had just met, or was about to meet, a Confederate officer at that point. It is evident that she was either taking him a dispatch or was there to receive one. Oak Run. (*Corporal Dunn and two soldiers enter, with Gertrude as a prisoner. They stop. Kerchival sits studying map. Gertrude glances at him and marches down with head erect; stops, with her back to him.*)

DUNN.   The prisoner, Colonel West!

KERCHIVAL.   Ah! Very well, Corporal; you can go. (*Rising; he motions the guard to retire. Corporal Dunn gives the necessary orders and exit with guard.*) Be seated, madam. (*Gertrude draws up, folding her arms and planting her foot, spitefully. Kerchival shrugs his shoulder. Aside.*) I wish they'd capture a tigress for me, or some other female animal that I know how to manage better than I do a woman. (*Aloud*) I am very sorry, madam; but, of course, my duty as a military officer is paramount to all other considerations. You have been captured within the lines of this army, and under circumstances which lead me to think that you have important dispatches upon your person. I trust that you will give me whatever you have, at once. I shall be exceedingly sorry if you compel me to adopt the extreme—and the very disagreeable course—for both of us—of having—you—I—I hesitate even to use the word, madame—but military law is absolute—having you—

GERTRUDE.   Searched! If you dare, Colonel West! (*Turning to him suddenly and drawing up to her full height*)

KERCHIVAL.   Gertrude Ellingham! (*Springs across to her, with his arms extended*) My dear Gertrude!

GERTRUDE.   (*Turning her back upon him*) Not "dear Gertrude" to you, sir!

KERCHIVAL.   Not?—Oh! I forgot.

GERTRUDE.   (*Coldly*) I am your prisoner.

KERCHIVAL.   Yes. (*Drawing up firmly, with a change of manner*) We will return to the painful realities of war. I am very sorry that you have placed yourself in a position like this, and, believe me, Gertrude—(*With growing tenderness*)—I am still more sorry to be in such a position myself. (*Resting one hand on her arm, and his other arm about her waist*)

GERTRUDE.   (*After looking down at his hands*) You don't like the position? (*He starts back, drawing up with dignity.*) Is that the paramount duty of a military officer?

KERCHIVAL.   You will please hand me whatever dispatches or other papers may be in your possession.

GERTRUDE.   (*Looking away*) You will *force* me, I suppose. I am a woman; you have the power. Order in the guard! A Corporal and two men—you'd better make it a dozen—I am dangerous! Call the whole regiment to arms! Beat the long roll! I won't give up, if all the armies of the United States surround me.

(*Enter General Buckthorn*)

KERCHIVAL.   General Buckthorn! (*Saluting*)

BUCKTHORN.   Colonel West.

GERTRUDE.   (*Aside*) Jenny's father! (*Buckthorn glances at Gertrude, who still stands looking away. He moves down to Kerchival.*)

BUCKTHORN.   (*Apart, gruffly*) I was passing with my staff, and I was informed that you had captured a woman bearing dispatches to the enemy. Is this the one?

KERCHIVAL.   Yes, General.

BUCKTHORN.   Ah! (*Turning, he looks at her.*)

GERTRUDE.   I wonder if he will recognize me. He hasn't seen me since I was a little girl. (*Turns toward him*)

BUCKTHORN.   (*Turning to Kerchival; punches him in the ribs*) Fine young woman! (*Turns and bows to her very gallantly, removing his hat. She bows deeply in return.*) A-h-e-m! (*Suddenly pulling himself up to a stern, military air; then gruffly to Kerchival, extending his hand*) Let me see the dispatches.

KERCHIVAL.   She declines positively to give them up.

BUCKTHORN.   Oh! Does she? (*Walks up the stage thoughtfully; turns*) My dear young lady! I trust you will give us no further trouble. Kindly let us have those dispatches.

GERTRUDE.   (*Looking away*) I have no dispatches, and I would not give them to you if I had.

BUCKTHORN.   What! You defy my authority? Colonel West, I command you! Search the prisoner! (*Gertrude turns suddenly towards Kerchival, facing him defiantly. He looks across at her aghast. A moment's pause.*)

KERCHIVAL.   General Buckthorn—I decline to obey that order.

BUCKTHORN.   You—you decline to obey my order! (*Moves down to him fiercely*)

KERCHIVAL.   (*Apart*) General! It is the woman I love!

BUCKTHORN.   (*Apart*) Is it? Damn you, sir! I wouldn't have an officer in my army corps who *would* obey me, under such circumstances. I'll have to look for those dispatches myself.

KERCHIVAL.   (*Facing him, angrily*) If you dare, General Buckthorn!

BUCKTHORN.   (*Apart*) Blast your eyes! I'd kick you out of the army if you'd *let* me search her; but it's my military duty to swear at you. (*To Gertrude*) Colonel West has sacrificed his life to protect you.

GERTRUDE.   His life!

BUCKTHORN.   I shall have him shot for insubordination to his commander, immediately. (*Gives Kerchival a huge wink and turns up stage*)

GERTRUDE.   Oh, sir! General! I have told you the truth. I have no dispatches. Believe me, sir, I haven't so much as a piece of paper about me, except—

BUCKTHORN.   Except? (*Turning sharply*)

GERTRUDE.   Only a letter. Here it is. (*Taking letter from the bosom of her dress*) Upon my soul, it is all I have. Truly, it is.

BUCKTHORN.   (*Taking letter*) Colonel West you're reprieved. (*Winks at Kerchival, who turns away, laughing. Buckthorn reads letter.*) "Washington"—Ho!—ho! From within our own lines!—"Colonel Kerchival West"—

KERCHIVAL.   Eh?

GERTRUDE.   Please, General!—Don't read it aloud.

BUCKTHORN.   Very well! I won't.

KERCHIVAL.   (*Aside*) I wonder what it has to do with me.

BUCKTHORN.   (*Reading. Aside.*) "If Kerchival West had heard you say, as I did-m-m—that you loved him with your whole heart—" (*He glances up at Gertrude, who drops her head coyly.*) This is a very important military document. (*Turns to last page*) "Signed, Constance Haverill." (*Turns to front page*) "My dear Gertrude!" Is this Miss Gertrude Ellingham?

GERTRUDE.   Yes, General.

BUCKTHORN.   I sent my daughter, Jenny, to your house with an escort this morning.

GERTRUDE.   She is here.

BUCKTHORN.   (*Tapping her under the chin*) You're an arrant little Rebel, my dear; but I like you immensely. (*Draws up suddenly, with an* Ahem!

Turns to Kerchival.) Colonel West, I leave this dangerous young woman in your charge. (*Kerchival approaches.*) If she disobeys you in any way, or attempts to escape—read that letter! (*Giving him the letter*)

GERTRUDE.   Oh! General!

BUCKTHORN.   But not till then.

KERCHIVAL.   (*Tenderly, taking her hand*) My—prisoner!

GERTRUDE.   (*Aside*) I could scratch my own eyes out—or his, either— rather than have him read that letter.

(*Enter Corporal Dunn with guard of four soldiers and Captain Ed- ward Thornton as a prisoner*)

KERCHIVAL.   Edward Thornton!

GERTRUDE.   They have taken him, also! He has the dispatch!

DUNN.   The Confederate Officer, Colonel, who was pursued by our troops at Oak Run, after they captured the young lady.

BUCKTHORN.   The little witch has been communicating with the enemy!

KERCHIVAL.   (*To Gertrude*) You will give me your parole of honor until we next meet?

GERTRUDE.   Yes. (*Aside*) That letter! I *am* his prisoner. (*She walks up the steps. Gertrude looks back at Thornton. Exit.*)

KERCHIVAL.   We will probably find the dispatches we have been looking for now, General.

BUCKTHORN.   Prisoner! You will hand us what papers you may have.

THORNTON.   I will hand you nothing.

BUCKTHORN.   Colonel! (*Kerchival motions to Thornton, who looks at him sullenly.*)

KERCHIVAL.   Corporal Dunn!—search the prisoner. (*Dunn steps to Thorn- ton, taking him by the shoulder and turning him rather roughly. Thorn- ton's back is to the audience. Dunn throws open his coat, takes paper from his breast, hands it to Kerchival, who gives it to Buckthorn.*) Pro- ceed with the search. (*Dunn continues the search. Buckthorn drops upon seat, lights a match, looks at the paper.*)

BUCKTHORN.   (*Reading*) "General Rosser will rejoin General Early with all the cavalry in his command, at—" This is important. (*Continues to read with matches. The Corporal hands a packet to Kerchival. He re- moves the covering.*)

KERCHIVAL.   (*Starting*) A portrait of Mrs. Haverill! (*He touches Corporal Dunn on the shoulder quickly and motions him to retire. Dunn falls back to the guard. Kerchival speaks apart to Thornton, who has turned front.*) How did this portrait come into your possession?

THORNTON.   That is my affair, not yours!

BUCKTHORN.   Anything else, Colonel?

KERCHIVAL.   (*Placing the miniature in his pocket*) Nothing!

THORNTON.   (*Apart, over Kerchival's shoulder*) A time will come, per- haps, when I can avenge the insult of this search, and also this scar.

(*Pointing to a scar on his face*) Your aim was better than mine in Charleston, but we shall meet again; give me back that picture.

KERCHIVAL.   Corporal! Take your prisoner!

THORNTON.   Ah! (*He springs viciously at Kerchival; Corporal Dunn springs forward, seizes Thornton and throws him back to the Guard. Kerchival walks to the right; Dunn stands with his carbine levelled at Thornton, looks at Kerchival, who quietly motions him out. Corporal Dunn gives the orders to the men and marches out with Thornton.*)

BUCKTHORN.   Ah! (*Still reading with matches*) Colonel! (*Rising*) The enemy has a new movement on foot, and General Sheridan has left the army! Listen! (*Reads from dispatches with matches*) "Watch for a signal from Three Top Mountain tonight."

KERCHIVAL.   We hope to be able to read that signal ourselves.

BUCKTHORN.   Yes, I know. Be on your guard. I will speak with General Haverill, and then ride over to General Wright's headquarters. Keep us informed.

KERCHIVAL.   I will, General. (*Saluting. Buckthorn salutes and exit.*)

KERCHIVAL.   "Watch for a signal from Three Top Mountain tonight." (*Looking up at Mountain*) We shall be helpless to read it unless Lieutenant Bedloe is successful. I only hope the poor boy is not lying dead, already, in those dark woods beyond the ford. (*He turns down, taking the miniature from his pocket.*) How came Edward Thornton to have this portrait of Mrs. Haverill in his possession? (*Gertrude runs in on veranda.*)

GERTRUDE.   Oh, Colonel West! He's here! (*Looks back*) They are coming this way with him.

KERCHIVAL.   Him! Who?

GERTRUDE.   Jack.

KERCHIVAL.   Jack!

GERTRUDE.   My own horse!

KERCHIVAL.   Ah, I remember! He and I were acquainted in Charleston.

GERTRUDE.   Two troopers are passing through the camp with him.

KERCHIVAL.   He is not in your possession?

GERTRUDE.   He was captured at the battle of Fair Oaks, but I recognized him the moment I saw him; and I am sure he knew me, too, when I went up to him. He whinnied and looked so happy. You are in command here —(*Running down*)—you will compel them to give him up to me?

KERCHIVAL.   If he is in my command, your pet shall be returned to you. I'll give one of my own horses to the Government as a substitute, if necessary.

GERTRUDE.   Oh, thank you, my dear Kerchival! (*Going to him; he takes her hand, looking into her eyes.*) I—I could almost—

KERCHIVAL.   Can you almost confess, at last, Gertrude, that you—love me? (*Tenderly; she draws back, hanging her head, but leaving her hand in his.*) Have I been wrong? I felt that that confession was hovering on your tongue when we were separated in Charleston. Have I seen that confession in your eyes since we met again today—even among the angry flashes which they have shot out at me? During all this terrible war—in the camp and the trench -in the battle—I have dreamed of a meeting like this. You are still silent? (*Her hand is still in his. She is looking down. A smile steals over her face, and she raises her eyes to his, taking his hand in both her own.*)

GERTRUDE.   Kerchival! I—(*Enter Benson. She looks around over her shoulder. Kerchival looks up. A trooper leading the large black horse of Act I, now caparisoned in military saddle, bridle, etc., follows Benson across; another trooper follows.*) Jack! (*She runs up stage, meeting the horse, Kerchival turns.*)

KERCHIVAL.   Confound Jack! That infernal horse was always in my way!

GERTRUDE.   (*With her arm about her horse's neck*) My darling old fellow! Is he not beautiful, Kerchival? They have taken good care of him. How soft his coat is!

KERCHIVAL.   Benson, explain this!

BENSON.   I was instructed to show this horse and his leader through the lines, sir.

KERCHIVAL.   What are your orders, my man? (*Moving up, the trooper hands him a paper. He moves a few steps down, reading it.*)

GERTRUDE.   You are to be mine again, Jack, mine! (*Resting her cheek against the horse's head and patting it.*) The Colonel has promised it to me.

KERCHIVAL.   Ah! (*With a start, as he reads the paper. Gertrude raises her head and looks at him.*) This is General Sheridan's horse, on his way to Winchester, for the use of the General when he returns from Washington.

GERTRUDE.   General Sheridan's horse? He is mine!

KERCHIVAL.   I have no authority to detain him. He must go on.

GERTRUDE.   I have hold of Jack's bridle, and you may order your men to take out their sabres and cut my hand off.

KERCHIVAL.   (*He approaches her and gently takes her hand as it holds the bridle.*) I would rather have my own hand cut off, Gertrude, than bring tears to your eyes, but there is no alternative! (*Gertrude releases the bridle and turns front, brushing her eyes, her hand still held in his, his back to the audience. He returns the order and motions troopers out; they move out with horse. Kerchival turns to move. Gertrude starts after the horse; he turns quickly to check her.*) You forget—that—you are my prisoner.

GERTRUDE.   I *will* go!

KERCHIVAL.   General Buckthorn left me special instructions—(*Taking out wallet and letter*)—in case you declined to obey my orders—

GERTRUDE.   Oh, Colonel! Please don't read that letter. (*She stands near him, dropping her head. He glances up at her from the letter. She glances up at him and drops her eyes again.*) I will obey you.

KERCHIVAL.   (*Aside*) What the deuce can there be in that letter?

GERTRUDE.   Colonel West! Your men made me a prisoner this afternoon;

tonight you have robbed me, by your own orders, of—of—Jack is only a pet, but I love him; and my brother is also a captive in your hands. When we separated in Charleston you said that we were enemies. What is there lacking to make those words true today? You *are* my enemy! A few moments ago you asked me to make a confession to you. You can judge for yourself whether it is likely to be a confession of—love—or of hatred!

KERCHIVAL. Hatred!

GERTRUDE. (*Facing him*) Listen to my confession, sir! From the bottom of my heart—

KERCHIVAL. Stop!

GERTRUDE. I will not stop!

KERCHIVAL. I command you.

GERTRUDE. Indeed! (*He throws open the wallet in his hand and raises the letter.*) Ah! (*She turns away; turns again, as if to speak. He half opens the letter. She stamps her foot and walks up the steps of the veranda. Here she turns again.*) I tell you, I—(*He opens the letter. She turns, and exits·with a spiteful step.*)

KERCHIVAL. I wonder if that document orders me to cut her head off! (*Returning it to wallet and pocket*) Was ever lover in such a position? I am obliged to cross the woman I love at every step.

(*Enter Corporal Dunn very hurriedly*)

DUNN. A message from Adjutant Rollins, sir! The prisoner, Captain Thornton, dashed away from the special guard which was placed over him, and he has escaped. He had a knife concealed, and two of the Guard are badly wounded. Adjutant Rollins thinks the prisoner is still within the lines of the camp—in one of the houses or the stables.

KERCHIVAL. Tell Major Wilson to place the remainder of the Guard under arrest, and to take every possible means to recapture the prisoner. (*Corporal Dunn salutes and exit.*) So! Thornton has jumped his guard, and he is armed. I wonder if he is trying to get away, or to find me. From what I know of the man, he doesn't much care which he succeeds in doing. That scar which I gave him in Charleston is deeper in his heart than it is in his face. (*A signal light suddenly appears on Three Top Mountain. The "Call."*) Ah!—the enemy's signal! (*Enter Captain Lockwood, followed by Lieutenant of Signal Corps*) Captain Lockwood! You are here! Are your Signalmen with you?

LOCKWOOD. Yes, Colonel; and one of my Lieutenants. (*The Lieutenant is looking up at the signal with a glass. Captain Lockwood does the same. Haverill enters, followed by two Staff Officers.*)

HAVERILL. (*As he enters*) Can you make anything of it, Captain?

LOCKWOOD. Nothing, General! Our services are quite useless unless Lieutenant Bedloe returns with the key to their signals.

HAVERILL. A-h! We shall fail. It is time he had returned, if successful.

SENTINEL. (*Without*) Halt! Who goes there? (*Kerchival runs up the stage and halfway up incline, looking off.*) Halt! (*A shot without*)

BARKET. (*Without*) Och!—Ye murtherin spalpeen!

KERCHIVAL. Sentinel! Let him pass; it is Sergeant Barket.

SENTINEL. (*Without*) Pass on.

KERCHIVAL. He didn't give the countersign. News from Lieutenant Bedloe, General!

BARKET. (*Hurrying in, up the slope*) Colonel Wist, our brave byes wiped out the enemy, and here's the papers.

KERCHIVAL. Ah! (*Taking papers—Then to Lockwood*) Is that the key?

LOCKWOOD. Yes, Lieutenant! (*Lieutenant hurries up to elevation looking through his glass. Lockwood opens book.*)

HAVERILL. What of Lieutenant Bedloe, Sergeant?

BARKET. Sayreously wounded, and in the hands of the inimy!

HAVERILL. (*Sighing*) A—h.

BARKET. (*Coming down stone steps*) It is reported that Captain Heartsease was shot dead at his side.

KERCHIVAL. Heartsease dead!

LIEUTENANT OF SIGNAL CORPS. (*Reading Signals*) Twelve—twenty-two—Eleven.

BARKET. Begorra! I forgot the Sintinil entirely, but he didn't forget me. (*Holding his left arm*)

HAVERILL. Colonel West! We must make every possible sacrifice for the immediate exchange of Lieutenant Bedloe, if he is still living. It is due to him. Colonel Robert Ellingham is a prisoner in this camp; offer him his own exchange for young Bedloe.

KERCHIVAL. He will accept, of course. I will ride to the front with him myself, General, and show him through the lines.

HAVERILL. At once! (*Kerchival crosses in front and exit on veranda.*) Can you follow the dispatch, Captain?

LOCKWOOD. Perfectly; everything is here.

HAVERILL. Well!

LIEUTENANT OF SIGNAL CORPS. Eleven—Twenty-two—One—Twelve.

LOCKWOOD. (*From book*) "General Longstreet is coming with—"

HAVERILL. Longstreet!

LIEUTENANT OF SIGNAL CORPS. One—Twenty-one.

LOCKWOOD. "With eighteen thousand men."

HAVERILL. Longstreet and his corps!

LIEUTENANT OF SIGNAL CORPS. Two—Eleven—Twenty-two.

LOCKWOOD. "Sheridan is away!"

HAVERILL. They have discovered his absence!

LIEUTENANT OF SIGNAL CORPS. Two—Twenty-two—Eleven—One—Twelve—One.

LOCKWOOD. "We will crush the Union Army before he can return."

HAVERILL. Signal that dispatch from here to our Station at Front Royal.

(*Pointing*) Tell them to send it after General Sheridan—and ride for their lives. (*Lockwood hurries out.*) Major Burton! We will ride to General Wright's headquarters at once—our horses! (*Noise of a struggle without*)

BARKET. What the devil is the row out there? (*Exit; also one of the Staff Officers*)

HAVERILL. What is this! Colonel West wounded!

(*Enter Kerchival West, his coat thrown open, with Ellingham and Barket assisting*)

ELLINGHAM. Steady, Kerchival, old boy! You should have let us carry you.

KERCHIVAL. Nonsense, old fellow! It's a mere touch with the point of the knife. I—I'm faint—with the loss of a little blood—that's all. Bob!—I— (*He reels suddenly and is caught by Ellingham as he sinks to the ground, insensible.*)

ELLINGHAM. Kerchival! (*Kneeling at his side*)

HAVERILL. Go for the Surgeon! (*To Staff Officer, who goes out quickly on veranda*) How did this happen? (*Enter Corporal Dunn and Guard with Thornton. He is in his shirt sleeves and disheveled, his arms folded. They march down stage.*) Captain Thornton!

ELLINGHAM. We were leaving the house together; a hunted animal sprang suddenly across our path, like a panther. (*Looking over his shoulder*) There it stands. Kerchival!—my brother!

DUNN. We had just brought this prisoner to bay, but I'm afraid we were too late.

HAVERILL. This is assassination, sir, not war. If you have killed him—

THORNTON. Do what you like with me; we need waste no words. I had an old account to settle, and I have paid my debt.

ELLINGHAM. General Haverill! I took these from his breast when he first fell. (*Handing up wallet and miniature to Haverill. Haverill starts as he looks at the miniature. Thornton watches him.*)

HAVERILL. (*Aside*) My wife's portrait!

THORNTON. If I have killed him—your honor will be buried in the same grave.

HAVERILL. Her picture on his breast! She gave it to him—not to my son! (*Dropping into seat. Captain Lockwood enters with a Signalman, who has a burning torch on a long pole; he hurries up the elevation. Captain Lockwood stands below facing him. Almost simultaneously with the entrance of the Signalman, Gertrude runs in on veranda.*)

GERTRUDE. They are calling for a surgeon! Who is it? Brother!—you are safe. Ah! (*Uttering a scream as she sees Kerchival, and falling on her knees at his side*) Kerchival! Forget those last bitter words I said to you. Can't you hear my confession? I do love you. Can't you hear me? I love you! (*The Signalman is swinging the torch as the curtain descends.*)

CURTAIN

ACT III

Scene, Same. It is now bright daylight, with sunshine flecking the foreground and bathing the distant valley and mountains. Jenny is sitting on a low stone post, looking to the left. As the curtain rises, she imitates a Trumpet Signal on her closed fists.

JENNY.   What a magnificent line! Guideposts! Every man and every horse is eager for the next command. There comes the flag! (*Trumpet Signal without*) To the standard! (*As the signal begins*) The regiment is going to the front. Oh! I do wish I could go with it. I always do, the moment I hear the trumpets. Boots and saddles! Mount! I wish I was in command of the regiment. It was born in me. (*Trumpet Signal without*) Fours right! There they go! Look at those horses' ears! (*Trumpet Signal without*) Forward. (*Military band heard without, playing "The Battle Cry of Freedom." Jenny takes attitude of holding bridle and trotting.*) Rappity—plap—plap—plap, etc. (*She imitates the motions of a soldier on horseback, stepping down to rock at side of post; thence to ground and about stage, with the various curvettings of a spirited horse. Chorus of soldiers without with the band. The music becomes more and more distant. Jenny gradually stops as the music is dying away, and stands, listening. As it dies entirely away, she suddenly starts to an enthusiastic attitude.*) Ah! If I were only a man! The enemy! On Third Battalion, left, front, into line, march! Draw sabres! Charge! (*Imitates a Trumpet Signal. As she finishes, she rises to her full height, with both arms raised, and trembling with enthusiasm.*) Ah! (*She suddenly drops her arms and changes to an attitude and expression of disappointment—pouting.*) And the first time Old Margery took me to papa, in her arms, she had to tell him I was a girl. Papa was as much disgusted as I was. But he'd never admit it; he says I'm as good a soldier as any of 'em—just as I am.

(*Enter Barket on the veranda, his arm in a sling*)

BARKET.   Miss Jenny!
JENNY.   Barket! The regiment has marched away to the front, and we girls are left here, with just you and a corporal's guard to look after us.
BARKET.   I've been watching the byes mesilf. (*Coming down*) If a little milithary sugar-plum like you, Miss Jenny, objects to not goin' wid' 'em, what do you think of an ould piece of hard tack like me? I can't join the regiment till I've taken you and Miss Madeline back to Winchester, by your father's orders. But it isn't the first time I've escorted you, Miss Jenny. Many a time, when you was a baby, on the Plains, I commanded a special guard to accompany ye's from one fort to anither, and we gave the command in a whisper, so as not to wake ye's up.

JENNY.   I told you to tell papa that I'd let him know when Madeline and I were ready to go.

BARKET.   I tould him that I'd as soon move a train of army mules.

JENNY.   I suppose we must start for home again today?

BARKET.   Yes, Miss Jenny, in charge of an ould Sargeant wid his arm in a sling and a couple of convalescent throopers. This department of the United States Army will move to the rear in half an hour.

JENNY.   Madeline and I only came yesterday morning.

BARKET.   Whin your father got ye's a pass to the front, we all thought the fightin' in the Shenandoey Valley was over. It looks now as if it was just beginning. This is no place for women, now. Miss Gertrude Ellingham ought to go wid us, but she won't.

JENNY.   Barket! Captain Heartsease left the regiment yesterday, and he hasn't rejoined it; he isn't with them, now, at the head of his company. Where is he?

BARKET.   I can't say where he is, Miss Jenny. (*Aside*) Lyin' unburied in the woods, where he was shot, I'm afraid.

JENNY.   When Captain Heartsease does rejoin the regiment, Barket, please say to him for me, that—that I—I may have some orders for him, when we next meet. (*Exit on veranda*)

BARKET.   Whin they nixt mate. They tell us there is no such thing as marriage in Hiven. If Miss Jenny and Captain Heartsease mate there, they'll invint somethin' that's mighty like it. While I was lyin' wounded in General Buckthorn's house at Washington, last summer, and ould Margery was taking care of me, Margery tould me, confidentially, that they was in love wid aitch ither; and I think she was about right. I've often seen Captain Heartsease take a sly look at a little lace handkerchief, just before we wint into battle. Here's General Buckthorn himself. He and I must make it as aisy as we can for Miss Jenny's poor heart.

(*Enter General Buckthorn*)

BUCKTHORN.   Sergeant Barket! You haven't started with those girls yet?

BARKET.   They're to go in half an hour, sir.

BUCKTHORN.   Be sure they do go. Is General Haverill here?

BARKET.   Yes, sir; in the house with some of his staff, and the Surgeon.

BUCKTHORN.   Ah! The Surgeon. How is Colonel West, this morning, after the wound he received last night?

BARKET.   He says, himself, that he's as well as iver he was; but the Colonel and Surgeon don't agray on that subject. The dochter says he mustn't lave his room for a month. The knife wint dape; and there's somethin' wrong inside of him. But the Colonel, bein' on the outside himsilf, can't see it. He's as cross as a bear, baycause they wouldn't let him go to the front this morning at the head of his regiment. I happened to raymark that the Chaplain was prayin' for his raycovery. The Colonel said he'd courtmartial him if he didn't stop that—quick; there's more important things for the Chaplain to pray for in his official capacity. Just at that moment the trumpets sounded, "Boots and Saddles." I had to dodge one of his boots, and the Surgeon had a narrow escape from the ither one. It was lucky for us both his saddle wasn't in the room.

BUCKTHORN. That looks encouraging. I think Kerchival will get on.

BARKET. Might I say a word to you, sur, about Miss Jenny?

BUCKTHORN. Certainly, Barket. You and old Margery and myself have been a sort of triangular mother, so to speak, to the little girl since her own poor mother left her to our care, when she was only a baby, in the old fort on the Plains. (*At his side and unconsciously resting his arm over Barket's shoulder familiarly. Suddenly draws up.*) Ahem! (*Then gruffly*) What is it? Proceed.

BARKET. Her mother's bosom would have been the softest place for her poor little head to rest upon, now, sur.

BUCKTHORN. (*Touching his eyes*) Well!

BARKET. Ould Margery tould me in Washington that Miss Jenny and Captain Heartsease were in love wid aitch ither.

BUCKTHORN. (*Starting*) In love!

BARKET. I approved of the match.

BUCKTHORN. What the devil! (*Barket salutes quickly and starts up stage and out. Buckthorn moves up after him; stops at post, Barket stops in road.*)

BARKET. So did ould Margery.

BUCKTHORN. March! (*Angrily. Barket salutes suddenly and exit.*) Heartsease! That young jackanapes! A mere fop; he'll never make a soldier. My girl in love with—bah! I don't believe it; she's too good a soldier herself.

(*Enter Haverill on veranda*)

Ah! Haverill!

HAVERILL. General Buckthorn! Have you heard anything of General Sheridan since I sent that dispatch to him last evening?

BUCKTHORN. He received it at midnight and sent back word that he considers it a ruse of the enemy. General Wright agrees with him. The reconnaissance yesterday showed no hostile force on our right, and Crook reports that Early is retreating up the valley. But General Sheridan may, perhaps, give up his journey to Washington, and he has ordered some changes in our line, to be executed this afternoon at four o'clock. I rode over to give you your instructions in person. You may order General Mac-Cuen to go into camp on the right of Meadow Brook, with the second division. (*Haverill is writing in his note-book.*)

(*Enter Jenny on veranda*)

JENNY. Oh, papa! I'm so glad you've come. I've got something to say to you. (*Running down and jumping into his arms, kissing him. He turns with her, and sets her down squarely on her feet and straight before him.*)

BUCKTHORN. And I've got something to say to you—about Captain Heartsease.

JENNY. Oh! That's just what I wanted to talk about.

BUCKTHORN. Fall in! Front face! (*She jumps into military position, turning towards him.*) What's this I hear from Sergeant Barket? He says you've been falling in love.

JENNY. I have. (*Saluting*)

BUCKTHORN. Young woman! Listen to my orders. Fall out! (*Turns sharply and marches to Haverill*) Order the Third Brigade of Cavalry, under Colonel Lowell, to occupy the left of the pike.

JENNY. Papa! (*Running to him and seizing the tail of his .coat*) Papa, dear!

BUCKTHORN. Close in Colonel Powell on the extreme left—(*Slapping his coat-tails out of Jenny's hands, without looking around*)—and hold Custer on the second line, at Old Forge Road. That is all at present. (*Turns to Jenny*) Goodbye, my darling! (*Kisses her*) Remember your orders! You little pet! (*Chuckling, as he taps her chin; draws up suddenly; turns to Haverill*) General! I bid you good-day.

HAVERILL. Good-day, General Buckthorn. (*They salute with great dignity. Buckthorn starts up stage; Jenny springs after him, seizing his coat-tails.*)

JENNY. But I want to talk with you, papa; I can't fall out. I—I haven't finished yet. (*Clinging to his coat, as Buckthorn marches out rapidly in the road, holding back with all her might*)

HAVERILL. It may have been a ruse of the enemy, but I hope that General Sheridan has turned back from Washington. (*Looking at his notebook*) We are to make changes in our line at four o'clock this afternoon. (*Returns book to pocket and stands in thought*) The Surgeon tells me that Kerchival West will get on well enough if he remains quiet; otherwise not. He shall not die by the hand of a common assassin; he has no right to die like that. My wife gave my own picture of herself to him— not to my son—and she looked so like an angel when she took it from my hand! They were both false to me, and they have been true to each other. I will save his life for myself.

(*Enter Gertrude on veranda*)

GERTRUDE. General Haverill! (*Anxiously, coming down*) Colonel West persists in disobeying the injuctions of the Surgeon. He is preparing to join his regiment at the front. Give him your orders to remain here. Compel him to be prudent!

HAVERILL. (*Quickly*) The honor of death at the front is not in reserve for him.

GERTRUDE. Eh? What did you say, General?

HAVERILL. Gertrude! I wish to speak to you, as your father's old friend;

and I was once your guardian. Your father was my senior officer in the Mexican War. Without his care I should have been left dead in a foreign land. He, himself, afterwards fell fighting for the old flag.

GERTRUDE.   The old flag. (*Aside*) My father died for it, and he—(*Looking to the left*)—is suffering for it—the old flag!

HAVERILL.   I can now return the kindness your father did to me, by protecting his daughter from something that may be worse than death.

GERTRUDE.   What do you mean?

HAVERILL.   Last night I saw you kneeling at the side of Kerchival West; you spoke to him with all the tender passion of a Southern woman. You said you loved him. But you spoke into ears that could not hear you. Has he ever heard those words from your lips? Have you ever confessed your love to him before?

GERTRUDE.   Never. Why do you ask?

HAVERILL.   Do not repeat those words. Keep your heart to yourself, my girl.

GERTRUDE.   General! Why do you say this to me? And at such a moment—when his life—

HAVERILL.   His life! (*Turning sharply*) It belongs to me!

GERTRUDE.   Oh!

KERCHIVAL.   Sergeant! (*Without. He steps into the road, looking back. Haverill comes down.*) See that my horse is ready at once. General! (*Saluting*) Are there any orders for my regiment beyond those given to Major Wilson in my absence this morning? I am about to ride on after the troops and reassume my command.

HAVERILL.   (*Quietly*) It is my wish, Colonel, that you remain here under the care of the Surgeon.

KERCHIVAL.   My wound is a mere trifle. This may be a critical moment in the campaign, and I cannot rest here. I must be with my own men.

HAVERILL.   (*Quietly*) I beg to repeat the wish I have already expressed. (*Kerchival walks to him and speaks apart, almost under his breath, but very earnest in tone.*)

KERCHIVAL.   I have had no opportunity, yet, to explain certain matters, as you requested me to do yesterday; but whatever there may be between us, you are now interfering with my duty and my privilege as a soldier; and it is my right to be at the head of my regiment.

HAVERILL.   (*Quietly*) It is my positive order that you do not reassume your command.

KERCHIVAL.   General Haverill, I protest against this—

HAVERILL.   (*Quietly*) You are under arrest, sir.

KERCHIVAL.   Arrest!

GERTRUDE.   Ah! (*Kerchival unclasps his belt and offers his sword to Haverill.*)

HAVERILL.   (*Quietly*) Keep your sword; I have no desire to humiliate you; but hold yourself subject to further orders from me. (*Kerchival moves to the left and goes up veranda.*)

KERCHIVAL.   My regiment at the front!—and I under arrest! (*Exit*)

HAVERILL.   Gertrude! If your heart refuses to be silent—if you feel that you must confess your love to that man—first tell him what I have said to you, and refer him to me for an explanation. (*Exit*)

GERTRUDE.   What can he mean? He would save me from something worse than death, he said. "His life—It belongs to me!" What can he mean? Kerchival told me that he loved me—it seems many years since that morning in Charleston—and when we met again, yesterday, he said that he had never ceased to love me. I will not believe that he has told me a falsehood. I have given him my love, my whole soul and my faith. (*Drawing up to her full height*) My perfect faith! (*Jenny runs in to the road and up the slope. She looks down the hill, then enters.*)

JENNY.   A flag of truce, Gertrude. And a party of Confederate soldiers, with an escort, coming up the hill. They are carrying someone; he is wounded.

(*Enter up the slope a Lieutenant of Infantry with an escort of Union Soldiers, their arms at right shoulder, and a party of Confederate Soldiers bearing a rustic stretcher. Lieutenant Frank Bedloe lies on the stretcher. Major Hardwick, a Confederate Surgeon, walks at his side. Madeline appears at veranda, watching them. Gertrude stands with her back to audience. The Lieutenant gives orders in a low tone, and the front escort moves to road. The Confederate bearers and the Surgeon pass through the gate. The rear escort moves to road, under Lieutenant's orders. The bearers halt, front; on a sign from the Surgeon, leave the stretcher on the ground, stepping back.*)

HARDWICK.   Is General Haverill here?

GERTRUDE.   Yes; what can we do, sir?

MADELINE.   The General is just about mounting with his staff to ride away. Shall I go for him, sir?

HARDWICK.   Say to him, please, that Colonel Robert Ellingham, of the Tenth Virginia, sends his respects and sympathy. He instructed me to bring this young officer to this point, in exchange for himself, as agreed upon between them last evening. (*Exit Madeline*)

JENNY.   Is he unconscious or sleeping, sir?

HARDWICK.   Hovering between life and death. I thought he would bear the removal better. He is waking. Here, my lad! (*Placing his canteen to the lips of Frank, who moves, reviving*) We have reached the end of our journey.

FRANK.   My father!

HARDWICK.   He is thinking of his home. (*Frank rises on one arm, assisted by the Surgeon.*)

FRANK.   I have obeyed General Haverill's orders, and I have a report to make.

GERTRUDE.   We have already sent for him. (*Stepping to him*) He will be here in a moment.

FRANK.   (*Looking into her face, brightly*) Is not this—Miss—Gertrude Ellingham?

GERTRUDE.   You know me? You have seen me before?

FRANK.   Long ago! Long ago! You know the wife of General Haverill?

GERTRUDE.   I have no dearer friend in the world.

FRANK.   She will give a message for me to the dearest friend I have in the world. My little wife! I must not waste even the moment we are waiting. Doctor! My note-book! (*Trying to get it from his coat. The Surgeon takes it out. A torn and blood-stained lace handkerchief also falls out. Gertrude kneels at his side.*) Ah! I—I—have a message from another—(*Holding up handkerchief*)—from Captain Heartsease. (*Jenny makes a quick start towards him.*) He lay at my side in the hospital, when they brought me away; he had only strength enough to put this in my hand, and he spoke a woman's name; but I—I—forgot what it is. The red spots upon it are the only message he sent. (*Gertrude takes the handkerchief and looks back at Jenny extending her hand. Jenny moves to her, takes the handkerchief and turns back, looking down on it. She drops her face into her hands and goes out sobbing.*)

(*Enter Madeline on veranda*)

MADELINE.   General Haverill is coming. I was just in time. He was already on his horse.

FRANK.   Ah! He is coming. (*Then suddenly*) Write! Write! (*Gertrude writes in the note-book as he dictates.*) "To—my wife—Edith;—Tell our little son, when he is old enough to know—how his father died; not how he lived. And tell her who filled my own mother's place so lovingly—she is your mother, too—that my father's portrait of her, which she gave to me in Charleston, helped me to be a better man!" And—Oh! I must not forget this—"It was taken away from me while I was a prisoner in Richmond, and it is in the possession of Captain Edward Thornton, of the Confederate Secret Service. But her face is still beside your own in my heart. My best—warmest, last—love—to you, darling." I will sign it. (*Gertrude holds the book, and he signs it, then sinks back very quietly, supported by the Surgeon, Gertrude rises and walks away.*)

MADELINE.   General Haverill is here. (*The Surgeon lays the fold of the blanket over Frank's face and rises.*)

GERTRUDE.   Doctor!

HARDWICK.   He is dead. (*Madeline, on veranda, turns and looks away. The Lieutenant orders the guard, "Present Arms." Enter Haverill on veranda. He salutes the guard as he passes. The Lieutenant orders, "Carry Arms." Haverill comes down.*)

HAVERILL.   I am too late?

HARDWICK.   I'm sorry, General. His one eager thought as we came was to reach here in time to see you. (*Haverill moves to the bier, looks down at it, then folds back the blanket from the face. He starts slightly as he first sees it.*)

HAVERILL.   Brave boy! I hoped once to have a son like you. I shall be in your father's place, today, at your grave. (*He replaces the blanket and steps back.*) We will carry him to his comrades in the front. He shall have a soldier's burial, in sight of the mountain-top beneath which he sacrificed his young life; that shall be his monument.

HARDWICK.   Pardon me, General. We Virginians are your enemies, but you cannot honor this young soldier more than we do. Will you allow my men the privilege of carrying him to his grave? (*Haverill inclines his head. The Surgeon motions to the Confederate Soldiers, who step to the bier and raise it gently.*)

HAVERILL.   Lieutenant! (*The Lieutenant orders the guard, "Left Face." The Confederate bearers move through the gate, preceded by Major Hardwick. Haverill draws his sword, reverses it, and moves up behind the bier with bowed head. The Lieutenant orders "Forward March," and the cortege disappears. While the girls are still watching it, the heavy sound of distant artillery is heard, with booming reverberations among the hills and in the valley.*)

MADELINE.   What is that sound, Gertrude?

GERTRUDE.   Listen! (*Another and more prolonged distant sound, with long reverberation*)

MADELINE.   Again! Gertrude! (*Gertrude raises her hand to command silence; listens. Distant cannon again.*)

GERTRUDE.   It is the opening of a battle.

MADELINE.   Ah! (*Running down stage. The sounds again. Prolonged rumble.*)

GERTRUDE.   How often have I heard that sound! This is war, Madeline! You are face to face with it now.

MADELINE.   And Robert is there! He may be in the thickest of the danger—at this very moment.

GERTRUDE.   Yes. Let our prayers go up for him; mine do, with all a sister's heart. (*Kerchival enters on veranda without coat or vest, his sash about his waist, looking back as he comes in.*) Kerchival!

KERCHIVAL.   Go on! Go on! Keep the battle to yourselves. I'm out of it. (*The distant cannon and reverberations rising in volume. Prolonged and distant rumble.*)

MADELINE.   I pray for Robert Ellingham—and for the *cause* in which he risks his life! (*Kerchival looks at her suddenly; also Gertrude.*) Heaven forgive me if I am wrong, but I am praying for the enemies of my country. His people are my people, his enemies are my enemies. Heaven defend him and his, in this awful hour.

KERCHIVAL.   Madeline! My sister!

MADELINE. Oh, Kerchival! (*Turning and dropping her face on his breast*) I cannot help it—I cannot help it!

KERCHIVAL. My poor girl! Every woman's heart, the world over, belongs not to any country or any flag, but to her husband—and her lover. Pray for the man you love, sister—it would be treason not to. (*Passes her, looks across to Gertrude*) Am I right? (*Gertrude drops her head. Madeline moves up veranda and out.*) Is what I have said to Madeline true?

GERTRUDE. Yes! (*Looks up*) Kerchival!

KERCHIVAL. Gertrude! (*Hurries across to her, clasps her in his arms. He suddenly staggers and brings his hand to his breast.*)

GERTRUDE. Your wound! (*Supporting him as he reels and sinks into seat*)

KERCHIVAL. Wound! I have no wound! You do love me! (*Seizing her hand*)

GERTRUDE. Let me call the Surgeon, Kerchival.

KERCHIVAL. You can be of more service to me than he can. (*Detaining her. Very heavy sounds of the battle; she starts, listening.*) Never mind that! It's only a battle. You love me!

GERTRUDE. Be quiet, Kerchival, dear. I do love you. I told you so when you lay bleeding here last night. But you could not hear me. (*At his side, resting her arm about him, stroking his head*) I said that same thing to—to—another, more than three years ago. It is in that letter that General Buckthorn gave you. (*Kerchival starts.*) No—no—you must be very quiet, or I will not say another word. If you obey me, I will repeat that part of the letter, every word; I know it by heart, for I read it a dozen times. The letter is from Mrs. Haverill.

KERCHIVAL. (*Quietly*) Go on.

GERTRUDE. "I have kept your secret, my darling, but I was sorely tempted to betray the confidence you reposed in me at Charleston. If Kerchival West—(*She retires backward from him as she proceeds.*)—had heard you say, as I did, when your face was hidden in my bosom, that night, that you loved him with your whole heart—"

KERCHIVAL. Ah! (*Starting to his feet. He sinks back. She springs to support him.*)

GERTRUDE. I will go for help.

KERCHIVAL. Do not leave me at such a moment as this. You have brought me a new life. (*Bringing her to her knees before him and looking down at her*) Heaven is just opening before me. (*His hands drop suddenly and his head falls back. Battle.*)

GERTRUDE. Ah! Kerchival! You are dying! (*Musketry. A sudden sharp burst of musketry, mingled with the roar of artillery near by. Kerchival starts, seizing Gertrude's arm and holding her away, still on her knees. He looks eagerly to the left.*)

KERCHIVAL. The enemy is close upon us!

(*Barket runs in, up the slope.*)

BARKET.   Colonel Wist! The devils have sprung out of the ground. They're pouring over our lift flank like Noah's own flood. The Union Army has started back for Winchester, on its way to the North Pole; our own regiment, Colonel, is coming over the hill in full retrate.

KERCHIVAL.   My own regiment! (*Starting up*) Get my horse, Barket. (*Turns*) Gertrude, my life! (*Embraces Gertrude*)

BARKET.   Your horse, is it? I'm wid ye! There's a row at Finnegan's ball, and we're in it. (*Springs to road and runs out*)

KERCHIVAL.   (*Turns away. Stops.*) I am under arrest. (*Retreat. Fugitives begin to straggle across stage from the left.*)

GERTRUDE.   You must not go, Kerchival; it will kill you.

KERCHIVAL.   Arrest be damned! (*Starts up, raises his arms above his head with clenched fist, rising to full height*) Stand out of my way, you cowards! (*They cower away from him as he rushes out among them. The stream of fugitives passing across stage swells in volume. Gertrude runs through them and up to the elevation, turning.*)

GERTRUDE.   Men! Are you soldiers? Turn back! There is a leader for you! Turn back! Fight for your flag—and mine!—the flag my father died for! Turn back! (*She looks out to the left and turns front.*) He has been marked for death already, and I—I can only pray. (*Dropping to her knees*)

(*The stream of fugitives continues, now over the elevation also. Rough and torn uniforms, bandaged arms and legs; some limping and supported by others, some dragging their muskets after them, others without muskets, others using them as crutches. A variety of uniforms, cavalry, infantry, etc.; flags draggled on the ground, the rattle of nearby musketry and roar of cannon continue; two or three wounded fugitives drop down beside the hedge. Benson staggers in and drops on rock or stump near post. Artillerists, rough, torn and wounded, drag and force a field-piece across. Corporal Dunn, wounded, staggers to the top of the elevation. There is a lull in the sounds of the battle. Distant cheers are heard without.*)

DUNN.   Listen, fellows! Stop! Listen! Sheridan! General Sheridan is coming! (*Cheers from those on stage. Gertrude rises quickly. The wounded soldiers rise, looking over hedge. All on stage stop, looking eagerly to the left. The cheers without come nearer, with shouts of "Sheridan! Sheridan!"*) The horse is down; he is worn out.

GERTRUDE.   No! He is up again! He is on my Jack! Now, for your life, Jack, and for me! You've never failed me yet. (*The cheers without now swell to full volume and are taken up by those on the stage. The horse sweeps by with General Sheridan.*) Jack! Jack!! Jack!!! (*Waving her arms as he passes. She throws up her arms and falls backward and is caught by Dunn. The stream of men is reversed and surges across the stage to the left in the road and on the elevation, with shouts, throwing up hats, etc. The field-piece is forced up the slope with a few bold, rough move-*

ments; the artillerists are loading it, and the stream of returning fugitives are still surging by in the road as the curtain falls.)

CURTAIN

ACT IV

Scene, Residence of General Buckthorn in Washington. Fireplace slanting upward from left to center. Small alcove upstage at the right. Opening to hall with staircase beyond, and also entrance from left. A wide opening with portieres to apartment. Upright piano. Armchair and low stool before fireplace. Small table for tea, etc. Ottoman. Other chairs, ottomans, etc. to taste. Mrs. Haverill in armchair is resting her face upon her hand and looking into the fire. Edith is on a low stool at her side, sewing a child's garment.

EDITH. It seems hardly possible that the war is over, and that General Lee has really surrendered. (*Fife and drum without*) There is music in the streets nearly all the time now, and everybody looks so cheerful and bright. (*Distant fife and drums heard playing "Johnnie Comes Marching Home." Edith springs up and runs up to window, looking out.*) More troops returning! The old tattered battle-flag is waving in the wind, and people are running after them so merrily. (*Music stops.*) Every day, now, seems like a holiday. (*Coming down*) The war is over. All the women ought to feel very happy, whose—whose husbands are—coming back to them.

MRS. HAVERILL. Yes, Edith; those women whose—husbands are coming back to them. (*Still looking into fire*)

EDITH. Oh! (*Dropping upon the stool, her head upon the arm of the chair*)

MRS. HAVERILL. (*Resting her arm over her*) My poor, little darling! *Your* husband will not come back.

EDITH. Frank's last message has never reached me.

MRS. HAVERILL. No; but you have one sweet thought always with you. Madeline West heard part of it, as Gertrude wrote it down. His last thought was a loving one, of you.

EDITH. Madeline says that he was thinking of you, too. He knew that you were taking such loving care of his little one, and of me. You have always done that, since you first came back from Charleston, and found me alone in New York.

MRS. HAVERILL. I found a dear, sweet little daughter. (*Stroking her head*) Heaven sent you, darling! You have been a blessing to me. I hardly

know how I should have got through the past few months at all without
you at my side.

EDITH.   What is your own trouble, dear? I have found you in tears so
often; and since last October, after the battle of Cedar Creek, you—you
have never shown me a letter from—from my—Frank's father. General
Haverill arrived in Washington yesterday, but has not been here yet. Is
it because I am here? He has never seen me, and I feel that he has never
forgiven Frank for marrying me.

MRS. HAVERILL.   Nonsense, my child; he did think the marriage was imprudent, but he told me to do everything I could for you. If General
Haverill has not been to see either of us since his arrival in Washington,
it is nothing that you need to worry your dear little head about. How are
you getting on with your son's wardrobe?

EDITH.   Oh! Splendidly! Frankie isn't a baby any longer; he's a man now,
and he has to wear a man's clothes. (*Holding up a little pair of trousers,
with maternal pride*) He's rather young to be dressed like a man, but I
want Frank to grow up as soon as possible. I long to have him old
enough to understand me when I repeat to him the words in which General Haverill told the whole world how his father died! (*Rising*) And yet,
even in his official report to the Government, he only honored him as
Lieutenant Bedloe. He has never forgiven his son for the disgrace he
brought upon his name.

MRS. HAVERILL.   I know him so well—(*Rising*)—the unyielding pride, that
conquers even the deep tenderness of his nature. He can be silent, though
his own heart is breaking. (*Aside*) He can be silent, too, though *my* heart
is breaking. (*Dropping her face in her hand*)

EDITH.   *Mother!* (*Putting her arm about her*)

(*Enter Jannette*)

JANNETTE.   A letter for you, Madam.

MRS. HAVERILL.   (*Taking note. Aside.*) He has answered me. (*Opens and
reads; inclines her head to Jannette, who goes out to hall. Aloud.*) General
Haverill will be here this afternoon, Edith. (*Exit up the stairs*)

EDITH.   There is something that she cannot confide to me, or to anyone.
General Haverill returned to Washington yesterday, and he has not been
here yet. He will be here today. I always tremble when I think of meeting him.

(*General Buckthorn appears in hall.*)

BUCKTHORN.   Come right in; this way, Barket. Ah, Edith!

BARKET.   As I was saying, sur—just after the battle of Sayder Creek began—

BUCKTHORN.   (*To Edith*) More good news! The war is, indeed, over, now!

BARKET.   Whin Colonel Wist rode to the front to mate his raytrating regiment—

BUCKTHORN. General Johnston has surrendered his army, also; and that, of course, does end the war.

EDITH. I'm very glad that all the fighting is over.

BUCKTHORN. So am I; but my occupation, and old Barket's, too, is gone. Always at work on new clothes for our little soldier?

EDITH. He's growing so, I can hardly make them fast enough for him. But this is the time for his afternoon nap. I must go now, to see if he is sleeping soundly.

BUCKTHORN. Our dear little mother! (*Tapping her chin*) I always claim the privilege of my white hair, you know. (*She puts up her lips; he kisses her. She goes out.*) The sweetest young widow I ever saw! (*Barket coughs. Buckthorn turns sharply; Barket salutes.*) Well! What the devil are you thinking about now?

BARKET. The ould time, sur. Yer honor used to claim the same privilege for brown hair.

BUCKTHORN. You old rascal! What a memory you have! You were telling me for the hundredth time about the battle of Cedar Creek; go on. I can never hear it often enough. Kerchival West was a favorite of mine, poor fellow!

BARKET. Just afther the battle of Sayder Creek began, when the Colonel rode to the front to mate his raytrating rigiment—

BUCKTHORN. I'll tell Old Margery to bring in tea for both of us, Barket.

BARKET. For both of us, sur?

BUCKTHORN. Yes; and later in the evening we'll have something else, together. This is a great day for all of us. I'm not your commander today, but your old comrade in arms—(*Laying his arm over Barket's shoulder*)— and I'm glad I don't have to pull myself up now every time I forget my dignity. Ah! you and I will be laid away before long, but we'll be together again in the next world, won't we, Barket?

BARKET. Wid yer honor's permission. (*Saluting*)

BUCKTHORN. Ha—ha—ha! (*Laughing*) If we do meet there, I'm certain you'll salute me as your superior officer. There's old Margery now. (*Looking to door, calls*) Margery! Tea for two!

MARGERY. (*Without*) The tay be waiting for ye, sur; and it be boilin' over wid impatience.

BUCKTHORN. Bring up a chair, Barket. (*Sitting in arm-chair*)

BARKET. (*Having placed table and drawing up a chair*) Do you know, Gineral, I don't fale quite aisy in my moind. I'm not quite sure that Margery will let us take our tay together. (*Sits down, doubtfully*)

BUCKTHORN. I hadn't thought of that. I—(*Glancing to the right*)—I hope she will, Barket. But, of course, if she won't—she's been commander-in-chief of my household ever since Jenny was a baby.

BARKET. At Fort Duncan, in Texas.

BUCKTHORN. You and Old Margery never got along very well in those days; but I thought you had made it all up; she nursed you through your wound, last summer, and after the battle of Cedar Creek, also.

BARKET. Yis, sur, bliss her kind heart, she's been like a wife to me; and that's the trouble. A man's wife is such an angel when he's ill that he dreads to get well; good health is a misfortune to him. Ould Margery and I have had anither misunderstanding.

BUCKTHORN. I'll do the best I can for both of us, Barket. You were telling me about the battle of—

BARKET. Just afther the battle of Sayder Creek began, whin Colonel Wist rode to the front to mate his raytrating rigiment—

(*Enter Old Margery with a tea-tray. She stops abruptly, looking at Barket. He squirms in his chair. Buckthorn rises and stands with his back to the mantel. Old Margery moves to the table, arranges things on it, glances at Barket, then at Buckthorn, who looks up at ceiling, rubbing his chin. Old Margery takes up one of the cups, with saucer.*)

OLD MARGERY. I misunderstood yer order, sur. I see there's no one here but yerself.

BUCKTHORN. Ah! Margery! (*She stops.*) Barket tells me that there has been a slight misunderstanding between you and him.

OLD MARGERY. Day before yisterday, the ould Hibernian dhrone had the kitchen upside down, to show anither old milithary vagabone loike himself how the battle of Sayder Creek was fought. He knocked the crame pitcher into the basket of clane clothes, and overturned some raspberry jam and the flat-irons into a pan of fresh eggs. There *has* been a misunderstanding betwane us.

BUCKTHORN. I see there has. I suppose Barket was showing his friend how Colonel Kerchival West rode forward to meet his regiment, when he was already wounded dangerously.

OLD MARGERY. Bliss the poor, dear young man! He and I was always good frinds, though he was somethin' of a devil in the kitchen himself, whin he got there. (*Wiping her eye with one corner of her apron*) And bliss the young Southern lady that was in love wid him, too. (*Changing the cup and wiping the other eye with the corner of her apron*) Nothing was iver heard of ayther of thim after that battle was over, to this very day.

BUCKTHORN. Barket was at Kerchival's side when he rode to the front. (*Old Margery hesitates a moment, then moves to the table, sets down the cup and marches out. Buckthorn sits in the arm-chair again, pouring tea.*) I could always find some way to get Old Margery to do what I wanted her to do.

BARKET. You're a great man, Ginerel; we'd niver have conquered the South widout such men.

BUCKTHORN. Now go on, Barket; you were interrupted.

BARKET. Just afther the battle of Sayder Creek began, whin—

(*Enter Jannette with a card, which she hands to Buckthorn*)

BUCKTHORN. (*Reading card*) Robert Ellingham! (*Rises*) I will go to him. (*To Jannette*) Go upstairs and tell Madeline to come down.

JANNETTE. Yes, sir. (*Going*)

BUCKTHORN. And, Jannette, simply say there is a caller; don't tell her who is here. (*Exit Jannette. Buckthorn follows her out to hall.*) Ellingham! My dear fellow! (*Extending his hand and disappearing*)

BARKET. Colonel Ellingham and Miss Madeline—lovers! That's the kind o' volunteers the country nades now!

(Enter Buckthorn and Ellingham)

BUCKTHORN. (*As he enters*) We've been fighting four years to keep you out of Washington, Colonel, but we are delighted to see you within the lines now.

ELLINGHAM. I am glad, indeed, General, to have so warm a welcome. But can you tell me anything about my sister, Gertrude?

BUCKTHORN. About your sister? Why, can't you tell us? And have you heard nothing of Kerchival West on your side of the line?

ELLINGHAM. All I can tell you is this: As soon as possible after our surrender at Appomatox, I made my way to the Shenandoah Valley. Our home there is utterly deserted. I have hurried down to Washington in the hopes that I might learn something of you. There is no human being about the old homestead; it is like a haunted house—empty, and dark, and solitary. You do not even know where Gertrude is?

BUCKTHORN. We only know that Kerchival was not found among the dead of his own regiment at Cedar Creek, though he fell among them during the fight. The three girls searched the field for him, but he was not there. As darkness came on, and they were returning to the house, Gertrude suddenly seized the bridle of a stray horse, sprang upon its back and rode away to the South, into the woods at the foot of Three Top Mountain. The other two girls watched for her in vain. She did not return, and we have heard nothing from her since.

ELLINGHAM. Poor girl! I understand what was in her thoughts, and she was right. We captured fourteen hundred prisoners that day, although we were defeated, and Kerchival must have been among them. Gertrude rode away, alone, in the darkness, to find him. I shall return to the South at once and learn where she now is.

(Jannette has re-entered, down the stairs.)

JANNETTE. Miss Madeline will be down in a moment. (*Exit*)

BARKET. (*Aside*) That name wint through his chist like a rifle ball.

BUCKTHORN. Will you step into the drawing-room, Colonel? I will see Madeline myself first. She does not even know that you are living.

ELLINGHAM. I hardly dared asked for her. Is she well?

BUCKTHORN. Yes; and happy—or soon will be.

ELLINGHAM.   Peace, at last! (*Exit to apartment*)

BUCKTHORN.   (*Closes portieres*) I ought to prepare Madeline a little,
Barket; you must help me.

BARKET.   Yis, sur, I will.

(*Enter Madeline down the stairs*)

MADELINE.   Uncle! Jannette said you wished to see me; there is a visitor
here. Who is it?

BARKET.   Colonel Robert Ellingham.

MADELINE.   Ah! (*Staggering*)

BUCKTHORN.   (*Supporting her*) You infernal idiot! I'll put you in the
guardhouse!

BARKET.   You wanted me to help ye, Gineral.

MADELINE.   Robert is alive—and here? (*Rising from his arms, she moves
to the portieres, holds them aside, peeping in; gives a joyful start, tosses
aside the portieres and runs through.*)

BUCKTHORN.   Barket! There's nothing but that curtain between us and
Heaven.

BARKET.   I don't like stayin' out o' Hiven, myself, sur. Gineral! I'll kiss
Ould Margery—if I die for it! (*Exit*)

BUCKTHORN.   Kiss Old Margery! I'll give him a soldier's funeral. (*Enter
Jenny from hall, demurely*) Ah! Jenny, my dear! I have news for you.
Colonel Robert Ellingham is in the drawing-room.

JENNY.   Oh! I am delighted. (*Starting*)

BUCKTHORN.   A-h-e-m!

JENNY.   Oh!—exactly. I see. I have some news for *you*, papa. Captain
Heartsease has arrived in Washington.

BUCKTHORN.   Oh! My dear! I have often confessed to you how utterly
mistaken I was about that young man. He is a soldier—as good a soldier
as you are. I'll ask him to the house.

JENNY.   (*Demurely*) He is here now.

BUCKTHORN.   Now?

JENNY.   He's been here an hour; in the library.

BUCKTHORN.   Why! Barket and I were in the library fifteen minutes ago.

JENNY.   Yes, sir. We were in the bay-window; the curtains were closed.

BUCKTHORN.   Oh! exactly; I see. You may tell him he has my full consent.

JENNY.   He hasn't asked for it.

BUCKTHORN.   Hasn't he? And you've been in the bay-window an hour?
Well, my darling—I was considered one of the best Indian fighters in the
old army, but it took me four years to propose to your mother. I'll go and
see the Captain. (*Exit to hall*)

JENNY.   I wonder if it will take Captain Heartsease four years to propose to me. Before he left Washington, nearly two years ago, he told
everybody in the circle of my acquaintance, except me, that he was in love
with me. I'll be an old lady in caps before our engagement commences.
Poor, dear mother! The idea of a girl's waiting four years for a chance to

say, "Yes." It's been on the tip of my tongue so often, I'm afraid it'll pop out, at last, before he pops the question.

(*Enter Buckthorn and Heartsease from hall*)

BUCKTHORN. Walk right in, Captain; this is the family room. You must make yourself quite at home here.

HEARTSEASE. Thank you.

BUCKTHORN. My dear! (*Apart to Jenny*) The very first thing he said to me, after our greeting, was that he loved my daughter.

JENNY. Now he's told my father!

BUCKTHORN. He's on fire!

JENNY. Is he? (*Looking at Heartsease, who stands quietly, stroking his mustache*) Why doesn't he tell *me?*

BUCKTHORN. You may have to help him a little; your mother assisted me. When you and Jenny finish your chat, Captain—(*Lighting a cigar at the mantel*)—you must join me in the smoking room.

HEARTSEASE. I shall be delighted. By the way, General—I have been in such a fever of excitement since I arrived at this house—

JENNY. (*Aside*) Fever? Chills!

HEARTSEASE. That I forgot it entirely. I have omitted a very important and a very sad commission. I have brought with me the note-book of Lieutenant Frank Bedloe—otherwise Haverill—in which Miss Gertrude Ellingham wrote down his last message to his young wife.

JENNY. Have you seen Gertrude?

BUCKTHORN. (*Taking book*) How did this note-book come into your possession?

HEARTSEASE. Miss Ellingham visited the prison in North Carolina where I was detained. She was going from hospital to hospital, from prison to prison, and from burial-place to burial-place, to find Colonel Kerchival West, if living—or some record of his death.

BUCKTHORN. Another Evangeline! Searching for her lover through the wilderness of this great war!

HEARTSEASE. I was about to be exchanged at the time, and she requested me to bring this to her friends in Washington. She had not intended to carry it away with her. I was not exchanged, as we then expected, but I afterwards escaped from prison to General Sherman's Army.

BUCKTHORN. I will carry this long-delayed message to the widowed young mother. (*Exit*)

JENNY. I remember so well, when poor Lieutenant Haverill took out the note-book and asked Gertrude to write for him. He—he brought me a message at the same time. (*Their eyes meet. He puts up his glasses. She turns away, touching her eyes.*)

HEARTSEASE. I—I remember the circumstances you probably allude to; that is—when he left my side—I—I gave him my—I mean your—lace handkerchief.

JENNY.   It is sacred to me!

HEARTSEASE.   Y-e-s—I would say—is it?

JENNY.   (*Wiping her eyes*) It was stained with the life-blood of a hero!

HEARTSEASE.   I must apologize to you for its condition. I hadn't any chance to have it washed and ironed.

JENNY.   (*Looking around at him, suddenly, then, aside*) What could any girl do with a lover like that? (*Turning up stage*)

HEARTSEASE.   (*Aside*) She seems to remember that incident so tenderly! My blood boils!

JENNY.   Didn't you long to see your—your friends at home—when you were in prison, Captain?

HEARTSEASE.   Yes—especially—I longed especially, Miss Buckthorn, to see—

JENNY.   *Yes!—to see—*

HEARTSEASE.   But there were lots of jolly fellows in the prison. (*Jenny turns away.*)

HEARTSEASE.   We had a dramatic society, and a glee club, and an orchestra. I was one of the orchestra. I had a banjo, with one string; I played one tune on it, that I used to play on the piano, with one finger. But, Miss Buckthorn, I am a prisoner again, tonight—your prisoner.

JENNY.   (*Aside*) At last!

HEARTSEASE.   I'll show you how that tune went. (*Turns to piano; sits*)

JENNY.   (*Aside*) Papa said I'd have to help him, but I don't see an opening. (*Heartsease plays part of an air with one finger, striking two or three wrong notes.*)

HEARTSEASE.   There are two notes down there, somewhere, that I never could get right. The fellows in prison used to dance while I played— (*Playing*)—that is, the lame ones did; those that weren't lame couldn't keep the time.

JENNY.   You must have been in great danger, Captain, when you escaped from prison.

HEARTSEASE.   Y-e-s. I was badly frightened several times. One night I came face to face, on the road, with a Confederate Officer. It was Captain Thornton.

JENNY.   Oh! What did you do?

HEARTSEASE.   I killed him. (*Very quietly, and trying the tune again at once. Enter Jannette from hall; she glances into the room and goes up the stairs.*) I used to skip those two notes on the banjo. It's very nice for a soldier to come home from the war, and meet those—I mean the one particular person—that he—you see, when a soldier loves a woman, as—as—

JENNY.   (*Aside*) As he loves me. (*Approaches him*)

HEARTSEASE.   As soldiers often do—(*Plays; she turns away, petulantly; he plays the tune through correctly.*) That's it!

JENNY.   (*Aside*) I'm not going to be made love to by piece-meal, like this, any longer. (*Aloud*) Captain Heartsease! Have you anything in particular to say to me? (*He looks up.*)

HEARTSEASE.   Y-e-s. (*Rising*)

JENNY.   Say it! You told my father, and all my friends, that you were in love with me. Whom are you going to tell next?

HEARTSEASE.   I *am* in love with you.

JENNY.   It was my turn.

HEARTSEASE.   (*Going near to her*) Do you love me?

JENNY.   (*Laying her head quietly on his breast*) I must take time to consider.

HEARTSEASE.   (*Quietly*) I assume that this means "Yes."

JENNY.   It isn't the way a girl says "No."

HEARTSEASE.   My darling!

JENNY.   Why! His heart is beating as fast as mine is!

HEARTSEASE.   (*Quietly*) I am frantic with joy. (*He kisses her. She hides her face on his breast. Enter Mrs. Haverill downstairs, followed by Jannette. Mrs. Haverill stops suddenly, Jannette stands in the doorway. Heartsease inclines his head to her, quietly looking at her over Jenny.*) I am delighted to see you, after so long an absence; I trust that we shall meet more frequently hereafter.

JENNY.   (*Looking at him*) Eh?

HEARTSEASE.   (*Looking down at her*) I think, perhaps, it might be as well for us to repair to another apartment, and continue our interview, there!

JENNY.   (*Dropping her head on his breast again*) This room is very comfortable.

MRS. HAVERILL.   Jenny, dear! (*Jenny starts up; looks from Mrs. Haverill to Heartsease.*)

JENNY.   Constance! I—'Bout face! March! (*Turns and goes out*)

MRS. HAVERILL.   I am glad to see you again, Captain, and happy as well as safe.

HEARTSEASE.   Thank you, Madam. I am happy. If you will excuse me, I will join—my father—in the smoking-room. (*Mrs. Haverill inclines her head, and Heartsease walks out.*)

MRS. HAVERILL.   Jannette! You may ask General Haverill to come into this room. (*Exit Jannette. Mrs. Haverill walks down stage, reading a note.*) "I have hesitated to come to you personally, as I have hesitated to write to you. If I have been silent, it is because I could not bring my hand to write what was in my mind and in my heart. I do not know that I can trust my tongue to speak it, but I will come."

(*Enter Haverill from hall; he stops.*)

HAVERILL.   Constance!

MRS. HAVERILL.   My husband! May I call you husband? After all these months of separation, with your life in almost daily peril, and my life— what? Only a weary longing for one loving word—and you are silent.

HAVERILL.   May I call you wife? I do not wish to speak that word except with reverence. You have asked me to come to you. I am here. I will be plain, direct and brief. Where is the portrait of yourself, which I gave you in Charleston, for my son?

MRS. HAVERILL. Your son is dead, sir; and my portrait lies upon his breast, in the grave. (*Haverill takes the miniature from his pocket and holds it towards her in his extended hand. She starts back.*) He gave it to you? And you ask me where it is?

HAVERILL. It might have lain in the grave of Kerchival West!

MRS. HAVERILL. Ah!

HAVERILL. Not in my son's. I found it upon *his* breast. (*She turns front, dazed.*) Well! I am listening! It was not I that sought this interview, madam; and if you prefer to remain silent, I will go. You know, now, why I have been silent so long.

MRS. HAVERILL. My only witnesses to the truth are both dead. I shall remain silent. (*Turning towards him*) We stand before each other, living, but not so happy as they. We are parted, forever. Even if you should accept my unsupported word—if I could so far forget my pride as to give it to you—suspicion would still hang between us. I remain silent. (*Haverill looks at her, earnestly, for a moment, then approaches her.*)

HAVERILL. I cannot look into your eyes and not see truth and loyalty there. Constance!

MRS. HAVERILL. No, John! (*Checking him*) I will not accept your blind faith!

HAVERILL. (*Looking down at the picture in his hand*) My faith is blind; blind as my love! I do not wish to see! (*Enter Edith. She stops; looks at Haverill. He raises his head and looks at her.*)

EDITH. This is General Haverill? (*Dropping her eyes*) I am Edith, sir.

HAVERILL. (*Gently*) My son's wife. (*Kisses her forehead*) You shall take the place he once filled in my heart. His crime and his disgrace are buried in a distant grave.

EDITH. And you have not forgiven him, even yet?

MRS. HAVERILL. Is there no atonement for poor Frank's sin—not even his death? Can you only bury the wrong and forget the good?

HAVERILL. The good?

MRS. HAVERILL. Your own words to the Government, as his commander!

HAVERILL. What do you mean?

MRS. HAVERILL. "The victory of Cedar Creek would have been impossible without the sacrifice of this young Officer."

HAVERILL. My own words, yes—but—

EDITH. "His name must take its place, forever, in the roll of names which his countrymen honor."

HAVERILL. Lieutenant Bedloe!

MRS. HAVERILL. Haverill! You did not know?

HAVERILL. My—son.

EDITH. You did not receive mother's letter?—after his death?

HAVERILL. My son! (*Sinking upon chair or ottoman*) I left him alone in his grave, unknown; but my tears fell for him then, as they do now. He died before I reached him.

EDITH. Father! (*Laying her hand gently on his shoulder*) You shall see Frank's face again. His little son is lying asleep upstairs; and when he wakes up, Frank's own eyes will look into yours. I have just received his last message. I will read it to you. (*She opens notebook and reads.*) "Tell our little son how his father died, not how he lived. And tell her who filled my own mother's place so lovingly." (*She looks at Mrs. Haverill, moves to her and hides her face in her bosom.*) My mother!

MRS. HAVERILL. Edith—my child! Frank loved us both.

EDITH. (*Reading*) "Father's portrait of her, which she gave to me in Charleston—(*Haverill starts.*)—helped me to be a better man."

HAVERILL. (*Rising to his feet*) Constance!

EDITH. (*Reading*) "It was taken from me in Richmond, and it is in the possession of Captain Edward Thornton."

HAVERILL. One moment! Stop! Let me think! (*Edith looks at him.*) Thornton was a prisoner—and to Kerchival West. A dispatch had been found upon him—he was searched! (*He moves to her and takes both her hands in his own, bowing his head over them.*) My head is bowed in shame.

MRS. HAVERILL. Speak to me, John, as you used to speak! Tell me you still love me!

HAVERILL. The—the words will come—but they are—choking me—now. (*Presses her hand to his lips*)

MRS. HAVERILL. We will think no more of the past, except of what was bright in it. Frank's memory, and our own love, will be with us always.

(*Enter Buckthorn, followed by Heartsease*)

BUCKTHORN. Haverill! You are back from the war, too. It begins to look like peace in earnest.

HAVERILL. Yes. Peace and home. (*Shaking hands with him; Mrs. Haverill joins Edith.*)

(*Enter Barket*)

BARKET. Gineral! (*Buckthorn moves to him. Haverill joins Mrs. Haverill and Edith. Barket speaks apart, twisting one side of his face.*) I kissed her!

BUCKTHORN. Have you sent for a surgeon?

BARKET. I felt as if the inimy had surprised us agin, and Sheridan was sixty miles away.

HAVERILL. This is old Sergeant Barket. (*Barket salutes.*) You were the last man of us all that saw Colonel West.

BARKET. Just afther the battle of Sayder Creek began—whin Colonel Wist rode to the front to mate his raytrating rigiment—the byes formed in line, at sight of him, to raysist the victorious inimy. It was just at the brow of a hill—about there, sur—(*Pointing with his cane*) and—here! (*He *takes tray from table and sets it on the carpet. Lays the slices of bread in a row.*) That be the rigiment. (*All interested. Madeline and Ellingham enter and look on. Barket arranges the two cups and saucers in a row.*) That be the inimy's batthery, sur. (*Enter Margery. She goes to the table, then looks around, sharply, at Barket.*)

OLD MARGERY.   Ye ould Hibernian dhrone! What are yez doin' wid the china on the floor? You'll break it all!

BUCKTHORN.   Ah—Margery! Barket is telling us where he last saw Colonel Kerchival West.

OLD MARGERY.   The young Colonel! The tay-cups and saucers be's the inimy's batthery? Yez may smash 'em, if ye loike!

BUCKTHORN.   Go on, Barket. (*Jenny and Heartsease have entered, as Barket proceeds; the whole party lean forward, intensely interested. Gertrude enters in hall, looks in, beckons. Kerchival follows. They move to the center of the stage, back of the rest, and stand unseen, listening.*)

BARKET.   Just as the rigiment was rayformed in line, and Colonel Wist was out in front—widout any coat or hat, and wid only a shtick in his hand—we heard cheers in the rear. Gineral Sheridan was coming! One word to the men—and we swept over the batthery like a whirlwind! (*Slashing his cane through the cups and saucers*)

OLD MARGERY.   Hoo—roo!

BARKET.   The attack on the lift flank was checked. But when we shtopped to take breath, Colonel Wist wasn't wid us. (*Gertrude turns lovingly to Kerchival. He places his arm about her.*) Heaven knows where he is now. Afther the battle was over, poor Miss Gertrude wint off by hersilf into the wilderness to find him.

KERCHIVAL.   My wife! You saved my life, at last! (*Embracing her*)

BARKET.   They'll niver come together in this world. I saw Miss Gertrude, myself, ride away into the woods and disappear behind a school-house on the battle-field, over there.

GERTRUDE.   No, Barket—(*All start and look.*)—it was the little church; we were married there this morning!

CURTAIN

MARGARET FLEMING*

by

James A. Herne

*From *Representative American Plays from 1767 to the Present Day*, Edited with Introductions and Notes by Arthur Hobson Quinn. Seventh Edition, Revised and Enlarged. Copyright 1953 by Arthur Hobson Quinn. Reprinted by permission of Appleton-Century-Crofts.

Introduction

James A. Herne (originally Aherne) was born in Cohoes, New York, on February 1, 1839. His father, though reared a Roman Catholic, had joined the Calvinistic Dutch Reformed Church and disapproved of his son's interest in the theatre. After working seven years in a brush factory, James made his acting debut as George Shelby in *Uncle Tom's Cabin* at the Adelphi Theatre, Troy, New York, in 1859. He acted in various Eastern companies, including one managed by his first wife, Helen Western, then went to San Francisco, where he became a leading actor and in 1876 became stage manager of the new Baldwin Theatre. In 1878 he married a young actress, Katherine Corcoran, who became his leading lady and undoubtedly assisted in the composition of some of his plays. Toward the end of the 1870's Herne began collaborating with young David Belasco on a series of romantic melodramas. The most successful of these plays, *Hearts of Oak* (1879), was an adaptation of an English play, *The Mariner's Compass* by Henry J. Leslie. After a disagreement with Belasco, Herne bought his half-share of the play and acted in the leading role for the next seven years.

Drifting Apart (1888), a temperance melodrama, brought Herne to the attention of young Hamlin Garland, who was living in Boston and writing realistic stories based on his prairie childhood. Garland introduced him to William Dean Howells and to Benjamin O. Flower, editor of the *Arena*, an *avant-garde* reform journal. Although he had little formal education, Herne became fascinated with the social, philosophical, and esthetic theories of his new friends. He and his wife read and discussed the writings of Tolstoy, Ibsen, and John Fiske, the American popularizer of the evolutionary theories of Darwin and Spencer. Herne at this time seems to have accepted an optimistic view of man's perfectibility and felt that it was the artist's function to expose the hypocrisy and evil that impeded progress. This led him to an emphasis on environmentalism, especially in his plays treating rural life. His essay "Art for Truth's Sake in the Drama" (*Arena*, February, 1897) was a significant statement in the development of a drama of ideas in America. As a corollary to his esthetic and social theories, Herne was converted to the Single Tax theory of Henry George and frequently made speeches supporting it. His vigorous participation in William Jennings Bryan's campaign for the Presidency in 1900 probably shortened his life. He also struggled against the control of American theatres by the Klaw-Erlanger Syndicate. Much of the financial profit from *Hearts of Oak* was devoted to attempts to produce *Margaret Fleming*, but the play failed to please American audiences, who preferred sentimental melodrama rather than penetrating character studies. Herne recouped some of his financial losses with *Shore Acres* (1892), a sentimental drama about rural Maine life in which he and his wife appeared. A realistic Civil War play, *Griffith Davenport* (1899), pleased the critics but was not a popular success. No text of the play exists because it was never published and all of Herne's manuscripts were lost when fire destroyed the family home in 1909. Herne was acting in his last play, *Sag Harbor*, when his health broke. He died of pneumonia on June 2, 1901. His daughters, Julie and Chrystal Herne, became successful actresses. The only full-length account of Herne's career is *James A. Herne: The Rise of Realism in the American Drama* (Orono, Maine, 1964) by Herbert J. Edwards and Julie A. Herne.

All of Herne's attempts to produce *Margaret Fleming* ended in frustration and disappointment. The play was first produced in Lynn, Massachusetts, for three performances beginning July 4, 1890, with the Hernes in the leading roles. No theatre manager was willing to produce such a daring play. On the advice of William Dean Howells, Herne rented Chickering Hall, a small auditorium in Boston seating about 500 people. Mrs. Herne sewed curtains; furniture and other properties from the Herne home were used for the Fleming living room. With support from Howells, Garland, Flower, Mary E. Wilkins, and others, Herne produced a slightly revised version of the play on May 4, 1891. He played Joe Fletcher, and his wife continued in the title role. Hamlin Garland later called this production somewhat extravagantly "the first of the so-called 'Little Theatres' in America." The first night audience included the most important literary and artistic people of Boston, but, even though Howells said that "it became the talk of the whole city wherever cultivated people met," the play closed after three weeks. It was revived briefly at Chickering Hall in October, 1891, and a matinee performance was given at Palmer's Theatre in New York on December 9, 1891. Herne then revised the play and produced it in Chicago in 1892 and in New York in 1894. Chrystal Herne starred in a Chicago revival in 1907, and Julie Herne played Margaret in a New York production in 1915.

In the Lynn, Massachusetts, production of 1890, four years elapse between Act III and Act IV. Joe Fletcher and Maria Bindley kidnap Lucy Fleming. Margaret goes insane. She has recovered her sanity but is blind when she meets Maria and tells her story without realizing to whom she is speaking. Maria tells her that she has found Lucy and gives her the child. Maria later tells Philip that she has sold Lucy to a woman who will train her as a professional thief. The last scene takes place in a police inspector's office. Maria has been arrested on Philip's complaint, and Margaret and Lucy are brought in. After an investigation Maria is released. Margaret agrees to let Philip visit her and Lucy, and he becomes a laborer in the mill he once owned.

In the 1891 Chickering Hall version, there was also a four-year lapse between Acts III and IV, during which time Joe and Maria kidnap Lucy. Margaret is blind in this version; she has lost and regained her memory but not her sanity. Philip has lost the mill and become a drunkard. He meets Joe Fletcher, who takes him to where Maria has hidden Lucy. The young child is said to demonstrate already her father's inclinations toward drinking and lying. Margaret, having found where Maria and Joe live, arrives to claim her child. After a violent quarrel between Maria and Joe, all five are arrested. At the police station Philip begs Margaret for forgiveness, which she refuses to grant. She will tolerate him as a friend but will never accept him as a husband.

Herne's revisions between 1890 and 1894 suggest that he wished to eliminate unnecessary plot complications, theatricality, and didacticism and to intensify the psychological realism. The final version was made much more dramatic by the unification of the setting. The four-year time span was reduced to nine days. Scenes that took place on Boston Common, in Maria's grocery store, and in a police station were eliminated, and all but two scenes take place in the Fleming living-room. The final version concentrates on the motivations and inner conflicts of the characters.

All manuscripts of *Margaret Fleming* were destroyed when the Herne home burned in 1909, but in 1914 Mrs. Herne, who had performed the role of Margaret in every production through 1894, reconstructed from memory the final version of the play. According to Julie Herne, her mother rewrote Act I, but "from then on the play is substantially as written by my father, though possibly some lines may be altered or missing, due to faults of memory and length of time that had elapsed since my mother acted in the play."

Margaret Fleming is the first significant American play to deal realistically with sociological themes. Although it is a profoundly original work, it reflects various secondary influences derived from Herne's reading and from his concern for social reform. He regards drinking as a social problem rather than a moral evil. Lena Schmidt is seen as "a product of her environment," and one feels that Philip's social position saves him from the fate of Joe Fletcher. The double standard of morality, soon to come under the heavier guns of Stephen Crane and Theodore Dreiser, is attacked when Margaret says to Philip, "You are a man—people will soon forget." In the second version of the play, Zola's theories of heredity are suggested by Lucy's manifesting her father's immoral proclivities. The characterization of Philip Fleming as an affable but morally weak sensualist may have been partially suggested by Howells' character Bartley Hubbard in *A Modern Instance* and *The Rise of Silas Lapham*. Julie Herne believed that Margaret Fleming was in some respects a portrait of her mother. Herne may also have been influenced by Bjornson's *The Letter* (1883) and Ibsen's *A Doll's House* (1879) and *Ghosts* (1881). Both Ibsen plays had been published in the United States, and Garland had praised Ibsen in *The Arena*. The action and the staging of the close of Act III of *Margaret Fleming* resemble the closing scene of *Ghosts*. Herne's play, however, is much more optimistic than those of the Norwegian playwrights. In the early versions Margaret recovers from her madness and amnesia and Philip reforms after his lapse into drunkenness. In the third version, printed here, one is led to expect that after a time Margaret will forgive Philip, she will have the operation suggested by Dr. Larkin in Act II, and the Flemings with their two children will have a reasonably happy life.

One of the most interesting aspects of *Margaret Fleming* is Herne's use of flower symbolism. Early in the play Margaret sings of blossoms told to go into the world of the wind and learn to weep, a prediction of her own fate once she leaves the sheltered environment of her home. Later Philip callously plucks the rose that Margaret had hoped would blossom on her daughter's birthday, the day when Philip was with Lena Schmidt. In the last act, Margaret, though blind, sees the truth about her husband and gives the doctor advice about spraying flowers: "Don't you know that the time to prevent trouble is to look ahead? From potatoes to roses, spray before anything happens—*then* nothing *will* happen." At the end of the play, Margaret seems to be symbolized by the flowers that surround her. She has learned to suffer and has conquered the life-destroying pestilences. In a crude and faltering fashion Herne anticipated 20th Century writers' preoccupation with symbolic details.

To a modern audience *Margaret Fleming* would seem rather mild, but late 19th century audiences found it shocking. Margaret's preparing to nurse the baby on stage repelled critics, managers, and spectators. A typical judgment was expressed in 1891 by Edward A. Dithmar, reviewer for the New York *Times:* "*Margaret Fleming* is, indeed, the quintessence of the commonplace. Its language is the colloquial English of the shops and the streets and the kitchen fire-place. Its personages are the everyday nonentities that some folks like to forget when they go to the theatre. . . . The life it portrays is sordid and mean, and its effect upon a sensitive mind is depressing . . . the stage would be a stupid and useless thing if such plays as *Margaret Fleming* were to prevail. . . . The text is simple and direct and contains many unpleasant expressions not often heard on the stage. The character of Margaret is strongly drawn, but if she is a logical personage, she is certainly a disagreeable one. Selfishness is her predominating trait." Obviously the truthful view of human nature, the simple language, and the use of everyday situations that Dithmar condemned would be considered marks of excellence by playwrights of the next generation. Although his achievement is now recognized by students of American drama, James A. Herne is not widely known. As often happens with a pioneer, the trail he broke has been widened and trampled flat by those who followed the route he made possible. Because *Margaret Fleming* was in the vanguard of the American realistic drama of ideas, one must turn to the work of such 20th century dramatists as Eugene O'Neill, Sidney Howard, Elmer Rice, Marc Blitzstein, and Arthur Miller for comparable plays.

James . A. Herne

Cordially Yours
Katharine C. Herne

**James A. Herne as Joe Fletcher and Katharine Corcoran Herne as
Margaret Fleming**

(From Arthur Hobson Quinn, *A History of the American Drama from the Civil
War to the Present Day*. Courtesy of Appleton-Century-Crofts)

PALMER'S THEATRE.

MR. A. M. PALMER........ ....SOLE LESSEE AND MANAGER

Wednesday Afternoon, December 9, 1891.

SPECIAL MATINEE

FOR THE PRODUCTION OF

MARGARET FLEMING

A Play of American Life, in five acts, by JAMES HERNE, Esq.

CAST OF CHARACTERS.

PHILLIP FLEMING...	E. M. BELL
DR. LARKIN..	E. M. HOLLAND
JOE FLETCHER..	CHAS. L. HARRIS
INSPECTOR OF POLICE...........................	WALDEN RAMSAY
DETECTIVE...	E. S. ABELES
OFFICER..	W. H. POPE
BILL HAGGERTY...	REUB. FAX
OFFICE BOY...	BENNIE SINGER
CHARLIE BURTON..	Master HUGHES
JOHNNIE LYNCH...............................	CAMPBELL MOWAT
MARGARET FLEMING....................................	Mrs. HERNE
MARIA BINDLY....................................	MATTIE EARLE
MRS. BURTON }	
ELLEN COOK }	HELEN GOOLD
MRS. BRADY.............................	NELLIE LINGARD
OLD LADY...	Mrs. BRITTON
MISS EDWARDS..	ADELAIDE ROWE
THE BABIES....................................	BY THEMSELVES
LITTLE LUCY	VIOLA NEILL

SYNOPSIS OF SCENERY.

ACT I.—Scene I.—Phillip Fleming's Office, Canton, Mass.
Curtain 1 minute.
Scene II.—House of Phillip Fleming, Canton, Mass.
ACT II.—Home of Phillip Fleming. Next morning.
ACT III.—Room in Mrs. Burton's Cottage.
Four years elapse.
ACT IV.—Scene I.—Boston Common.
Scene II.—Mrs. Fletcher's Grocery at North End, Boston.
ACT V.—Office of Inspector of Police.

The Orchestra under Direction of Mr. HERMANN BRODE will perform the following Selections:

OVERTURE...................................	Comedy........	.................FUNCK
SERENADE...............................		..........JENSEN
WALTZ............................	The Tyrolean.................................	ZELLER
SELECTION......	Clover.................	SUPPE
PIECE DE SALON......................	At the Fountain.........	.........EILENBERG

EXECUTIVE STAFF OF PALMER'S THEATRE.

BUSINESS MANAGER.........................Mr. F. A. LOVECRAFT.
STAGE MANAGER........ ....Mr. GENE W. PRESBREY.
SCENIC ARTIST. ....Mr. RICHARD MARSTON | MACHINIST............Mr. FRED. DORRINGTON
PROPERTY MAN...................Mr. ED. SEIDLE | GAS MAN....................Mr. JOSEPH DRISCOLL

Ladies' Toilet Room in Balcony Foyer.

The Pianos used in this Theatre are from the establishment of CHICKERING & SONS, 130 Fifth Ave.

The MASON & HAMLIN Liszt Organ used in this theatre.

MARVIN SAFE Co. furnished Safes for this House.

OPERA GLASSES FOR HIRE IN THE LOBBY.

(Harvard Theatre Collection)

Cast of Characters

PHILIP FLEMING, mill owner.
DOCTOR LARKIN
JOE FLETCHER
MR. FOSTER, manager of the mill.
WILLIAMS, foreman.
BOBBY, office boy.
CHARLIE BURTON
MARGARET FLEMING, wife of Philip Fleming.
MARIA BINDLEY, a nurse.
MRS. BURTON
HANNAH, the cook.
JANE, a maid.

ACT I

Scene 1—Philip Fleming's private office at the mill.
Scene 2—The living-room in Margaret's home.

ACT II

The living-room in Margaret's home.

ACT III

A room in Mrs. Burton's cottage.

ACT IV

The living-room in Margaret's home.

The action takes place in Canton, Mass., in 1890.

ACT FIRST
Scene 1

It is a morning in Spring in Philip Fleming's private office at the mill. Bright sunlight floods the room at first. Later it becomes cloudy until at the end of the act, rain is falling fitfully. The room is handsomely furnished. There is a table in the center at the back between two windows. Above the table and attached to the wall is a cabinet with a mirror in the door. In the right corner is an umbrella-stand and hat-rack beside a door leading to the street. There are two windows be-low the door. A little to the right of the center of the room is an arm-chair, and in the same position on the left is a flat-top office desk, with a chair on either side. Behind it on the left is a door lead-ing to the mill. There are a bunch of flowers on the desk and two silver frames holding pictures of Margaret and Lucy. There are also pictures on the wall, including one of the mill and one of Philip's father as a young man.

As the curtain rises, Bobby enters from the left with a desk-basket of mail, which he places on the desk. He rearranges the chairs slightly. As he is about to go out a key is heard in the door on the right. Bobby pauses expectantly. Philip Fleming, carrying an um-brella and a rain-coat, enters from the street door on the right. He is a well dressed, prosperous, happy-looking man about thirty-five. He hangs up his hat and coat, and places his umbrella in the stand. Then he glances carelessly into the hat-rack mirror and runs his hand lightly over his hair.

PHILIP. (*In a friendly manner*) Good morning, Bobby.
BOBBY. (*Grinning appreciatively*) Good morning, sir.

(*Philip goes to his desk and, shifting one or two articles out of his way, begins the duties of the day.*)

PHILIP. Did you get wet this morning in that big shower?
BOBBY. Yes, sir, a little, but I'm all right now.

(*Philip glances rapidly through the letters and with an eager manner selects two large envelopes, opens one, glances through a document it contains and places it in his inside coat-pocket with a satisfied smile.*)

PHILIP. (*Chatting, as he continues his work*) Still doing the four mile sprint?
BOBBY. Yes, sir. Oh, I like it, sir—when it don't rain.

(*Philip opens other letters rapidly, glancing with a quick, compre-hensive eye through each before placing it in the growing heap on the desk.*)

PHILIP. How about the bicycle?
BOBBY. Well, sir, Mr. Foster says he thinks he'll be able to recommend me for a raise pretty soon, if I keep up my record.
PHILIP. (*Looking at him quizzically*) A raise, Bobby?

BOBBY.   Yes, Mr. Fleming, and my mother says I can save all I get and I guess I'll have a bicycle pretty soon then.
PHILIP.   How long have you been here?
BOBBY.   Six months the day after tomorrow.
PHILIP.   (*Smiling kindly*) I guess I'll have to talk to Foster, myself.
BOBBY.   Oh, thank you, Mr. Fleming.

(*Philip opens a letter which appears to disturb him. He pauses over it with a worried frown.*)

PHILIP.   Ask Mr. Foster to come here at once, please. (*As Bobby starts to go*) And tell Williams I want to see him.
BOBBY.   Yes, sir. (*He goes out the door on the left. There is a moment's pause, and then Foster enters from the same door. He is a bright, active young man about twenty-eight or thirty.*)
PHILIP.   Good morning, Foster.
FOSTER.   Good morning, Mr. Fleming.
PHILIP.   Here's a letter from the receiver for Reed and Vorst. He wants to know if we'll accept an immediate settlement of forty percent.
FOSTER.   (*Becoming serious*) Gee, Mr. Fleming, I don't see how we can. I was depending on at least fifty percent to carry us through the summer. It's always a dull season, you know, and—
PHILIP.   Why, we have more orders now than we had this time last year.
FOSTER.   Yes, I know, sir. But, I was going to speak to you. The Cotton Exchange Bank doesn't want to renew those notes.
PHILIP.   Doesn't, eh? Well, then, we'll have to accept Reed and Vorst's offer.
FOSTER.   I think it would be a mistake just now, sir. If we hold out they've got big assets.
PHILIP.   Can't be helped. I'm hard-pressed. We're short of ready money.
FOSTER.   I don't understand it. We've had a better winter than we've had for years.
PHILIP.   (*Smiling*) That last little flier I took wasn't as successful as the former ones.
FOSTER.   You've been too lenient with the retailers.
PHILIP.   "Live and let live" 's my motto.
FOSTER.   I'd hate to see anything happen to the mill.
PHILIP.   Nothing's going to happen. Let me do the worrying. Our credit's good. I'll raise the money tomorrow.
FOSTER.   I hope so, sir. Anything else?
PHILIP.   (*Giving him the letters*) Wire the answers to these right away. That's all.
FOSTER.   All right, sir. (*He goes out.*)

(*Philip takes up a large sheet of paper which contains a report from one of the departments of the mill. He scans it closely and makes some calculations upon a sheet of paper. Williams enters.*)

PHILIP. (*Looking up*) Good morning, Williams.

(*Williams is quite an old man, but has the attitude of one who knows his business and can do things. He stands with bent shoulders and arms hanging limp. He is chewing tobacco, and speaks with a quick, sharp, New England accent.*)

WILLIAMS. Good morning, Mr. Fleming.

PHILIP. (*Holding the report in his hand*) Williams, a short time ago you told me that the main supply belt in the finishing room was only repaired a few times during the last six months. I find here from your report that it has broken down about twice a week since last January. How long does it take to make a repair?

WILLIAMS. Oh, sometimes about ten minutes—other times again, twenty minutes. We have done it in five minutes.

PHILIP. There are about one hundred and ten operators in that room?

WILLIAMS. One hundred and seven.

PHILIP. Why, you should have reported this condition the first week it arose. Poor economy, Williams. (*He makes a few, rapid calculations upon the back of a report.*) Twelve hundred dollars lost time. (*He shakes his head.*) We could have bought a new belt a year ago and saved money in the bargain.

WILLIAMS. I told Mr. Baker several times, sir, in the beginning and he didn't seem to think anything of it.

PHILIP. Well, report all such details to me in the future. (*He writes a few lines rapidly and rings the bell. Bobby enters briskly.*) Tell Mr. Foster to get those firms over long distance, and whichever one can make the quickest delivery to place orders there—see?

BOBBY. Yes, sir. (*He has a soiled card in his hand, which he offers to Philip with a grin.*) A man outside told me to hand you his visiting card.

WILLIAMS. Is that all, sir?

PHILIP. Yes. (*He smiles as he reads the card.*) Joe Fletcher! Tell him to come in. (*He resumes work at his desk. Williams goes out.*)

BOBBY. Yes, sir. (*He follows Williams.*)

(*After a moment Joe Fletcher enters. He is a man of middle age, well made but heavy and slouching in manner. He has a keen, shrewd eye in a weak and dissipated face, which is made attractive, nevertheless, by a genial and ingratiating smile. He is wearing a shabby linen coat called a "duster," which hangs, crushed and limp, from his neck to his ankles. Strung from his left shoulder is a cord hung with sponges of various sizes. Several lengths of chamois are dangling with the sponges across his breast and back, draping his right hip and leg. In one hand he has a weather-beaten satchel. He carries by a leather thong a heavy stone hanging from a cracked plate. There are two holes in the rim of the plate through one of which runs the thong by which it is carried. The other, the big stone, is fastened*)

*to it with a piece of chain. He carries it unconscious of its weight.
There is a pervading sense of intimacy between the man and his
equipment, and from his battered hat to his spreading shoes the
stains of the road, like a varnish, bind them together in a mellow
fellowship.)*

PHILIP.   Hello, Joe. (*He looks at him with humorous curiosity.*)

JOE.   (*Light-heartedly*) How d'do, Mr. Fleming. (*His voice is broken
and husky. He gives a little, dry cough now and then in an ineffectual
attempt to clear it. He crosses to the corner of the table, and shows by
his step that his feet are sore and swollen.*)

PHILIP.   What are you doing now, Joe?

JOE.   (*Indicating his effects. While he talks he places the stone against
a corner of the table on the floor, and puts the valise on the edge of the
table.*) Traveling merchant; agent for Brummell's Giant Cement; professional corn doctor—soft and hard corns—calluses—bunions removed instantly, ingrowing nails treated 'thout pain or loss of blood—or money
refunded. Didn't ye read m'card? (*He coughs.*)

PHILIP.   (*Laughing*) Well, not all of it, Joe.

JOE.   (*Reminiscently*) Inventor of Dr. Fletcher's famous cough mixture,
warranted to cure coughs—colds, hoarseness and loss o' voice. An infalli-
ble remedy fur all chronic conditions of the *pull-mon*-ary organs. (*He
coughs again.*) When not too fur gone. (*He takes a labelled bottle, containing a brown mixture from his inside pocket, shakes it and holds it
up proudly before Philip.*) Kin I sell ye a bottle? (*He smiles ingrati-
atingly.*)

PHILIP.   (*Smiling but shaking his head*) No, Joe, I guess not today.

JOE.   (*Opening the satchel insinuatingly*) Mebbe a few boxes o' corn
salve? It's great. (*Philip shakes his head.*) Would ye like to consider a
box o' cement?

PHILIP.   (*Still smiling*) No, but I'll take one of those big sponges.

JOE.   I thought I could sell ye something. (*He unhooks a large sponge
and lays it upon the desk. Philip hands him a bill. He takes it carelessly,
looks at it, shakes his head regretfully and puts it into his pocket. Then
he feels in his other pocket and taps his vest pockets.*) Gosh, I'm sorry,
but I ain't got a bit of change.

PHILIP.   Oh, never mind the change, Joe. (*He laughs indulgently.*)

JOE.   (*Regretfully*) Well, I'd feel better if I hed the change. (*Joe has been
standing to the left of the desk.*) Kin I set down fur a minnit, Mr. Fleming? M'feet gets so tired.

PHILIP.   Yes, Joe, sit down.

JOE.   I got pretty wet a while ago in that shower. My, but it did come
down.

PHILIP.   (*Warmly*) Perhaps you'd like a hot drink? (*He indicates with a
nod of the head, the cabinet back of Joe, as the latter is about to sit
down. Joe shows a lively interest.*)

JOE.   (*Glancing at Philip with a shy twinkle in his eye*) Oh, kin I, Mr.

Fleming? Thank ye. (*He shuffles over to the cabinet, opens the door and gloats over the vision of joy which greets him. He selects a bottle.*)

PHILIP.   Hold on, Joe. Wait for some hot water.

JOE.   (*Hastily*) No, thank ye. I'm afraid I'd be like the Irishman in the dream.

PHILIP.   What was that, Joe?

JOE.   (*As he pours out a generous portion*) Well, the Irishman was dreaming that he went to see the priest, and the priest asked him to have a drink. "I will, thank ye kindly," says Pat. "Is it hot or cold ye'll have it?" says the priest. "Hot, if ye plaze, yer Riverence," says Pat, and while they were waiting fur the hot water, Pat wakes up. "Bad luck to me," says he, "why didn't I take it cold?" (*He drains the glass, smacks his lips and chuckles.*) My, but that's good stuff! Mr. Fleming, are ye as fond of it yourself as ye used to be?

PHILIP.   (*Smiling and shaking his head*) No, Joe. I've got through with all that foolishness. I've sowed my wild oats.

JOE.   (*Chuckling as he sits in the chair*) You must have got a pretty slick crop out o' yourn.

PHILIP.   Every man gets a pretty full crop of those, Joe, before he gets through.

JOE.   Ye've turned over a new leaf, eh?

PHILIP.   Yes—married.

JOE.   Married?

PHILIP.   Yes, and got a baby.

JOE.   Thet so! Did ye marry out'n the mill?

PHILIP.   Oh, no. She was a Miss Thorp, of Niagara. (*He hands the picture of the child to Joe.*)

JOE.   (*Showing interest immediately, and gazing at the picture, while gradually a gentle responsive smile plays over his features. He says, admiringly.*) By George! that's a great baby! (*He gives a chuckling laugh at it.*) Boy?

PHILIP.   (*Proudly*) No. Girl!

JOE.   Thet so! Should a thought you'd a wanted a boy. (*With sly significance, and chuckling at his own joke*) Ye've hed so many girls.

PHILIP.   (*He laughs lightly.*) Tut, tut, Joe, no more of that for me. (*He hands him the frame containing Margaret's picture.*) My wife.

JOE.   (*His expression becoming grave as the sweetness and dignity of the face touches him. He takes a long breath.*) My, but that's a fine face. Gee, if she's as good as that, you're a lucky man, Mr. Fleming.

PHILIP.   Yes, Joe, I've got more than I deserve, I guess. (*He becomes serious for the first time and a shadow flits over his face. He sighs.*)

JOE.   (*Sympathetically*) Oh, I understand just how you feel. I'm married m'self. (*He sits down facing the audience, his hands clasped, his thumbs gently rolling over each other. A far-away tender look comes into his eyes.*)

PHILIP.   (*Surprised*) Married? (*Joe nods his head.*) Where's your wife?

JOE. Left me. (*He gives a sigh of self pity.*)

PHILIP. (*Touched*) Left you! (*He shakes his head compassionately, then the thought comes to him.*) If my wife left me I'd kill myself.

JOE. (*Philosophically*) Oh, no, no, ye wouldn't. You'd get over it, just as I did. (*He sighs.*)

PHILIP. How did it happen? What did you do?

JOE. (*Innocently*) Not a durn thing! She was a nice, German woman, too. She kept a gent's furnishing store down in South Boston, and I married her.

PHILIP. (*Recovering himself and speaking gaily*) Oh, Joe. (*He shakes his head in mock reproval.*) You married her for her money, eh? (*He laughs at him.*)

JOE. (*Ingenuously*) No, I didn't, honest. I thought I might get a whack at the till once in a while, but I didn't.

PHILIP. (*Quizzing him*) Why not, Joe?

JOE. She fixed me up a pack and sent me out on the road to sell goods, and when I got back, she was gone. There was a new sign on the store, "Isaac Litchenstein, Ladies and Gents' Drygoods." (*He draws a big sigh.*)

PHILIP. And you've never seen her since?

JOE. (*Shaking his head sadly*) No, siree, never!

PHILIP. (*Serious again, impressed by Joe*) That's pretty tough, Joe.

(*Bobby enters*)

BOBBY. Doctor Larkin would like to see you, sir.

JOE. (*Gathering himself and his merchandise together*) Well, I guess I'll get out and drum up a few sales. Much obliged to you, Mr. Fleming.

PHILIP. Oh, stop at the house, Joe. Mrs. Fleming might want something. It's the old place on Linden Street.

JOE. Got a dog?

PHILIP. Yes.

JOE. That settles it.

PHILIP. Only a pug, Joe.

JOE. Oh, a snorer. I'll sell him a bottle of cough mixture. (*As Dr. Larkin enters*) Hello, Doc! How are you? Raining?

(*Joe goes to the door on the right, crossing the doctor who is walking toward Philip on the left.*)

DOCTOR. (*Looking at him, mystified*) Good morning, sir. No, it's not raining. (*Joe goes out. Dr. Larkin is a tall, gaunt man who looks older than he is, with quite a stoop in his shoulders. He has dark brown hair and a beard, streaked with grey, and soft, kind blue eyes. He carries the medicine satchel of a homeopathic physician. His manner is usually distant and cold but extremely quiet and gentle. In the opening of this scene he is perturbed and irritated, later he becomes stern and authoritative.*)

PHILIP.   Good morning, Doctor Larkin.

DOCTOR.   (*Turning to Philip*) Who is that fellow? (*He looks after Joe as he goes out.*)

PHILIP.   Don't you remember him? That's Joe Fletcher. (*Philip is standing to the right of the desk, and Doctor Larkin at the left center of the stage.*)

DOCTOR.   Is that Joe Fletcher? Why he used to be quite a decent sort of fellow. Wasn't he a foreman here in your father's time?

PHILIP.   Yes, he was one of the best men in the mill.

DOCTOR.   (*Shaking his head*) He is a sad example of what liquor and immorality will bring a man to. He has indulged his appetites until he has no real moral nature left.

PHILIP.   (*Lightly*) Oh, I don't think Joe ever had much "moral nature."

(*The sunlight leaves the room. It is growing cloudy outside.*)

DOCTOR.   Every man has a moral nature. In this case it is love of drink that has destroyed it. There are some men who are moral lepers, even lacking the weakness of the tippler as an excuse.

PHILIP.   Have you been to the house, doctor? About midnight Margaret thought little Lucy had a fever. She was going to call you up—but—

DOCTOR.   (*Abruptly*) She would not have found me in at midnight.

PHILIP.   Ah, is that so? Someone very ill? (*The telephone rings.*) Excuse me, doctor. Hello. Oh, is that you, Margaret? How is Lucy now? Good! I knew she'd be all right. Yes, of course. Do—bring her. (*To the Doctor*) She's bringing baby to the 'phone. Hello, Lucy. Many happy returns of the day. Good-bye. Yes, I'll be home at twelve sharp. Apple pie? Yes, of course, I like it. That is, *your* apple pie. (*He leaves the phone with a joyous air.*) This is baby's birthday, you know, doctor.

DOCTOR.   I've just left a baby (*He speaks bitterly, looking at Philip significantly.*) that should never have had a birthday.

PHILIP.   (*Without noticing the doctor's manner, he goes to the cabinet and, taking a box of cigars, offers the box to the doctor.*) Why, Doctor, you're morbid today. Take a cigar, it will quiet your nerves.

(*The rain begins to fall, beating heavily against the windows.*)

DOCTOR.   No, thank you. (*With a subtle shade of repugnance in his tone*) I'll smoke one of my own.

(*Philip smiles indulgently, goes to the desk, sits in the chair to the left of it, lights a cigar, leans back luxuriously, with his hands in his pockets, and one leg over the other, and tips back the legs of the chair.*)

PHILIP.   (*Carelessly*) What's the matter, doctor? You used to respect my cigars.

DOCTOR. (*Hotly*) I used to respect you.

PHILIP. (*Rather surprised but laughing good-naturedly*) Well, doctor, and don't you now? (*He is bantering him.*)

DOCTOR. (*Quietly but sternly*) No, I don't.

PHILIP. (*Smoking placidly*) Good Lord—why?

DOCTOR. (*His satchel resting upon his knees, his hands clasping the metal top, he leans over a trifle and, looking impressively into Philip's face, says, in a low, calm voice.*) At two o'clock last night Lena Schmidt gave birth to a child.

PHILIP. (*Becoming livid with amazement and fear, and staring blankly before him, the cigar dropping from his parted lips*) In God's name, how did they come to send for you?

DOCTOR. Doctor Taylor—he called me in consultation. He was frightened after the girl had been in labor thirty-six hours.

PHILIP. (*Murmuring to himself*) Thirty-six hours! Good God! (*There is a pause, then he partly recovers himself.*) I suppose she told you?

DOCTOR. She told me nothing. It was a lucky thing for you that I was there. The girl was delirious.

PHILIP. Delirious! Well, I've done all I could for her, doctor.

DOCTOR. Have you? (*His tone is full of scorn.*)

PHILIP. She's had all the money she wanted.

DOCTOR. Has she? (*He speaks in the same tone.*)

PHILIP. I tried to get her away months ago, but she wouldn't do it. She was as stubborn as a mule.

DOCTOR. Strange she should want to remain near the father of her child, isn't it?

PHILIP. If she'd done as I told her to, this thing would never have happened.

DOCTOR. You'd have forced some poor devil to run the risk of state's prison. By God, you're worse than I thought you were.

PHILIP. Why, doctor, you must think I'm—

DOCTOR. I don't think anything about it. I know just what brutes such men as you are.

PHILIP. Well, I'm not wholly to blame. You don't know the whole story, doctor.

DOCTOR. I don't want to know it. The *girl's* not to blame. She's a product of her environment. Under present social conditions, she'd probably have gone wrong anyhow. But you! God Almighty! If we can't look for decency in men like you—representative men,—where in God's name are we to look for it, I'd like to know?

PHILIP. If my wife hears of this, my home will be ruined.

DOCTOR. (*Scornfully*) Your home! Your home! It is just such damn scoundrels as you that make and destroy homes.

PHILIP. Oh, come now, doctor, aren't you a little severe?

DOCTOR. Severe! Severe! Why, do you realize, if this thing should become known, it will stir up a stench that will offend the moral sense of every man, woman and child in this community?

PHILIP.   Well, after all, I'm no worse than other men. Why, I haven't seen the girl for months.

DOCTOR.   Haven't you? Well, then suppose you go and see her now.

PHILIP.   (*He springs to his feet.*) I'll do nothing of the sort.

DOCTOR.   Yes, you will. She shan't lie there and die like a dog.

PHILIP.   (*He walks around the room greatly perturbed.*) I tell you I'll not go!

DOCTOR.   Yes, you will.

PHILIP.   (*He comes over to the Doctor and looks down upon him.*) What'll you do if I don't?

DOCTOR.   I don't know, but you'd best go and see that girl.

PHILIP.   (*He turns away.*) Well, what do you want me to say to her?

DOCTOR.   Lie to her as you have before. Tell her you love her.

PHILIP.   I never lied to her. I never told her I loved her.

DOCTOR.   Faugh!

PHILIP.   I tell you I never did!

DOCTOR.   (*Rising from his chair*) You'd better get Mrs. Fleming away from here until this thing blows over. When I think of a high-minded, splendid little woman like her married to a man like you—ugh! (*The doctor goes out quickly.*)

(*Philip, left alone, walks about like an old man, seems dazed for a moment, then goes mechanically to the telephone.*)

PHILIP.   Lindon, 3721. Margaret. (*He speaks in a broken, hushed voice.*) Margaret! Yes, it's I, Philip. Yes! Well, I'm tired. No, I can't come home now. I will not be home for luncheon. I have a business engagement. No, I cannot break it off. It's too important. Eh? Why, with a man from Boston. Yes, certainly, I will, just as soon as I can get away. Yes, dear—I will—good-bye. (*Just before he finishes, Foster enters.*) Hello, Foster.

FOSTER.   (*Consulting a memorandum*) I couldn't get the Harry Smith Company, New York, until noon, sir. They say that the belting can be shipped by fast express at once. The Boston people want ten cents a square foot more than they ask, but we can save that in time and express rates.

PHILIP.   When would the New York shipment get here?

FOSTER.   At the earliest, tomorrow afternoon.

PHILIP.   White and Cross can ship at once, you say?

FOSTER.   Yes, sir.

PHILIP.   Well, give them the order. Their stuff is better, anyhow. Have a covered wagon at the station for the four-ten train. Keep enough men over time tonight to put it up.

FOSTER.   Yes, sir, the sooner it's done, the better.

PHILIP.   Yes, Williams is getting old. He's not the best man for that finishing room. Put him where you can keep an eye on him. He's all right. I have an appointment and will not be in the office again today. Get the interest on those notes off.

FOSTER. Yes, I've attended to that already. Anything else?
PHILIP. No.
FOSTER. All right, sir. Good morning.

(*Philip, who has braced himself for this, relaxes again. The rain continues. He goes about the room, lights a cigar, puts on a rain-coat, looks at his watch, buttons his coat, all the while sunk in deep thought. He takes his umbrella and hat and goes out quietly, shutting the door so that the click of the latch is heard, as the curtain falls.*)

Scene 2

The scene is the living-room in Margaret's home. At the back large glass doors open on to a spacious porch with a garden beyond. There is a fire-place with logs burning, in the corner on the left, and beside it a French window opening on the garden. Below it is a door leading to another room. There is another door on the right going to the main part of the house. There is a table in the center, a baby grand piano on the lower right, and a baby carriage close by the doors at the back. The room is furnished in exquisite taste showing in its distinct character the grace and individuality of a well-bred woman.

Margaret is seated in a low rocking-chair near the fire with the baby in her lap. A large bath towel is spread across her knees. She is exquisitely dressed in an evening gown.

Maria Bindley, the nurse-maid, is dressed in a black dress, cap and apron. She is a middle-aged German woman, dark in complexion, and of medium build and height. She speaks with a not too pronounced German accent. She is gathering up the baby's garments which are scattered about Margaret's feet. She is furtively weeping and makes an occasional effort to overcome her emotion. Margaret is putting the last touches to the baby's night toilet. She is laughing and murmuring mother talk to her.

A shaded lamp is burning on the table to the right. The effect of the light is subdued. The glare of the fire is the high note, making a soft radiance about Margaret and the child. Maria is in the shadow, except as she flits into the light whenever she moves near Margaret. The sound of the rain beating against the windows, is heard now and then.

MARGARET. (*In a low, laughing tone*) No—no—no! You little beggar. You've had your supper! (*She fastens the last two or three buttons of her dress.*) No more! Time to go to sleep now! No use staying awake any longer for naughty father. Two, whole, hours—late! No, he doesn't care a bit about you; not a bit! (*She shakes her head.*) No, nor me either. Never mind, darling, we'll punish him well for this. Yes, we will. Perhaps we'll leave *him* some day, and then we'll see how he likes being left alone. Naughty, bad father—isn't he? *Yes he is!* Staying away all day! Never mind, ladybird—hush, go to sleep now—Mother loves her! Go to sleep—close your eyes. (*This is all said in a cooing, soothing voice. She begins to sing a lullaby.*) Go—to—sleep—blossom—go to sl—

(*Maria comes close to Margaret and picks up two little socks. As she rises, she sniffs in an effort to suppress her tears. This attracts Margaret's attention, and immediately she is all commiseration.*)

MARGARET.   Don't cry, Maria—please don't—it distresses me to see you cry.

MARIA.   (*Smiling a little at Margaret's sympathy. As she talks, she smooths the socks and folds them.*) I cannot help it, Mrs. Fleming—I am an unhappy woman. I try not to cry, but I cannot keep back de tears. (*She puts the socks in the basket on the table.*) I have had an unhappy life —my fadder vas a brute. (*She picks up the dress and shakes it.*) My first husband, Ralph Bindley, vas a goot, honest man. (*She puts the dress in the basket.*) Und my second husband vas dot tramp vot vas here dis morning. Vat I have told you aboudt already. (*She gathers together the other garments.*) Und now my sister—my little Lena—is dying.

MARGARET.   (*In dismay*) Dying! Why, you didn't tell me *that*, Maria!

MARIA.   Vell, she is not dying yust this very moment, but the doctor says she vill never leave dot bed alive. My sweet little Lena! My lovely little sister. I have nursed her, Mrs. Fleming, yust like you nurse your baby now.

MARGARET.   (*Holding the child to her breast*) What did you say her name was?

MARIA.   (*Working mechanically and putting the things neatly away*) Lena,—Lena Schmidt. She does not go by my name—she goes by my fadder's name.

MARGARET.   And, you say, she ran away from you?

MARIA.   Ya—I tried to find her every place. I hunted high und low, but she does not come, und von day I meet an olt friend on Vashington Street, Chris Anderson, und Chris, he tell me that two or three weeks before he see her by the public gartens. Und she vas valking by the arm of a fine, handsome gentleman—und she look smiling and happy, und Chris, he says dot he knows *dot* gentleman—*dot* he vas a rich man vot lives down in Canton where Chris vonce worked when he comes to dis country first.

MARGARET.   And didn't you ask the man's name?

MARIA.   Ach, I forget. Und Chris go back to de olt country, und I never find out. Und den I tink maybe she is married to dot man—und she is ashamed of me and dot miserable husband of mine. I say to myself, "I vill go and see—und find oudt if she is happy." Den I vill go far away, where she vill never see me again. Und I come here to Canton, und at last I find her—und Ach Gott! She is going to be a mutter—und she is no man's vife! (*She has been weeping silently but has continued to work, only pausing at some point in her story that moved her.*)

MARGARET. (*Deeply touched*) Did she tell you the man's name?

MARIA. Ach! No! You could not drag dot oudt of her mit red-hot irons. She says she loves dis man, und she vill make him no trouble. But, by Gott, I vill find dot man oudt, und I vill choke it from his troat. (*She is beside herself with vindictive passion.*)

MARGARET. (*Terrified at her ferocity and crushing her child to her breast*) Oh, Maria—don't—please don't! You frighten me!

MARIA. (*At once all humility*) Excuse me, Mrs. Fleming. I did not mean to do dot.

MARGARET. (*Kindly*) You need not remain any longer. I can manage baby myself. You had best go to your sister at once. If I can be of any help to you, please tell me, won't you?

MARIA. Ya, Mrs. Fleming, I tank you. Und if she is vorse maybe I stay all night.

MARGARET. Yes, certainly. You need not come back tonight.

MARIA. (*Very softly and humbly*) I am much obliged to you, Mrs. Fleming.

MARGARET. (*As Maria is going*) Oh! You had best take my rain-coat.

MARIA. Ah, you are very goot, Mrs. Fleming. (*She has finished her work and is going but hesitates a moment and turns back.*) If you please, don't tell Mr. Fleming about me und my poor sister!

MARGARET. (*Slightly annoyed*) Decidedly not! Why should I tell such things to him?

MARIA. Vell—men don't have sympathy mit peoples like us. He is a fine gentleman, und if he knowed about *her*—he might not like to have *me* by his vife und child. He might tink *I* vas as badt as she was. Good night, Mrs. Fleming.

MARGARET. Good night, Maria. No need to hurry back in the morning. (*There is a wistful sympathy in her face. As her eyes rest upon the door through which Maria has passed, she is lost in thought. Presently a door slams, then she is all alert with expectation. There is a moment's pause, she listens then quickly puts the child in the baby carriage and runs to the door.*) Is that you, Philip?

JANE. (*Outside*) No, ma'am, it is not Mr. Fleming. It was only the post man.

(*Margaret turns away with a sigh of disappointment, goes to the French window and peers out at the rain. The maid enters with several letters, leaves them on the table and goes out. Margaret turns from the window, brushes the tears away impatiently, and drifts purposelessly across the room toward the right, her hands clasped behind her back. Finding herself at the piano she listlessly sits before it and plays a plaintive air, softly. Then suddenly she dashes into a prelude to a gay love song. As she sings half through a stanza, the song gradually loses spirit. Her hands grow heavy over the keys, her voice breaks, and the words come slow and faltering. She ends by breaking into tears, with her head lowered and her fingers resting idly upon the keys. The child attracts her and she goes quickly to her. She laughs through her tears into the wide-open eyes, and begins scolding her for not going to sleep. Soft endearing notes come and go in her voice. A tender joy takes possession of her spirit. She takes the child in her arms.*)

MARGARET.   Well, my lady, wide awake! Come, come, no more nonsense, now! No. Go to sleep! Late hours—will—certainly spoil—your beauty. Yes! Close up your eyes—quick! Come! There, that's nice. She's a sweet, good child! (*She hums.*) Go—to—sleep! (*She sways slowly from right to left, then swinging with a rhythmic step with the lullaby, she lilts softly.*) Blow, blow, Blossom go—into the world below—I am the west wind wild and strong—blossoms must go when they hear my song. (*She puts out the lamp, leaving the room in the warm glare of the firelight.*) Go, little blossom, go—into the world below. Rain, rain, rain is here. Blossoms must learn to weep. (*She reaches the French window. As she turns Philip is seen through the filmy curtains. He enters unnoticed.*) I am the east wind, bleak and cold, poor little blossoms their petals must fold. Weep, little blossoms, weep, into your cradles creep. (*She is unconscious of Philip's presence. His rain-coat and hat are dripping wet. He is pale and weary, his manner is listless and abstracted and he looks as though he had been wandering about in the rain for hours. He drifts into the room. Margaret turns around and takes a step, her eyes upon the child, then her lullaby grows indistinct as she notices that the baby is asleep. Another step takes her into Philip's arms. She gives a cry of alarm.*)
MARGARET.   Oh, Philip! You frightened me! Why did you do that?
PHILIP.   Why are you in the dark, Margaret? (*He goes toward her as if to take her in his arms.*) Dearest!
MARGARET.   (*Drawing back from him with a shade of petulance*) You're all wet. Don't come near baby. She was wakeful. I've put her to sleep. Where have you been all day?
PHILIP.   Didn't I tell you over the 'phone I had an engagement?
MARGARET.   (*As she flits swiftly into the room on the left*) Did it take you all day to keep it? (*She remains in the room long enough to put the child in the crib and then returns.*)
PHILIP.   Yes. A lot of things came up—that I didn't expect. I've been detained. (*He is still standing where she left him.*)
MARGARET.   (*Turning up the lamp*) Why, dear, look! Your umbrella is dripping all over the floor.
PHILIP.   (*Noticing the little puddle of water*) Oh, how stupid of me! (*He hurries out the door on the right, removes his hat and rain-coat, leaves the umbrella, and returns quickly.*)

(Margaret meanwhile has mopped up the water. Then she turns on the lamp on the table to the right.)

MARGARET. *(Reproachfully)* We've been awfully lonesome here all day, baby and I!

PHILIP. *(By the fire)* Forgive me, sweetheart. I've had a very hard day.

MARGARET. Did you forget it was Lucy's birthday?

PHILIP. *(Smiling gravely)* No, I didn't forget. You have both been in my mind the whole day.

MARGARET. *(Glowing with love and a welcome that she refused to give until now)* Oh, Philip! *(She throws herself in his arms.)* It's good to get you back. So good! *(After a moment she rings the bell. The maid answers.)* Jane, I wish you would serve dinner in here.

JANE. Yes, Mrs. Fleming.

PHILIP. *(Drawing her close to him again)* Dear little wife! *(As though a long time had passed since he parted from her)*

JANE. *(Coming in with a tray containing food and silver, and going to the center table)* Shall I lay the table here, Mrs. Fleming?

MARGARET. No—here—cosy—by the fire. *(Jane dresses the table deftly and without bustle. She goes away and returns with the dinner.)* You need not return, Jane. I'll ring if we need you.

JANE. Very well, Mrs. Fleming. *(She goes off.)*

PHILIP. *(Sitting to the right of the table, and taking a large envelope from his pocket, he withdraws a bank book and hands it to Margaret, who is about to sit down on the left.)* Here, Margaret—I want you to look over that.

MARGARET. *(Taking the book and reading the cover)* Margaret Fleming in account with Boston Providence Savings Bank. *(She opens the book and reads.)* "By deposit, May 3, 1890, $5,000." Five thousand dollars! Oh, Philip!

PHILIP. *(Smiling complacently)* There's something else.

MARGARET. Yes? *(Philip nods his head, and hands her a large envelope which he has taken from his pocket. She looks at it and reads.)* "Margaret Fleming, guardian for Lucy Fleming." *(She takes a document from the envelope.)* A certificate for $20,000 worth of United States bonds, maturing 1930. Why, Philip! How wonderful. But, can you afford it? *(He smiles and nods his head, and then begins to serve the dinner. Margaret, in childish joy, rushes to the door of the room where the child is.)* Oh, baby! Lucy! You are rich, rich! *(She stops and peeps in.)* Oh, my, I must not wake her. *The little heiress!* *(She sits at the table and begins to serve.)*

PHILIP. *(Handing her another envelope. Tenderly.)* For you Margaret!

MARGARET. *(Taking it and becoming breathless as she reads it)* It's a deed for this house and all the land! Ah, Philip, how generous you are, and this is what has kept you away all day! And I was cross with you. *(Tears come to her eyes.)* Forgive me, dear, please do. *(She goes to him and kneels by his side.)* But, why do you do all this? What need? What necessity for me to have a deed of property from you?

PHILIP. Well, things have not been going just our way at the mill. The new tariff laws may help some, but I doubt it. At all events, before anything serious—

MARGARET. (*A little awed*) Serious?

PHILIP. Well, you never can be sure. At any rate, in times of stress a business man should protect his family.

MARGARET. Is there danger—of—trouble?

PHILIP. No! I hope not. I think I'll be able to tide it over.

MARGARET. But, dear—you—this property, is worth a lot of money. Why not sell it? Wouldn't that be a great help? A resource in case—

PHILIP. Sell the home?

MARGARET. No, sell the house. The home is where we are. (*She rises and stands partly back of his chair with her arms about his neck.*) Where *love is*—no matter *where*, just so long as we three are there together. A big house—a little house—of course, I do love this place, where you were born, and baby— (*Taking a long breath*) It's very precious—but—(*She has moved back to the head of the table and now lays down the deed.*) I cannot take it, dear. It frightens me. It's too valuable—all this—land—no—let us guard it together and if bad times come, it will be—a fine thing to have--

PHILIP. (*Protesting*) Now, my dear!

MARGARET. I don't want the responsibility. Suppose something happened to me. (*She sits at the table, on the left.*)

PHILIP. Ah—Margaret—

MARGARET. (*Laughing*) Well—I just said "suppose."

PHILIP. (*Laughing*) Well—*don't say it*. We'll think of nothing "suppose." *Nothing*, but bright—*beautiful* things.

MARGARET. Come, dear, eat. I should think you were famished. You've touched nothing yet.

PHILIP. I don't feel hungry. I'm tired—awfully tired.

MARGARET. No wonder, after all you've been through today. I'll make you a cup of tea. (*She rings the bell. Jane enters.*) Boiling water, Jane, please, and bring the tea things. (*While she is busy over the tea things she stops and looks at him quizzically.*) Who was that tramp you sent here this morning?

PHILIP. (*Innocently*) What tramp?

MARGARET. Why, the one with the plate and the big stone—the cough medicine,—the sponges and *the voice*. (*She imitates Joe.*)

PHILIP. (*Laughing*) Ah, he's not a tramp—that's Joe Fletcher.

MARGARET. Did you know that he was Maria's husband?

PHILIP. (*Amazed*) What! Maria's husband? What did he say to her?

MARGARET. (*Smiling reminiscently*) He didn't say much—*She* did all the talking.

PHILIP. What did *she* say?

MARGARET. I don't know. She spoke in German. I think, she was swearing at him. When I came she had him by the ears and was trying to pull his head off. Then she got him to the floor and threw him down the front steps. It was the funniest thing I ever saw. I couldn't help laughing, yet my heart ached for her.

PHILIP. Poor Joe! That's the second time she's thrown him out.

MARGARET. She never did that before.

PHILIP. He says she did.

MARGARET. Well, she didn't. He robbed her and left her.

PHILIP. What?

MARGARET. She went out on the road to sell goods and left him in charge of the shop. When she came back he was gone and he had sold out the place to a secondhand dealer.

PHILIP. (*In wonderment*) What a liar that fellow is!

MARGARET. Well, if he told you any other story—he certainly is. (*She notices a change in his face.*) Why, Philip! You look awfully white! Are you ill? Are you keeping anything from me? Oh, please tell me—do. Let me share your trouble. (*She goes to him, and puts her arms about his shoulders, with her face against his as she finishes the last line.*)

PHILIP. No—no—dear heart—nothing! There's nothing more to tell. I'm very tired.

MARGARET. Oh, how selfish of me. You should have gone to bed the moment you came.

PHILIP. I'll be all right in the morning. I must have caught a chill. (*He shudders.*) My blood seems to be congealed.

MARGARET. (*Alarmed*) Oh, my dear—my poor boy! It was a dreadful thing you did. (*He starts guiltily.*) Going about in the rain all day. (*She goes swiftly into the room on the left and returns with a handsome dressing gown and slippers. Philip has gone over to the fire.*) I must give you some aconite. A hot drink—and a mustard foot bath. (*She fusses over him, helps him to get into his dressing gown, and warms his slippers by the fire.*)

PHILIP. I don't think I need anything, dear, but a hot drink, perhaps, and a night's rest. I'll be all right in the morning. I think I'll take a little brandy.

MARGARET. (*Quickly*) I'll get it for you, dear. Keep by the fire. (*She rushes out the door on the right, and returns quickly with a silver tray holding a cut-glass decanter of brandy and a glass. She pours out some and holds up the glass.*) Is that enough?

PHILIP. Plenty—thank you! (*He drinks it, while Margaret replaces the tray on the small table at the back.*)

MARGARET. Now, dear, I'll look after that mustard bath.

PHILIP. (*Protesting*) Oh, Margaret, please don't bother. I really don't need it.

MARGARET. (*Laughing at him*) Yes, you do. (*She shakes her finger threateningly at him.*) You might just as well make up your mind that you've got to have it.

PHILIP. (*Smiling resignedly*) All right—"boss."

MARGARET.   (*Laughing at him as she starts to go*) You know, Philip, dear, you gave me the strangest feeling when you stood there—the rain dripping from you—you didn't look a bit like yourself. (*She gives an apologetic laugh.*) You gave me a dreadful fright. Just like a spirit! A lost spirit. (*She laughs again.*) Now, wasn't that silly of me? (*She runs off to the right, still laughing.*)

(*Philip sits in the fire-light looking sadly after her as the curtain falls.*)

ACT SECOND

The scene is the same as the Second Scene of the First Act. The large doors at the back are open showing a luxuriant garden in brilliant sunshine. The baby is in her carriage by the garden door. Margaret, in a dainty house dress, is seated in a low chair in the center of the room, mending one of the baby's dresses. Dr. Larkin, sitting at the table on the left with his back turned to her, is folding little packages of medicine. Margaret looks happy and contented as she chats with him.

DOCTOR.   You say you have no pain in the eyes?
MARGARET.   No pain at all . . . only, once in awhile there is . . . a . . . sort of a dimness.
DOCTOR.   Yes, a dimness.
MARGARET.   As if my eyes were tired.
DOCTOR.   Yes!
MARGARET.   When I read too long, or . . .
DOCTOR.   (*Turning about and looking at her*) Do you know what would be a good thing for you to do?
MARGARET.   What, doctor?
DOCTOR.   Wear glasses.
MARGARET.   Why, doctor, aren't you dreadful! (*She laughs at him.*) Why, I'd look a sight.
DOCTOR.   Well, it would be a good idea, all the same. You should wear glasses when you are reading or sewing, at least.
MARGARET.   (*Laughing gaily at him*) Well, I'll do nothing of the sort. Time enough for me to wear glasses, years and years from now.
DOCTOR.   (*Smiling indulgently*) It would be a good thing to do now. How is "Topsy" this morning?
MARGARET.   (*Glancing proudly in the direction of the baby*) Oh, she's blooming.
DOCTOR.   Mrs. Fleming, any time you want to sell that baby, Mrs. Larkin and I will give you ten thousand dollars for her.

MARGARET. (*Laughing and beaming with pride*) Yes . . . doctor . . . *when* we *want* to sell her. How is Mrs. Larkin?

DOCTOR. She's doing very nicely. I'm going to try to get her up to the mountains this summer. (*He finishes the packages.*) There . . . take one of these powders three times a day. Rest your eyes as much as possible. Don't let anything fret or worry you, and keep out-doors all you can. (*He closes the bag after putting a couple of bottles and a small medicine case in it.*)

MARGARET. Oh, doctor, aren't you going to leave something for Philip?

DOCTOR. (*Giving a dry, little grunt*) Hum! I forgot about him. (*Standing by the table, he takes a small case from his satchel, removes two large bottles of pellets from it, fills two phials from them and makes a number upon the cork of each with a fountain pen.*) You say he was pretty wet when he came home last night?

MARGARET. Yes, and tired out. He had a very hard day, I think. I never saw him so completely fagged. It seemed to me he had been tramping in the rain for hours. I gave him a good scolding too, I tell you. I doctored him up as well as I could and put him to bed. (*Smiling contentedly*) He's as bright as a lark this morning, but all the same, I insisted upon his remaining home for a rest.

DOCTOR. You take good care of him, don't you? (*He beams upon her kindly.*)

MARGARET. (*Playfully*) I've got to . . . he's all I have, and men like Philip are not picked up every day, now, I tell you.

DOCTOR. (*Drily*) No, men like Philip Fleming are certainly not to be found easily.

MARGARET. I hope there's nothing wrong with him. I was worried last night. You know, he has been working awfully hard lately.

DOCTOR. (*Kindly*) Now, don't fret about imaginary ills. He's probably a little over-worked. It might be a good idea to have him go away for a week or two.

MARGARET. (*Entering into the suggestion*) Yes . . . a little trip somewhere would help him a lot, I'm sure.

DOCTOR. (*Holding up his finger*) But, you must go with him, though.

(*Margaret, by this time, is standing up, with the baby's dress tucked under her arm. She takes stitches as she talks.*)

MARGARET. (*Eagerly*) Of course! I wouldn't let him go alone. Somebody might steal him from me. (*She smiles.*)

DOCTOR. (*Snapping the clasp of his satchel, vehemently murmurs under his breath*) Hum! They'd bring him back mighty quick, I guess. (*He turns to her.*) Give him these. Tell him to take two alternately every hour.

MARGARET. (*Taking the phials, and nodding her head as if to remember*) Two every hour—thank you.

(*Philip enters from the garden, gaily humming an air. He has a freshly plucked rose in his hand.*)

PHILIP. Good morning, doctor.

DOCTOR. (*Coldly*) Good morning.

MARGARET. (*Noticing the rose, regretfully*) Oh, Philip, you plucked that rose.

PHILIP. Yes, isn't it lovely? It's the first of the season. (*He smells it.*)

MARGARET. Yes, and I've been watching it. I wanted it to open yesterday for baby's birthday.

PHILIP. (*Playfully*) It saved itself for today for baby's mother. (*He puts it on her breast.*)

MARGARET. (*Pleased*) Well, I'd rather it had bloomed yesterday for her. Excuse me, doctor, I must run into the kitchen. We have a new cook and she needs watching.

PHILIP. (*Gaily*) And she's a dandy. (*He breaks into a chant.*) Oh, I'm glad we've got a new cookie. I'm glad we've got a new cook. She's . . .

MARGARET. (*Laughing at him*) Hush! Hush! Philip, stop—be quiet! (*She puts her hand over his mouth. He tries to sing through her fingers.*) She'll hear you. Oh, doctor, isn't he terrible? He's poking fun at her all the time, but she is funny, though. (*She runs off joyously to the right.*)

PHILIP. What a glorious morning, after yesterday.

DOCTOR. (*Eyeing him coldly*) Yes—it is—you're in high feather this morning, eh?

PHILIP. (*Cheerily*) Of course I am. What's the good in worrying over things you can't help?

DOCTOR. Have you seen . . . ?

PHILIP. (*Quickly*) Yes. (*In a low voice*) I've made arrangements for her to go away as soon as she is well enough.

DOCTOR. *Humph!*

PHILIP. It's a terrible mess. I'll admit I never realized what I was doing, but, I shall make things all right for this girl, and her child. (*He sits on the edge of the table to the left. The doctor is standing to the right of him.*) Doctor, I'm going to tell my wife this whole, miserable story.

DOCTOR. (*Aghast*) What?

PHILIP. (*Hastily interrupting*) Ah, not now—in the future. When we both have grown closer together. When I have shown her by an honest and decent life that I ought to be forgiven—when I feel sure of her faith and confidence—then I shall confess and ask her to forgive me.

DOCTOR. (*Shaking his head*) That would be a mighty hazardous experiment. You would draw a woman's heart strings closer and closer about you—and then deliberately tear them asunder. Best keep silent forever.

PHILIP. There would be no hazard. I know Margaret—of course if she found me out now—I admit it—it would be a terrible thing, but—

DOCTOR. (*Abruptly*) You'd better get Mrs. Fleming away from here for a few weeks.

PHILIP. (*Surprised*) Away? (*He smiles confidently.*) What need?

DOCTOR. She is threatened with a serious affection of the eyes.

PHILIP. (*His smile fading away, then recovering quickly and laughing lightly*) Aren't you trying to frighten me, doctor?

DOCTOR. (*Annoyed by his levity*) I don't care anything about you, but, I tell you, your wife has a tendency to an affection of the eyes called glaucoma.

PHILIP. (*Interested*) Glaucoma? Affection of the eyes? Why, Margaret has magnificent eyes.

DOCTOR. Yes, she has magnificent eyes, but, her child is the indirect cause of the development of an inherent weakness in them.

PHILIP. In what way?

DOCTOR. Conditions incident to motherhood. Shock. She is showing slight symptoms now that if aggravated would cause very serious consequences.

PHILIP. (*Puzzled*) I do not understand.

DOCTOR. The eye—like other organs, has its own special secretion, which keeps it nourished and in a healthy state. The inflow and outflow of this secretion is equal. The physician sometimes comes across a patient of apparently sound physique, in whom he will find an abnormal condition of the eye where this natural function is through some inherent weakness, easily disturbed. When the patient is subject to illness, great physical or mental suffering—the too great emotion of a sudden joy or sorrow,—the stimulus of any one of these causes may produce in the eyes a superabundant influx of this perfectly healthy fluid and the fine outflowing ducts cannot carry it off.

PHILIP. Yes. What then?

DOCTOR. The impact continues—until the result—is—

PHILIP. Yes? What is the result?

DOCTOR. Blindness.

PHILIP. (*Awed*) Why—that is horrible—is there no remedy?

DOCTOR. Yes. A very delicate operation.

PHILIP. Always successful?

DOCTOR. If performed under proper conditions—yes.

PHILIP. And my wife is in danger of this? (*He walks up and down the room.*)

DOCTOR. There is no danger whatever to Mrs. Fleming, if the serenity of her life is not disturbed. There are slight, but nevertheless serious symptoms that must be remedied at once, with ordinary care. She will outgrow this weakness. Perhaps you will understand now, how necessary it is that she leave Canton for a few weeks.

PHILIP. (*Deeply impressed by the doctor's recital*) Yes, I do. I will set about getting her away at once. I can leave the mill for a while in Foster's hands.

DOCTOR. Yes, he is an honest, capable fellow. Above all things, do not let Mrs. Fleming suspect that there is anything serious the matter. Keep her cheerful.

PHILIP. Ah, Margaret is the sunniest, happiest disposition—nothing troubles her.

DOCTOR. Well, you keep her so. (*Philip takes out his cigar case and offers it to the doctor. The latter refuses laconically.*) Thank you, I have my own. (*He has taken a cigar from his vest pocket. Philip strikes a match and offers it to the doctor. At the same time, the doctor is lighting his cigar with his own match, ignoring Philip's attention. Philip shrugs his shoulders indulgently, lights his cigar and good-naturedly watches the doctor, who takes up his satchel and leaves the room hastily with a curt Good morning.*)

PHILIP. (*Genially*) Good morning, Dr. Larkin. (*He sits in the armchair to the right and comfortably contemplates the convolutions of the cigar smoke.*)

(*The closing of the front door is heard. Joe Fletcher appears at the French window, stealthily peering into the room. He sees Philip and coughs.*)

JOE. Hello, Mr. Fleming!

PHILIP. (*Looking up*) Hello, Joe—come in.

JOE. (*In a whisper*) Is it safe?

PHILIP. (*Laughing*) Yes, I guess so.

JOE. (*Slouching inside*) Where's Maria?

PHILIP. Gone out.

JOE. (*Relieved*) Say, that was a damn mean trick you played on me yesterday.

PHILIP. What trick?

JOE. Sending me up here—you knew durn well she'd go fer me.

PHILIP. (*Laughing*) I didn't know Maria was your wife, honest I didn't.

JOE. Oh, tell that to the marines. I want my sign. (*As Philip looks puzzled*) The sample of giant's cement with the plate.

PHILIP. (*Remembering*) Oh, yes. (*He chuckles to himself, goes to the door at the right and brings back the cracked plate with the big stone hung to it. Joe takes it and turns to go.*) Why did you lie to me yesterday?

JOE. I didn't lie to you.

PHILIP. You told me your wife ran away from you.

JOE. So she did.

PHILIP. *She* says you robbed her and left her.

JOE. She's a liar, and I'll tell it to her face.

PHILIP. (*Laughing*) Come, Joe, you wouldn't dare.

JOE. She's a liar. I'm not afraid of her.

PHILIP. She made you run yesterday.

JOE. (*Holding up the sign*) Didn't she have this? What chance has a fellow got when a woman has a *weapon* like this?

PHILIP. (*Laughing at him*) And you were in the war.

JOE. Yes, and I was in the war! The Johnnies didn't fight with things like this.

PHILIP. (*Enjoying the situation*) Come, Joe, I believe she'd make you run without that.

JOE. She's a liar. I can lick her. (*With conviction*) I have licked her. (*He grows bolder.*) An' I'll lick her again.

PHILIP. (*Laughing heartily*) Come, Joe, that'll do. The best way for you to lick 'er is there. (*He points to the decanter upon the side table. Joe gazes upon it tenderly and chuckles with unctuous satisfaction.*)

JOE. That's a great joke, Mr. Fleming. *Kin* I? (*He shuffles over to the decanter.*)

PHILIP. Yes, go ahead.

(*Joe pours the liquor into a glass. Maria walks hastily in through the window and sees Philip.*)

MARIA. (*Diffidently*) Excuse me, Mr. Fleming, I did not know you vas here. I always come in dot way mit de baby. (*Joe is in the act of carrying the glass to his lips. He hears Maria's voice and stands terrified. Maria sees him and becomes inflamed with indignation. She puts her hands on her hips and glares at him.*) Vell, you dom scoundrel!

JOE. (*Soothingly extending a hand to her*) There now, Maria, keep cool. Don't lose your temper.

MARIA. (*Mocking him*) Yah, don't lose my temper. Didn't I tell you never to darken dis house again? Du teufel aus Hölle! (*She makes a lunge at him. He dodges and hops on tip-toe from side to side in a zig-zag.*)

JOE. Just a minute, Maria! (*He gulps.*) I can—I can explain—the whole—thing. (*He makes a desperate bolt, but Maria is on his heels. He stumbles and falls sprawling upon his hands and face, with his head to the front, in the center of the room. She swoops upon him, digs her hands into the loose folds of his coat between the shoulders and drags him to his feet. He limps with fright, puffing and spluttering, awkwardly helping himself and dropping the sign.*) Maria, for God's sake, don't! I ain't ever done anything to you.

MARIA. (*Dragging him toward the window*) Ach, Gott! No, you have never done nutting to me.

JOE. I'll make it all right with you. Let me go. I want my sign! Ugh! (*She throws him through the French window. He stumbles and staggers out of sight. Maria picks up the sign and flings it after him. All the time she is scolding and weeping with anger.*)

MARIA. Don't you dare come here no more to a decent house, you loafer. You can't explain nutting to me, you tief—you loafer— (*She sinks into the chair at the right of the table, leans her arms across the table, buries her face in them and sobs bitterly. All her fury has vanished and she is crushed and broken.*)

PHILIP. (*Laughing and calling after Joe*) Joe, come back! Joe! (*He goes out through the window.*) Joe!

MARGARET.   (*Rushing in and up to the garden door, afraid some harm has come to the child*) What on earth is the matter? An earthquake?

MARIA.   (*Sobbing*) No, Mrs. Fleming. It vas dot miserable husband of me.

MARGARET.   What?

MARIA.   Yah, I yust came in now, und I find him dere drinking of Mr. Fleming's brandy.

MARGARET.   Good gracious—what did you do, Maria?

MARIA.   I skipped dot gutter mit him, I bet my life. (*She is still weeping.*)

MARGARET.   (*A smile flickering about her lips*) There, Maria, don't cry. Don't let him trouble you so. How is your sister?

MARIA.   Vorse, Mrs. Fleming.

MARGARET.   Worse. Oh, I'm so sorry.

MARIA.   Yah. I don't tink she vill ever leave dot bed alive. My poor little Lena. Mrs. Fleming, I ask you—mebbe you vill come to see her. She talks about you all de time now.

MARGARET.   (*Surprised*) Talks about me? Why, how does she know me?

MARIA.   Vell, she ask about you—a lot—und I tell her of you and your beautiful home und your little baby, und now she says she'd like yust once to look into your face.

MARGARET.   (*Hesitating a moment*) Well, I'll go. If I only could do anything for her, poor girl.

MARIA.   Yah, she is a poor girl, Mrs. Fleming. Mebbe she vill tell you the name of dis man vot—

MARGARET.   (*With repugnance*) Oh, no, no! I don't want to know the brute, or his name.

MARIA.   (*Vindictively*) Oh, Gott! If I vould know it—

MARGARET.   (*Breaking in upon her, kindly*) But, I'll go to see her.

MARIA.   Tank you, Mrs. Fleming. You are a goodt lady.

MARGARET.   Where did you say she lives?

MARIA.   (*Still quietly weeping*) Forty-two Millbrook St. By Mrs. Burton's cottage.

MARGARET.   Very well. (*Philip's voice is heard outside, laughing.*) Oh, there's Mr. Fleming. Come, Maria, don't let him see you crying. Come, go to the kitchen and tell Hannah— (*She has urged Maria to her feet and is pressing her toward the door.*)

MARIA.   Is dot new girl come?.

MARGARET.   Yes.

MARIA.   Hannah is her name?

MARGARET.   (*Pressing her*) Yes, tell her to make you a nice cup of tea, and then you'd best go back to your sister.

MARIA.   Tank you, Mrs. Fleming. I don't want no tea. Mebbe she needs me. I go right back to her. You'll come sure, Mrs. Fleming?

MARGARET.   (*Putting her through the door on the right as Philip comes in through the window on the left*) Yes, I'll come in a little while.

PHILIP.   Oh, Margaret, I wish you'd been here. (*He begins to laugh.*) Such a circus. The funniest thing I ever saw.

MARGARET. Yes, Maria told me. Poor thing. I'm sorry for her. (*Philip laughs. She goes to her work basket which is on the center table, and takes out the two phials. Philip crosses to the right and Margaret goes to him.*) Here, dear—some medicine Dr. Larkin left for you.

PHILIP. (*Pushing her hand away gently*) Oh, I don't want any medicine. There's nothing the matter with me. (*He begins to chuckle again.*) If you could—

MARGARET. (*Shaking him by the lapels of his jacket*) Yes, there is a great deal the matter with you. (*She looks at him seriously and he becomes serious.*) Doctor says you're all run down. You've got to have a rest. Here, now, take two of these pellets, alternating every hour. (*He takes the phials and puts them in his vest pocket.*) Take some now!

PHILIP. Oh! Now? Must I?

MARGARET. (*Shaking him*) Yes, this minute. (*He takes two pellets and pretends to choke. She shakes him again.*) Look at your watch. Note the time.

PHILIP. Yes'm.

MARGARET. Well, in an hour, take two from the other phial.

PHILIP. Yes'm. (*He lights a fresh cigar, and Margaret gives a cry of reproval.*)

MARGARET. Philip! What are you doing? (*She rushes at him and takes the cigar from him.*) Don't you know you mustn't smoke when you are taking medicine.

PHILIP. Why not?

MARGARET. It'll kill the effect of it. You may smoke in an hour.

PHILIP. I've got to take more medicine in an hour?

MARGARET. Well, I guess you'll have to give up smoking.

PHILIP. What!

MARGARET. Until you're well.

PHILIP. But, I'm well now.

MARGARET. (*Going through the door on the left*) Until you have stopped taking those pellets!

PHILIP. All right. I'll forget them.

MARGARET. Philip!

PHILIP. (*Going to the baby in the garden doorway*) The cigars! What are you doing?

MARGARET. Changing my gown. I'm going out.

PHILIP. Where are you going?

MARGARET. Oh, just a little errand.

PHILIP. Well, hurry back.

MARGARET. Yes, I won't be long. (*She gives a little scream.*) Oh!

PHILIP. What's the matter?

MARGARET. Nothing. Stuck a pin into my finger, that's all.

PHILIP. My! You gave me a shock. (*He puts his hand to his heart playfully.*)

MARGARET. (*Laughing*) Sorry. Did you see my gloves?

PHILIP. Yes.

MARGARET. Where?

PHILIP. On your hands, of course.

MARGARET. Now don't be silly!

PHILIP. (*Playing with the baby*) Margaret, you know, baby's eyes are changing.

MARGARET. No.

PHILIP. Yes. They're growing like yours.

MARGARET. Nonsense. She has your eyes.

PHILIP. (*Eyeing the baby critically*) No, they're exactly like yours. She's got my nose though.

MARGARET. (*Giving a little cry of protest*) Oh, Philip—don't say that.

PHILIP. Why?

MARGARET. It would be terrible if she had your nose. Just imagine my dainty Lucy with a great big nose like yours.

PHILIP. (*Feeling his nose*) Why, I think I have a very nice nose.

MARGARET. (*Coming in, laughing*) Oh, yes, it's a good enough nose—as noses go—but— (*She touches the bell.*)

PHILIP. (*Noticing her gown*) Your new suit?

MARGARET. (*Gaily*) Yes. Like it?

PHILIP. It's a dandy. Turn around. (*She dances over to him and twirls about playfully.*) Wait, there's a thread. (*He picks it off her skirt.*)

(*Jane enters.*)

MARGARET. Jane, please tell Hannah to come here.

JANE. Yes, ma'am. (*She goes.*)

(*Philip begins to chuckle.*)

MARGARET. Now, Philip, I implore you to keep still. Please don't get me laughing while I'm talking to her.

PHILIP. (*Indignantly*) I'm not going to say anything.

(*Hannah appears. She is very large, stout and dignified.*)

MARGARET. (*Hurriedly, in haste to be off*) Hannah! I'm going out and I shall not be able to look after the baking of the bread. When the loaves have raised almost to the top of the pans put them in the oven.

HANNAH. (*Who has been studying admiringly Margaret's costume.*) Yes, Ma'am. I does always put the bread in when it's almost up to the top in the pans.

MARGARET. And bake them just one hour.

HANNAH. Ah! Yes, Ma'am. I always bakes 'em an hour.

(*Philip smothers a laugh in a cough. Margaret stares at him.*)

MARGARET. And, have luncheon on at half past twelve, please.

HANNAH. Yes, I always has the lunch on at half past twelve, sharp.

MARGARET. (*Who has been putting on her gloves*) Thank you, Hannah, that's all. Well, I'm off. (*To Philip*) Good-bye, dear. (*She starts off hastily.*)

HANNAH. Good-bye, ma'am. (*She goes out.*)

MARGARET. (*Pausing to look at Philip as he plays with the baby in the carriage*) Oh, how dear you both look there together.

PHILIP. (*Looking at his watch*) You'd best hurry if you want to get back at *half past twelve sharp*. (*He imitates Hannah.*)

MARGARET. (*Rapturously gazing at them*) Oh, if I could paint, what a picture I would make of you two!

PHILIP. Are you going?

MARGARET. Yes, I'm going. (*She notices Philip giving the baby his watch, and giving a little scream of alarm, she rushes at him.*) Philip, what are you doing?

PHILIP. That's all right. She won't hurt it.

MARGARET. Suppose she'd swallow it.

PHILIP. Well!

MARGARET. (*Mocking him*) Well! There, put it in your pocket. And have some sense. (*She picks up the rattle and the big rubber ball and puts them in his hands.*) There, you can play with these. (*They both laugh with the fun of it all.*)

PHILIP. Oh! Go on Margaret, and hurry home.

MARGARET. (*Kissing him and the baby*) All right. Won't be long. Don't forget your medicine, and please don't smoke when my back is turned. (*She dances out through the French window, overflowing with fun and animation. This scene must be played rapidly, with a gay, light touch.*)

ACT THIRD

The scene is a neat, plainly furnished sitting-room in Mrs. Burton's cottage. The walls are covered with old-fashioned wall paper of a faded green color. Sunlight streams in through two windows at the back. In one there is a small table holding a few pots of geraniums, and in the second, a hanging basket of ivy. A few straggling vines creep about the window-frame. There are doors at the left center, down left and on the right. In the center of the room stands a table with a chair to the right of it, and a few haircloth chairs are here and there. A sofa stands against the left wall below the door, and there is a low rocking-chair on the left.

The room is empty and after a moment the stillness is broken by the wail of an infant. The hushed notes of a woman's voice are heard from the open door on the left, soothing the child. A low knock is heard at the door to the right. The door opens slowly and Doctor Larkin enters. Mrs. Burton emerges from the room on the left with a tiny baby wrapped in a soft white shawl in her arms. She is a motherly woman, large and placid, with a benign immobility of countenance. She speaks with a New England drawl.

MRS. BURTON.   Good morning, doctor. I didn't hear ye knock.

DOCTOR.   How is your patient this morning?

MRS. BURTON.   Why, ain't yer seen Dr. Taylor? Didn't he tell ye?

DOCTOR.   No. She's—?

MRS. BURTON.   (*Nodding her head*) Yes.

DOCTOR.   When did it happen?

MRS. BURTON.   About an hour ago. She seemed brighter this morning. After her sister went out she slept for a while. When I came in the room she opened her eyes and asked me for a pencil and paper. I brought 'em to her and she writ for quite a spell. Then she lay 'back on the pillow. I asked her if she wouldn't take a little nourishment. She smiled and shook her head. Then she gave a long sigh—an'—an'—that was all there was to it.

DOCTOR.   How's the child?

MRS. BURTON.   Poor little critter— (*She looks down at it.*) I can't do nothing for it. I've tried everything. It ought to have mother's milk— that's all there is to it. Be quiet, you poor little motherless critter.

DOCTOR.   It would be better for it if it had gone with her.

MRS. BURTON.   Why, doctor, ain't ye awful?

DOCTOR.   Why, what chance has that child got in this world? I'll send you something for it. (*He turns to go.*)

MRS. BURTON.   Don't ye want to see her?

DOCTOR.   No! What good can I be to her now, poor devil?

(*Charley Burton, a sturdy lad of ten, breaks boisterously into the room from the door on the right, carrying a baseball and bat.*)

CHARLEY.   Ma! Ma! Here's a woman wants to see Mrs. Bindley.

MRS. BURTON.   (*Reprimanding him*) Lady! And take your hat off.

(*Dr. Larkin and Mrs. Burton look expectantly toward the door. Margaret enters slowly, her eyes bent upon her glove which she is unfastening. Dr. Larkin is dumbfounded at the sight of her. She takes a few steps toward him and looks up.*)

MARGARET.   (*Pleasantly surprised at seeing him*) Why, doctor! I didn't know that you were on this case.

DOCTOR.   (*Confused*) I'm not. Dr. Taylor—he—called me in consultation. But, what in the name of all that's wonderful brings you here?

MARGARET.   Maria!

DOCTOR. What Maria? Not—

MARGARET. Yes, our Maria—this sick girl is her sister. (*She removes her hat and places it with her gloves on the table.*)

DOCTOR. (*In consternation.*) Her sister! Then you know?

MARGARET. I know that there is a poor sick girl here who wants—

DOCTOR. (*Going to her, brusquely*) Mrs. Fleming, you'd best not remain here—the girl is dead. Go home.

MARGARET. (*Pityingly*) Dead? Poor thing!

DOCTOR. Yes. Does your husband know you are here?

MARGARET. (*Shaking her head*) Oh, no!

DOCTOR. Come, you must go home! (*He almost pushes her out of the room in his urgency.*)

MARGARET. (*Resisting him gently*) Ah, no, doctor. Now that I am here, let me stay. I can be of some help, I know.

DOCTOR. No, you can be of no use. Everything has been done.

MARGARET. Well, I'll just say a word to Maria. Where is she?

DOCTOR. I don't know—I don't know anything about Maria.

MRS. BURTON. She's in there. (*She nods toward the door on the left.*)

(*The doctor has crowded Margaret almost through the door in his eagerness to have her out of the house. She is reluctantly yielding to him, when Mrs. Burton's voice arrests her. She turns quickly and, looking over the doctor's shoulder, notices the child in Mrs. Burton's arms. She impulsively brushes the doctor aside and goes toward her, her face beaming with tender sympathy.*)

MARGARET. Oh, is this the baby?

MRS. BURTON. Yes'm.

MARGARET. (*Going close to her on tip-toes and gazing with maternal solicitude down upon the child*) Poor little baby! What a dear mite of a thing it is.

MRS. BURTON. Yes'm.

MARGARET. (*Impulsively*) Doctor, we must take care of this baby.

DOCTOR. (*Impatiently*) You've got a baby of your *own*, Mrs. Fleming.

MARGARET. Yes, and that's why I pity this one, I suppose. I always did love babies, anyhow. They are such wonderful, mysterious little things, aren't they?

MRS. BURTON. Yes'm.

DOCTOR. (*Spurred by a growing sense of catastrophe*) Mrs. Fleming, there is danger to your child in your remaining here.

MARGARET. (*Alarmed*) Oh, doctor!

DOCTOR. I hated to tell you this before—but—there is contagion in this atmosphere.

MARGARET. (*Hastily taking her hat from the table*) Doctor, why didn't you— (*She is hurrying away when she is checked by a poignant moan.*

She turns a frightened face and sees Maria coming from the room on the left with a letter in her hand. Maria's face is distorted by grief.)

MARIA. Ah, Mrs. Burton, I have found out who dot man is. He is— (*She sees Margaret and smiles bitterly upon her.*) So,—you have come, Mrs. Fleming?

MARGARET. (*Making a movement of sympathy*) Maria!

MARIA. Vell, you may go back again. You can do nutting for her now. She is dead. (*Perversely*) But, ven you do go, you vill take dot baby back mit you. He shall now have two babies instead of one.

MARGARET. (*Smiling*) What do you mean, Maria? Who shall have two babies?

MARIA. (*Fiercely*) Philip Fleming—dot's who.

(*Margaret stares at her, only comprehending half what Maria means. Dr. Larkin goes quickly to her.*)

DOCTOR. Come away, Mrs. Fleming—the woman is crazy. (*He tries to draw her away.*)

MARIA. (*Contemptuously*) No, I ain't crazy! (*She shakes the letter at Margaret.*) You read dot letter and see if I vas crazy!

(*Margaret, in a dazed way, reaches for the letter, and tries to read it, turning it different ways.*)

MARGARET. I cannot make it out. (*She hands it to the doctor, and says helplessly.*) Read it—to me—doctor—please.

DOCTOR. (*Beside himself and snatching the letter*) No, nor shall you. (*He makes a motion to tear the letter.*)

MARIA. (*Threateningly*) Don't you tear dot letter, doctor.

MARGARET. (*Putting her hand out gently*) You must not destroy that letter, doctor. Give it back to me. (*Dr. Larkin returns the letter reluctantly. Margaret attempts to read it, fails, becomes impatient and hands it to Maria, helplessly.*) You read it to me, Maria.

(*Maria, whose passion has subsided, takes the letter in an awed manner and begins to read it. The doctor is in a daze. Margaret sinks into the chair to the right of the table. She has recovered her calm poise, but does not seem to be at all the same Margaret.*)

MARIA. (*Reading in a simple, unaffected manner*)

Canton, June 10,

DEAR MR. FLEMING:

You was good to come to see me, and I thank you. I will not trouble you no more. I am sorry for what has happened. I know you never loved me and I never asked you to, but I loved you. It was all my fault. I will never trouble you no more. You can do what you like with the baby. I do not care. Do not be afraid, I shall never tell. They tried to get me to but I never shall. Nobody will ever know. No more at present, from your obedient servant,

LENA SCHMIDT.

MARGARET. (*Turning to the doctor, who is standing close to her chair*) Did you know—anything of this—doctor?

DOCTOR. (*Evasively*) Well—I knew—something of it—but, this girl may be lying. Such as she is—will say anything sometimes.

MARIA. (*Fiercely*) Don't you say dot, doctor. She would not tell nutting to hurt him, not to save her soul.

DOCTOR. (*With finality*) Well, now that you know the worst, come away from here—come home.

MARIA. (*Bitterly*) Oh! Ya! She can go home. She have alvays got a home und a husband und fine clothes, because she is his vife, but my poor sister don't have any of dese tings, because she is only de poor mistress. But, by Gott, she shall not go home unless she takes dot baby back mit her.

DOCTOR. She shall do nothing of the sort.

MARIA. Vell, den, I vill take it, und fling it in his face.

MARGARET. (*Calmly, and rising from the chair*) You shall not go near him. You shall not say—one word to him!

MARIA. Von't I? Who is going to stop me? I vould yust like to know dot?

MARGARET. (*Quite calmly*) I am!

MARIA. (*Mockingly*) You—you vill take his part, because you are his vife! (*Fiercely*) Vell! (*She draws a pistol from her dress pocket.*) Do you see dot gun? Vell, I buy dot gun, und I swore dot ven I find out dot man I vill have his life. Und, if you try to stop me, I vill lay you stiff und cold beside her.

MARGARET. (*Calmly, pityingly, holding out her hand as though to quiet her*) Maria! Stop! How dare you talk like that to me? Give me that pistol. (*Maria, awed by Margaret's spirit, meekly hands her the weapon.*) You think—I—am happy—because I am his wife? Why, you poor fool, that girl (*She points to the door on the left.*) never in all her life suffered one thousandth part what I have suffered in these past five minutes. Do you dare to compare her to me? I have not uttered one word of reproach, even against her, and yet she has done me a wrong, that not all the death-bed letters that were ever written can undo. I wonder what I have ever done to deserve this! (*She loses control of herself and sinks sobbing, into the chair, her arms upon the table, and her head dropping upon them.*)

DOCTOR. (*Overcome by the situation, throws his arms about her and tries to draw her to her feet*) For God's sake, Mrs. Fleming, let me take you out of this hell.

MARGARET. (*Gently resisting him*) Ah, doctor, you cannot take *this hell* out of my breast. (*Suddenly her manner changes. She says with quick decision.*) Maria, get me a sheet of writing paper. Doctor, give me a pencil.

(*Doctor Larkin puts his hand into his vest pocket. Maria, who seems dazed, looks helplessly about as though the paper might be within reach. Then suddenly thinking of the letter in her hand, she tears off the blank half of it and quickly lays it on the table before Margaret.*)

DOCTOR.　(*Giving her the pencil*) What are you going to do?
MARGARET.　Send—for *him!*
DOCTOR.　No—not here!
MARGARET.　Yes—here— (*She writes nervously, mumbling what she writes.*) "Philip: I am waiting for you, here. That *girl* is *dead.*" (*She folds the letter.*) Where's that boy?

(*Maria and Mrs. Burton both make a movement in search of Charley.*)

MARIA.　Charley! (*She goes to the door at the back and calls again in a hushed voice.*) Charley! (*Charley enters. She whispers to him that the lady wants him.*) You, go quick! (*Charley goes to Margaret.*)
MARGARET.　(*In tense nervousness*) Charley, do you know Mr. Fleming?
CHARLEY.　Yes'm.
MARGARET.　Do you know where he lives?
CHARLEY.　Yes'm—on Canton Street.
MARGARET.　Yes—go there—don't ring the bell—go through the garden— you will find him there, playing with the baby. Give him this.
CHARLEY.　Any answer?
MARGARET.　(*At nervous tension*) No! Go quick! Quick! (*She springs to her feet.*) Now, doctor—I want you to leave me!
DOCTOR.　Mrs. Fleming, for God's sake don't see him here.
MARGARET.　Yes, here—and—alone! Please go. (*The doctor does not respond.*) I don't want you or any other living being to hear what passes between him and me, and, (*She points to the room.*) that dead girl. Please go!
DOCTOR.　Mrs. Fleming, as your physician, I order you to leave this place at once.
MARGARET.　No, doctor—I must see him, *here.*
DOCTOR.　(*With gentle persuasion*) Mrs. Fleming, you have no right to do this. Think of your child.
MARGARET.　(*Remembering*) My baby! My poor, little innocent baby! Oh, I wish to God that she were dead. (*She is beside herself and not realizing what she says. She crosses to the left.*)
DOCTOR.　(*Following her*) Mrs. Fleming, in God's name, calm yourself! I have tried to keep it from you, but, I am forced to tell you— (*He is so deeply moved that he is almost incoherent.*) If you continue in this way, dear lady, you are exposing yourself to a terrible affliction—this—trouble—

with your eyes. You are threatened with—if you keep up this strain—a sudden blindness may fall upon you.

MARGARET. (*Appalled*) Blind! Blind! (*She speaks in a low terrified voice.*) Oh, no doctor, not *that*—not *now*—not until after I've seen him.

DOCTOR. Not only that, but if you keep up this strain much longer, it may cost you your life.

MARGARET. I don't care—what happens to me, only, let me *see* him, and then, the sooner it all comes the better. (*She crosses to the left with the doctor following her.*)

DOCTOR. (*Growing desperate, and throwing his arms about her*) Mrs. Fleming, you must leave this place! Come home.

MARGARET. No. Doctor, please leave me alone. (*She draws herself from him.*) I tell you I've got to see him here. (*Then with a sweet intimacy, she goes to him.*) A woman has a strange feeling for the physician who brings her child into the world—I love you—I have always obeyed your orders, haven't I? (*She speaks brokenly.*)

DOCTOR. (*Quietly*) Always.

MARGARET. Then, let me be the doctor now, and I order you to leave this house at once.

DOCTOR. (*Hopelessly*) You are determined to do this thing?

MARGARET. (*With finality*) Yes.

DOCTOR. Very well then—good-bye. (*He holds out his hand, which she takes mechanically. He holds her hand warmly for a moment. She clings to him as though afraid to let him go, then slowly draws away.*)

MARGARET. Good-bye!

(*The doctor leaves the room quickly. Margaret takes a step after him until she touches the left side of the table in the center. She stands there gazing into space, the calmness of death upon her face. The sunlight streaming through the window falls upon her. Mrs. Burton is sitting in a rocking-chair in the corner of the room. Marie is sitting on the sofa at the left, weeping silently, with clasped hands, her arms lying in her lap, her body bent. She makes a plaintive moan before she speaks.*)

MARIA. Ah—Mrs. Fleming, you must not do dis ting. Vat vas I—vot was she, I'd like to know—dot ve should make dis trouble for you? You come here, like an angel to help us, und I have stung you like a snake in dot grass. (*She goes to Margaret and falls upon her knees beside her.*) Oh, Mrs. Fleming, on my knees I ask you to forgive me.

(*Margaret stands immobile at the table, her right hand resting upon its edge—her left hand partly against her cheek. She is lost in spiritual contemplation of the torment she is suffering. She shows impatience at the sound of Maria's voice as though loath to be disturbed. She replies wearily.*)

MARGARET. I have nothing to forgive. Get up, Maria. You have done nothing to me—go away!

MARIA. (*In a paroxysm of contrition*) Oh, I beg, Mrs. Fleming, dot you vill take dot gun and blow my brains out.

MARGARET. Don't go on like that, Maria! (*Maria's weeping irritates her.*) Get up! Please go away. Go away! I say.

(*Maria slinks away quietly into the back room. Margaret takes a long, sobbing breath, which ends in a sigh. She stares into space and a blank look comes into her face as though she were gazing at things beyond her comprehension. Presently the silence is broken by a low wail from the infant. It half arouses her.*)

MARGARET. What is the matter with that child? (*Her voice seems remote. Her expression remains fixed.*) Why don't you keep it quiet?

MRS. BURTON. (*In a hushed voice*) It's hungry.

MARGARET. (*In the same mood, but her voice is a little querulous.*) Well, then, why don't you feed it?

MRS. BURTON. I can't get nothing fit for it. I've tried everything I could think of, but it's no use. (*She gets up and places the child upon the sofa to the left.*) There, be still, you poor little critter, an' I'll see what I ken get fer ye. (*As she goes to the door at the back, Margaret speaks wearily.*)

MARGARET. Bring a lamp—it's getting dark here. (*She is still in the same attitude by the table. There is a silence, then the child's wail arouses her. She half turns her head in its direction—and tries to quiet it.*) Hush—child —hush— (*Then she reaches out her hand as if to pat it.*) There—there— poor little thing. Don't fret—it's no use to fret, child—be quiet now—there —there, now. (*She turns and slowly gropes her way to the sofa, sits on the edge of it, and feels for the child and gently pats it. She murmurs softly.*) Hush—baby—go to sleep.

(*There is a silence while a soft flood of sunshine plays about her. A pitying half smile flits across her face. She utters a faint sigh and again drifts away into that inner consciousness where she evidently finds peace. Again the child is restless—it arouses her and, hopeless of comforting it, she takes it in her arms. After a moment, she rises to her feet and stumbles toward the table. She knocks against the low chair. At the same moment, Philip Fleming dashes breathlessly into the room through the door on the right. He pauses in horror as Margaret raises her head, her eyes wide open, staring into his—her face calm and remote. She hushes the child softly, and sits in the low chair. Philip stands in dumb amazement watching her. The child begins to fret her again. She seems hopeless of comforting it. Then scarcely conscious of what she is doing, suddenly with an impatient, swift movement she unbuttons her dress to give nourishment to the child, when the picture fades away into darkness.*)

ACT FOURTH

*The scene is the same as the Second Act. The doors and window
leading into the garden are open.*
   *Maria is seated close to the open door, sewing. She occasionally
looks into the garden as if guarding something. She is neatly dressed,
fresh and orderly looking. Her manner is subdued. A bell rings and
a closing door is heard. Then Dr. Larkin enters. Maria goes to meet
him and scans his face anxiously.*

MARIA.   Goot morning, doctor.
DOCTOR.   Good morning. Well! Any news?
MARIA.   (*Losing interest and shaking her head sadly*) No, doctor. No
vord from him yet. It is seven days now—I hoped—mebbe you might have
some.
DOCTOR.   No—nothing. How is Mrs. Fleming?

(*Maria sits down to the left of the center of the room and the doctor
to the right.*)

MARIA.   Yust the same as yesterday, und the day before, und all the
udder days. Ach, so bright, und so cheerful, but I tink all the same she
is breaking her heart. Ach, ven I look into her sad eyes—vot cannot see
me—I am ashamed to hold my head up. (*She brushes away the tears.*)
DOCTOR.   Does she talk about him at all?
MARIA.   No, she never speaks his name.
DOCTOR.   How is the child?
MARIA.   (*Brightening*) She is fine. Dot little tooth came trough dis morning und she don't fret no more now.
DOCTOR.   And, the *other* one?
MARIA.   (*Indifferently*) Oh, he's all right. I put him beside Lucy in her
crib dis morning und she laughs and pulls at him und plays mit him yust
like he vas a little kitten. Dis is no place for him, doctor. Ven Mr. Flem-
ing comes home he vill fix tings, und I vill take him away by myself—
vere she no more can be troubled mit him.
DOCTOR.   Things will come out all right. You'd best keep quiet. Have
nothing whatever to say in this matter.
MARIA.   Ya. I make enough trouble already mit my tongue. You bet I
keep it shut in my head now. Shall I call Mrs. Fleming? She is in the
garden.
DOCTOR.   She's there a great deal now, isn't she?
MARIA.   Ya, she is always dere by the blossoms, und the babies. (*She
goes to the door and says in slow, deferential voice.*) Mrs. Fleming, Doctor Larkin is here.

MARGARET. (*Outside*) Yes, I'll come. (*She slowly emerges from the garden into the doorway, her arms filled with flowers. She is daintily dressed and there is a subtle dignity and reserve about her. She smiles cheerily.*) Good morning, doctor. Maria, there are some daffodils out by the yellow bed. Bring them, please. (*She slowly enters the room.*)

(*The doctor goes to her and gently leads her to the table on the right where she puts the flowers, after carefully locating a place to lay them.*)

DOCTOR. Well, well, where did you get such a lot of roses? I couldn't gather so many in a month from my scrubby bushes. The bugs eat 'em all up.

MARGARET. Why don't you spray them? (*Maria brings a large loose bunch of daffodils.*) Bring some jars, Maria.

DOCTOR. I did spray them.

MARGARET. When?

DOCTOR. When I saw the rose bugs.

MARGARET. (*Smiling*) That's a fine time to spray bushes. Don't you know that the time to prevent trouble is to look ahead? From potatoes to roses, spray before anything happens—*then* nothing *will* happen.

DOCTOR. (*Laughing*) Yes, of course, I know, but I forgot to do it until I saw two big, yellow bugs in the heart of every rose and all the foliage chewed up.

MARGARET. There's no use in it now. You are just wasting time. Start early next year before the leaves open.

DOCTOR. (*Admiringly*) What a brave, cheery little woman you are.

MARGARET. What's the use in being anything else? I don't see any good in living in this world, unless you can live right.

DOCTOR. And this world needs just such women as you.

MARGARET. What does the world know or care about me?

(*The bell rings and the door opens and shuts.*)

DOCTOR. Very little, but it's got to feel your influence. (*He pats her hand.*)

(*The maid enters.*)

MAID. Mr. Foster wishes to see you for a moment, Mrs. Fleming.

MARGARET. Tell him to come in. (*The maid goes out. In a moment Foster enters, flurried and embarrassed.*) Good morning, Mr. Foster. (*She holds out her hands to him.*) Anything wrong at the mill?

FOSTER. Good morning, Mrs. Fleming. Oh, no—not at all, not at all. How do you do, doctor? (*He shakes hands with the doctor with unusual warmth.*)

DOCTOR. (*Somewhat surprised and looking at him quizzically*) Hello, Foster.

MARGARET. Will you sit down, Mr. Foster?

FOSTER. Thank you—yes, I will. What beautiful flowers. Mother says you have the loveliest garden in Canton.

MARGARET. (*Pleased*) That's awfully nice of her. I had a delightful visit with her yesterday.

FOSTER. (*Nervously*) Yes, she told me so.

MARGARET. We sat in the garden. What a sweet, happy soul she is.

FOSTER. (*Fussing with his hat and getting up and moving his chair close to the doctor's*) Yes. Mother always sees the bright side of the worst things.

MARGARET. She's very proud of you.

FOSTER. (*Laughing foolishly*) Oh, yes, she is happy over anything I do. (*He looks at Margaret furtively, then at the doctor. He evidently has something to say. Suddenly in a tense whisper he speaks to the doctor.*) Mr. Fleming has come back.

DOCTOR. Hush! Where is he? At the mill?

FOSTER. No. Here—outside.

DOCTOR. How does he look?

FOSTER. He's a wreck. He wants to see her.

DOCTOR. Well, tell her—I'll go— (*He rises.*)

FOSTER. No! (*He grabs him by the coat.*) For God's sake don't go. You tell her—you're her doctor.

(*Margaret, who has been busy with the flowers, becomes suddenly interested.*)

MARGARET. What are you two whispering about?

FOSTER. (*Laughing nervously*) Oh, just a little advice, that's all. (*He goes to Margaret.*) I'll say good morning, Mrs. Fleming. Glad to see you— er—looking—ah—so well. (*He shakes hands and rushes out.*)

(*Margaret stands a little mystified. The doctor approaches her gently.*)

DOCTOR. (*Very tenderly*) Mrs. Fleming—I have something to say to you.

MARGARET. (*Standing tense and with ominous conviction*) Philip is dead!

DOCTOR. No. He is not dead.

MARGARET. Where is he?

DOCTOR. *Outside.*

MARGARET. Why doesn't he come in?

DOCTOR. He's ashamed—afraid.

MARGARET. This is his home. Why should he be afraid to enter it? I will go to him. (*She starts toward the door, and then staggers. The doctor puts an arm around her.*)

DOCTOR. There now. Keep up your courage. Don't forget, everything depends upon you.

MARGARET. (*Brokenly*) I'm brave, doctor. I—perhaps it's best for you to tell him to come here.

DOCTOR. (*Patting her on the shoulder*) Remember, you are very precious to us all. We cannot afford to lose *you*.

(*Margaret stands by the table, calm and tense. Philip comes in from the right, carrying his cap in his hands. He looks weary and broken. He crosses behind Margaret to the center of the stage and standing humbly before her, murmurs her name softly.*)

PHILIP. Margaret!

MARGARET. Well, Philip. (*After a slight pause*) You have come back.

PHILIP. (*Humbly*) Yes.

MARGARET. (*Gently*) Why did you go away?

PHILIP. (*Overwhelmed with shame*) I couldn't face you. I wanted to get away somewhere, and hide forever. (*He looks sharply at her.*) Can't you see me, Margaret?

MARGARET. (*Shaking her head*) No!

PHILIP. (*Awed*) You are blind! Oh!

(*Margaret sits down in a chair by the table. Philip remains standing.*)

MARGARET. Don't mind. I shall be cured. Doctor Norton sees me every day. He will operate as soon as he finds me normal.

PHILIP. You have been suffering?

MARGARET. Oh, no. (*After a pause*) Philip, do you think that was right? To run away and hide?

PHILIP. I did not consider whether it was right or wrong. (*He speaks bitterly.*) I did not know the meaning of those words. I never have.

MARGARET. Oh, you are a man—people will soon forget.

PHILIP. (*Fiercely*) I do not care about others. It is you, Margaret—will you ever forget? Will you ever forgive?

MARGARET. (*Shaking her head and smiling sadly*) There is nothing to forgive. And, I want to forget.

PHILIP. (*Bewildered by her magnanimity but full of hope*) Then you will let me come back to you? You will help me to be a better—a wiser man?

MARGARET. (*Smiling gently*) Yes, Philip.

(*A quick joy takes hold of Philip. He makes a warm movement to go to her, then checks himself, and approaches her slowly while speaking, overcome by the wonder and beauty of her kindness.*)

PHILIP. All my life, Margaret, I will make amends for what I have done. I will atone for my ignorance—Oh, my wife—my dear, dear wife. (*He hangs over her tenderly, not daring to touch her.*)

(At the word "wife" Margaret rises, shrinking from him as though some dead thing was near her. A look of agony flits across her face.)

MARGARET.   No! Philip, not that! No! *(She puts out her hands to ward him off.)*

PHILIP.   *(Beseechingly)* Margaret!

MARGARET.   *(Her face poignant with suppressed emotion, she confesses, brokenly.)* The wife-heart has gone out of me.

PHILIP.   Don't—don't say that, Margaret.

MARGARET.   I must. Ah, Philip, how I worshipped you. You were my idol. Is it my fault that you lie broken at my feet?

PHILIP.   *(With urgency)* You say you want to forget—that you forgive! Will you—?

MARGARET.   Can't you understand? It is not a question of forgetting, or of forgiving— *(For an instant she is at a loss how to convince him.)* Can't you understand? Philip! *(Then suddenly)* Suppose—I—had been unfaithful to you?

PHILIP.   *(With a cry of repugnance)* Oh, Margaret!

MARGARET.   *(Brokenly)* There! You see! You are a man, and you have your ideals of—the—sanctity—of—the thing you love. Well, I am a woman —and perhaps—I, too, have the same ideals. I don't know. But, I, too, cry "pollution." *(She is deeply moved.)*

PHILIP.   *(Abashed)* I did not know. I never realized before, the iniquity— of my—behavior. Oh, if I only had my life to live over again. Men, as a rule, do not consider others when urged on by their desires. How you must hate me.

MARGARET.   No, I don't—I love you—I pity you.

PHILIP.   Dear, not now—but in the future—some time—away in the future—perhaps, the old Margaret—

MARGARET.   Ah, Philip, the old Margaret is dead. The truth killed her.

PHILIP.   Then—there is no hope for me? *(There is a dignity and a growing manliness in his demeanor as the scene progresses.)*

MARGARET.   *(Warmly)* Yes. Every hope.

PHILIP.   Well, what do you want me to do? Shall I go away?

MARGARET.   No. Your place is here. You cannot shirk your responsibilities now.

PHILIP.   I do not want to shirk my responsibilities, Margaret. I want to do whatever you think is best.

MARGARET.   Very well. It is best for us both to remain here, and take up the old life together. It will be a little hard for you, but you are a man— you will soon live it down.

PHILIP.   Yes—I *will* live it down.

MARGARET.   Go to the mill tomorrow morning and take up your work again, as though this thing had never happened.

PHILIP.   Yes. All right. I'll do that.

MARGARET.   Mr. Foster, you know, you have an unusually capable man there?

PHILIP. Yes, I appreciate Foster. He's a nice chap, too.

MARGARET. He has carried through a very critical week at the mill.

PHILIP. Don't worry, Margaret, everything will be all right there now. I will put my whole heart and soul into the work.

MARGARET. Then, you must do something for your child.

PHILIP. Yes, our dear child.

MARGARET. No, not our child—not Lucy. Your son.

PHILIP. My son?

MARGARET. Yes.

PHILIP. Where is he?

MARGARET. Here.

PHILIP. (*Resentfully*) Who brought him here?

MARGARET. I did.

PHILIP. (*Amazed*) You brought that child here?

MARGARET. Yes, where else should he go?

PHILIP. You have done that?

MARGARET. What other thing was there for me to do? Surely if he was good enough to bring into the world, he is good enough to find a shelter under your roof.

PHILIP. (*Moved by her magnanimity*) I never dreamed that you would do that, Margaret.

MARGARET. Well, he is here. Now, what are you going to do with him?

PHILIP. (*Helplessly*) What can I do?

MARGARET. Give him a name, educate him. Try to make atonement for the wrong you did his mother. You must teach him never to be ashamed of her, to love her memory—motherhood is a divine thing—remember that, Philip, no matter when, or how. You can do fine things for this unfortunate child.

PHILIP. (*Contemptuously*) Fine things for him! I am not fit to guide a young life. A fine thing I have made of my own.

MARGARET. There is no use now lamenting what was done yesterday. That's finished. Tomorrow? What are you going to do with that?

PHILIP. There does not seem any "tomorrow" worth while for me. The past—

MARGARET. The past is dead. We must face the living future. Now, Philip, there are big things ahead for you, if you will only look for them. They certainly will not *come* to *you*. I will help you—we will fight this together.

PHILIP. Forgive me, please. I'll not talk like that any more.

MARGARET. Of course, there will be a lot of talk—mean talk—but they will get tired of that in the end. Where have you been all this time?

PHILIP. In Boston.

MARGARET. What have you been doing?

PHILIP. Nothing—I've been—in the hospital.

MARGARET. (*Stretching out her arms to him with an infinite tenderness*) Ah, Philip, you have been ill?

PHILIP. No!

MARGARET. What was it? (*He is silent.*) Please tell me.

PHILIP. (*Rather reluctantly reciting his story*) I was walking across the bridge over the Charles river one night—I was sick of myself—the whole world—I believed I should never see your face again. The water looked so quiet, it fascinated me. I just dropped into it and went down. It seemed like going to sleep. Then I woke up and I was in a narrow bed in a big room.

MARGARET. (*Breathless*) The hospital?

PHILIP. Yes.

MARGARET. Oh, that was a cruel thing to do. Were they kind to you there?

PHILIP. Yes. There was an old nurse there—she was sharp. She told me not to be a fool, but to go back to my wife. She said—"If she's any good, she will forgive you." (*He smiles whimsically.*) Margaret, some day I am going to earn your respect, and then—I know, I shall be able to win you back to me all over again.

MARGARET. (*Smiling sadly*) I don't know. That would be a wonderful thing. (*She weeps silently.*) A very wonderful thing. (*Then suddenly she springs to her feet.*) Ah, dreams! Philip! Dreams! And we must get to work.

(*Philip is inspired by her manner, and there is a quickening of his
spirit, a response to her in the new vibration in his voice.*)

PHILIP. Work! Yes—I'll not wait until tomorrow. I'll go to the mill now.

MARGARET. That's fine. Do it.

PHILIP. Yes, I'll take a bath and get into some fresh clothing first.

MARGARET. Do. You must look pretty shabby knocking about for a week without a home.

PHILIP. Oh, I'll be all right. I'd like to see Lucy. (*He looks about.*) Where is she?

(*Margaret is at the table occupied with the flowers.*)

MARGARET. They are both out there. (*She indicates with a turn of her head.*) In the garden.

(*Philip goes quickly to the door opening upon the garden and gazes
out eagerly. Margaret, at the table, pauses in her work, gives a long
sigh of relief and contentment. Her eyes look into the darkness and a
serene joy illuminates her face. The picture slowly fades out as
Philip steps buoyantly into the garden.*)

THE END OF THE PLAY